THE COMPLETE THYROID BOOK

W9-CAU-011

Other Books by M. Sara Rosenthal

The Thyroid Sourcebook (1st edition, 1993; 4th edition, 2000)
The Gynecological Sourcebook (1st edition, 1994; 4th edition, 2003)
The Pregnancy Sourcebook (1st edition, 1995; 3rd edition, 1999)
The Fertility Sourcebook (1st edition, 1995; 3rd edition, 2002)
The Breastfeeding Sourcebook (1st edition, 1995; 3rd edition, 2000)
The Breast Sourcebook (1st edition, 1996; 2nd edition, 1999)
The Gastrointestinal Sourcebook (1997)
Managing Your Diabetes (1998)
The Thyroid Sourcebook for Women (1st edition, 1999; 2nd edition, 2004)
The Type 2 Diabetes Sourcebook for Women (2005)
Women and Depression (2000)
Women and Passion (2000)
Managing PMS Naturally (2001)
The Canadian Type 2 Diabetes Sourcebook (1st edition, 2002; 2nd edition, 2005)
Women Managing Stress (2002)
The Hypothyroid Sourcebook (2002)
The Natural Woman's Guide to Preventing Diabetes Complications (2002)
The Natural Woman's Guide to Hormone Replacement Therapy (2003)
The Thyroid Cancer Book (1st edition, 2002; 2nd edition, 2003)
The Skinny on Fat (2004)

50 Ways Series

50 Ways to Prevent Colon Cancer (2000)
50 Ways Women Can Prevent Heart Disease (2000)
50 Ways to Manage Ulcer, Heartburn and Reflux (2001)
50 Ways to Prevent and Manage Stress (2001)
50 Ways to Prevent Depression Without Drugs (2001)

THE COMPLETE THYROID BOOK

KENNETH AIN, M.D.

M. SARA ROSENTHAL, Ph.D.

McGraw·Hill

New York   Chicago   San Francisco   Lisbon   London   Madrid   Mexico City
Milan   New Delhi   San Juan   Seoul   Singapore   Sydney   Toronto

Library of Congress Cataloging-in-Publication Data

Ain, Kenneth.
    The complete thyroid book / by Kenneth Ain and M. Sara Rosenthal.
        p.   cm.
    ISBN 0-07-143526-3
    1. Thyroid gland—Diseases—Popular works.   I. Rosenthal, M. Sara.   II. Title.

    RC655.A36   2005
    616.4′4′—dc22   2005000840

Copyright © 2005 by Kenneth Ain and M. Sara Rosenthal. All rights reserved. Printed in the United States of America. Except as permitted under the United States Copyright Act of 1976, no part of this publication may be reproduced or distributed in any form or by any means, or stored in a database or retrieval system, without the prior written permission of the publisher.

8 9 0   DOC/DOC   0 9

ISBN 0-07-143526-3

McGraw-Hill books are available at special quantity discounts to use as premiums and sales promotions, or for use in corporate training programs. For more information, please write to the Director of Special Sales, Professional Publishing, McGraw-Hill, Two Penn Plaza, New York, NY 10121-2298. Or contact your local bookstore.

The purpose of this book is to educate. It is sold with the understanding that the authors and publisher shall have neither liability nor responsibility for any injury caused or alleged to be caused directly or indirectly by the information contained in this book. While every effort has been made to ensure its accuracy, the book's contents should not be construed as medical advice. Each person's health needs are unique. To obtain recommendations appropriate to your particular situation, please consult a qualified health-care provider.

This book is printed on acid-free paper.

Contents

PART 1 The Basics

PART 2 People in Special Circumstances

CONTENTS

PART 4 Complications of Thyroid Disease

Acknowledgments

We'd like to thank the team at McGraw-Hill for supporting us through this huge project. Judith McCarthy helped us conceive this book, while Meg Leder, our editor, and Nancy Hall, our project editor, helped deliver this baby. Each of us would like to acknowledge other individuals who played a role in shaping who we are, which is what has made this book come to fruition.

Ken: I thank the following individuals for my formative development and inspiration: Samuel Refetoff and Jacob Robbins for their mentorship, Theodore and Florence Ain for creating me, Max and Jake Ain for their love and need for college tuition funding, and Sara Rosenthal for everything beautiful in my life. This book could not have been written without Sara's inspiration, expertise, and frequent reminders. She is my collaborator in life and research, as well as my motivation for happiness.

Sara: I am forever grateful to Dr. Robert Volpe, a world expert in autoimmune thyroid disease who was my very first medical advisor on the first edition of my first book in 1992, *The Thyroid Sourcebook*. I am also grateful to the unwavering support of my mentor in bioethics, Dr. William Harvey. Larissa Kostoff and Laura Tulchinsky remain pillars for me in my personal and professional life. This book would not have been possible without my access to my coauthor, mentor, soul mate, and of course, the best medical advisor I ever had: my husband, Kenneth Ain.

Introduction

Why We're Passionate About Thyroid Disease

Roughly 12 percent of the adult population suffers from some form of thyroid disease. The most common thyroid diseases are autoimmune thyroid diseases, which affect women much more frequently than men, especially when they are pregnant or after delivery. These comprise Hashimoto's disease (see Chapter 5) and Graves' disease (see Chapter 6). Subclinical hypothyroidism and hyperthyroidism are also becoming more of a concern, particularly with an aging population, and in light of the fact that so many early signs of thyroid disease can be masked by or mimic a host of other disorders. More and more people are now being definitively diagnosed with an underlying thyroid disease instead of being misdiagnosed with other diseases.

Thyroid cancer, still considered a rare cancer, comprising only about 2 percent of all cancers, is now considered the fastest rising cancer among women in the United States, rising in incidence faster than lung or breast cancers. And in both sexes, thyroid cancer diagnoses have increased precipitously. Part of the rise in incidence likely has to do with better screening and information about early signs of thyroid cancer. In the past, many patients with thyroid cancers were not diagnosed early enough, and some of these cancers were missed until they were very aggressive and hard to treat.

Thyroid disease in the developing world is still widespread because of iodine deficiency. This is something we discuss in both Chapters 1 and 3. Poor mental development, caused by hypothyroidism in infants and children, is partly to blame for the depressed economies of many third world nations, with more than 500 million people at risk.

All in all, thyroid disease constitutes one of the most significant categories of health problems, notable for its frequency, its dramatic effects on world society, its spectacular consequences on individuals' well-being, and its remarkable response to appropriate treatment.

Who We Are: Meet Ken and Sara

Thyroid books such as this become the friend you can turn to for answers, advice, and reassurance. As the authors whose voices you may be relying on for your thyroid information, we think it's valuable to introduce ourselves to you and share our individual thyroid stories with you—including an unusual thyroid story that also led to our marriage.

Ken's Story

I have always been fascinated by biology and medicine, spending weekends in high school volunteering at the Mütter Museum in the Philadelphia College of Physicians and summers working in labs at a nearby medical school. My interest in the thyroid began during my third year of medical school at Brown University. It seemed that the most astute physician at the local hospital where I spent my medicine clerkship was a new endocrinologist on the faculty. The dean gave me permission to spend six weeks under the endocrinologist's tutelage, and he introduced me to academic endocrinology, critical thinking, and the thyroid gland.

As a new intern, my first intensive care patient was a comatose gentleman whose illness had defied understanding for three weeks. What a triumph for a new physician to diagnose myxedema (hypothyroid) coma and see my patient awaken after sufficient treatment with thyroid hormone! My interest in thyroid disease persisted and grew through medical residency, then blossomed under the mentorship of Dr. Samuel Refetoff at the University of Chicago during three years of an endocrinology fellowship. It progressed further during my time as a senior staff fellow working with Dr. Jacob Robbins at the National Institutes of Health, where I began to specialize in treating patients with thyroid cancer and continued my basic and clinical research on thyroid diseases.

Since the end of 1990, I've been on the faculty of the University of Kentucky in Lexington, founding and directing the Thyroid Oncology Program, as well as running the Thyroid Clinic at the Veterans Affairs Medical Center (VAMC). In addition, I have a thyroid cancer research laboratory at the VAMC, investigating the molecular and cellular biology of the thyroid and thyroid cancer.

My personal life has also been affected by my interest in thyroid issues. My first marriage was blessed with two sons, but my wife and I grew apart, and we divorced in 2001. The next June, I received an e-mail from a remarkable woman, well known as an author of medical resource books for patients. I had briefly met her at a Thyroid Cancer Survivors' Association (ThyCa) conference in Washington, D.C., in late 2000, but, being married at the time, our meeting was completely businesslike; I answered medical questions for a few minutes before she precipitously departed. Now that I was single, the e-mail evoked the image of a beautiful and intelligent woman.

I was asked to review her new book, *The Thyroid Cancer Book*. First I reviewed the book, and then I intensely reviewed its author, spending hours on the telephone. A romantic weekend in Cleveland at the end of June resulted in my proposal two weeks later and our marriage at the end of May 2003. Our collaborations, melding mutual personal and professional interests and goals, continue to increase, bringing much joy. My boys are also enthralled with their stepmother. Sara and I look forward to our future together, enjoying this rare opportunity knowing that our lives completely mesh in every positive way. Much thanks to the thyroid gland!

Sara's Story

Many of you reading this book may already have in your thyroid libraries past works I have written on thyroid disease, such as *The Thyroid Sourcebook* (now in its fourth edition), *The Thyroid Sourcebook for Women* (now in its second edition), or *The Hypothyroid Sourcebook*. Those books were inspired from family members with autoimmune thyroid diseases, my own experiences with thyroid cancer, and my living my entire adult life without a thyroid gland.

When I wrote the first edition of *The Thyroid Sourcebook* in 1992, I was working as a health journalist on an article about thyroid disease and was surprised to find there were no books for patients on thyroid disease written in plain language. All I could find were some outdated M.D.-authored books that were either too brief or too technical to be of any use to me. With two bachelor's degrees—one in English literature, the other in education—I still couldn't understand medical-speak and required information without the technical jargon. It occurred to me that I could write the book I wished I had when my thyroid problem was first diagnosed. It was a tough sell to a publisher because I was not an M.D. One small publisher in California was willing to take a chance. They had begun a "sourcebook" series and thought I could write *The Thyroid Sourcebook*. Even if only a handful of readers benefited, I felt it would be well worth the effort. I learned a valuable lesson early in life: follow your passion and it will take care of you.

Today, hundreds of thousands of thyroid patients have benefited from that book, which has been updated four times and translated into several languages, including Chinese. Between 1993 and 1996 I created seven health sourcebooks while holding down various writing jobs in advertising and journalism. As I saw how powerful a tool accessible information could be for informed consent and patient education, I started to become passionate about another area: bioethics, also known as medical ethics. In 1997, I went back to graduate school and began a second career as an academician: I completed my master's and Ph.D. in medical sociology and bioethics.

By 1999, I had written more than eleven books, and ended my nine-year marriage. During this time, no matter where I went or what I wrote, I was deluged with e-mail from my thyroid book readers. It became clear that the topic of thyroid disease required more of my attention and focus. I tried to convince my publisher that a book on thyroid cancer was the next thing to focus on, but the hard truth was that it's too small a disease to "sell" to a publisher. It was amidst the dot-com era, and e-publishing was just gaining momentum and popularity. It suddenly occurred to me that I could publish a book on thyroid cancer using these new technologies, financing the project with my royalties. In 2000, after developing my first website (sarahealth.com), which provided original health content to browsers, I thought about starting a health publishing company catering to orphan diseases, such as thyroid cancer. Several friends who were savvy in business implored me not to do this; I was told that this venture would be a financial loser. I ignored the advice and plunged ahead. Once again, I followed my passion.

That fall, I spoke at the annual ThyCa conference. When I was first diagnosed with thyroid cancer in 1983, there were virtually no dedicated thyroid cancer specialists. At this conference, there were more thyroid cancer specialists than I had ever seen. One doctor in particular, Kenneth Ain, was the only thyroid cancer specialist who dealt with aggressive, hard-to-treat thyroid cancers. I asked him some questions about my own case, disguising the case as a friend's, and he essentially advised that whomever I was talking about had not been followed properly and was in danger of a missed recurrence. I learned more about thyroid cancer in ten minutes than I had from researching it all those years. But since what he said upset me so much, all I could manage to do was get his card and get out of the room.

The next ThyCa conference was in September 2001. Because of the 9/11 terrorist attacks, I canceled my trip to the conference. Other work interfered with my getting down to the business of writing the book on thyroid cancer. In early 2002, I was finally ready to contact a potential medical advisor for the book. I immediately knew that Dr. Ain would be ideal, but I was concerned that a top researcher who ran various federally funded clinical trials would probably not be interested in my little patient book on thyroid cancer. So I contacted ThyCa and asked for another specialist's name. At the last minute, the advisor planned for the book couldn't work on it, and I was stuck.

I decided, nervously, to send a friendly e-mail to Dr. Ain, requesting his assistance. He wrote back immediately, and not only remembered who I was but warmly agreed to review the chapters that needed his medical attention, as long as I could adjust the deadline. I responded with my contact information, feeling completely relieved that he agreed. Ten minutes later, he called.

Since we had met in 2000, he had been through a divorce. He told me, frankly, that he was probably too busy to do the book, but that his interest was personal. After chatting for a long time, we realized we had a lot more in common than thyroid cancer. When I quoted the little-known statistic on a rare type of thyroid cancer (anaplastic), which, unbeknownst to me, came from an article he wrote, I think we fell in love. In that same phone call, we made arrangements to meet in Cleveland because it was halfway between Toronto and Lexington, Kentucky. Six weeks later, we were engaged. *The Thyroid Cancer Book* was published shortly after that.

We were married in 2003. I noted with interest that the Kentucky state license plate artistic version sports a butterfly, frequently used as the symbol for the thyroid gland, as it is butterfly shaped. I was truly living in the land of thyroid.

Through this journey, where my professional and personal lives have fused, I have come to a much deeper understanding of the thyroid and the many factors that affect thyroid health. Since Ken and I both share such a passion for this gland, and for one another, it was only natural that we pass on our thyroid passion to you.

Our Goals for Our Readers

We've been told that we are a unique pairing in the thyroid world. Together, we bring you a wealth of information from quite opposite perspectives. We share a common goal to bring our readers much fuller information about the biology and biochemistry of the thyroid gland, thyroid hormone, diagnostic tests, and treatments. We have observed that most thyroid patients are forced to self-educate about thyroid disease, without the benefit of a medical education or even sufficient health literacy.

This creates enormous problems with genuine informed consent, and many people are vulnerable to misinformation. Misinformation can be shared by extremely well-intentioned patient advocates, but it can also be a vehicle with which to confuse you and sell you drugs, products, and services you don't need.

Added to this problem, many primary care doctors and even endocrinologists are not as immersed in thyroid disease as dedicated thyroidologists. They may not order the appropriate tests or understand how to interpret certain test results, and they may misconstrue facts and confuse patients further. Some may even have their own non-standard "thyroid health miracle treatments," which they advocate in their own books for their own financial gain. There is also the continuing problem of how to identify helpful complementary therapy versus genuine quackery, which can have harmful health effects.

We've done a thorough literature review on thyroid misinformation, which we present in this book. We've tried to provide you with the correct information in language you can understand. The table of contents should be self-explanatory, but we urge each reader to especially visit Chapter 2 (on thyroid tests and labs) and Chapter 10 (on thyroid hormone), which will be your guideposts for the lifelong chore of staying properly balanced, or properly TSH-suppressed if you have had thyroid cancer. If you are one of those who frequently collect information from the Internet, we encourage you to read Chapter 19, "Thyroid Misconceptions and Misinformation."

A Word About Our Voice

We have a lot to say in this book. In most cases, both of us are speaking to you within each chapter. Since we've spent our lives and careers immersed in thyroid disease, sometimes we felt it necessary to share experiences, personal insights or opinions, and perspectives from our individual academic disciplines. In some cases, there is a principal chapter author. We will indicate in parentheses who is speaking to you when you see *my* or *I*, as in "I (Ken)" or "I (Sara)." Otherwise, we've tried to present you with a united voice when possible. One thing is clear: we think that, for a book this large and comprehensive, two heads are better than one!

THE
COMPLETE
THYROID
BOOK

PART

1

The Basics

THERE ARE MANY types of thyroid
diseases and disorders. This section
covers the scope of common thyroid
problems you have likely encountered,
including autoimmune diseases, such as
Hashimoto's disease or Graves' disease,
and the symptoms of hypothyroidism or
hyperthyroidism. All possible diagnostic
and laboratory tests used in thyroid
disease are covered in this section, as
are all medications and treatments used
in thyroid disease.

1 What Is the Thyroid, and What Does It Do?

I (Ken) am often amazed, when talking with educated and articulate patients, some of whom have received years of medical treatments for a thyroid disorder, how little they know about their thyroid gland. This chapter describes the thyroid gland, covering its development, location in the body, and function. You will see how it produces thyroid hormone and what role this critical hormone plays in your body. I discuss the body's natural control systems, including the pituitary "thermostat," which regulates the thyroid. In addition, you will see how your diet and the environment affect this gland's function.

This critical knowledge enables you to understand what underlies diseases or dysfunctions of the thyroid. Rather than merely memorizing or reading long lists of signs and symptoms to learn about thyroid problems, it's helpful to gain an insight into the causes of such problems. It is hard to know what is wrong unless you know how it should be right.

How It Formed, Where It Is, What It Does

When my youngest son was nearly four years old, a preschool teacher gave him a standardized test to assess his vocabulary and basic knowledge. Halfway through a successful test session, Jake was told, "Point to your thigh." Jake triumphantly touched the center of his neck, just above his breastbone. "Wrong!" exclaimed the teacher. Watching the test, I was surprised. "What do you mean?" I said, "He thought you meant his thyroid gland." "Where is the thyroid gland?" she asked me, clearly at a loss to conceive that such a young child knew something about anatomy that had eluded her graduate education. Unfortunately, her situation is much too common.

In the Beginning

The first sign of the developing thyroid gland can be seen near the developing tongue in a seventeen-day-old embryo. Of course, this tiny embryo is crowded with many tiny little structures destined to become all of the major organs of the future person. The developing heart is just nearby and, over the next couple of weeks as the heart descends in the chest, the main portion of the early thyroid gland follows, downward from the tongue toward its eventual position at the base of the neck. A thin stalk of thyroid material, remnant of the descending thyroid, is left connecting the base of the tongue with the thyroid gland, which comes to be located just under the Adam's apple (the thyroid cartilage).

Although this stalk, called the *thyroglossal duct*, usually disintegrates by the sixth week, remnants can still remain in some adults. Sometimes diseases that affect the thyroid gland can also affect remnant thyroid material in this duct, showing up as swellings or lumps anyplace between the base of the tongue and the breastbone. In some cases, the thyroid does not descend all the way, remaining near the tongue or anyplace in between there and its proper location. In very rare circumstances, the thyroid may descend too far and be found in the middle of the chest. Any abnormal location of the gland is called an *ectopic thyroid*.

It is believed that 10 percent of the thyroid gland cells, the parafollicular cells that make the hormone calcitonin, come from a different part of the embryo to merge with the rest of the thyroid in the two-month-old embryo. When the fetus is at least three months old, its thyroid gland first starts making thyroid hormone. The fetus requires thyroid hormone to permit its brain and nervous system to develop, and it appears that a small but significant contribution from the mother's thyroid is most important before this time. Recent studies suggest that the children of hypothyroid (low- or nonfunctioning thyroid) mothers who did not take thyroid hormone during the first trimester of pregnancy had measurably lower intelligence than children whose hypothyroid mothers received thyroid hormone treatment. For such obvious and important reasons, it is very important to be certain that a woman who may become pregnant is not hypothyroid or, if receiving thyroid hormone therapy, has proper thyroid hormone levels.

Location, Location

We like to think that the thyroid looks like a butterfly, although the ancient Greeks thought it looked like their shields, giving it the current English name (*thyroid* comes from the Greek word for "shield-shaped"). (See Figure 1.1.) Likewise, the German name for this gland, *Schilddrüse*, also means "shield gland." It is typically located in front of the windpipe (trachea) just above the midline bony notch in the top of the breastbone (sternal notch). Both of its "wings," the right and left thyroid lobes, wrap backward around the trachea and are attached to the upper front of the trachea and the lower part of the voice box (larynx). Each lobe is around 4 centimeters (1.6 inches) from top to bottom (pole to pole). The middle part of the gland, connecting the two lobes and

FIGURE 1.1

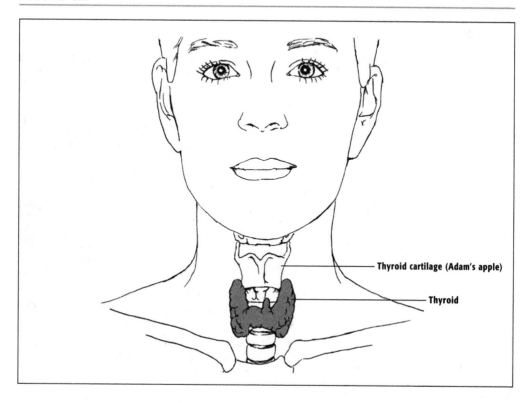

Thyroid cartilage (Adam's apple)

Thyroid

corresponding to the body of the butterfly, is the *isthmus*. Often, a pencil-thin bit of thyroid, known as the *pyramidal lobe* (the head of the "butterfly"), comes from the middle of the isthmus. When you swallow, the entire thyroid gland moves upward and back, just as the Adam's apple (thyroid cartilage) moves.

How Does It Feel?

A normal adult thyroid weighs around 15 to 20 grams (0.5 to 0.75 ounces). In some situations, when the gland is stimulated to grow by certain conditions (described in later chapters), the enlarged gland is called a *goiter*. A goiter is considered *diffuse* when the entire gland is symmetrically enlarged and *nodular* when there are one or more distinct lumps that can be distinguished from the rest of the gland. Ribbon-thin muscles overlie the thyroid, and a thick muscle on either side of the sternal notch runs to a point behind each ear (the sternocleidomastoid muscles).

I find that it is easier for me to feel the thyroid gland on another person when I'm standing just to the side, facing the individual. I usually begin, standing to the person's right side, with the fingers of my right hand feeling for the Adam's apple, then moving

TABLE 1.1 Thyroid Self-Exam

Examination Step	What to Do	What to Look For
1	Facing a mirror, place the fingers of your right hand over your Adam's apple while your chin is slightly out. Slowly and carefully feel the middle of your neck, working your way gradually down toward your breastbone.	Just as you pass downward from your Adam's apple, you will feel the firm cartilage rings of your windpipe. Feel the middle of each ring, moving downward until you feel a softer, flattened fleshy area overlying a ring. This is the middle portion of the thyroid gland, called the isthmus.
2	Keep your fingers on the thyroid isthmus and move them slowly toward the left side along the windpipe, pushing them under any loose flesh or muscle.	You should be feeling your left thyroid lobe, alongside your windpipe and sometimes, if enlarged, extending toward the left upper side of your neck.
3	Keep your fingers on your left thyroid lobe (you might have to feel down toward your collarbone). While your fingers are still, swallow.	You should feel the left thyroid lobe moving upward under your fingertips as you swallow. It should be fairly smooth and moderately soft. Any firm lumps or nodules should be noted and called to the attention of your physician.
4	Repeat these instructions, starting at step 1, but substitute right for left and left for right.	This should permit you to examine your right thyroid lobe.

downward over the windpipe until I feel the flattened, soft, spongy thyroid isthmus. With my fingers maintaining contact with the gland, I slide them toward the person's left neck, pushing under the sternocleidomastoid muscle and moving upward and downward slightly to feel the entire left thyroid lobe. Often I have to place my fingers over the lowest portion of the left thyroid lobe that I can reach, then ask the person to swallow to permit me to feel the lower left thyroid pole slide upward beneath my fingers. I use the same process to feel the right thyroid lobe, facing the person and standing at his or her left side, then using my left hand to feel the right side of the thyroid. With this technique and some practice, most thyroid glands can be felt unless the individual's neck is extremely short and thick or the gland is abnormally small or in an unusual location.

We encourage all readers to perform a thyroid self-exam at least once a year, which can help you find suspicious thyroid lumps (called *nodules*) or an enlargement of the thyroid that should be evaluated by your doctor. Table 1.1 describes how to do a thyroid self-exam and what to look for. Thyroid nodules are discussed in detail in Chapter 8.

More About Structure

There are a number of additional interesting features of thyroid gland structure. It is well supplied with blood from four major thyroid arteries. Under usual conditions, the flow through these arteries carries the equivalent of the entire body's blood volume each hour. Under some circumstances in which the thyroid is stimulated to become enlarged and hyperactive, such as in Graves' disease, the entire blood volume passes through the thyroid each half minute.

The thyroid gland is also supplied with nerves that provide sensation from the gland. When the thyroid gland is irritated, you may feel discomfort in the front of the neck; however, sometimes the sensation is felt in the ear. This is known as *referred pain*, much as one may feel pain in the left arm when experiencing a heart attack.

Near each thyroid lobe is a special nerve that supplies the voice box and vocal cords, the *recurrent laryngeal nerves*. Because of their proximity to the thyroid, these nerves may be damaged during thyroid surgery or directly injured by a thyroid cancer. If one nerve is damaged, then the vocal cord on the same side may be permanently paralyzed, resulting in a weak or hoarse voice. If both nerves are damaged, then both paralyzed vocal cords might block the windpipe, requiring an opening to be made in the neck so that the person can breathe (a tracheostomy).

Besides blood vessels and nerves in the thyroid, tiny, thin-walled tubes, called *lymph vessels*, can be found throughout the thyroid and the neck. Along the path of these lymph vessels are small nodules (*lymph nodes*) containing small white blood cells (lymphocytes). Lymph nodes function as filters for anything carried through the lymph vessels. In this way, bacteria that may infect the thyroid are carried first to lymph nodes, activating the lymphocytes there to stimulate the immune system to fight the infection. Likewise, in the event of thyroid cancer cells being present, some cancer cells may be passed through the lymph vessels and stop in these lymph node filters, growing there as lumps, which are removed during the course of thyroid cancer surgery.

The Parathyroid Glands

Four (in some cases, three to six) other glands are located very close to the thyroid gland; they're called *parathyroid glands*, which means "near the thyroid." These glands do not produce thyroid hormone but rather make parathyroid hormone, which causes the kidneys to retain calcium in the blood while releasing phosphorus into the urine. At the same time, parathyroid hormone increases the activation of vitamin D, which enhances the absorption of calcium and phosphorus from food and beverages.

Parathyroid glands are sometimes damaged or accidentally removed during surgery on the thyroid gland. Although only one functioning parathyroid gland is needed, loss or damage to all four glands results in loss of parathyroid hormone. Loss of parathyroid hormone will cause calcium to be lost into the urine and reduce its absorption from the diet, causing calcium levels in the blood to fall. The symptoms of low calcium include muscle cramps and spasms, numbness, and sometimes seizures, if severe. With the loss of parathyroid hormone, phosphorus levels would remain high because the kidneys would not be able to release it into the urine.

Inside the Thyroid Cell

The smallest living unit of the human body is the cell. All of the parts of the body are made of large numbers of these tiny cells, organized into body tissues and organs. A single cell is so small that a powerful microscope is needed to see it, and it takes around a million cells in a single lump before it is visible to the eye. Cells have a "skin" called the *cell membrane*. Inside the membrane is a relatively large ball (the *nucleus*) that contains the chromosomes, composed of genes that are responsible for controlling the cell's functions and the blueprints for all of its parts, as well as many smaller balls (the *organelles*) that perform vital functions of energy production and moving proteins and nutrients within the cell.

In the thyroid, the cells that produce thyroid hormone are called *follicular cells*. They are arranged in groups so that the follicular cells form a hollow ball (*thyroid follicles*), with its center (the *follicular lumen*) containing stored thyroid hormone (called *colloid*). All these thyroid follicles are contained within the fibrous capsule of the thyroid gland like bunches of tiny microscopic grapes. Between neighboring thyroid follicles are tiny blood vessels, lymph vessels, and collections of other cells called *parafollicular cells*. These parafollicular cells (also known as *C cells*) make additional hormones, such as calcitonin and somatostatin.

Thyroid follicular cells have special proteins in their membranes that are docking stations, or *receptors*, for special hormones that control the thyroid gland. One such hormone is thyroid stimulating hormone, also known as *TSH*. TSH (as will be discussed later in this chapter) sticks to the TSH receptor in the membrane. This causes a signal to be sent to the nucleus of the cell to activate the genes that result in the cell making proteins that work as iodine pumps. Once these iodine pumps are placed in the follicular cell membrane, they actively suck iodine (in the form of iodide) into the follicular cell.

The TSH receptor signal also activates the genes that control the production of thyroglobulin. *Thyroglobulin* is a protein that is unique to thyroid cells and is the early form of thyroid hormone. The iodine that was pumped into the follicular cell is joined to the thyroglobulin at certain places. These portions of thyroglobulin are broken off, becoming thyroid hormone (*thyroxine*, also known as *T4* because it contains four iodine atoms for each hormone molecule). The follicular cell releases both thyroxine and thyroglobulin into the blood. The best way to think about this complex process is to imagine a domino effect; when TSH in the blood reaches the thyroid follicular cell and sticks to the TSH receptor, it unleashes a chain of events inside the follicular cell: it manufactures iodine pumps, concentrates iodine from the blood, makes thyroglobulin, joins iodine to the thyroglobulin, breaks off thyroxine, and then releases both thyroxine and thyroglobulin into the bloodstream. Some of the thyroglobulin is stored inside the lumen of the thyroid follicles as colloid, ready to be taken back into the follicular cells and combined with iodine for release into the blood, should it be needed.

An Introduction to Thyroid Hormone

Here, we'll introduce you to thyroid hormone, a key player in understanding how the thyroid works. In Chapter 10, we'll discuss thyroid hormone used as replacement hormone for treating various thyroid diseases in much greater detail.

Thyroid hormone is essential for our existence, affecting every single cell in the body. In a very simplified view, thyroid hormone serves as the speed control for cells, controlling their speed of life. There are a few different forms of this hormone. As already discussed, it is made from portions of the thyroglobulin protein that are combined with iodine and then broken off. Iodine is the critical ingredient used by the thyroid to make thyroid hormone. In fact, without sufficient iodine in the diet, the thyroid gland is unable to produce enough thyroid hormone. (See Chapter 3 for more about iodine deficiency, which causes hypothyroidism.) Without sufficient iodine, a goiter (an enlarged thyroid gland) can also develop. (See Chapter 7.) Most people need at least 100 micrograms of iodine each day to produce enough thyroid hormone and avoid goiter.

Thyroxine (T4) is the predominant form of thyroid hormone. It's called T4 because it contains four iodine atoms for each hormone molecule. When thyroxine is provided as a medication in pill form, it is known as *levothyroxine*. It is debatable whether T4 has any direct effect on the cells of the body. When one specific iodine atom is removed from the T4 molecule, it becomes *T3 (triiodothyronine)*, the form necessary for doing the thyroid's job for the body's cells.

Nearly all cells have special enzymes inside of them (deiodinases) that remove an iodine from T4 to make it into T3. It seems likely that this is one way that each cell customizes how much T3 it will get, even though the blood supply to all of the cells generally provides the same level of T4 at the same time. If a different iodine atom is removed from T4, it makes an inactive molecule that does not work as an effective thyroid hormone.

The thyroid gland usually releases around 80 percent of its thyroid hormone as T4 and 20 percent as T3. (The T3 made by the thyroid is only a tiny portion of the T3 that is found in the body's cells—most is made from T4 within the cells.) When this T4 and T3 enter the blood, most of these hormones stick to blood proteins made by the liver, called *thyroid hormone transport proteins*. The three major thyroid hormone transport proteins are thyroxine-binding globulin (note that this is *not* the thyroglobulin that is made by the thyroid, even though the words appear similar), thyroxine-binding prealbumin, and albumin (as well as assorted other proteins, including cholesterol-carrying lipoproteins). Of the total T4 in the blood, 99.97 percent is stuck to these proteins. Unfortunately, the T4 and T3 stuck to these proteins generally do not get inside the body's cells, making them unavailable to be effective thyroid hormone. Only 0.03 percent of the total T4 is traveling around in the bloodstream in the free form, not stuck on anything. This *free T4* is the only portion of all of the T4 that is able to be taken up into each body cell and do the job of effective thyroid hormone.

Once the free T4 passes into a body cell of any kind, it is changed into T3 by the deiodinase enzymes. This T3 is taken into the nucleus of the cell. Inside the nucleus are special T3-receptor proteins that are made to stick to distinct spots in the genes of the chromosomes, and also stick to T3. When enough T3 is taken into the nucleus, it sticks to these T3 receptors and controls the genes that they are stuck to. Some genes are turned on and some genes are turned off. This shows the great power of thyroid hormones, working directly at the genetic controls of cells. It also shows how fundamentally important it is to have proper amounts of thyroid hormone in the body. Lastly, it explains how giving pure levothyroxine (T4) provides all of the benefits of thyroid hormone in the body by letting each cell convert the correct proportion to T3 for its own needs.

There is some evidence that T4 and T3 do additional tasks in each cell besides affecting the genes. Some of these tasks include affecting the support structure of cells, affecting the energy factory of cells (the mitochondria), and changing the way that the cell membrane permits a variety of chemicals to enter the cell. The many effects of thyroid hormones are still being discovered and seem to be important for every type of cell in the body.

Keeping It Right: The Body's Natural Thyroid Hormone "Thermostat"

It's clear that the body needs to tightly control thyroid hormone. Even very small changes in the amount of thyroid hormone that enters each cell affects the cells' function.

To keep the amount of thyroid hormone regulated, your body relies on the pituitary gland, a gland that hangs down from the underside of the brain, in the center of the head behind the eyeballs (see Figure 1.2). The pituitary gland serves as the "thermostat" for some of the body's hormones. It is constantly measuring the level of thyroid hormone in the blood. Just as the house's thermostat sends an electrical signal to the furnace if the house air is cold, the pituitary gland sends a hormone signal through the bloodstream to stimulate the thyroid gland if the thyroid hormone level in the blood is too low. This hormone signal is called *thyroid stimulating hormone*, also known by its initials as *TSH*, as discussed earlier. The TSH stimulates the thyroid to take up iodine from the blood and make thyroid hormone, just as the thermostat's electrical signal to the furnace stimulates it to take up fuel and make heat. When the thyroid hormone level in the blood rises to the proper level, it causes the pituitary to reduce its release of TSH, just as the house's thermostat turns off its electrical signal to the furnace when

FIGURE 1.2

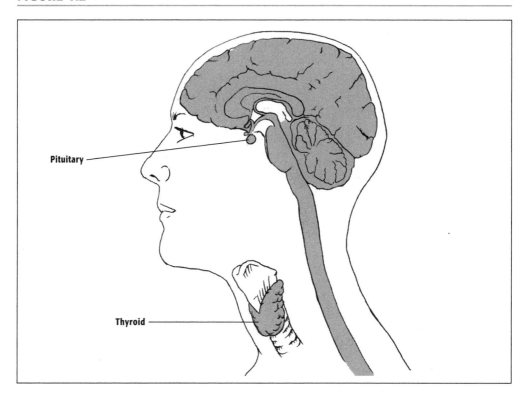

Pituitary

Thyroid

the air reaches the desired temperature. This results in the thyroid hormone level staying at the proper level in the blood, similar to way the thermostat regulates the air temperature in a house. For this reason, if the pituitary gland is working properly, a high level of TSH indicates there needs to be more thyroid hormone in the blood, a low level of TSH indicates there's too much thyroid hormone in the blood, and a normal level of TSH indicates a normal level of thyroid hormone.

While this analogy explains how to interpret many of the blood tests used in diagnosis of thyroid problems, the actual control system in the body has additional layers of complexity. The hypothalamus is a part of the brain that is just above the pituitary gland. It is connected to the pituitary by a thin stalk that carries hormones that help control the pituitary. A part of the hypothalamus also works like a thyroid hormone "thermostat," releasing its own signal, *TSH-releasing hormone* (also known as *TRH*), to the pituitary when the thyroid hormone levels are low. In this way, there is a "double-thermostat" control of thyroid hormone in the body, a superbly precise control system in a healthy person.

2 Tests and Labs: Diagnosing Thyroid Disease

When trying to determine if fatigue, weight gain, dry skin, and other conditions are caused by a thyroid condition, other health disorders, or simply normal life variations, it all comes down to blood tests. These tests help doctors determine if you have appropriate amounts of thyroid hormone in your blood.

A normal and healthy amount of thyroid hormone is known as *euthyroidism*. If the thyroid hormone levels are insufficient to be euthyroid, we call this *hypothyroidism* (described in Chapter 3). If the thyroid hormone levels are too high, the condition is termed *thyrotoxicosis* (described in Chapter 4). Sometimes thyrotoxicosis is present because the thyroid is overactive, making too much thyroid hormone, a situation known as *hyperthyroidism*. However, thyrotoxicosis can also be present without hyperthyroidism, such as when someone takes too high a dose of thyroid hormone tablets. In this case the thyroid itself is not overactive (thus not hyperthyroid); however, the levels of thyroid hormone in the blood are too high.

Often, when I'm (Ken) lecturing to large audiences of physicians, usually late in the evening, I ask, "Who is tired? Who is a bit overweight? Who suffers from constipation? Who has dry skin?" Each question results in a large number of raised hands. Then I ask, "Is anyone here hypothyroid and not taking thyroid hormone?" No one raises his or her hand. Yet many of these symptoms are the same as those of hypothyroidism. The symptoms of hypothyroidism completely overlap with those of normal life variations or those of unrelated health disorders. The proper laboratory test acts as an "honest broker," providing objective evidence for making the correct diagnosis. Know, however, that such tests are not infallible.

This chapter will take you through all of the laboratory tests that can be useful in providing diagnostic answers with respect to your thyroid gland. We'll first visit the tests that measure the levels of thyroid hormones, including measuring free T4. Then we'll discuss how to assess the pituitary gland's responses to these thyroid hormone levels through measuring thyroid stimulating hormone. This will be followed by a review of tests that evaluate the function of the thyroid gland itself. Finally, we'll see how thyroid disease affects laboratory tests that assess other parts of the body. After this, we'll fit all of these different tests into a framework based on the different types of thyroid disease.

Throughout this chapter (and in much of this book), we use the term *protein*. Proteins are one of the major types of substances that make up the body. Proteins are made of amino acids that are connected together. Nearly all hormones, enzymes, and body structures are made of different types of proteins. Some of these proteins are dissolved in the bloodstream and some form solid structures in the body. In addition, through the actions of protein enzymes, the body's cells can produce a wide range of nonprotein chemicals to perform a variety of functions.

Three other major types of substances make up the body. *Carbohydrates*, another name for sugars, can be dissolved in the blood and used as fuel for the body's cells, or they can be attached to some proteins to become part of their structure. *Fats*, also known as *lipids*, can be found in the blood as free fatty acids, attached to proteins (sometimes known as *lipoproteins*), or in solid lumps as body fat. Lastly, *minerals* can be found in the bones of the body, forming the fourth type of body substance.

Besides forming proteins, some amino acids are used to form hormones, such as the amino acid tyrosine, which forms thyroid hormones when combined with iodine. The thyroid hormones, thyroxine and triiodothyronine, are members of the steroid hormone superfamily, which also includes cortisol, estrogen, progesterone, androgen, aldosterone, and vitamin D. All of these different hormones stick to special proteins in the nucleus (center part) of the cell called *nuclear receptor proteins*, which then stick to particular parts of different genes to do their own particular jobs. (See Chapter 1.) Proper use of laboratory tests ensures that hormones are doing their jobs.

Tests That Measure Thyroid Hormone Levels

As we discussed in Chapter 1, the major thyroid hormone made by the thyroid gland is thyroxine (T4), which is known as *levothyroxine (L-T4)* when given as a medication. T4, called this because each T4 molecule has four iodine atoms, is converted within each cell of the body to triiodothyronine (T3, containing only three iodine atoms for each molecule). T3 is the active thyroid hormone that activates genes and does the job of thyroid hormone. When additional iodines are removed (for example, forming T2 or T1), inactive degradation products with no thyroid hormone–like effects are created.

In the bloodstream, 99.97 percent of the T4 is stuck to a variety of blood proteins with only a small portion (0.03 percent) floating free and able to enter cells to be converted to active T3. Most of these binding proteins are made by the liver and serve as a circulating reservoir of T4 and some T3 in the blood. Nonetheless, since these binding proteins cannot enter the body's cells with their T4 and T3, only the levels of the free and unattached T4 and T3 are important to know. Doctors can perform different tests that measure the free T4, including a *free T4 test*, a *free thyroxine index*, or an *equilibrium dialysis free T4*. The free T4 test is the most appropriate test for measuring the effective thyroid hormone level in most people. The free thyroxine index is now considered outdated, but it can give physicians a reasonable estimate of the free T4 level. The equilibrium dialysis free T4 is the "gold standard" measure of the actual free T4 level. It is a bit expensive and takes a while for the lab to complete the test, but it is most useful for severely ill people in whom the typical free T4 test may not be accurate.

While blood tests that measure the total T4 level cannot be used to give an accurate picture of the effective (free) T4 level, there are still some physicians who try to use a total T4 test to evaluate their patients. Sometimes it gives them sufficient information to make a diagnosis, but there are many situations in which the total T4 is misleading. In pregnancy, when blood proteins are much higher than usual because of increased levels of estrogen, the total T4 level can seem twice as high as normal despite the free T4 being completely normal. Likewise, in conditions of starvation, some types of liver disease, and in some types of kidney disease, the blood proteins are much lower than normal, making the total T4 abnormally low despite normal free T4 levels. For these reasons, your physician should not be using a total T4 test to assess a thyroid problem.

The T3 level can be useful to assess thyroid hormone levels in the case of thyrotoxicosis. This is because there are some cases of hyperthyroidism in which T3 release from the thyroid is the cause of the high thyroid hormone levels, a condition called *T3 toxicosis*. Although a free T3 test is the most accurate and can be ordered, a total T3 level is usually sufficient to assess for this condition. However, a total T3 is not useful in evaluating for hypothyroidism.

The T3 level in the blood cannot accurately tell you about the actual level of T3 inside each of your body cells, which is the critical feature of thyroid hormone activity. This is because most of the T3 inside your cells is actually produced right in the cells, whereas the T3 in the blood comes from T3 leaking from the body's cells and being released from the thyroid gland. Tests that determine the amount of T3 in the blood level are only useful when there are excessive amounts of T3 in the cells as in thyrotoxicosis.

TSH: The Most Sensitive Test to Assess Thyroid Hormone Status

Another way to assess the adequacy of thyroid function in the body is by assessing the level of thyroid stimulating hormone (TSH) produced by the pituitary gland. This test is by far the most valuable, and perhaps the most misunderstood by thyroid patients. This section looks at TSH testing in detail.

Why Is TSH Necessary?

One problem with trying to use the free T4 level to diagnose hyperthyroidism or hypothyroidism is that it is not very sensitive for an individual. This is because the normal range of the free T4 is "normal" in respect to large groups of people, but not to individual persons. For example, the normal range of the free T4, in some labs, is 0.8 to 2.1 ng/dL. However, for one particular person, the normal level for free T4 could be 1.2 precisely. If that person is given extra thyroid hormone pills to raise the free T4 to 2.0 (still within the "normal range"), he or she will have symptoms of thyrotoxicosis. Another person whose individual normal free T4 is 1.7, after receiving sufficient antithyroid medication (see Chapters 6 and 11) to lower the free T4 to 0.9, would become truly hypothyroid, even though the free T4 is still in the "normal range."

The most sensitive way to see how the body "feels"—euthyroid, hypothyroid, or thyrotoxic—is to look at the body's own natural "thermostat" for thyroid hormone, the pituitary gland. If the blood going to the pituitary gland (and the rest of the body) contains the proper amount of free T4, the level of thyroid stimulating hormone (TSH) will be normal (0.5 to 4.0 mU/L). If you are hypothyroid, the TSH level will be higher than normal, as the pituitary seeks to stimulate your thyroid gland, even if it isn't there or working anymore. If you are thyrotoxic, the TSH level will be much lower than normal, since the pituitary is reflecting its need to diminish its stimulation of your thyroid gland.

What Is a Normal Range?

The definitions of normal, high, and low TSH levels have been changing because of refinements in our appreciation of thyroid function testing. For nearly all laboratory blood tests, the "normal range" is figured out by taking a large group of "normal" people and performing the test on them. The average result is defined as the middle of the "normal range," and the upper and lower limits come from a statistical calculation (plus or minus 2 standard deviations). However, we're now learning that many of the people in this "normal" group actually had mild cases of thyroid disease, most apparent in older people who have greater risk of subclinical or hidden thyroid problems. For this reason, although your own laboratory might print its "normal range" for the TSH as something close to 0.5 to 5.0, these refinements are likely to make the normal range a level ranging from 0.5 to 2.0.

What Are Abnormal TSH Levels?

TSH levels that are elevated, yet lower than 10, are in the range called *early* or *subclinical* hypothyroidism. Most people with TSH levels in this range do not have any symptoms that clearly suggest they're hypothyroid. However, many medical research studies have shown that such individuals have subtle unhealthy changes in their bodies. These can be corrected by taking sufficient thyroid hormone (levothyroxine) to lower the TSH into the normal range and to prevent future problems with worsening hypothyroidism.

People with slightly lowered TSH levels, ranging from just beneath the normal range down to 0.2, may have early thyrotoxicosis; however, unless they are elderly or have heart rhythm problems (see Chapter 25) it is not useful to do much more than to monitor them closely until they either become normal or the TSH lowers further. People with TSH levels from less than 0.2 to beneath the lowest measurable number are in the *thyrotoxic* range. Sometimes, in people with thyroid cancer (see Chapter 9), sufficient levothyroxine is given to keep the TSH low on purpose, while trying to avoid thyrotoxic symptoms. In other cases, TSH levels this low warrant careful evaluation and treatment. Many doctors will check the free T4 and the TSH levels a few weeks after noting a subtly low TSH to see if this TSH has spontaneously become normal or has lowered into the definitively thyrotoxic range.

Exceptions to the Rule

The "rule" that hypothyroidism comes with high TSH levels and thyrotoxicosis comes with low TSH levels is not always accurate. It assumes that the pituitary gland and hypothalamus are completely normal and that any abnormalities come from the thyroid gland. This is not always the case.

When the Pituitary Is "Broken"

Sometimes, the pituitary gland is not working properly. This can result from a tumor growing in the gland and preventing it from making TSH. This can also happen if the portion of the brain that controls the pituitary gland, the hypothalamus, is damaged from a tumor, trauma, or stroke. In both of these situations, the pituitary gland cannot make sufficient TSH to stimulate the thyroid gland to make T4, causing the person to be hypothyroid. In such a case, the free T4 levels would be quite low, but the TSH level would be inappropriately in the normal range or lower than normal. This combination of a low free T4 level and a normal or low TSH level should prompt your physician to begin a careful evaluation of your pituitary gland and all of the other hormones that it regulates. The pituitary gland also regulates the adrenal glands, which make cortisol; the sex glands (testes in men and ovaries in women), which make either testosterone or estrogen; and the control of urine flow, by releasing vasopressin (antidiuretic hormone, ADH). In this case, it would be dangerous to give you levothyroxine treatment without evaluating all of the potential hormone deficiencies and correcting them with proper hormone therapy.

Rare Pituitary Tumors That Make TSH

There are very, very rare pituitary tumors that make too much TSH. They do this even though the free T4 level is way too high and the person probably has symptoms of thyrotoxicosis. Such tumors usually require a combination of special medications or external beam radiation treatments, even after a surgeon has performed surgery to remove them. Their treatment and evaluation requires the care of a very experienced endocrinologist.

Thyroid Hormone Resistance Syndrome

Certain rare inherited diseases result in people being born with a resistance to their own thyroid hormone. This is caused by a mutation in the gene that makes the receptors for thyroid hormone within the nucleus of each body cell. Because of these abnormal thyroid hormone receptors that don't stick to T3 as well as they should, far higher than normal levels of thyroid hormone are necessary to do the things that normal levels of thyroid hormone usually do. In this situation, despite high levels of free T4, the TSH may be inappropriately high or normal and the person will show no symptoms of thyrotoxicosis. If this situation is suspected, it is important that your physician consult one of a very few academic specialists in this thyroid condition to confirm the suspicion and screen the family for other affected individuals. We'll discuss thyroid hormone resistance more in Chapter 18.

Thyroglobulin: The Specific Thyroid Protein

The thyroid gland makes a special protein called *thyroglobulin*. No other body organ has been found to make it. When TSH is released by the pituitary gland to stimulate the thyroid gland, it stimulates each thyroid follicular cell to make thyroglobulin. Some of the thyroglobulin is stored within the interior of the thyroid follicles as colloid (see Chapter 1). Some is combined with iodine within the thyroid cell, releasing fragments that become T4 and T3 in the bloodstream. Some of the thyroglobulin is released directly into the bloodstream.

The measurement of thyroglobulin can be very useful in diagnosing thyroid conditions. In general, the level of thyroglobulin in the blood reflects the amount of thyroid tissue in the body. When the TSH level is very high, as when a person is hypothyroid, each thyroid cell makes more thyroglobulin. On the other hand, when levothyroxine tablets are given in high enough dosages to keep the TSH level very low, each thyroid cell makes much less thyroglobulin.

Measuring the thyroglobulin level in the blood has several uses. In thyrotoxic people, it can discriminate between people taking too many thyroid hormone pills, in which case the thyroglobulin level would be very low, and those who are hyperthyroid with overactivity of the thyroid gland, in which the thyroglobulin level would be high. In situations when the thyroid gland is inflamed (thyroiditis), release of thyroglobulin that had been stored in the gland accounts for high thyroglobulin levels during blood tests.

Thyroglobulin levels have the most importance in the follow-up of people with a history of thyroid cancer. For people with thyroid cancer, surgical removal of the thyroid gland and any noticeable tumor, along with destruction of any remnant thyroid cells using radioactive iodine, should result in the elimination of any measurable thyroglobulin in the blood. On the other hand, in such situations, the ability to measure thyroglobulin levels to any degree indicates the persistence of thyroid cancer cells in the body (since there is no normal thyroid tissue to account for the thyroglobulin). However, around 20 percent of women have autoimmune antibodies that stick to their own thyroglobulin and interfere with the blood tests that measure the thyroglobulin levels. See Chapter 9 for further details on thyroglobulin levels in thyroid cancer.

Thyroid Hormone-Binding Proteins

Several proteins in the blood, produced by the liver, stick to thyroid hormones. They include thyroxine-binding globulin (TBG), thyroxine-binding prealbumin (TBPA), and albumin. In addition, several cholesterol-containing particles in the blood, lipoproteins, are able to bind T4 and T3.

Before good tests were available to measure the free T4, it was useful to measure the TBG level as a way to estimate the portion of the total T4 that was free. Since modern laboratory tests no longer need this estimate, the TBG level is not usually used for diagnosis of thyroid problems. *It is important to note that the TBG level is frequently mistaken for a thyroglobulin level (often abbreviated as TG) with the result that the TBG is wrongly obtained in following thyroid cancer patients who need the TG level measured.* The only way to ensure that you are getting a TG test (or have had one) and not a TBG test is to request a copy of all of your lab reports. If you suspect this common error was made, you must educate your doctor about this mix-up, and if need be, photocopy a passage of this book to help bring the matter to your doctor's attention.

In some unusual cases, there may be abnormal thyroid binding protein levels, or altered binding proteins, which can change other thyroid function tests. For example, some people make abnormal TBG, no TBG, or too much TBG. This can result in the total T4 levels being low or high, without having much effect upon the free T4 levels and absolutely no effect upon the TSH. Likewise, altered albumin can stick to T4 much more than normal and cause the total T4 to be much higher than normal, without affecting the person or changing the TSH level. This is another reason why it is very important to avoid using the total T4 level, rather than the free T4 level, as the method to evaluate your thyroid hormone.

Table 2.1 summarizes appropriate thyroid blood tests and their expected results for various thyroid conditions.

TABLE 2.1. Thyroid Conditions and Appropriate Thyroid Blood Tests

Thyroid Condition	Free T4	T3 or Free T3	TSH	Thyroglobulin
Normal thyroid function (euthyroidism) in a person with a normal thyroid gland	Normal	Normal	Normal	Normal
Normal thyroid function (euthyroidism)in a person *without* a thyroid gland	Normal	Normal	Normal	Very low or none
Early or subclinical hypothyroidism	Normal or low	Not used	Slightly high	Not used
Hypothyroidism	Low	Not used	High	Not used
Mild or subclinical thyrotoxicosis	Normal or high	Normal or high	Slightly low but greater than 0.2	Not used
Thyrotoxicosis	High	High	Low (less than 0.2)	Not used
Thyrotoxicosis from thyroid pills	High	High	Low	Low
Thyrotoxicosis from hyperthyroidism (Graves' disease or toxic thyroid nodule)	High	High	Low	High

Measuring Thyroid Antibodies

The body has an immune system that is important to help it fight infectious diseases. There are several parts of the immune system, but the portions of the body responsible for this are the white blood cells. Some kinds of white blood cells, *neutrophils*, engulf bacteria and viruses. Other white blood cells, *lymphocytes*, make and release special proteins called antibodies that are tailor-made to stick to specific types of invading bacteria or viruses. Sometimes, some of the lymphocytes get mixed up and make antibodies that target parts of your own body. When this causes an illness, it is called an *autoimmune* (self-immune) disease. If the antibodies target the joints, this causes rheumatoid arthritis. If the antibodies target the muscles, this causes myasthenia gravis. Antibodies that target the thyroid can cause thyroid disease.

There are three major kinds of antithyroid antibodies. *Antithyroid peroxidase (TPO) antibodies* used to be called anti-microsomal antibodies. TPO antibodies attack the portion of the thyroid cell responsible for making thyroid hormones. The thyroid disease that is associated with these antibodies is *Hashimoto's thyroiditis* (also known as *Hashimoto's disease*). Hashimoto's thyroiditis is classically diagnosed by examining the thyroid gland or a piece of the thyroid gland (from a biopsy) under a microscope. Since more than 95 percent of people with Hashimoto's thyroiditis have TPO antibodies in their blood, the presence of these antibodies is usually sufficient to make this diagnosis without doing a thyroid biopsy. (Hashimoto's disease is discussed more in Chapter 5.)

Another antibody associated with Hashimoto's thyroiditis is one that sticks to thyroglobulin, the *antithyroglobulin antibody*. This particular antibody is important because its presence, in people with thyroid cancer, interferes with the ability of a laboratory to measure the level of thyroglobulin in the blood.

The third major type of thyroid antibody is called *thyroid stimulating immunoglobulin* (*TSI*, also known as *thyroid stimulating antibody* or *TSA*). Normally, TSH from the pituitary will stick to the TSH receptor (a "docking station" for TSH) to turn on each thyroid cell to start to suck up iodine and make thyroid hormone. However, in this case, TSI will stick to the TSH receptors and do all of the thyroid cell stimulation that TSH would have done. Unlike TSH, however, TSI is not turned off when thyroid hormone levels become too high. The continued stimulation of the TSH receptor by TSI causes thyrotoxicosis. This is known as *Graves' disease*, discussed more in Chapter 6. TSI will also stick to parts of the eye muscles, causing eye irritation and swelling of these muscles sufficient to make the eyeballs protrude from the eye socket, another feature of Graves' disease, called *orbitopathy* or *exophthalmopathy*. In patient circles it is known as *thyroid eye disease* (*TED*) or *Graves' ophthalmopathy* (*GO*), discussed more in Chapter 23.

Graves' disease antibodies are usually a mixture of TPO antibodies and thyroglobulin antibodies that help destroy the thyroid gland, and TSI antibodies that stimulate the thyroid gland. This is why all three of these antibodies can be measured in the blood of people with Graves' disease, while only TPO antibodies and thyroglobulin antibodies are seen in people with Hashimoto's thyroiditis.

Different labs report results on these antibodies using different units with different normal ranges. Your doctor should pay close attention to the details of the lab report to know if these antibodies are present in high enough amounts to be significant. Again, you can request copies of your lab reports, which will have the normal range for that particular lab listed; then you can compare whether your own levels are higher than normal, meaning that you indeed have antibodies in significant amounts. Copies of your lab reports also help in cases where you seek out a specialist, or a second or even third opinion. Almost one-quarter of women in North America show significant levels of TPO antibodies at some time in their life, accounting for a high prevalence of hypothyroidism. Elevated levels of TPO antibodies are also associated with a higher risk of postpartum thyroiditis (an inflammation of the thyroid gland occurring in moth-

TABLE 2.2. Lab Tests Used to Measure Thyroid Function

Laboratory Tests	Normal Range Common Units (International Units)	How It's Used (Condition)
Free T4	0.9–1.6 ng/dL (12–21 pmol/L)	Measures thyroid hormone available to enter cells (hypothyroidism, thyrotoxicosis)
T3	80–180 ng/dL (1.2–2.8 nmol/L)	Measures total T3 (thyrotoxicosis)
Free T3	2.2–4.0 ng/L (3.4–6.1 pmol/L)	Measures free (unbound) T3 (thyrotoxicosis)
Reverse T3	90–350 pg/mL (140–538 pmol/L)	Measures reverse T3, an inactive degradation product of T4, increased in illness (not used)
TSH	0.6–4.5 µU/mL (0.6–4.5 mU/L)	Most sensitive measure of thyroid status (hypothyroidism, thyrotoxicosis, thyroid cancer care)
Thyroglobulin (TG)	less than 35 ng/mL (less than 35 µg/L)	Measures thyroglobulin, a unique protein from thyroid cells (thyroiditis, thyroid cancer care)
Thyroxine-binding globulin (TBG)	13–30 µg/mL (13–30 mg/L)	Measures TBG, a protein in blood, made in the liver, that sticks to thyroid hormone (not used)
TPO antibody	0–70 IU/mL	Measures TPO, an autoimmune antibody in thyroid disease (Hashimoto's, Graves' disease, pregnancy)
Thyroglobulin antibody	0–2.2 IU/mL	Measures autoimmune antibody to thyroglobulin (Hashimoto's, thyroid cancer—check TG)
Thyroid-stimulating immunoglobulin (TSI or TSA)	Less than 130% of basal activity	Measures autoimmune antibody to TSH receptor (Graves' disease)

ers after giving birth) and a higher risk of miscarriage as compared to other women, both discussed in Chapter 13.

Table 2.2 shows units used and normal ranges for various thyroid blood tests.

Dynamic Tests of Thyroid Function

The pituitary gland is stimulated to make its hormones, including TSH, by hormones released by the portion of the brain just above it, the hypothalamus. In the case of TSH, the particular stimulating hormone is called *TSH-releasing hormone (TRH)*. Before the mid-1980s, TSH tests were not able to measure values low enough to distinguish low from normal levels. To see if there was evidence of thyrotoxicosis (which would lower TSH levels) people were often given injections of TRH. Several TSH levels were measured from the time of the injection to two hours later. If there was thyrotoxicosis, then the TSH levels would remain low despite the stimulation of the TRH. A normal test would result in the TSH levels rising to around 20 and then returning back to baseline levels by one hour. Since TSH tests became much improved and more sensitive, they have been able to discern low TSH levels (thyrotoxicosis) from normal TSH levels (euthyroid), making TRH tests obsolete. The only current use for TRH testing is to check for abnormalities of the pituitary or hypothalamus. (Unfortunately, the company that made TRH no longer does so, making this test impossible to perform and only of historical interest. Although some patient literature still refers to TRH tests being available, and in some cases, even offers contact information for certain labs, this information is now outdated and inaccurate.)

Tests of Metabolism

The classic test of the body's metabolism, its speed of life, is called the *basal metabolic rate*, the *BMR*. Before there were blood tests to measure TSH levels or thyroid hormone levels, the only way physicians could objectively assess thyroid status was to check the BMR. This test involves the patient resting comfortably in bed, preferably early in the morning, and then having a plastic hood placed over his or her head. A machine would then sample air from the hood and measure the rate that oxygen was used up, providing a rough estimate of the person's metabolic rate.

Unfortunately, many, many things can affect the BMR that have nothing to do with thyroid hormone. Everything from a cup of coffee to a menstrual period makes far greater changes in the BMR than do changes in thyroid hormone levels. Reputable physicians no longer use this test to diagnose their patients' thyroid disorders. Its only value is in the context of research studies, with investigators fully aware of its limitations. Measuring the BMR cannot unmask hidden thyroid disease that modern laboratory testing fails to detect. We deal more with this and other thyroid treatment myths in Chapter 19.

Radioactive Thyroid Tests

Many of us have come to fear radioactive substances, sometimes correctly, with so many terrible historical associations: Hiroshima, Nagasaki, the Marshall Islands, Three

Mile Island, and Chernobyl, to name just a few. Indeed, a very important guideline in the field of radiation safety is to make sure that anyone's exposure to radiation is "as low as reasonably achievable" (this phrase is referred to by its acronym, *ALARA*). On the other hand, thyroid disease was the first type of illness in which radioactive substances proved essential for both diagnosis and treatment, providing the starting basis for the entire field of nuclear medicine. Radioactive iodine isotopes have played major roles in understanding normal physiology of the thyroid and the nature of thyroid diseases. Particularly in Graves' disease, toxic nodular disease, and thyroid cancer, radioiodine has provided unique diagnostic insights and therapeutic opportunities. In this section, we'll explore the diagnostic uses of radioisotopes, starting with tests of thyroid function and ending with tests to detect and characterize thyroid diseases.

Radioactive Iodine Uptake Measurements

Each thyroid cell takes up iodine to make thyroid hormone. The average thyroid gland weighs around 20 grams, with each gram taking up around 1 percent of the iodine available from the diet. Usually, if the thyroid gland is stimulated and has become hyperthyroid, it takes up more iodine. Likewise, thyroid glands that are not working well and do not make thyroid hormone usually take up less iodine. To measure this, a person is given a small dose of radioactive iodine (I-123 or I-131) to swallow. One day later, a radiation detector is placed near the person's thyroid gland. The portion of the total dose of radioactive iodine that was swallowed that is measured in the thyroid gland is called the *24-hour radioactive iodine uptake (RAIU)*. Although a normal RAIU is between 15 and 25 percent, this result can be greatly affected by the person's diet. People who eat foods that are high in iodine (iodized salt, dairy products, kelp, seafood, and so on), will have a lower RAIU. This is because, although their thyroid's ability to suck up iodine has not been altered, the nonradioactive dietary iodine dilutes out the portion of the radioactive iodine that goes into the thyroid gland, resulting in a lower RAIU.

The RAIU is useful under certain circumstances. It is most useful when evaluating people with thyrotoxicosis. If the RAIU is high, then hyperthyroidism (usually from a toxic thyroid nodule or Graves' disease) will be diagnosed as the cause of the excess thyroid hormone. If the RAIU is low, then the cause of thyrotoxicosis is from excess ingestion of thyroid hormone or release of stored thyroid hormone from an inflamed thyroid gland (thyroiditis). If you have Graves' disease, then your physician may use the RAIU result to calculate the amount of radioactive iodine to give you to treat the hyperthyroidism. (Chapter 6 discusses Graves' disease in more detail.)

Radioactive Scans and Imaging

Radioactive isotopes, given to people with thyroid disease, may concentrate within the thyroid gland or, in the case of thyroid cancer, in any tumor cells spread anywhere in the body. After the radioactive isotope is administered by mouth or into a vein (iodine isotopes are usually swallowed and other element isotopes are intravenous), the person is placed in front of a machine that is able to detect the gamma rays (x-rays) that come from the radioactive isotope in the thyroid gland or in tumor cells. This machine or camera puts together a picture or scan based upon the x-rays coming from the person's body. There are a variety of types of radioactive isotopes and scans used.

When to Use Thyroid Scans

Thyroid scans are used to see how much of the thyroid gland is taking up iodine, representing parts of the gland that are functioning normally, overfunctioning by taking up higher amounts of iodine (looking "hot" on the scan), or underfunctioning and not taking up iodine well (showing up as "cold" areas on the scan). Prior to the scan, the person is given a small dose of a radioactive tracer. The best tracer is the I-123 isotope of iodine because using radioactive iodine for the scan best represents the natural processes of the thyroid gland and I-123 exposes a person to less radiation than the other useful iodine isotope, I-131; however, I-123 is more expensive than I-131. Alternatively, many scans are done using an isotope of technetium, 99m-Tc. Technetium is most readily available to nuclear medicine departments and it can provide a useful scan image; however, it does not always give the same picture as an iodine isotope scan.

When Not to Use Thyroid Scans

It's unfortunate, but most of the thyroid scans that physicians order are unnecessary. There are only a few appropriate reasons for undergoing a thyroid scan. First, if you are thyrotoxic (low TSH and normal or high free T4), a thyroid scan can show if the entire thyroid gland is overactive ("hot") or if there is a distinct nodule that is overactive ("hot" nodule). Many times, thyroid scans are used to evaluate thyroid glands with nodules, distinct lumps, or masses. This is useful only if the TSH is low (lower than 0.2), so that you can see if the nodule is "hot" or "cold." A "hot" nodule (if the TSH is low) is known as a *toxic thyroid nodule* and treated with radioactive iodine or surgery.

If the TSH is *not* low, then a doctor should *not* use a scan to evaluate a thyroid nodule. This is because, no matter what the scan shows, it will not answer the critical question, is the nodule a thyroid cancer? The only way that this question can be reliably answered, short of having surgery, is by a fine (thin) needle biopsy. Sometimes thyroid scans are used inappropriately to check out the size of the thyroid gland or to look for nodules. Determining the size of the thyroid gland or looking for nodules is best done by physical examination or with an ultrasound of the thyroid gland. We discuss thyroid nodules and fine needle biopsy more in Chapter 8.

Radioactive Iodine Whole Body Scans (WBS) and Thyroid Cancers

Radioactive iodine scans of the entire body are used to evaluate you for thyroid cancer only *after* you have had your thyroid gland removed by surgery and have been suitably prepared to have this scan done. A much rarer use of such scans is to look for ectopic (in a different place than usual) thyroid tissue, such as is sometimes seen in the ovary or in the chest.

Preparation for Whole Body Scans

There are three important requirements for adequate radioactive iodine WBS preparation: a sufficiently high TSH level (greater than 30) to stimulate thyroid and thyroid cancer cells, depletion of nonradioactive iodine from the body (low-iodine diet and avoiding intravenous contrast dye used for CT scans), and a determination that you are not pregnant if you are a fertile woman.

The low-iodine diet (see Chapter 20) is critical in all methods of scan preparation and can enhance the sensitivity of the scan around tenfold. This is because the cancer cells, stimulated by TSH, suck up iodine regardless of whether it is radioactive or nonradioactive. The amount of iodine in the average American diet exceeds the amount of iodine in the radioactive tracer dose by several hundredfold and can dilute the uptake of the radioactive iodine, making the scan much less effective for detecting tumor. Of course, it is important to avoid radiation exposure to a fetus in a pregnant woman and appropriate contraception is necessary to guard against this.

Three different methods ensure that the TSH is high enough for a WBS, all of which should be conducted under your physician's guidance:

The Hypothyroid Withdrawal Preparation: The "Gold Standard." The classic, "gold standard" method of raising the TSH level sufficient to be ready for a radioactive iodine WBS requires not taking levothyroxine medication for around six weeks or avoiding starting levothyroxine after the surgical removal of the thyroid gland (thyroidectomy). Since the half-life of levothyroxine (the time it takes for the blood levels to fall to half of the starting level after the medication is stopped) is a week, it takes roughly six "half-lives" (six weeks) of time to get the free T4 level low enough so that the TSH is above 30. To avoid hypothyroid symptoms for the first four weeks, you should be given T3 in tablet form (Cytomel) twice daily, since the last two weeks of the six-week period are sufficient to get rid of the Cytomel. (T3 and Cytomel are discussed more in Chapters 3 and 10.)

This approach is the "gold standard" by which the next two methods are compared. The main disadvantage of this hypothyroid withdrawal scan preparation is that you become severely hypothyroid with all of its disadvantages (see Chapter 3). You should not be operating motor vehicles nor performing any critical tasks requiring you to have optimal mental function. For many people, three to four weeks of medically excused absence from work is required. This method will not work if there are pituitary diseases that reduce the ability of the pituitary to make its own TSH.

On the other hand, this hypothyroidism is actually a big advantage in enhancing the sensitivity of the scan, since hypothyroid kidneys do not get rid of the radioactive iodine from the blood as rapidly as kidneys with normal thyroid hormone levels, permitting the radioactive iodine greater availability to be taken up by tumor cells. There is no other current method of WBS preparation that provides better sensitivity than the hypothyroid withdrawal method. In addition, as will be discussed later in Chapter 9, the hypothyroid withdrawal preparation is the best method of preparation for radioactive iodine therapy of thyroid cancer should the WBS reveal its presence. In this way, the same preparation permits both scanning and treatment. One way to balance the negative aspects of being hypothyroid with the positive aspect of more sensitive scans is to use hypothyroid withdrawal scans less and less frequently as long as scan results remain clean (cancer-free). This reduces the need to become hypothyroid any more than is optimal.

The "Moderate Hypothyroidism" Preparation: An Alternative. Another method of raising the TSH to a level sufficient to perform an I-131 WBS uses a gradual approach toward hypothyroidism. Instead of stopping the levothyroxine medication completely for six weeks and using Cytomel for the first four weeks, the *moderate hypothyroidism* approach is to continue to take the usual levothyroxine medication *every other* day instead of every day. A variation of this approach is to reduce the levothyroxine dose to one-fourth of the usual dose, taking it daily. After four weeks, the TSH level should be measured. It should be checked weekly from then, usually exceeding 30 mU/L by the fifth to eighth week. The low-iodine diet needs to be started by the fourth week of the preparation and continued for as many weeks as it takes to reach a TSH greater than 30. The advantage to this method is that there are diminished hypothyroid symptoms.

It is still advisable to avoid driving an automobile during this time. Other difficulties you may encounter with this method include difficulty predicting when the scan would take place (making significant scheduling problems for the patient and the physician), the likelihood of a prolonged time on the low-iodine diet, and the possibility that you may not be able to raise your TSH sufficiently within a reasonably short time and may still suffer prolonged, though diminished, hypothyroid symptoms.

Thyrogen: Artificial TSH Injections Without Hypothyroidism. Over the past decade, physicians have been trying new methods to prepare for the WBS without making people stop their levothyroxine medication and becoming hypothyroid. Since one of the intentions of hypothyroidism is to raise the TSH enough to stimulate thyroid cells and thyroid cancer cells to take up the radioactive iodine, it makes a great deal of sense that injecting TSH into the person directly would take away the need to stop thyroid hormone treatment. Thyrogen is the brand name of TSH made in vats of floating animal cells carrying the human TSH gene. The correct generic term for this is *recombinant human TSH (rhTSH)*. As with the other radioactive iodine WBSs, it is important to be on a low-iodine diet for at least a week or more for a Thyrogen-stimulated WBS.

Usually, Thyrogen is injected into the muscles of your arm or buttocks on the first and second days of a five-day test. On the third day, you swallow an I-131 tracer dose, (should be at least 4 mCi) and will undergo a WBS on the fourth and fifth day as well as a blood test to measure the thyroglobulin level on the fourth day. The single over-riding advantage to this approach is that you remain on your thyroid hormone med-ication and do not feel hypothyroid. This enables you to drive your car, work in your job, and feel relatively good. For the rare people with both thyroid cancer and pituitary disease, unable to make their own TSH, Thyrogen use is absolutely necessary for a WBS. Likewise, some people with severe psychiatric disturbances or extremely severe reactions to hypothyroidism may require a Thyrogen preparation.

On the other hand, there are several disadvantages. Thyrogen is very expensive and may not be covered on some insurance plans. Some people experience side effects of headache and nausea with Thyrogen, although it's fair to say that Thyrogen-related side effects are dwarfed by the side effects of hypothyroidism. Even more important, since the entire body, particularly the kidney, is not hypothyroid, the radioactive iodine tracer is quickly lost in the urine. This reduces the opportunity for tumor cells to take up this tracer and makes the scans less sensitive than similar scans prepared by hypothyroid withdrawal. For this reason, the recommendations of the U.S. Food and Drug Administration (FDA) are to: (1) give a high enough tracer dose (at least 4 mCi of I-131), (2) take a much longer time to perform the scan pictures (at least thirty min-utes for each view compared to ten minutes for the hypothyroid withdrawal prepara-tion method), (3) obtain a thyroglobulin level to assess for persistent thyroid cancer at the same time as the scan (as should be done for all scan preparation methods), and (4) limit the use of Thyrogen to people with clean bills of health on previous scans and thyroglobulin tests, who are unlikely to have persistent thyroid cancer.

Physicians who use Thyrogen for scanning their thyroid cancer patients should have some patients on hypothyroid withdrawal preparation, including patients getting I-131 treatments, patients with aggressive thyroid cancers, patients with elevated thy-roglobulin levels, and patients who don't yet have a clean bill of health showing nor-mal previous WBSs and undetectable thyroglobulin levels. For that reason, you should be cautious of physicians who *always* use Thyrogen for their patients, as they may be using it inappropriately. Also, many nuclear medicine departments use the same ten-minute scans for people getting Thyrogen scans as those getting hypothyroid with-drawal scans. There are not many people who would complain about their "clean" Thyrogen scan; however, it wouldn't be to their advantage if the scan was falsely "clean" because the scan time wasn't long enough to see the tumor.

My Own Practice

Since you may be curious about what I (Ken) do in my own practice, we thought we would share this information here. I usually use hypothyroid withdrawal preparation for most of my patients. This is because I prefer to gradually increase the interval time between doing I-131 WBSs, sometimes as much as five years for patients with clean bills of health, making each scan a "gold standard" rather than using more frequent Thyrogen scans. In addition, I like to have the opportunity to immediately give a radioactive iodine treatment if the scan shows the presence of tumor; since I deal with so many patients who have had aggressive thyroid tumors, this method has proved useful. On the other hand, I frequently use Thyrogen to evaluate the stimulated thyroglobulin level in people whose tumors no longer take up radioactive iodine. In addition, I believe patients with previously clean studies and low chances of persistent cancer should always have the opportunity to use Thyrogen if they prefer it and can afford it.

Types of Radioactive Iodine for WBSs: I-131 Versus I-123

There is a significant debate between nuclear medicine physicians using I-123 for whole body scans for thyroid cancer versus using I-131 scans.

The classic and standard type of radioactive iodine for whole body scans is I-131. This specific radioactive iodine isotope has a physical half-life of 8.1 days, meaning that if a vial of I-131 is stored for 8 days, 50 percent of the I-131 has decayed to a non-radioactive form; after 16 days only 25 percent of the I-131 is left; and after 24 days, only 12.5 percent of the I-131 remains. This provides an optimal situation for scanning. There are a number of things to be determined from the scan. First, comparing the amount of I-131 in tumor deposits on the scan at 24 hours (from when the tracer was swallowed) to the I-131 present at 48 hours lets me figure out if the tumor is discharging the I-131 fast enough to interfere with effective I-131 treatment of the cancer (rapid tumor turnover). If the scan seems clean at 24 hours, there might be sufficient background radiation from I-131 in the blood to hide potential tumor deposits. By 48 hours enough I-131 may be cleared from the bloodstream to reveal these deposits.

On the other hand, I-123 has a half-life of half a day. This means that after 24 hours only 25 percent of the I-123 remains in a sealed vial and after 48 hours only 6 percent of the I-123 remains. This makes it extremely difficult to reliably calculate how long radioactive iodine stays in the tumor or to evaluate delayed scan images (for enhanced sensitivity) since there is very little I-123 left by 48 hours to create a scan image. Some nuclear medicine physicians advocate using I-123 since it exposes patients to a lower radiation dose than I-131. Unfortunately, I-123 cannot provide the same information as I-131 since it doesn't stay in the tumor long enough to evaluate delayed scans. In addition, it is significantly more expensive than I-131. For these reasons, I continue to prefer I-131 as a scanning isotope.

Alternative Scans for Following Up on Thyroid Cancer

Radioactive iodine scans depend upon the ability of thyroid cancer to take up radioactive iodine, in much the same way that the normal thyroid would take up iodine to make thyroid hormone. Unfortunately, some thyroid cancers lose the ability to take up iodine. In such a case, the I-131 WBS would appear clean, even when there was considerable disease present. One clue to this possibility is the presence of thyroglobulin despite the absence of any abnormal sites seen on I-131 WBS. Another clue might be awareness that some types of thyroid cancer (Hurthle cell variants of follicular and papillary cancer, tall cell variants of papillary thyroid cancer, and tumors that were aggressively invasive into surrounding tissues at the time of the initial thyroid surgery) might have a greater chance to lose the ability to take up radioactive iodine. Additionally, medullary thyroid cancers never take up iodine and require alternative scanning agents.

One such alternative nuclear scanning agent is technetium-99m-SESTAMIBI (hexakis 2-methoxy isobutyl isonitrile). It is injected into your vein, and whole body scan images are taken at two different times within the next couple of hours. Other types of scanning agents include thallium-201 (Tl-201) and technetium-99m-tetrofosmin.

Positron-Emission Tomography (PET) Scans for Difficult Tumors

Sometimes, aggressive thyroid cancers that have spread in the body have a metabolism (speed of life) that is faster than surrounding normal parts of the body. These cancers often take in sugar at a greater rate to feed their metabolism. In such cases, doctors can perform a special scan using radioactive sugar (glucose) to look for these tumors. The scanning agent is fluorine-18 fluorodeoxyglucose (18-FDG), a radioactive form of glucose that releases positrons. Special scanning equipment detects these positrons and can construct a detailed image of these tumors in the body. Often, Thyrogen is injected into the person to stimulate the thyroid cancer to take in the 18-FDG in greater amounts to improve the scan quality.

X-Rays, Ultrasounds, and Other Diagnostic Pictures

Nuclear scans, as discussed previously, provide a way to find out about the thyroid gland or thyroid cancers based upon the function of the thyroid or thyroid cancer cell. This function involves taking up one or more of the scanning agents used for nuclear imaging. Besides such function, it is critical to know about the form and structure of the thyroid gland or to be able to locate thyroid cancer deposits in the body that may no longer take up radioactive scanning agents.

Obviously, the first and most important tools for this anatomical search are the fingers. A physical examination of the thyroid gland is the best way to see if the thyroid gland is normal in size, shape, and location (see Chapters 1 and 8 for information on self-examinations). The careful examiner will be able to tell if there are any thyroid nodules that should be investigated further. The examination should also include a careful search of the entire neck, looking for enlarged lymph nodes that could represent a thyroid cancer spread in the neck. The texture of the thyroid gland, either firm and *bosselated* (like the surface of a golf ball, suggesting Hashimoto's thyroiditis) or with a normal soft and fleshy quality, provides information that may prove helpful in diagnosis.

An enlarged thyroid gland, known as a *goiter*, may cause a blockage in the neck by pushing on vital structures, such as the windpipe (trachea), food tube (esophagus), carotid arteries, or jugular veins. This condition, known as *thoracic inlet obstruction*, is best seen by raising the arms straight up in the air against the ears, a technique known as the *Pemberton's maneuver*. If there is thoracic inlet obstruction, the person's face becomes red and the neck veins bulge. This can involve one or both sides of the neck. Sometimes, using a stethoscope or placing your ear against the person's neck, you can hear a "swooshing" or rumbling sound with each beat of the pulse. This is called a *vascular thrill* or *bruit* and is often heard in Graves' disease.

Beyond the physical examination, a number of devices have been useful to evaluate structural features of people with thyroid problems. They include ultrasounds (usually of the neck), x-rays (plain films of the chest, bones, and abdomen), computerized axial tomography scans (CT scans), and magnetic resonance imaging (MRI) studies.

Ultrasounds

An ultrasound is a simple and easy device that uses high-frequency sound waves to produce an "echo picture" of structures in your neck. It is the same type of machine used to look at a fetus within a mother's womb. A jelly lubricant is smeared on the neck to allow the ultrasound transducer to slide easily over your skin. The picture produced by the ultrasound machine provides an excellent view of the thyroid gland, permitting assessment and measurement of any nodules or masses. A thin needle biopsy can be performed with the ultrasound to obtain samples of cells from the nodule or mass, allowing the physician to find out whether it is malignant. Although most thyroid nodules can be biopsied by a skilled physician without an ultrasound, sometimes thyroid nodules are discovered accidentally while performing an ultrasound evaluation of the carotid arteries (known as a carotid duplex study) and the nodule can be found only with the ultrasound.

A major problem with thyroid ultrasound evaluations is that such devices are much too sensitive. Most normal people can be shown to have very tiny thyroid nodules using a thyroid ultrasound. When the physical examination is used to find thyroid nodules to evaluate for possible cancer, only large and clinically significant nodules (usually greater than 1 centimeter in diameter) can be found. Such nodules have a 10 percent chance of being malignant and warrant a biopsy. On the other hand, very tiny nodules, found in nearly all people with ultrasound exams, have such a low chance of representing a clinical risk of thyroid cancer that evaluating each of them would not be effective, causing substantial anxiety and expense. For that reason, doctors don't use thyroid ultrasounds to screen for thyroid nodules in most people. An exception to this would be for a person with a history of childhood exposure to radiation therapy in the neck region or radiation fallout from nuclear testing. In such individuals, the risk of thyroid cancer is increased threefold, making it reasonable to use ultrasounds to assist in a search for thyroid nodules to be biopsied.

In people with thyroid cancer, after a surgeon has removed the thyroid gland, the ultrasound complements a physical examination in the search for recurrent disease in the neck. I've found that it is particularly helpful if the physician performing the ultrasound has been asked to biopsy anything that is seen that is suspicious for thyroid cancer deposits. If the thyroglobulin level is detectable in the blood, despite a clean I-131 whole body scan, thyroid cancer is still present somewhere in the body. An ultrasound search of the neck can be successful in finding the cancer in the neck around half of the time. In some physicians' offices, ultrasound examination of the neck is routinely performed to check for recurrent tumor; however, it is up to you and your doctor to decide if this added expense is warranted because of insufficient confidence in the physical examination.

Plain X-Rays, Including Chest X-Rays

Several decades ago, the chest x-ray was routinely performed in people with thyroid cancer to check for tumor that may have spread to the lung. Chest x-rays are quick, inexpensive, and easily obtained; however, they can be quite insensitive. Thyroid cancers that have spread (metastasized) to the lung have to be quite large (nodules exceeding 1 centimeter in diameter) to be detected by the chest x-ray. I (Ken) typically obtain chest x-rays as a simple screen for obvious problems in patients receiving radioactive iodine treatment for their thyroid cancer, while using CT scans of the chest as a more sensitive test for metastatic tumors in the lung.

X-rays of all of the major bones in the body, called a *metastatic survey*, are very useful to look for thyroid cancer metastasized to bones. Metastatic surveys are particularly helpful if the thyroglobulin is very elevated and the radioactive iodine whole body scans fail to show the site of the cancer. In other types of cancer, such as breast cancer or prostate cancer, nuclear bone scans are used for this purpose. In thyroid cancer, nuclear bone scans are insensitive and usually useless in showing such disease in bones.

CT and MRI Scans

CT scans are both useful and dangerous in evaluating people with thyroid cancer. They are useful because of their great sensitivity and their ability to look everywhere in the body. They can be coupled to PET scanners for something known as a "fusion study" that shows tumor sites in the body and characterizes each one by its metabolic rate of glucose consumption. On the other hand, the contrast dye that is injected into a person's veins when the CT scan is performed floods the entire body with nonradioactive iodine that can stay there for two to eleven months. This can result in a failure of radioactive iodine scans to detect tumor in the body and a failure of the radioactive iodine to kill the cancer cells. There is no type of contrast dye for CT scans that does not contain iodine. If a CT scan is performed with such contrast dye, there is a simple way to determine if your body has gotten rid of the iodine, sufficient for radioactive iodine scans or treatments. This entails going on a careful low-iodine diet (see Chapter 20) for one week, then collecting a full twenty-four-hour urine sample on the last day of the diet. Your physician will send this urine to a special clinical laboratory, such as the Mayo Clinic Laboratory in Rochester, Minnesota, for measurement of the total iodine in the urine. If the total amount of iodine in the urine is under 100 micrograms, then the contrast dye iodine has sufficiently departed from your body. If the amount is higher, then the urine collection (and diet) should be repeated once each month until it is low enough.

I find the CT scan of the chest, *without* contrast dye, to be the best way to evaluate the lung for metastatic thyroid tumors, complementing the radioactive iodine whole body scans. Unfortunately, CT scans are not very helpful in other parts of the body unless contrast dye is used. If you have medullary thyroid cancer, anaplastic thyroid cancer, or other types of thyroid cancer that do not (or have lost the ability to) take up radioactive iodine, then CT scans *with* contrast are perfectly acceptable. When you have a papillary or follicular thyroid cancer that is being evaluated or treated with radioactive iodine, MRI scans can be used to look at parts of the body other than the lungs. The contrast dye used for MRI scans, gadolinium, does not contain any iodine and is perfectly safe for any person with thyroid cancer because it does not interfere with radioactive iodine. MRI scans are often superior to other tests when looking at the spine or parts of the brain.

A number of additional x-ray tests may use contrast dye with iodine that can interfere with radioactive iodine. Most blood vessel x-rays, called *angiograms* (including cardiac catheterizations), and special gallbladder x-rays use iodine dyes. If your physician considers your chest pain to be an emergency, needing a heart catheterization evaluation, or you have a severe headache that makes your doctor worry about an aneurysm in your brain, then you should permit the doctor to use any iodine contrast dye needed to evaluate and take care of you. On the other hand, if it isn't a life-threatening situation, ask the physician to avoid using iodine contrast dye until your thyroid cancer physician can be consulted.

Pathology: Do You Need Surgery? What Did the Surgeon Find?

Laboratory blood tests are useful to determine thyroid diseases that result in too much thyroid hormone or too little thyroid hormone. On the other hand, the only way to determine whether the thyroid gland contains a malignancy (cancer) is to examine a piece of it under the microscope. The method of evaluating the thyroid gland (or a lymph node in the neck) before surgery is by a fine needle biopsy. After surgery, the pathologist has the thyroid itself to analyze (sometimes a difficult task).

Fine Needle Aspiration (FNA) Biopsy of Thyroid Nodules

Proper evaluation of thyroid nodules, particularly if you are not thyrotoxic, usually requires fine needle biopsy (see Chapter 8). This is a simple way to see if a thyroid nodule or enlarged portion of a thyroid could be a cancer. I (Ken) usually perform these biopsies in my office with minimal, if any, discomfort to my patient.

When undergoing a fine needle biopsy, you lie down on your back, and the skin over the thyroid nodule is carefully cleaned with alcohol. A very thin needle (27 gauge) attached to a plastic syringe is pushed through your skin and into the nodule while the syringe plunger is gently pulled back, taking out a tiny bit of reddish material. The needle is quickly pulled out of your neck for the physician to smear the material on some glass slides. I usually do this at least five times in different parts of the thyroid nodule. Although some physicians use anesthetic in the skin, I've found that my patients prefer the biopsy without it, since it is usually more uncomfortable injecting the anesthetic than doing the entire biopsy. Not every physician uses the same technique. Some find it useful to use ultrasounds to guide their biopsies, and all nodules that cannot be clearly felt that exceed 1 centimeter in diameter should be biopsied using ultrasound guidance.

A cytologist (a particular type of pathologist) evaluates the biopsy slides. First, the cytologist determines if there are enough thyroid cells on the slides to examine. One way that a biopsy can be faulty is if the absence of thyroid cancer cells on the slides is wrongly presumed to be an absence of thyroid cancer cells in the patient. There have to be sufficient *normal* thyroid cells on the slides to know that enough of a sample is present to determine that the nodule is not cancer and that the biopsy is adequate.

Next, the cells are evaluated to determine a diagnosis. There are generally three major types of diagnosis: *benign*, *malignant*, or *indeterminate*. When the nodule has been accurately sampled during the biopsy and an experienced cytologist evaluates the slides, a diagnosis of benign colloid nodule is greater than 95 percent accurate. If the diagnosis is that the nodule is cancerous, this is almost always the case. On the other hand, if the diagnosis is indeterminate, then the nodule has a reasonable chance of being cancerous and there is no other test, short of surgery, that would give more definite information. In this circumstance, it is usually advisable for a thyroid surgeon to remove the half of the thyroid containing the nodule, as well as the middle of the gland (the isthmus). Further surgical removal of the gland is warranted if the nodule proves to be cancer.

Most of the time, papillary thyroid cancers are easily distinguished by FNA biopsy. Follicular thyroid cancers are almost never diagnosed by FNA biopsy because they will usually appear as a type of indeterminate classification, *follicular neoplasia.* If a nodule is classified as benign, it may need to be rebiopsied after several months if it continues to enlarge. If it remains the same size or gets smaller, it is confirmed as benign. The pathologist further evaluates any nodules found to be malignant or indeterminate when the surgical specimen becomes available after thyroid surgery.

It is very important to know that cytologists are not all the same. Some have more or less expertise in thyroid disease than others. The interpretation of FNA biopsy slides by a cytologist may not be definitive, and second opinions from other experienced cytologists may be both cost-effective and wise.

Thyroid Pathology: What Did It Reveal from My Surgery?

It may seem strange to you, but the most important diagnostic test you will ever have in your entire life, with regard to your thyroid, is the evaluation of the body parts removed during your thyroid surgery (surgical specimen). The pathologist's decision on the name of the thyroid disease revealed by your surgical specimen will determine the course of your medical care for the rest of your life. The decision may result in the use of treatments and diagnostic tests that entail significant time, commitment, and expense. It may affect your health insurance, life insurance, and employment opportunities. If a thyroid cancer is missed by the pathologist, you may fail to receive appropriate care from other excellent physicians and you risk having that cancer reveal itself, years later, having spread to the lung, spine, bones, or brain. On the other hand, the diagnosis of thyroid cancer justifies lifelong diagnostic testing and medical follow-up, as well as possible treatments with radioactive iodine. It is in your best interest to play an active role in making sure that your surgical specimen is properly evaluated.

I (Ken) direct a thyroid oncology (thyroid cancer) program and see more than two hundred new thyroid cancer patients each year, in addition to my care of a far larger group of longtime patients. I will not see a new patient unless the original slides from the patient's thyroid surgery have been sent to the expert pathologists at my hospital whom I've learned to trust, often spending time with me on a multiheaded microscope, to verify (and sometimes change) the diagnosis from outside hospitals. Every couple of years we find a person who, having received years of treatment for a thyroid cancer at numerous outside hospitals, never had that cancer in the first place. This can be avoided if your physician insists on having the slides from your original surgery reviewed by another pathologist, rather than relying on uncertain medical records or hearsay diagnoses. Even more common are the calls from other physicians (looking for advice) and attorneys (looking for an expert witness for their malpractice case) concerning people with thyroid surgeries ten or twenty years earlier, told they had benign tumors, and now revealing metastatic thyroid cancer in their spine, brain, or other sites.

Very few pathologists can rightly call themselves "thyroid pathologists" and, even among expert pathologists, distinguishing types of thyroid cancers can be their most difficult of tasks. It is important, particularly if your surgery has been performed at a small, community, or nonacademic hospital, for you to insist that the pathology slides of your surgical specimen be sent to an outside academic pathologist for a second opinion.

Certain types of thyroid diagnoses are "red flags" for requesting a second opinion from an outside pathologist. First, the only difference between a benign follicular adenoma and a follicular carcinoma is the complete absence of any evidence of the tumor cells pushing their way through the capsule of the thyroid tumor or into a blood vessel in the tumor. This diagnosis "by exclusion" is wholly dependent on the compulsiveness of the pathologist in evaluating the entire thyroid tumor and making enough microscope slides to exclude such findings with confidence.

Next, any thyroid cancer that has pushed its way outside of the thyroid gland, involving other parts of the neck, has extensively spread into lymph nodes in the neck, or has spread to body regions outside of the neck, should be sent for a second opinion. Experienced pathologists sometimes see features in such tumors that change the way that your thyroid cancer physician should treat you.

Lastly, if you are unfortunate enough to have the diagnosis of an anaplastic thyroid cancer, this is sufficiently rare and dangerous as to warrant obtaining extreme confidence in this classification prior to embarking on aggressive, experimental treatments.

3 Hypothyroidism: The Most Common Problem

Being *hypothyroid* is one of the most common health problems in North America. The term means that you don't have enough thyroid hormone in your body to function normally. Usually this is because the thyroid gland is underactive and is not making enough thyroid hormone for your body's requirements. Hypothyroidism can be mild, moderate, or severe. People most at risk for hypothyroidism are women, older individuals (over sixty), those with a family history of thyroid disease, or those with other autoimmune diseases (such as pernicious anemia, type 1 diabetes, rheumatoid arthritis, or lupus).

The most recent population screening studies show that the prevalence of mild hypothyroidism in the general population is 4 to 10 percent, and in people over sixty, 7 to 26 percent. And in those population studies, hypothyroidism indeed affects women much more frequently than men.

If you've been diagnosed with a thyroid disorder of any kind, you will probably experience hypothyroidism at some point because the treatments for other thyroid conditions usually result in hypothyroidism (quite deliberately). This chapter explains the many possible causes of hypothyroidism, the symptoms of hypothyroidism, and treatment with thyroid hormone. It also discusses the many conditions that can mimic, or mask, hypothyroidism, such as depression.

Why Am I Hypothyroid?

There are two categories of people who become hypothyroid. The first category is called *primary hypothyroidism*. By this, we refer to people who develop hypothyroidism as a condition because of the primary failure of the thyroid gland itself; in essence, "a broken thyroid" is primary hypothyroidism. This group includes people who develop

Hypothyroidism at a Glance

You might notice the following:

- Changes in skin pigmentation
- Chest pain after physical activity
- Constipation
- Depression
- Difficult-to-manage hair, brittle nails
- Difficulty concentrating
- Dry skin
- Extreme tiredness and slowness
- Eyelids that feel sticky
- Feeling cold
- Headaches and problems focusing
- Irregular periods or infertility
- Loss of appetite
- Loss of interest in sex
- Milk leaking from breasts (when you're not breast-feeding)
- Muscle spasms
- Poor memory
- Shortness of breath
- Slow healing, frequent infections
- Tingling in hands and feet
- Weakness and muscular aches and pains
- Weight gain

thyroiditis (inflammation of the thyroid gland) from Hashimoto's disease or other causes; babies born without a thyroid gland; or people who stop making as much thyroid hormone as they used to because of aging.

People who develop *iatrogenic hypothyroidism* (meaning "doctor-caused") as a result of having their thyroid glands surgically removed or receiving radioactive iodine therapy for the purpose of ablating the thyroid gland also have primary hypothyroidism because their thyroid glands no longer work. Also, roughly 25 to 50 percent of all people who have received external radiation therapy to the head and neck area for cancers such as Hodgkin's disease tend to develop hypothyroidism from thyroid gland failure within ten years after their treatment. It's recommended that this group have an annual thyroid stimulating hormone (TSH) test, as discussed in the previous chapter.

Others might say:

- "You look pale."
- "Your face is puffy."
- "Your eyes are swollen."
- "Your hair looks/feels coarse." or "Are you losing hair?"
- "Your voice is husky."
- "You're talking more slowly than usual."
- "You snore."
- "You used to *love* doing X or Y but aren't interested anymore."
- "You can't hear well."

Your doctor should look for:

- Delayed reflexes
- Goiter (enlarged thyroid)
- High cholesterol levels
- Increased blood pressure
- Muscle weakness
- Slowed pulse
- Tingling or numbness in the hands (sign of carpal tunnel syndrome)
- TSH tests, performed appropriately for any suspicion of thyroid trouble

Congenital and Neonatal Hypothyroidism

Roughly one out of four thousand babies is born with either neonatal or congenital hypothyroidism. With congenital hypothyroidism, the baby is born without a thyroid gland. In neonatal hypothyroidism, the baby is born with what appears to be a normal thyroid gland, but then develops symptoms of hypothyroidism after its first twenty-eight days of life. While the condition was present at birth, the symptoms may not manifest until later. Neonatal hypothyroidism is treated no differently from congenital hypothyroidism.

Neonatal and congenital hypothyroidism are very serious conditions, which can lead to severe brain damage and developmental impairment. Either condition can occur from an iodine deficiency in the mother's diet. This is common in remote or mountainous areas of the world where iodine is not readily available. In fact, iodine deficiency is the most common cause of mental retardation in underdeveloped countries. Fortunately, this is not a problem in North America, where our salt is iodized. (And low-salt diets still contain enough iodine for our needs.) Furthermore, since neonatal screening for hypothyroidism in newborns was introduced in the mid-1970s through the heel-pad test, we can now treat congenital hypothyroidism early. For more information on congenital and neonatal hypothyroidism, see Chapter 15.

Thyroiditis

Thyroiditis means "inflammation of the thyroid gland." Hypothyroidism can develop from thyroiditis, and the most common cause of thyroiditis is an autoimmune disease known as *Hashimoto's thyroiditis*, which we discuss thoroughly in Chapter 5. In fact, Hashimoto's disease is the most common cause of hypothyroidism in North America. There are other kinds of thyroiditis that are different from Hashimoto's thyroiditis that can cause either hypothyroidism or hyperthyroidism (see Chapter 5), including postpartum thyroiditis (see Chapter 13).

Subclinical Hypothyroidism

Now also known as *mild hypothyroidism*, subclinical hypothyroidism refers to hypothyroidism that has not progressed very far, meaning that you have few or no symptoms. As you might guess, the most common cause of this is Hashimoto's thyroiditis. On a blood test, your free T4 (free thyroxine) readings would be normal or very close to normal, but your thyroid stimulating hormone (TSH) readings would be higher than normal.

Right now, there is much discussion in clinical circles about doing routine TSH testing in certain groups of people for subclinical hypothyroidism. This would include anyone with a family history of thyroid disease, women over forty, women after childbirth, and anyone over age sixty. Because the TSH test is simple and can be added to any blood laboratory package, it presents an opportunity to catch hypothyroidism before serious symptoms develop, and hence prevent it and all the symptoms discussed in this chapter. The following groups of people should be screened for subclinical hypothyroidism by having an annual TSH test:

- Anyone with a family history of thyroid disease
- Women planning pregnancy
- Pregnant women (very important!)
- Women who have just given birth (very important!)
- Women over forty
- Anyone over sixty
- Anyone with symptoms of depression (especially postpartum depression) or who has been diagnosed with depression (see Chapter 24)
- Anyone with symptoms of chronic fatigue syndrome or fibromyalgia or who has been diagnosed with one or both conditions (see Chapter 26)

- Anyone diagnosed with "new" PMS (premenstrual syndrome) or perimenopause symptoms (see Chapter 14)
- Anyone diagnosed with premature menopause, early menopause, or premature ovarian failure
- Anyone with another autoimmune disease, especially rheumatoid arthritis, lupus, or type 1 diabetes

Drug Interactions

Certain drugs can trigger hypothyroidism. For example, lithium can trigger Hashimoto's-induced hypothyroidism. In other words, if you have underlying Hashimoto's disease with no symptoms, and take lithium to manage bipolar disorder, lithium may unveil hypothyroidism. We discuss drug interactions in detail in Chapters 10 and 11.

Secondary Hypothyroidism: Pituitary Problems

Sometimes hypothyroidism occurs because of a pituitary gland disorder that may interfere with the production of thyroid stimulating hormone (TSH). This is fairly unusual, however. Tumors or cysts on the pituitary gland can also interfere with production of hormones from the gonads and the adrenal glands.

A common type of pituitary tumor is one that makes large quantities of a hormone called *prolactin*, known as a *prolactinoma*. These can occur in both men and women, often causing milk to come from the breasts or interfering with fertility. In most cases, prolactinomas are treated with medication to shrink them rather than surgery or radiation therapy. This may result in restoration of normal pituitary function, fixing the hypothyroidism.

The other common type of pituitary tumor is one that doesn't seem to produce any particular hormone in excess, merely blocking the normal hormone production of the pituitary gland. This type of pituitary tumor must be removed by a neurosurgeon, usually through an incision under the upper lip (a transsphenoidal hypophysectomy).

Often, tumors can recur, requiring external beam radiation therapy to prevent further enlargement. Rarely, some pituitary tumors make a hormone known as ACTH, causing Cushing's disease in which high levels of steroids (cortisol) are made. This dangerous condition is also treated by a transsphenoidal hypophysectomy, possibly resulting in hypothyroidism from pituitary damage. Many years ago, before improved obstetrical care, excessive loss of blood during childbirth could cause a drop in blood pressure that caused part of the pituitary to die and sometimes bleed, a condition known as Sheehan's syndrome. This can still happen to anyone with an unsuspected thyroid tumor who has a rapid drop in his or her blood pressure, resulting in destruction of the remaining pituitary, called *pituitary apoplexy*.

Tertiary Hypothyroidism: Hypothalamus Problems

There are rare problems with the portion of the brain that is just above the pituitary, attached to the pituitary by a stalk. The most frequent is called a *craniopharyngioma*. This is a collection of skin cells that were left behind during fetal development and became stuck in this part of the brain. Although not cancerous, these skin cells start to grow and form cysts, which push upon the sensitive brain tissue of the hypothalamus. This portion of the brain transmits hormones down its stalk into the pituitary gland, responsible for stimulating the pituitary gland to release its own hormones. In the case of the thyroid system, this means that TRH (TSH-releasing hormone) is not sent to the pituitary gland. Consequently, the pituitary fails to make sufficient TSH to stimulate the thyroid gland, causing the thyroid to "go to sleep" and hypothyroidism to develop. A similar problem can happen if there is trauma (such as from an auto accident) to that portion of the brain or if a malignant tumor grows there.

Iodine Deficiency

As discussed in Chapter 1, iodine is the critical ingredient used by the thyroid to make thyroid hormone. Without enough iodine in the diet, the thyroid gland cannot produce enough thyroid hormone. If this happens, the pituitary gland makes more TSH, continuing to stimulate the thyroid gland and causing it to enlarge (a condition called a goiter, discussed in Chapter 7). Most people need at least 100 micrograms of iodine each day to produce enough thyroid hormone and avoid goiter. Unfortunately, much of the world's population lives in regions that have very low levels of iodine in the soil and water.

You may be familiar with the term *goiter belt*, which refers to regions that typically suffer from insufficient iodine. The Great Lakes region, for example, used to be a goiter belt. The term originated because inhabitants of these regions would often develop goiters from a lack of iodine. Goiter belts are located far from seawater. In regions close to seawater, iodine gets into the soil and water supply from the wind and rain off the ocean. It also gets into plants. It then travels into the milk and meat in our diet.

The introduction of iodized salt in our diet has virtually eliminated goiters resulting from iodine deficiencies in North America. But the problem of iodine deficiency is far from solved in other parts of the world. In fact, more than one billion people are at risk for iodine deficiency–related hypothyroidism, which is reversible with either sufficient quantities of iodine, or iodine and thyroid hormone. Three hundred million people in Asia alone suffer from goiters, while twenty million people suffer from brain damage because of iodine deficiency in pregnancy and infancy. Goiters from iodine deficiency are regularly found in Asia, Africa, South America, parts of Holland, and especially in mountainous regions such as the Himalayas and the Andes, the Alps, portions of mainland China, central Mexico, and much of Greece. This phenomenon is very disturbing because these problems could be completely prevented by the simple addition of iodized salt or iodized oil (proposed in some regions) to the diet. Without iodine supplements, people in iodine-deficient regions have insufficient iodine to maintain their health. If this deficiency is severe, newborn children can suffer from a condition known as "cretinism" characterized by mental retardation, short stature, hypothyroidism, and goiter. Even in the absence of all the signs of cretinism, low iodine levels in early development can be responsible for decreased brain development and mental retardation. In regions with iodine deficiency, reduced brain development contributes to poor social and economic productivity, poverty, and underdevelopment.

The first International Goiter Congress was held in 1929 in Bern after Switzerland and the United States introduced iodized salt. Many countries soon followed suit, and iodine deficiency has disappeared in most parts of the world. But not much happened to eliminate iodine deficiency in underdeveloped nations until 1985, when thyroid specialists established the International Council for Control of Iodine Deficiency Disorders (ICCIDD), a group of about four hundred members from seventy different countries.

While in North America only about one in four thousand newborns is born with hypothyroidism, in iodine-deficient areas 10 percent of all newborns are hypothyroid. Worse still, up to 70 percent of iodine-deficient populations are severely hypothyroid; lack of thyroid hormone prevents proper brain development. As a result, iodine deficiency is now recognized as the most common cause of preventable mental defects. ICCIDD works with the World Health Organization and UNICEF to develop national programs in Africa, Asia, Latin America, and Europe with the goal of eliminating iodine deficiency in the near future. Most recently, the salt industry has joined the fight, too.

When iodine-deficient populations are supplemented with adequate iodine, there are certainly less goiters from iodine-deficient hypothyroidism, but on the flip side, you will also see an increase in these populations in autoimmune thyroid disease (both Hashimoto's and Graves' disease). You will also see a higher ratio of certain types of thyroid cancer over others (more papillary versus follicular thyroid cancers, for example)—discussed more in Chapter 9.

Iodine Excess

Too much iodine is believed to be responsible for triggering goiters and thyroid disorders, too. On the other hand, in countries where iodine has been made plentiful in the food supply, such as in the United States, hypothyroidism from iodine deficiency has disappeared while hypothyroidism from autoimmune disease has skyrocketed. It seems that excess iodine in the diet stimulates the immune system to create antibodies that attack the thyroid gland and causes it to stop making normal amounts of thyroid hormone, a condition called Hashimoto's thyroiditis (named after the Japanese physician who first described it). Also, among people who get thyroid cancer, iodine supplementation has changed the types of thyroid cancer, decreasing the number of follicular thyroid cancers and increasing the proportion of papillary thyroid cancers. The reasons why iodine supplementation does these things are unknown. In healthy people who take very high doses of iodine once in a while, such as using iodine-containing water-purification tablets on a camping trip, excess iodine temporarily shuts off the thyroid gland and reduces its production of thyroid hormone. Healthy thyroids will usually regain the ability to make thyroid hormone despite continued exposure to high iodine levels. That's one reason why taking kelp (seaweed) as a preventive measure is not recommended. If you live in North America, you're getting enough iodine in your diet from your food. Taking kelp in the belief that it will prevent a thyroid problem is simply bad practice. Not only will it not prevent a thyroid problem, but it could trigger one.

Hong Kong's Consumer Council had concerns about seaweed snacks that were popular with Hong Kong children. Apparently, the amount of iodine in two small packages of roasted seaweed exceeded the World Health Organization's recommended daily iodine intake for children under age twelve. The council was concerned that the snacks could trigger goiters and thyroid disorders.

In North America, other than recommending against taking kelp, physicians do not generally issue warnings to people at risk for a thyroid disorder about avoiding iodine-containing food. That's because you'll find iodine in a host of different foods that offer important nutrients, as already discussed.

Your thyroid gland will use about a milligram of iodine per week (or approximately 90 to 100 micrograms per day) to make thyroid hormone; that is a tiny amount, so it is easy to understand that a balanced diet provides more than enough iodine for the average thyroid gland. A healthy thyroid gland can store enough iodine to last for three months. How much food do you need to eat to reach 90 micrograms? Well, one small carton of yogurt contains 125 grams of iodine, which is equivalent to 125,000,000 micrograms. Don't let any of this scare you, though. A healthy thyroid gland is designed to take only what it needs from your daily diet.

According to some sources, a diet too high in fiber may prevent your gut from absorbing *enough* iodine, and a strict sodium-free or salt-free diet may also prevent you from absorbing enough. However, given that iodine is present in so many foods, it's unlikely that you're suffering from iodine deficiency in North America.

Low-iodine diets are necessary for thyroid cancer patients undergoing thyroid scans. (See Chapters 9 and 20 for more information.)

Goitrogens

Goitrogens are chemicals that block, or interfere with, iodine absorption, often causing a goiter (see Chapter 7). One type of goitrogens, the *thiocyanates*, comes from foods such as yellow turnips, cassava, maize, bamboo shoots, sweet potatoes, and lima beans. Another type, the *flavenoids*, is found in millet, sorghum, beans, and ground nuts. Unless your diet is also severely iodine deficient, however, there is no need to worry about having these foods as they are excellent sources of fiber, important vitamins, and cancer-fighting agents.

Additionally, some other goitrogens enter the water supply from coal deposits, particularly resorcinols, phenols, and polycyclic aromatic hydrocarbons. Similarly, thiocyanates, flavenoids, and hydroxypyridines are goitrogenic chemicals that enter the body from cigarette smoke.

Other Waterborne Concerns

Perchlorate is a major ingredient in rocket fuel, and perchlorates have been found as contaminants in the water supply of parts of the western United States. Recently, large areas of Southern California and Nevada have been found to have their water supplies contaminated. Although there has not been any evidence of adverse health effects from this environmental contaminant, additional studies have been undertaken since there are possibilities of legal actions (called *toxic torts*) should such evidence be found. These studies document the absence of any ill effects of perchlorate when taken in the amounts measured in the water supply.

Slowing Down: Signs of Hypothyroidism

When you are hypothyroid, everything slows down—including your reflexes and your ability to respond to your environment. The slowing down occurs from head to toe. We'll discuss these symptoms alphabetically so that you can find the information you need faster. These symptoms disappear once the thyroid hormone level is restored to normal.

Cardiovascular Changes

Hypothyroid people will have an unusually slow pulse rate (between forty-five and sixty beats per minute) and blood pressure that may be too high.

More severe or prolonged hypothyroidism could raise your cholesterol levels as well, and this can aggravate blockage of coronary arteries. In severe hypothyroidism, the heart muscle fibers may weaken, which can lead to heart failure. This scenario is rare, however, and one would have to suffer from severe and obvious hypothyroid symptoms long before the heart would be at risk.

But even mild hypothyroidism may aggravate your risk for heart disease if you have other risk cofactors. For example, if you are hypothyroid, it's not unusual to notice chest pain (which may be confused with angina), shortness of breath when you exert yourself, or calf pain (which is caused by dysfunction of the muscles in the leg). Fluid may also collect, causing swollen legs and feet. For more on cardiovascular disease see Chapter 25.

Cold Intolerance

You may not be able to find a comfortable temperature and may often wonder, "Why is it always so freezing in here?" Hypothyroid people carry sweaters with them all the time to compensate for continuous sensitivity to cold. You'll feel much more comfortable in hot, muggy weather and may not even perspire in the heat. This is because your entire metabolic rate has slowed down.

Depression and Psychiatric Misdiagnosis

Hypothyroidism is linked to psychiatric depression more frequently than hyperthyroidism. The physical symptoms associated with unipolar depression (discussed more in Chapter 24) overlap with hypothyroidism and can cause the psychiatric misdiagnosis. Sometimes, psychiatrists find that hypothyroid patients can even exhibit certain behaviors linked to psychosis, such as paranoia or aural and visual hallucinations (hearing voices, seeing things that are not there). This used to be called *myxedema madness*. Interestingly, roughly 15 percent of all patients suffering from depression are found to be hypothyroid. Chapter 24 discusses depression and unmasked hypothyroidism, as well as simultaneous depression and hypothyroidism. Bipolar disorder and lithium are also discussed in detail.

Digestive Changes and Weight Gain

Because your system has slowed down, you'll suffer from constipation, hardening of stools, bloating (which may cause bad breath), poor appetite, and heartburn.

Depression or Thyroid?

The following symptoms can indicate mild, moderate, or severe depression as well as hypo- or hyperthyroidism:

- Feelings of sadness and/or "empty mood"*
- Difficulty sleeping (waking up frequently in the middle of the night)†
- Loss of energy and feelings of fatigue and lethargy*
- Change in appetite (usually a loss of appetite)*†
- Difficulty thinking, concentrating, or making decisions*
- Loss of interest in formerly pleasurable activities, including sex*
- Anxiety or panic attacks (characterized by racing heart)†
- Obsessing over negative experiences or thoughts
- Feeling guilty, worthless, hopeless, or helpless
- Feeling restless and irritable†
- Thinking about death or suicide

*Represents signs of hypothyroidism
†Represents signs of hyperthyroidism

The heartburn results because your food is not moving through the stomach as quickly, so acid reflux (where semidigested food comes back up the esophagus) may occur.

Because the lack of thyroid hormone slows down your metabolism, you might gain weight as well. But often—because your appetite may decrease radically—your weight will stay the same. Hypothyroid patients can experience some, or all, of these symptoms, and sometimes, if the hypothyroidism is caught early enough, patients may not be conscious of any of these symptoms until their doctor specifically asks if they have noticed a particular change in their metabolism or energy. You'll need to adjust your eating habits to compensate, which is discussed in more detail in Chapter 16. The typical scenario is to gain roughly ten pounds during a period of about a year, even though you may not be eating as much. Some of the weight gain, however, is because of bloating from constipation.

Enlarged Thyroid Gland

Your thyroid gland often enlarges, known as a *goiter*, either because it is scarred from Hashimoto's thyroiditis (discussed in Chapter 5) or from constant stimulation from high TSH levels. In some cases, however, the destruction of the thyroid tissue can actually cause the thyroid gland to shrink. A goiter can also develop from Graves' disease, when too much thyroid hormone is produced, discussed in Chapter 4.

Fatigue and Sleepiness

The most classic symptom is a distinct, lethargic tiredness or sluggishness, causing you to feel unnaturally sleepy, even though you slept well more than twelve hours the night before. Your doctor may also notice that you exhibit very slow reflexes. Researchers now know that when you are hypothyroid, you are unable to reach the deepest stage 4 level of sleep. This is the most restful kind of sleep. Lack of it will explain why you will remain tired, sleepy, and unrefreshed. See Chapter 26 for more on coping with fatigue.

Fingernails

Fingernails become brittle and develop lines and grooves to the point where applying nail polish may become impossible.

Hair Changes

When you are hypothyroid, hair may become thinner, dry, and brittle, causing you to need additional hair conditioner. Hair loss may also occur to the point where balding sets in. (See "Hair Changes" under the list of symptoms in Chapter 4 for more details.) You will also lose body hair such as eyebrow, leg, and arm hair, as well as pubic hair. Much of this grows back after some time on thyroid hormone replacement. If you have your thyroid hormone levels change over a short time, such as going from hypothyroidism to normal (euthyroidism) or from euthyroidism to hypothyroidism, you may experience transient increased hair loss, which will grow back.

High Cholesterol

Hypothyroid people often have high cholesterol that can lead to a host of other problems, including heart disease. This should be controlled through diet until your thyroid problem is brought under control. It's generally recommended that anyone with high cholesterol be tested for hypothyroidism. Cholesterol-lowering medications should not be started unless the high cholesterol levels persist a few months after sufficient thyroid hormone replacement therapy. We discuss cholesterol more in Chapter 25.

Menstrual Cycle Changes

In women, menstrual periods become much heavier and more frequent than usual, and sometimes ovaries can stop releasing an egg each month. This can make conception difficult if you are trying to have a child. Anemia, resulting from heavy periods, may also develop.

Milky Discharge from Breasts

Hypothyroidism may cause women to overproduce prolactin, one of the hormones responsible for milk production. Too much prolactin can also block estrogen production, which will interfere with regular periods and ovulation. As a general rule, when you notice discharge coming out of your breast by itself and you are not lactating or deliberately expressing your breasts, please have it checked by a breast specialist or gynecologist (who should also perform a thorough breast exam to rule out other breast conditions).

Muscle Problems

Common complaints from hypothyroid people are muscular aches and cramps (which may contribute to crampier periods). Joints may also start to hurt. In fact, many people believe they are experiencing arthritic symptoms, when, in fact, this condition completely clears up once hypothyroidism is treated. But the aching can be severe enough to wake you up at night. Muscle coordination is also a problem, causing you to feel "klutzy" all the time while finding it increasingly difficult to perform simple motor tasks. This can result from the effects of hypothyroidism on the coordination center in the brain, the cerebellum.

Numbness

Numbness is combined with a sensation of "pins and needles" as well as a tendency to develop carpal tunnel syndrome, characterized by tingling and numbness in the hands. The carpal tunnel syndrome is caused, in this case, by compression on nerves in the wrist because of thickening and swelling of the body tissues under the skin. Carpal tunnel syndrome can also be a repetitive strain injury and can be aggravated by working

Hypothyroidism or PMS?

The following PMS symptoms can also be confused with symptoms of hypo- or hyperthyroidism:

- Abdominal bloating*
- Backache*
- Breast swelling and tenderness†
- Brittle fingernails*
- Changes in sex drive* (either more or less)
- Chills*
- Clumsiness and poor coordination*
- Constipation*
- Depression*
- Diarrhea†
- Dizziness*
- Eye problems*†
- Fatigue*
- Feeling cold*
- Headaches*
- Heart pounding†
- Heavier periods*
- High cholesterol*
- Hoarseness*
- Increased appetite†
- Insomnia†
- Irregular periods or infertility*†
- Joint and muscle pain*
- Muscle spasms*
- Nausea, menopausal-like hot flashes†
- Poor memory and concentration*
- Shakiness†
- Skin eruptions*
- Sugar and salt cravings*

*Represents signs of hypothyroidism
†Represents signs of hyperthyroidism

at a computer keyboard, for example. Numbness also plagues pregnant women who suffer from water retention. This condition should resolve itself once your hypothyroidism is treated.

Poor Memory and Concentration

Hypothyroidism causes a "spacey" feeling, where you may find it difficult to remember things or to concentrate at work. This is especially scary for seniors, who may feel as though dementia is settling in. In fact, one of the most common causes of so-called "senility" has been undiagnosed hypothyroidism. If it seems a loved one is experiencing dementia, consider setting up a thyroid function test before declaring it's Alzheimer's. See Chapter 17 for more details about thyroid disease and aging.

Skin Changes

Skin may feel dry and coarse to the point where it flakes like powder when you scratch it. Cracked skin will become common on your elbows and kneecaps. Your skin will also sport a yellowish hue as the hypothyroidism worsens. The yellow color results from a buildup of carotene, a substance in our diet that is normally converted into vitamin A but slows because of hypothyroidism. Because your blood vessels are more tightly constricted, diverting blood away from your skin, you will appear pale and washed out.

Other symptoms, more obvious to a physician, will be the presence of a condition known as *myxedema*, a thickening of skin and underlying tissues. Myxedema is characterized by a puffiness around the eyes and face, and can even involve the tongue, which will also swell. This is very different from the *pretibial myxedema* seen in Graves' disease, caused by an effect of autoantibodies upon the skin. Also see the section "Easy Bruising" in Chapter 4.

Stunted Growth in Children

The classic scenario is wondering why your twelve-year-old son still looks like he's only nine years old. So you take him to the doctor—and find out that his thyroid petered out and he has stopped growing! This will completely reverse itself once treatment with thyroid hormone begins. (For more information, see Chapter 15.)

Voice Changes

If your thyroid is enlarged, it may affect your vocal cords and cause your voice to sound hoarse or husky.

Diagnosing Hypothyroidism

The most important clue in diagnosing hypothyroidism is looking at possible symptoms and screening people who are vulnerable to subclinical hypothyroidism. Typically, people who have four or more of the symptoms of hypothyroidism outlined earlier should be screened. On the other hand, hypothyroidism is common enough so that TSH tests performed during a regular yearly checkup may detect hypothyroidism way before there are any discernible symptoms.

The next task in diagnosing hypothyroidism is to evaluate results of a TSH test properly. Abnormally high levels of TSH are a sign of hypothyroidism, while abnormally low levels of TSH are a sign of too much thyroid hormone, or thyrotoxicosis. It is important to note that the laboratory tests for people with symptoms of hypothyroidism should consist of both a free T4 level and a TSH level (see Chapter 2). This is because some people have trouble with their pituitary gland or brain that interferes with proper TSH production. In such situations, the free T4 level would be low while the TSH would be inappropriately normal or low.

Driving While Hypothyroid

People who are moderately to severely hypothyroid, with TSH levels higher than 10, should not be driving a vehicle of any kind, flying a plane, or operating heavy machinery. These rules do *not* apply to the vast majority of those who are mildly hypothyroid (usually with levels 5 to 10). Thyroid cancer patients preparing for withdrawal scans (see Chapters 2 and 9), whose TSH levels will typically go above 30 while in preparation, *should most definitely not be driving while hypothyroid.*

Clearly, this is more of a problem for people who do not have access to public transit or taxis, and in some cases, doctor's notes may be necessary. Indeed, there have been several cases of hypothyroid patients being seriously injured or killed in car acci-

---

The Hypo Reflection: A View of Blatant Hypothyroidism

If you look in the mirror, you may notice the following changes in your appearance when you are hypothyroid, compared to a photo taken in the past when your thyroid was functioning normally:

- **Face:** Full and puffy, with pads of skin around the eyelids, as well as little yellow lumps around the eyes (called *xanthelasma*), which are caused by cholesterol buildup.
- **Complexion:** Pale and porcelain-like, with a pink flush in the cheeks. It may also have a yellowish tint to it, because of a buildup of carotene.
- **Lips:** They may appear to be swollen and a little purple because of poor circulation. Your tongue may also be slightly enlarged.
- **Eyebrows:** You may notice that you have fewer brow hairs.
- **Expression:** Sad, lackluster.
- **Hair:** It may lose its sheen, becoming dull and limp.
- **Skin:** Thick, dry, and peeling with possible patches of pigmentation loss.

dents. There is also the legal issue to consider. Should a hypothyroid driver be in an accident, particularly with loss of life occurring, even if absolutely blameless for causing the accident, the driver could be legally defenseless. An opposing attorney or prosecutor could argue that the hypothyroidism was a factor in the accident, even if this was not true. Likewise, should the insurance company find out about the hypothyroid status of the driver, it might be difficult (if not impossible) to obtain financial payments that would have otherwise been easily obtained. It is important to verify with your doctor whether or not it is safe for you to drive.

Treating Hypothyroidism

Treating hypothyroidism involves taking thyroid hormone, which either replaces the thyroid hormone you're no longer making or supplements thyroid hormone to compensate for the inadequate amount your thyroid is making. What isn't so simple is finding the right dosage and restoring your thyroid levels to normal, determined by the TSH test discussed in the previous chapter.

In fact, finding "normal" for each individual can be so tricky, it has led to a hypothyroid patients' movement, demanding more attention be paid to adequate balancing and less rigidity in labeling certain TSH levels "normal" when there is a wide range. As discussed in the previous chapter in the TSH section, the normal euthyroid range used to be indicated as 0.5 to 5.0 for TSH results. However, since these were based on men instead of women (who make up the majority of hypothyroid patients), and some of the men were likely subclinically hypothyroid (appearing healthy with no reported symptoms of hypothyroidism), the "normal" range was probably driven up.

The American Association of Clinical Endocrinologists (AACE) revised its TSH targets in 2002, down to 0.3 to 3.0. But the TSH targets that knowledgeable thyroid specialists aim for is now 0.5 to 2.0. This is based on their clinical research as well as published data. Because it takes a lot of time to complete research studies on TSH targets, published guidelines are slow to reflect the targets used by thyroidologists practicing state-of-the-art standards of care. Indeed, most people who are euthyroid sit between 0.4 and 2.5. Revising the "normal" target to more realistic ranges for women has helped many hypothyroid patients negotiate better care with their doctors, instead of the past scenarios where patients would voice that they "feel hypo" only to be told they were "normal" and sent home. Newer targets will also help to eliminate the hunt for bizarre (and incorrect) theories that attempt to explain why some people still "feel" hypothyroid within the normal ranges. In fact targets between 3.0 and 5.0 may indicate mild hypothyroidism in some people, but there are no studies that show these findings as of this writing. Some endocrinologists report that they have seen patients with mild hypothyroidism with TSH levels of 2.1 to 4.4, but this remains unsupported in any peer-reviewed medical literature. All that being said, the normal range according to most labs does remain 0.5 to 5.0, but many labs now use 4.0 as the upper limit. Most people will feel mild hypothyroid symptoms at numbers above 10. Mild hypothyroidism would present at TSH levels ranging between 10 and 20, while severe hypothyroidism would be at levels above 30. Hypothyroidism that can be mild to moderate has TSH values between 10 and 20.

Thyroid Hormone Replacement

Although we will get into thyroid hormone replacement in much greater detail in Chapter 10, this section is designed to give you a beginning understanding of thyroid hormone therapy for hypothyroidism. Treatment for hypothyroid children and the elderly is discussed in greater detail in Chapters 15 and 17.

In the United States, more than fifteen million prescriptions of thyroid hormone per year are sold. Even if only part of your thyroid gland was surgically removed, thyroid hormone replacement may be prescribed.

A prescription for thyroid hormone replacement pills costs anything from $30 to $80 for a three-month supply, depending on the brand. If you have a very rare problem with dyes used to color the pills, most brands offer their 50-microgram strength as a plain white pill, without dye. You can take your thyroid hormone using the white pills only. For example, if you were on a dosage of 150 micrograms, you'd take three white pills instead of the usual one blue pill that represents 150. See the section "What Is in This Stuff, Anyway?" (later in this chapter) for more information.

Today's thyroid replacement hormone, or synthetic thyroid hormone, comes in colored tablet form. The generic name is *levothyroxine sodium*, or *T4*, which, as discussed in Chapter 1, converts into T3 inside each cell of the body. Sufficient levels of T3 then shut off TSH production by the pituitary gland. Under natural circumstances, the conversion of T4 into T3 is how we wind up with T3 in the first place, and it has been shown over many years of study that allowing the body to convert T3 naturally from T4 is far smoother and easier on your body than just adding T3. Adding T3 to T4 is not advised as of this writing, and we discuss why later in this chapter (see "The T3 Issue") and in Chapter 10.

Since we are all individuals, dosing may vary greatly from one person to the other. Indeed, people of the same gender, age, and weight may require different doses. The goal of thyroid hormone replacement therapy is to restore thyroid hormone levels to a level that results in a normal TSH value.

When your symptoms persist in spite of normal TSH levels, this means that those symptoms are caused by something other than hypothyroidism and will need to be investigated further. Feeling hypo while having a normal TSH reading is probably not as common as it once was because of revised TSH targets. In short, with more people on target, fewer people are walking around with mild or subclinical hypothyroidism. If you still feel hypothyroid in spite of the new target ranges discussed in this book, it's important to remember that there are other things going on in your life and your body besides hypothyroidism.

It is critical to understand that a normal TSH level means you are making adequate amounts of T3 from the T4 that enters each body cell. We know this because within the pituitary cells, the gene that makes TSH will make high levels of TSH unless there is sufficient T3 inside the cell to shut off the TSH production. The normal TSH response from the pituitary cells shows that there is a normal amount of T3 and reflects the same normal T3 level inside the rest of your body's cells. (You may read on the Internet and in other patient materials that in some people T4 does not convert into T3 properly. This statement is not accurate, and we will explain why in Chapter 19.)

Mixed preparations of T3 and T4 are also available, which we don't recommend as of this writing. One such drug is liotrix, sold under the brand name of Thyrolar. This drug is discussed more in Chapter 10, which covers thyroid hormone.

Brand-name thyroid hormone replacement pills (levothyroxine) are color-coded, and each pill should have the actual dosage strength printed on the tablet in micrograms (for example, 100 micrograms, which equals 0.1 milligram).

The Right Dosage

If you are on too high a dosage of levothyroxine, you will develop symptoms of thyrotoxicosis, discussed in the next chapter. (In this case, TSH readings would be below 0.2.) If this happens notify your doctor; your dosage will be adjusted downward accordingly. Again, the correct dosage of levothyroxine sodium is determined by a normal TSH reading. The correct clinical laboratory tests (which sometimes are not done) are highly sensitive in determining hypothyroidism at even subclinical levels. (Some material on the Internet suggests that clinical laboratory blood tests are inaccurate in determining hypothyroidism or that subtle rises in body temperature or other nonstandard tests are the best ways to measure hypothyroidism. This is inaccurate, and we explain why in Chapter 19.)

When treating full-blown hypothyroidism or after treatment for hyperthyroidism that results in hypothyroidism, the average replacement dose of thyroid hormone is roughly 1.6 micrograms per kilogram of body weight each day. Most people will be able to find the right dose for them in the twelve dosage strengths that various brands offer, which range from 25 to 300 micrograms (specifically 25, 50, 75, 88, 100, 112, 125, 137, 150, 175, 200, and 300 micrograms).

If You Are Elderly or Have Heart Disease

To avoid any risk of being over-replaced (overdosed to the point where you are thyrotoxic) if you are elderly or have heart disease, dosages of thyroid hormone in your case may start fairly low, at around 50 micrograms. Dosages should be adjusted very, very slowly, in increments of 25 micrograms monthly, until you reach the proper thyroid hormone level that makes a normal TSH. We discuss treatment of thyroid disease in older individuals in Chapter 17.

What Brand of Thyroid Hormone Should I Take?

The key phrase in a quality thyroid hormone replacement pill is *precise dosing*. This enables your doctor to prescribe the lowest and most effective dose without overdoing it or "underdoing" it. It's also important to keep in mind that thyroid hormone brands are not interchangeable. Endocrinologists have seen significant differences in thyroid function after patients have switched brands. The right dose for you on Brand A may not be the right dose on Brand B.

That said, some pharmacologic studies to date indicate no significant differences between the four most commonly dispensed brands of levothyroxine. In "clinical speak," they were found to be *pharmacologically equivalent* (absorbed in the blood in precisely the same way) and are considered equivalent under current FDA guidelines. This means that the brands studied were found to be interchangeable in the majority of patients receiving thyroid hormone replacement therapy. But disagreement persists regarding *bioequivalency* among thyroid brands. This is because many thyroid experts believe that bioequivalence requires comparing TSH responses, rather than just T4 levels. One manufacturer had to recall some of its batches from the market because the drug was not being manufactured in a previously standardized way. Very simple changes in the manufacturing of levothyroxine tablets can make a big difference in performance. In addition, when the batch of thyroid pills that you receive from your pharmacist has been on the shelf for too long or exposed to heat, the pills may not be as potent as they were when first shipped. Therefore, it's crucial to always ask when your pills expire and be alert to poor storage conditions (for example, a pharmacy stockroom that is not air-conditioned in the summertime). Experts also warn that a bottle of pills that expires in March 2010 and is dispensed in December 2009 should be rejected by the buyer as a batch that is not sufficiently fresh.

The shortest route to maintaining thyroid hormone function with your thyroid pill is to:

- Choose a brand of thyroid hormone pill that offers precise dosing. This is particularly important for women over age forty who may be approaching menopause, and anyone over age sixty as well as people with heart conditions. Most branded, nongeneric levothyroxine tablets are available in this fashion.
- Stay on one brand; don't switch around. Request that your doctor write "do not substitute" on your prescriptions.
- Watch for signs of thyrotoxicosis (see next chapter). These symptoms may mean that you're on too high a dosage of thyroid hormone.

- Watch for signs of hypothyroidism. These are signs that you may be on too low a dosage of thyroid hormone.
- Get a thyroid function test every four months for the first year or two after you begin your pills; then graduate to six months; then get tested annually.
- Always find out when the pills expire and how and where they have been stored in the pharmacy.
- If you miss a pill, don't worry; take two the next day. Thyroid hormone pills have a very long half-life, and missing a pill every now and then won't make any difference *as long as you make up for it by taking the missed tablets.*
- Take your pill on an empty stomach if you can. Don't take it at the same time as a multivitamin; take the vitamin at bedtime and the thyroid pill in the morning.

What Is in This Stuff, Anyway?

Thyroid hormone pills contain a number of excipients (substances added to a medicine that allow it to be formed into a shape having consistency, which include diluents, lubricants, binders, and disintegrants). The pills may contain acacia, lactose, magnesium stearate, povidone, confectioners' sugar (which has cornstarch), talc, and various coloring agents. The lactose used in thyroid hormone pills is minimal; there is approximately one hundred times the amount of lactose in one-half cup of whole milk as in one tablet of Synthroid, for example. In theory, if you are highly lactose intolerant, you could take your thyroid hormone pill together with a lactase enzyme; however, we've never heard of anyone needing to do so.

When Thyroid Hormone Doesn't Work

There are rare cases when thyroid hormone doesn't work. In this case, you would have high TSH levels in spite of taking thyroid hormone, but this has nothing to do with T4/T3 conversion. Clearly, when you don't have enough T4 in your body, or it is being poorly absorbed from your pills, you won't make sufficient amounts of T3 either. Here are the common reasons why thyroid hormone doesn't work:

Thyroid Hormone Resistance (a.k.a. Refetoff Syndrome)

Thyroid hormone resistance is a rare genetic disorder in which the receptors that stick to T3 (then stick to specific parts of the chromosomes of each body cell) are mutated so that they don't stick to T3 very well. Because of this, much, much more T4 is needed to enter each cell and change to T3 to make up for this abnormal T3 receptor. In this case, you would have either high TSH levels, despite normal or high levels of free T4 or free T3 (making you hypothyroid), or normal TSH levels and very high levels of T4 and T3 (making you euthyroid because the high levels compensate for the resistance). In either case, just as in normal individuals, a high TSH reflects too little thyroid hormone and a normal TSH reflects sufficient thyroid hormone. We devote a separate chapter to thyroid hormone resistance (Chapter 18). If you have thyroid hormone resistance, a highly trained thyroid specialist needs to be on the case; as of 1997, only about 350 cases were seen worldwide! That means most endocrinologists have never seen a case. (Some material on the Internet refers to a nonexistent disorder called "thyroxine resistance." This appears to be a distorted and misunderstood interpretation of the literature on thyroid hormone resistance. We deal with this and other distortions of thyroid hormone resistance in Chapter 19.)

Not Taking Thyroid Hormone Properly

Many people take thyroid hormone with too much food or with hot liquids, take it at irregular times on successive days, or just skip pills. All of these things can dramatically affect proper absorption of thyroid hormone or its efficacy. In these cases, you would have high TSH, and low levels of free T4 and free T3. See Chapter 10 on thyroid hormone, which outlines the correct way to take T4 for maximum efficacy and optimum absorption.

Taking Certain Medications or Supplements That Interfere with Absorption

If you take multivitamin pills or iron supplements such as ferrous sulphate, take your thyroid hormone pill at least five hours in advance or take the multivitamin at bedtime and your thyroid hormone tablet in the morning. Iron appears to bind to thyroid hormone, thus making less of it available for absorption into your body. In this case you would have high TSH levels. This is discussed more in Chapter 10.

Pill Storage Issues

Thyroid pills become inactive when they are exposed to heat. Use the "chocolate bar rule"; if you wouldn't store a chocolate bar in a given place for fear of it melting, don't store your thyroid hormone pills there, either.

Individuals with Malabsorption Syndromes

Very rarely, certain malabsorption problems such as celiac disease can interfere with thyroid hormone absorption. In this case you would have high TSH levels.

Natural Thyroid Hormone

Natural thyroid hormone, consisting of dried extracts of pig thyroid glands, is available by prescription under the brand name Armour. This is what my grandmother took years ago, along with millions of other thyroid patients of yesteryear. The patients who take it usually do just fine, but patients on natural thyroid hormone remain less balanced than those taking pure levothyroxine sodium, which offers precise dosing designed to keep people well balanced. The problem with natural thyroid hormone is that it is still a bit of a mixed bag of compounds, which include a variety of thyroid hormone breakdown products that may not be useful. (In many patient materials, and on the Internet, natural thyroid hormone is touted for containing "all four thyroid hormones: T1, T2, T3, and T4." T1 and T2 are what T4 degrades into, and have no activity, offering absolutely no benefit to you. We deal with these claims in Chapter 19.)

Advocates of natural thyroid hormone have created a business out of their advocacy, exploiting the suffering of hypothyroid patients whose symptoms of hypothyroidism may be persisting for reasons having nothing to do with what brand of thyroid hormone they're on. Similarly, there is no good clinical reason to take natural thyroid hormone, and the patients who request it have usually read misleading material extolling its virtues. The plain truth is this: natural thyroid hormone is available and may not be dangerous if from a reputable manufacturer, but it's certainly not superior. Top endocrinologists will prescribe it only if forced to by a patient's insistence. We discuss natural thyroid hormone more in Chapter 10.

The T3 Issue

In recent years, it became in vogue for thyroid patients to request supplementation with a combination of T3 (Cytomel) and T4 (levothyroxine sodium). Certain books and articles about T3 supplementation reported that it helped with "brain fog," depression, and other apparent symptoms of hypothyroidism. There was also a trend that began in psychiatry, where T3 was added to antidepressants, which reportedly helped alleviate depression, but which has been disputed by most endocrinologists as not helpful and potentially harmful.

A small pilot study on T3 supplementation was done in Kaunas, Lithuania, which involved 33 participants. Published in the February 11, 1999, issue of the *New England Journal of Medicine*, it reported that participants felt better and performed better according to their scores on standardized psychological tests. The small study suggested that a combination of T3 and T4 improved results of various psychological tests that assessed concentration and depression in hypothyroid patients. Unfortunately, the study was wrongly interpreted to verify that T3 supplementation improved quality of life for all hypothyroid patients. In my (Sara's) revised thyroid books from that period (1999 to 2002), I enthusiastically informed readers of this study, encouraged them to discuss it with their doctors if they thought they might benefit, but also expressed concerns over the potential risks as there were many groups of patients who might not be good candidates for T3 supplementation.

Since then, larger, well-designed clinical trials, published in 2003, investigating whether the T3/T4 combination offers any benefit to hypothyroid patients, *failed* to verify that there is any value in the combination T3/T4 therapy. In addition, a post-analysis of the 1999 study revealed many flaws in its design and interpretation. For example, half of the participants were thyroid cancer patients and not representative of the majority of people with hypothyroidism because they were on TSH suppression doses of T4, which sometimes create other problems. The reality is that many patient advocates were too quick to embrace the study as the solution for the hypothyroid masses.

From an ethics perspective, the mass dispensing of T3/T4 combination therapy is fraught with problems, since the risk of thyrotoxicosis (see next chapter) with T3 hormone is not insignificant. This can occur even under careful monitoring—something that is hard to enforce in a climate with fewer and fewer endocrinologists in practice, and overloaded primary care physicians.

What preceded these studies was an explosion of interest in T3 supplementation, and many doctors (some with questionable training in thyroid disease) began patients on T3. Doctors, who anecdotally reported improvement with T3 in patients with depression or other features of mild hypothyroidism, were actually reporting improvement when treating subclinical hypothyroidism *itself* rather than observing that T3 conferred particular benefits over T4. These patients had never been on the appropriate dosages of T4 to make their TSH levels normal in the first place.

Although there are rare endocrinologists who use T3 without T4, as a treatment for depression or other symptoms of mild hypothyroidism in the presence of normal TSH levels, this is not considered a standard of care that makes sense in light of the most current physiology knowledge and research. We devote more discussion to the use of T3 therapy in Chapter 10, which covers thyroid hormone in more detail. What's important to understand here is that top thyroidologists do not support the routine use of T3 in treating hypothyroidism—not because they do not have an open mind but because it doesn't seem to offer benefit and may offer some risks.

Thyroid patient advocates and thyroid patients on Internet listservs continue to cling to the T3/T4 combination therapy as the answer to living well with hypothyroidism, while doctors who don't agree with this approach are labeled "closed minded" or too conventional. The only patients who should be on the T3/T4 combination therapy are those patients who have just had a withdrawal scan that checks for thyroid cancer recurrence and are temporarily climbing back up to normal levels of thyroid hormone, discussed more in Chapters 2 and 9. There may be rare cases in people who are severely hypothyroid who may be started on T3 until enough T4 builds up in their system, or T3 may be used in treating thyroid hormone resistance (see Chapter 18), but these situations do not represent the majority of hypothyroid people.

As of this writing, anyone that suggests to you that T3 should be routinely added to your T4, other medications you might be taking, or as a solo therapy, is not up to date.

Why Do I Still Feel Hypothyroid?

If you have normal TSH levels but still have symptoms of hypothyroidism, then you will be relieved to know that the symptoms that persist are not likely to be related to your hypothyroidism and you can, at last, investigate other causes and remedies. The goal of treating hypothyroidism is to restore your thyroid levels to normal (indicated by normal TSH). The hypothyroid state in your body may exist along with other problems. Ask people who are not hypothyroid if they're tired, depressed, constipated, or have muscular aches and pains, and a huge majority will say yes to at least one of those complaints in spite of normal thyroid levels and no history of thyroid disease.

It's been suggested in some thyroid patient literature that some people fail to properly convert T4 into T3, which is why you may still feel hypothyroid. Again, this is completely erroneous (see Chapter 19). We've seen numerous false and bizarre theories put forth about why "hidden hypothyroidism" persists in spite of normal TSH. It's not hidden hypothyroidism, but hidden causes for your symptoms, which can mimic (or in most cases, mask) hypothyroidism. In other words, you can continue to feel "hypothyroid" when you're not (meaning that your lab results show normal TSH levels) because all of the symptoms of hypothyroidism overlap with multiple causes not related to thyroid problems. For example, fatigue (see Chapter 26), depression (see Chapter 24), poor concentration, and poor digestion are common complaints among many adults in the absence of a thyroid problem.

Other potential causes of these ailments include physical and emotional stress, sleep deprivation, normal aging (including menopause), sedentary living (the older we get, the less active we become), poor diet, obesity or obesity-related diseases (such as diabetes or cardiovascular disease), and other diseases we should be managing. Remember, too, that bouts of hypothyroidism seriously interfere with your normal activities. Many people become more sedentary, gain weight, and may consequently feel bad even after their thyroid hormone levels are restored. Bouts of hypothyroidism can leave us out of the loop at work and socially, and we may feel the consequences of having to catch up or the long absence of engagement in our community or our social network, in turn, that can trigger real depression. (See Chapter 24.) In that way we can feel worse or unwell in spite of normal thyroid hormone and TSH levels.

It's important to understand that you can't blame all of your symptoms of poor health on your thyroid condition, especially when you have cofactors for other diseases, including possibly poor social support systems at home, which can predispose people to depression. In short, there are things going on in your life and body other than hypothyroidism, and indeed, many people have multiple health conditions simultaneously.

4 Too Much Thyroid Hormone: Thyrotoxicosis

n Chapter 1, we outlined how thyroid hormone is produced, why it's necessary in life, and how it is regulated in the body. When you make too much thyroid hormone, a cascade of symptoms develops, and you feel unwell until the problem is resolved. This chapter looks at those symptoms in detail and outlines why they may be occurring, who is vulnerable, how to verify the condition through testing, and how to treat it.

Many thyroid patients (and doctors) confuse two distinct terms: *hyperthyroidism*, which refers to an overactive thyroid gland, and *thyrotoxicosis*, which means "too much thyroid hormone." Hyperthyroidism and thyrotoxicosis are two cousins that often pass as twins. All of the "hyperthyroid" symptoms you may have read about, or heard about, are, in fact, symptoms of too much thyroid hormone, which may indeed result from an overactive thyroid gland (hyperthyroid). But too much thyroid hormone can also result from other thyroid diseases, as well as too high a dosage of thyroid hormone taken as a medication. We use the accurate term, *thyrotoxicosis*, throughout this book, which means "having too much thyroid hormone in your body"—for any number of reasons.

Symptoms of Too Much Thyroid Hormone

Before we get into the many causes of thyrotoxicosis, let's review the symptoms.

When you have too much thyroid hormone in your body, everything speeds up. As a result, you can experience numerous physical symptoms that we'll discuss alphabetically. The good news is that the vast majority of these symptoms disappear once the cause of thyrotoxicosis is treated and your thyroid hormone levels are restored to normal.

Adrenaline Rush

An important hormone system in the body called the *adrenergic* system is formed from parts of the brain, nervous system, and adrenal glands (small glands that sit on top of each kidney). The hormones released by the adrenergic system are called *catecholamines*. Two of these hormones are adrenaline (also known as epinephrine) and noradrenaline (norepinephrine). You might remember that adrenaline is a "fight or flight" hormone, released when you are scared, shocked, or highly excited. When this happens you feel jittery or nervous, your heart beats very fast, you sweat profusely, and your eyes appear wide open because your lids are pulled back (retracted). Just like with many other hormones, special receptors are present in the body's cells that stick to these hormones to stimulate the cells. Two types of these adrenergic receptors are alpha receptors, which make blood vessels squeeze together tightly and raise the blood pressure, and beta receptors, which make the heart beat faster.

High levels of thyroid hormones increase the numbers of beta-adrenergic receptors in your body's cells. This makes you much more sensitive to the effects of your own adrenaline. Consequently, when thyroid hormone levels increase, the heart speeds up and beats very fast from the combined effects of both adrenaline and thyroid hormone. This is why special types of medications, called *beta-blockers*, are so very useful to help slow the heart down and prevent severe heart symptoms that can make thyrotoxicosis dangerous.

Many of the symptoms of thyrotoxicosis are related to this adrenaline effect and sometimes, especially in older people, they are the only obvious symptoms of too much thyroid hormone. There can also be very rare tumors of the adrenal glands, which release too much adrenaline, called *pheochromocytomas*. Since the symptoms of rapid heartbeat and lid retraction are similar in thyrotoxic people and in those with pheochromocytomas, they may be confused for each other before blood test results are available. A major difference is that blood pressure is usually very high in people with pheochromocytomas (an alpha-adrenergic effect), but thyrotoxicosis is not likely to cause high blood pressure since it causes beta-adrenergic stimulation. There is an uncommon type of thyroid cancer, medullary thyroid cancer, which can be part of an inherited disease (caused by a genetic mutation) associated with pheochromocytomas. This inherited disease is called *multiple endocrine neoplasia, type 2a or type 2b*, and is discussed in greater detail in Chapter 9.

The rapid heartbeat in thyrotoxicosis may be very obvious to you or it may be unnoticed. Sometimes, it is noticed only at bedtime when you are lying quietly and trying to go to sleep. Once in a while it may be severe enough to cause a heart rhythm problem called *atrial fibrillation*. A fine tremor from thyrotoxicosis may not be noticed except as it affects your signature or when your arm is stretched out in front of you. Both of these symptoms usually respond to beta-blockers (see Chapter 11) and get better when the thyroid hormone level becomes normal. See the section "Heart Palpitations" later in this chapter for additional detail.

Behavioral and Emotional Changes

You may experience a host of emotional symptoms such as irritability, restlessness, sleeplessness, anxiety, depression, and sadness. See the sections "The Emotional Effects of Thyrotoxicosis" and "Psychiatric Misdiagnosis" later in this chapter.

Bowel Movements

Increased frequency of bowel movements, known as *hyperdefecation*, is another sign of thyrotoxicosis. This is different from diarrhea because the bowel movements will not be liquid-like but appear to be normal. They'll just appear more often—even if your diet is normal and hasn't changed. Because your digestion speeds up, so does your bowel habit. Sometimes the buildup of thyroid hormone will prevent your small intestine from absorbing certain nutrients from food as well. If you suffered from chronic constipation prior to your thyroid problem, you may notice simple regularity without laxatives or fiber. You may even notice that you have magically lost seven to ten pounds, although you have been eating more than usual. You may also crave sweets.

Easy Bruising

Platelet disorders tend to be more common in people with either thyrotoxicosis or hypothyroidism because such disorders are often because of autoimmune problems that tend to be more common when autoimmune thyroid diseases are present. This may cause bruising, and aspirin can make the bruising worse. If there are no associated platelet problems, easy bruising can be seen because capillaries (very small blood vessels) are more fragile in thyrotoxicosis.

Enlarged Thyroid Gland

As discussed in Chapter 1, an enlarged thyroid gland is called a *goiter*, where your thyroid will enlarge and may swell in the front of your neck. Thyrotoxic goiters develop because of hyperthyroidism. Here, a goiter develops because too much stimulation of the thyroid causes the gland to enlarge. In extreme cases, a goiter can swell to the diameter of a grapefruit. The appearance of the thyroid gland is very helpful for determining the cause of the thyrotoxicosis. In Graves' disease (see Chapter 6) there is usually a symmetrical goiter that can vary from slightly larger than normal to five times larger than normal. On the other hand, if there is a distinct nodule in the thyroid or asymmetry of the goiter, it suggests that there may be a *toxic nodular thyroid*. For more details about nodules, see Chapter 8, and for details about goiters, see Chapter 7.

Exhaustion

When your body is overworked as a result of too much thyroid hormone, this can lead to exhaustion, which will affect your energy level and your general emotional well-being. Difficulty sleeping, resulting in sleep deprivation, may be partly to blame. Weak muscles, discussed later, are another important factor. Although popular mythology might suggest that increased levels of thyroid hormone give you more energy, the opposite effect is much more common.

Eye Problems

Eye changes seen with thyrotoxicosis from any cause are related to the adrenergic effects discussed earlier in this chapter. This is called the *thyroid stare* and is because of lid retraction. Additional changes, which point to Graves' disease as a cause of the thyrotoxicosis, include protrusion of the eyeball (*proptosis*), swelling of the skin around the eyes (*periorbital edema*), and reddened irritation (*chemosis*). Swelling of the muscles surrounding the eyeballs causes the proptosis. It may be sufficiently severe as to prevent the eyes from moving together when you look at something, resulting in double vision (*diplopia*). The chemosis may be associated with feelings of burning, grittiness, or inability to tolerate bright lights (*photophobia*). These discomforts become worse as the proptosis becomes worse because the eyelids don't cover the eyes at night, letting them become too dry. See Chapter 23 for more details.

Fingertips and Fingernail Changes

Many thyrotoxic people notice that they have swollen fingertips to the point where they look clubbed. This is known as *acropachy* or clubbing. Nail growth also increases, while the nails become soft and easy to tear off. In addition, a condition known as *onycholysis* can occur where the upper edges of the fingernails become partially separated from the fingertips.

Hair Changes

Hair often becomes softer and finer and may not be as easy to style as it once was. Curly hair tends to become straighter. In some cases you may notice some hair loss and find clumps of it on your pillow, clothing, tub, or hairbrush. This usually happens when there are big changes in the thyroid hormone levels. It may also become grayer and may not take to perms or color. In appearance, there could be a general thinning of your hair, but once your thyroid hormone levels are restored to normal, your hair should grow as it once did. To create less stress on the hair, you should avoid coloring or perms until your hair follicles are stronger.

Heart Palpitations

One of the first signs of thyrotoxicosis is a rapid, forceful heartbeat. Increased levels of thyroxine released from the thyroid gland stimulate the heart to beat faster and stronger. In addition, as discussed earlier in this chapter, there is an enhanced sensitivity to your own adrenaline resulting in further stimulation of the heart rate. Initially, you will not notice an increase in your heart rate until it becomes severe.

When a heartbeat is noticeably fast, and you are conscious of it beating in your chest, you will experience what is called a *palpitation*. Generally, palpitations can occur from excessive exercise, sexual activity, alcohol, caffeine, or smoking. Yet, it is abnormal for a palpitation to occur when your body is inactive, not anxious, or not exposed to substances known to increase your heart rate. Thyrotoxic individuals often experience palpitations when they are reading, sleeping, or involved in other relaxing activities. Palpitations caused by thyrotoxicosis do not mean you have a serious heart condition, however. Once your thyroid hormone levels are restored to normal, your heart will resume its normal rate.

Untreated palpitations can, however, lead to serious heart problems and, if they are associated with severe thyrotoxicosis or a weakened heart, can cause heart failure. Normally, thyrotoxicosis is caught in its early stages—long before any serious heart problem develops from palpitations. In fact, permanent changes in the heart are unusual in patients with normal, healthy hearts, unless thyrotoxicosis is particularly severe and prolonged. This can cause thickening of the walls of the heart's left ventricle.

A minority of all thyrotoxic people experience atrial fibrillation, a common heart rhythm abnormality. This means that your heart may have an irregular heart rhythm with random pauses and bursts of heartbeats. While this may be only an occasional symptom, it is not unusual for it to be continuous until thyroid hormone levels are restored to normal. This condition is serious and should be treated by a cardiologist. Atrial fibrillation puts you at significant risk of spontaneous blood clots that could cause a stroke. Often, atrial fibrillation associated with thyrotoxicosis is associated with some degree of underlying heart disease.

Another problem with a fast pulse rate (which may be as high as 150 beats per minute) is that the speed of the heartbeat may create congestive heart failure that can cause swollen ankles and even a collection of fluid in the chest. Shortness of breath may also develop, particularly if you are over age sixty-five or have underlying heart problems. For this reason, it is not unusual for hyperthyroidism to be misdiagnosed as asthma, bronchitis, or heart disease.

Thyroid-related heart problems are treated with beta-blockers that slow the heart down. Beta-blockers are discussed in Chapter 11. A large portion of thyroid patients are misdiagnosed as cardiac patients for obvious reasons. (See Chapter 25 for more information on heart complications.)

Heat Intolerance

A classic sign of thyrotoxicosis is intolerance to heat. Your body temperature may rise a bit; however, even normal room temperatures feel too warm. In addition, you will sweat far more than usual. This combination is unpleasant and you feel isolated in your discomfort. Typically, someone who is thyrotoxic is constantly wondering, "Is it me or is it really hot in here?"

This single symptom is responsible for misdiagnosis of thyrotoxicosis in women approaching menopause whose complaints of "feeling hot" are mistaken for hot flashes, a classic menopausal symptom.

Infertility

Too much thyroid hormone can interfere with a woman's ovulation cycle resulting in temporary infertility. Once thyroid hormone levels are restored to normal, in the absence of other barriers (such as endometriosis or blocked ovarian tubes), fertility is restored.

Thyrotoxicosis in early pregnancy can lead to miscarriage; repeated miscarriage is often considered a form of infertility. If this is a problem for you, it's important to insist that your TSH levels are checked to rule out an underlying thyroid problem. For more information about thyroid disorders and pregnancy, see Chapter 13.

Menstrual Cycle Changes

Thyrotoxic women will find that their periods are lighter and scantier, and they may even skip periods. This is why thyroid problems can affect fertility—because they interfere with ovulation and regular cycles. When thyroid hormone levels are restored to normal, cycles should return to normal. See *The Thyroid Sourcebook for Women* (second edition), for more information on this topic.

Muscle Weakness

Muscle weakness is especially noticeable in the shoulders, hips, and thighs, which can make it difficult to climb stairs. Thigh muscles may in fact ache or feel soft. Shoulder weakness is noticed when you brush your hair or do upper arm movements for long periods of time. Muscle symptoms are greatly exacerbated by worsening of arthritis or osteoporosis (see Chapter 14). Muscle weakness may be due partly to an overworked, exhausted body; however, there is good reason to believe that thyrotoxicosis has direct effects upon muscle function, sometimes causing wasting of skeletal muscles.

Myasthenia gravis is an autoimmune disease that afflicts muscles, causing profound weakness. In both Graves' disease and Hashimoto's thyroiditis, there is a greater incidence of myasthenia gravis, making it important to have your physician check for this problem if your muscle weakness is very severe. Interestingly, one sign of myasthenia gravis is drooping of the eyelids (*ptosis*), the opposite of the lid retraction seen in thyrotoxicosis. Any ptosis seen with thyrotoxicosis, particularly if other muscles are weak, should make one alert to this possibility. Another unusual muscle problem, periodic paralysis, is dealt with in the next section.

Periodic Paralysis

Periodic paralysis is a rare symptom found in thyrotoxicosis, where you may experience episodes of paralysis following exercise or after eating a lot of starches and sugars. This particularly affects people of Asian descent, but once Graves' disease is brought under control, the paralysis will resolve. Once it's resolved, the level of potassium in the blood usually changes; however, the precise reason for this is not well understood.

Sexual Function and Libido

Thyrotoxic men can experience a decreased libido, which seems to be related to increased signs of estrogen effects, including abnormally enlarged breasts (*gynecomastia*). Some of this may be because thyrotoxicosis increases the amounts of sex hormone binding proteins made by the liver, reducing the amount of male sex hormone (testosterone) available to enter body cells. Men with hyperthyroidism may complain of impotence. Some men may also experience low sperm count and thus impaired fertility. If a young adolescent male develops hyperthyroidism, he may experience a delay in development during normal puberty. Some men do not seem to have any negative effects on their libido during thyrotoxicosis. Of course, the complex effects of thyrotoxicosis on brain function, altering thoughts and behavior, might have additional and differing effects on libido.

The effects of thyrotoxicosis on women's sexuality are unclear. Some women may have an increased desire for sex because of the effects of thyrotoxicosis on brain function and behavior. On the other hand, thyrotoxicosis-associated weakness and menstrual irregularities may combine to reduce a woman's sense of well-being and sex drive.

Skin Changes

Thyrotoxicosis may cause your skin to develop a fine, silky texture and feel moist with remarkably few wrinkles. Because of enhanced perspiration, the constant moisture may cause a rash from inflamed pores. Sometimes there may be areas of the skin that darken, particularly in the creases of the palms and areas that become abraded. There may be areas that itch, and sometimes the skin becomes sensitive to touch, swelling with minimal contact so that you can seemingly write your name on the skin (*dermatographism*).

Some specific changes are not related to thyrotoxicosis and may be associated with autoimmune diseases, such as Graves' disease. Loss of pigmentation (*vitiligo*) is an autoimmune attack on melanin-containing skin cells. Likewise, some people with Graves' disease develop thickening in the skin over the lower legs called *pretibial myxedema*. The skin becomes firm and swollen and slightly darker in color. This is thought to be a reaction to the autoimmune antibodies of Graves' disease and is sometimes treated with steroid creams or ointments. Sometimes the skin under the fingernails becomes remarkably thick, causing the ends of the fingers to thicken, called *thyroid acropachy*. In addition, loss of hair from autoimmune disease may be permanent and result in baldness over the entire body (*alopecia areata* or *totalis*).

Tremors

Trembling hands is one of the classic signs of thyrotoxicosis. You may notice that you have a tremor—meaning that you feel a little nervous and shaky all the time. This is a part of the adrenaline-like effect of thyrotoxicosis discussed earlier in this chapter. It can improve with normalization of the thyroid hormone levels or treatment with beta-blocker medication.

Weight Loss

Sometimes the increased bowel activity (hyperdefecation), combined with an increased metabolic rate, contributes to weight loss—in spite of a healthy appetite. Overweight thyrotoxic people find this an unexpected bonus, but it is this single tendency that is responsible for a misunderstanding of thyroid and weight issues, and the misuse of thyroid hormone as a weight loss drug. Usually, weight loss is limited to ten to twenty pounds, and not all patients necessarily lose weight. Thyrotoxicosis often causes severe exhaustion, and some patients end up gaining weight because they become less active and their appetite is stimulated by their thyrotoxicosis. Unfortunately, some people with normal thyroid function take thyroid hormone pills to induce weight loss. This is a big mistake and can cause (among a host of other unpleasant side effects) heart trouble. Weight is discussed in more detail in Chapter 16.

The Emotional Effects of Thyrotoxicosis

Many people very poorly understand the concept of "energy" as it relates to thyrotoxicosis and your emotional state. There is an assumption that having higher than normal thyroid hormone levels can make you more energetic, less tired, and less

---

The Thyrotoxic Reflection

If you look in the mirror, you may notice the following changes in your appearance when you are thyrotoxic, compared to a photo taken when your thyroid was functioning normally:

- **Face:** A little gaunt because of weight loss (in most cases).
- **Eyes:** They may appear to be bulging with the lids slightly retracted. This is a sign of Graves' disease or thyroid eye disease. (See Chapter 23.)
- **Complexion:** You may notice soft, sweaty skin that is almost silky because you are sweating more. You may also notice that it is either increasingly "tanned" or that you have patches of pigmentation loss.
- **Expression:** Staring and almost "mad" looking because of your eyes.
- **Hair:** It may become softer and finer, and you may even notice it is falling out. It may become grayer as well and not take to being colored or permed.

depressed. This assumption is completely false. The physical effects of thyrotoxicosis are usually closer to a state of exhaustion, rather than increased vigor. Many thyrotoxic people also have difficulty getting to sleep (insomnia). This is the paradox of thyrotoxicosis: on the one hand, bodily functions speed up; on the other, mental and physical energy levels are literally exhausted. The combination of exhaustion and insomnia distinguishes thyrotoxic people from people with mania, who usually have increased energy with insomnia. If a thyrotoxic person feels an increased energy level, there is a chance that he or she has an additional problem of a bipolar affective disorder.

Thyrotoxic patients experience a range of emotional symptoms. Symptoms of nervousness, restlessness (unable to keep still, to sit quietly and calmly), anxiety, irritability, sleeplessness (not able to sustain sleep for long periods of time—waking up every hour), or insomnia are common problems. A thyrotoxic person may exhibit some, all, or none of these features; it depends on the individual.

Some thyrotoxic people are emotionally labile and easily angered. Others may have disordered thoughts, sometimes severe enough to become frank paranoia. Although it is rare, some people have such severe behavioral problems that their thoughts become bizarre and delusional. This may be coupled with agitation and, if present, makes it critical to get good psychiatric care.

Older people with thyrotoxicosis sometimes have a condition called *apathetic thyrotoxicosis*. This is an unusual situation in which a person appears to be depressed and withdrawn. The weight loss and apathy could be mistaken for a clinical depression rather than thyrotoxicosis. This is further explored in Chapter 17.

Psychiatric Misdiagnosis

Psychiatrists see so many thyroid patients who have been referred to them as psychiatric patients that thyroid function tests have now become standard industry practice for most psychiatric referrals.

When people experience the exhaustion of too much thyroid hormone and the natural anxiety that accompanies it, but do not notice or report other physical manifestations such as a fast pulse or hyperdefecation (which can also be attributed to anxiety), they are often misdiagnosed with anxiety disorders. Unfortunately, it is women especially who may suffer from continuous and classic psychiatric misdiagnoses. One reason for this is that thyroid disorders occur much more frequently in women. Another reason is that thyrotoxic symptoms can mimic either unipolar depression or bipolar disorder, both diagnosed in women more frequently than men (see Chapter 24).

Unipolar depression can manifest with irritability and sadness, poor appetite, weight loss, sleeplessness, no energy, a lack of sex drive, anxiety, and panic. Thyrotoxic symptoms unfortunately mimic these same manifestations. Finally, thyrotoxicosis can sometimes cause euphoric mood swings, a characteristic of a mania, which is present in bipolar disorder (formerly known as manic depression). These issues are discussed more in Chapter 24, which covers depression.

Generalized Anxiety Disorder (GAD) and Thyrotoxicosis

A lot of people suffer from generalized anxiety disorder (GAD), but it can also suddenly develop if you're thyrotoxic for a prolonged period of time. In fact, you may be misdiagnosed with GAD, which is characterized by extreme worry about things that are unlikely to happen. You may worry about whether your child is safe or whether your partner is going to get into a car accident on the way home. You may begin to worry about health problems (for good reason if you are thyrotoxic and have other symptoms). The worries begin to be persistent and interfere with your normal functioning. Always there is a sense of dread—a constant fretting, restlessness, and uneasiness about your personal security or safety. You may also suffer from physical symptoms, some of which are also signs of thyrotoxicosis (indicated by an asterisk):

- Clenching of teeth or jaw
- Tightened muscles
- Sleeping problems*
- Racing heartbeat*
- Breathing difficulties*
- Chest pain*
- Hyperventilation

Anxiety can also accompany depression. (See Chapter 24.)

It's normal to worry about a lot of things. Worry crosses over into anxiety when the worry persists after the problem you worried about has resolved or ended. Normally, after a problem has been resolved, there is a calm or even satisfaction that follows. When there is no relief from persistent worry, this is anxiety. When you're under emotional stress or under unusual physical stress, which occurs with thyrotoxicosis, normal worries can cross over into anxiety, and low-level anxiety can also worsen or heighten.

You may also have other social causes for your anxiety; in the euthyroid population, when anxiety suddenly appears, it is often because of new life stresses or pressures, such as being a victim of a crime or accident, moving or changing jobs, loss or grief, having a baby, or going through a divorce.

Panic Disorder and Thyrotoxicosis

Panic attacks are so named because they are an "attack"—they come on suddenly without warning. Because there is no warning, once you've had one panic attack, you can easily begin to worry about when the next one will strike. The fear of having a panic attack in public can become so overwhelming, you may be afraid to leave your house. When you're home, you're in a safe place for a panic attack. But when you're in public, the panic is heightened, and so are the symptoms of the attack.

The symptoms of a panic attack are brought on by a rush of adrenaline—a stress hormone that gets pumped out in a "fight or flight" response, *and that has greater effect in thyrotoxicosis*. For example, people with diabetes who suffer from episodes of low blood sugar have the same response, as adrenaline gets pumped out when blood sugar is low; this is why people can confuse thyrotoxicosis for seeming low blood sugar reactions.

When the adrenaline is pumped out and the "fight or flight" response is triggered—regardless of what caused the adrenaline rush—you will first feel an accelerated heart rate, which often feels like a palpitation or a "fluttery" heartbeat; it can also feel racing, pounding, or skipping. This is accompanied by a cold sweat or excessive sweating, chills or flushes (also known as cold or hot flashes), and possibly tremors or nervousness. What happens next is quite variable: some people begin to feel vertigo symptoms: extreme dizziness, lightheadedness, shakiness, nausea, and other stomach problems. Other people begin to feel choking symptoms: rapid breathing or hyperventilating, a perception of difficult breathing, choking or smothering sensation, or a lump in the throat; others feel chest pain, pressure, or discomfort.

Whether the symptoms are vertigo or choking, there is also a feeling of unreality about panic attacks; you may feel you are in a nightmare or dream or that you are detached from your body while it's occurring with distorted perceptions. A fear of losing control or embarrassing yourself, a sense of impending doom, or a fear of dying may also be part of the experience. You may also pass out, and you can vomit or have seizures during this phase. When you begin to notice panic attack symptoms, you can start to panic even more because the situation is so frightening and jarring.

Roughly 2 percent of North Americans ages eighteen to fifty-four suffer from panic attacks each year, occurring twice as often in women as in men; it is not known how many people who suffer from panic disorder are thyrotoxic. If you begin to suffer from panic attacks, however, have your thyroid checked to rule out thyrotoxicosis as an underlying cause.

Low Blood Sugar or Thyrotoxicosis?

Low blood sugar, also known as *hypoglycemia*, triggers the very same adrenaline rush reaction that can occur in a panic attack. Low blood sugar can be measured, and a reading below 50 mg/dl (or in Canada, 3.5 mmol/L) is considered too low. But many people assume they suffer from "low blood sugar" even when their blood sugar levels are normal because they feel shaky and irritable when hungry, which is relieved by food. In fact, the common feature to panic attacks and true hypoglycemic attacks is a rapid activation of the adrenergic system (adrenaline release), the same system enhanced by thyrotoxicosis. In this way, thyrotoxicosis can be confused for both panic attacks and hypoglycemia. Treatment of these adrenergic symptoms by beta-blockers can relieve most of these symptoms, and correction of the underlying thyrotoxicosis relieves the rest of them.

Thyroid Storm

In some cases, symptoms of severe thyrotoxicosis can manifest into a "storm" of severe thyrotoxic symptoms—particularly cardiovascular symptoms that warrant emergency attention and admission to an intensive care unit. This used to happen more frequently, but since the development of the TSH test, as well as more active screening for earlier signs of thyrotoxicosis or subclinical thyrotoxicosis (before serious or noticeable symptoms develop), it is unusual for people with thyrotoxicosis to progress to such severe thyroid storm symptoms.

No intrinsic difference exists between the thyroid hormone levels in people with severe thyrotoxicosis with or without thyroid storm. The main difference is the side effects on their bodies, particularly their hearts, and whether they are compensated or in severe crisis (the thyroid storm). Changes in medical management, including the introduction of beta-blockers, have significantly reduced the number of people with thyroid storm, to the point that it is now an exceedingly rare diagnosis.

Causes of Thyrotoxicosis Without Hyperthyroidism

Because hypothyroidism is the most common thyroid disease, we'll first look at causes of thyrotoxicosis *without* hyperthyroidism.

Thyroid Hormone Overdose

Thyroid hormone overdose is a common problem. This is because dosages of thyroid hormone used for treatment of hypothyroidism may be selected empirically and not sufficiently monitored using appropriate laboratory tests. This results in some people remaining hypothyroid with inadequate thyroid hormone dosages and some becoming thyrotoxic with too much thyroid hormone.

Poor compliance is the second most common reason for overdose. An occasional scenario is in thyroid patients who have memory loss problems; they may forget that they have taken their thyroid hormone pill and repeat the dosage. Or, many seniors, who are managing multiple health problems and daily medications, may become confused and take too many thyroid pills. Frequently, people don't understand what pills they have and what they're for, and they may be dealing, too, with multiple pharmacies for their prescriptions, which can confuse matters. Some people have mistaken beliefs that purposely taking excessive thyroid hormone doses will alleviate symptoms of tiredness and lack of energy. Ironically, these are symptoms worsened by this deliberate overdose.

People treated for thyroid cancer need to be on higher doses of thyroid hormone to suppress TSH. If poorly adjusted, these higher doses can result in thyrotoxicosis. Thyroid cancer and TSH suppression dosing is discussed more in Chapters 9 and 10.

Misuse of Thyroid Hormone

Thyroid hormone has a shady history of inappropriate use in the past. Throughout the 1950s, 1960s, and even 1970s, overweight women were frequently prescribed levothyroxine sodium as a weight loss drug and told that it would speed up their metabolisms, resulting in the desired weight loss. This practice is known as *off-label* prescribing and was the source of countless cases of thyrotoxicosis, which frequently went untreated, harming these women. It also led to many women being misdiagnosed with psychiatric illnesses. Similarly, amphetamines or "speed" were widely prescribed to women, which were also dangerous.

It is still not unusual for women to be prescribed an array of off-label drugs for weight loss, and many people can obtain them through Internet sources.

Unfortunately, many women, in particular, continue to abuse thyroid hormone as a weight loss drug. Young women may help themselves to pills they find in Mom's medicine cabinet or may discover another relative's or friend's supply. This practice is dangerous and risky behavior, which can lead to health problems down the road—particularly heart problems. Levothyroxine sodium is a dangerous drug for anyone who has a healthy thyroid gland.

Thyroiditis

Again, *thyroiditis* means "inflammation of the thyroid gland," and some types of thyroiditis can cause thyrotoxicosis. In Hashimoto's disease, the most common cause of autoimmune thyroiditis, the thyroid gland can leak out too much thyroid hormone, creating thyrotoxic symptoms. Then the gland usually is unable to make any more thyroid hormone, causing hypothyroidism. This is known as *Hashitoxicosis* or *silent thyroiditis*. Hashimoto's disease is discussed in Chapter 5, as are other types of thyroiditis, such as subacute (De Quervain's) thyroiditis. Thyroiditis from drugs (particularly amiodarone) can also cause thyrotoxicosis, and this is discussed in Chapter 11.

Thyroid Tissue in the Wrong Place

In extremely rare cases, a woman's ovary can contain a teratoma, a piece of the ovary containing an assortment of tissues that resemble other body parts. These teratomas can contain thyroid tissue (*struma ovarii*) that becomes spontaneously overactive and produces enough thyroid hormone to cause thyrotoxicosis. Sometimes these teratomas are cancerous and can spread within a woman's body.

Thyroid cancers can take up iodine and make thyroid hormone; however, they are usually so inefficient in producing thyroid hormone that it is exceedingly rare for them to be the cause of thyrotoxicosis.

Hamburger Toxicosis

There have been rare cases where ingesting ground meat (hamburger) containing thyroid tissue can cause isolated outbursts of thyrotoxicosis. In one incident in the mid-

1980s, some members of a community suddenly developed thyrotoxicosis and, upon investigation, it was linked to a meat packing plant that had made hamburger from the neck muscles of cattle, contaminated with thyroid tissue.

Thyrotoxicosis with Hyperthyroidism

Again, *hyperthyroidism* means "overactive thyroid gland." Although there can be several reasons why a thyroid gland would become overactive, in around 80 percent of cases the cause is an autoimmune disorder known as Graves' disease, discussed in detail in Chapter 6.

Other Causes for Hyperthyroidism

Very rare types of pituitary tumors make excessive amounts of TSH. The thyroid hormone levels do not properly regulate TSH secretion in these tumors, unlike the normal pituitary gland. This is one cause of inappropriate TSH secretion resulting in thyrotoxicosis despite normal or elevated thyroid hormone levels.

Another case of inappropriate TSH secretion is even less common: selective pituitary resistance to thyroid hormone. In this situation, there are mutations in the thyroid hormone receptors in pituitary cells, making them less able to bind thyroid hormone than normal, and resulting in excessive amounts of TSH being made by them. Other parts of the body appear normally responsive to thyroid hormone, and the person gets symptoms of thyrotoxicosis.

Sometimes there are additional hormones that stimulate the thyroid gland to produce thyroid hormones. There are situations in which cells from the placenta from a pregnancy persist despite the end of the pregnancy (known as *trophoblastic tumors*). They secrete a hormone called *human chorionic gonadotropin (HCG)* that, if produced in high quantities, stimulates the thyroid gland. Around one in two thousand pregnancies result in a benign trophoblastic tumor called a *hydatidiform mole* (also known as a *molar pregnancy*). One out of sixty thousand pregnancies results in a cancerous trophoblastic tumor called a *choriocarcinoma* that can spread inside the body. Both of these conditions are suspected when the HCG levels are very high and a pregnancy is not present.

Intrinsic Thyroid Autonomy: Independent Thyroid Hormone Manufacturers

As discussed in Chapter 1, it's not uncommon for the thyroid to enlarge and/or develop lumps or nodules that make their own supply of thyroid hormone—in addition to the usual supply made by the rest of the thyroid gland. As soon as the nodule(s) starts to make more than normal amounts of thyroid hormone, it suppresses the pituitary's production of TSH. This causes the normal (non-nodular) portions of the thyroid gland to "go to sleep" since there is no TSH to wake them up. The degree of thyrotoxicosis depends upon the ability of this autonomous thyroid nodule to make thyroid hormone.

Toxic Adenoma

Single thyroid nodules that independently make too much thyroid hormone without the need for TSH to stimulate them are called *autonomously functioning thyroid nodules* or *toxic adenomas*. These toxic adenomas are suspected when the TSH level is low, the person is thyrotoxic, and the person's thyroid gland has a lump or nodule. A radioactive iodine thyroid scan will show that this nodule takes up most of the radioactive iodine (a *hot nodule*), while the rest of the thyroid takes up much less radioactive iodine than normal. Some of these toxic adenomas form because their TSH receptors have mutations that keep them turned on, even if there isn't any TSH in the blood. These are discussed further in Chapter 8.

Toxic Multinodular Goiter

There are people whose thyroid glands form multiple nodules, usually detectable through a physical examination of their thyroid. For much the same reason as in the singular toxic adenomas, these multiple thyroid nodules produce too much thyroid hormone and do not require TSH to do so. In such a situation, the radioactive iodine thyroid scan will show multiple toxic thyroid nodules, termed a *toxic multinodular goiter*.

Diagnosing Thyrotoxicosis and/or Hyperthyroidism

Thyrotoxicosis can be easily discovered with elevated free T4 or T3 levels and a TSH level that is lower than normal (usually less than 0.2). See Chapter 2 for more details on lab testing for TSH and free T4 and T3.

The challenge for diagnosing either hyperthyroidism and/or thyrotoxicosis is similar for hypothyroidism: the symptoms can overlap with stress, anxiety, panic disorder, low blood sugar, and cardiovascular diseases. For women, PMS and perimenopause can mask, or be mistaken for, thyrotoxicosis; miscarriage or infertility can also result from thyrotoxicosis.

In my (Sara's) case, I suffered from thyrotoxic symptoms for more than four years, in the belief that I had low blood sugar and panic disorder. Having been on a TSH-suppression dosage of thyroid hormone most of my adult life, as I aged, I became less tolerant but didn't realize it. A few years later, after Ken and I were married (and he witnessed a few of these episodes), he also noticed one day that my heart was racing. Ken suggested my panic attacks and "hypoglycemic" reactions might be caused by thyrotoxicosis, which, as discussed previously, makes people oversensitive to their own adrenaline. Of course, this would be the logical result of being on a high dosage of T4 all of those years. After starting a beta-blocker, which blocks the adrenaline rush symptoms of thyrotoxicosis, my panic attacks and "hypoglycemia" vanished. Anyone under the belief that he or she is suffering from panic disorder or low blood sugar should request a thyroid screening to rule out thyrotoxicosis.

Testing for Antibodies

If you are not hypothyroid, and medication balancing is not an issue, then it's important to find out whether you have autoimmune thyroid disease, the most common cause of hyperthyroidism, which causes thyrotoxicosis. You may have the beginnings of Hashimoto's disease (and Hashitoxicosis as discussed earlier), or you may have Graves' disease. Although there are blood tests for detecting the antibodies associated with these thyroid diseases, sometimes the physician, if experienced, is able to make the correct diagnosis and treatment without measuring them in the blood. In other situations, these antithyroid antibodies may prove useful to aid in the diagnosis and management of your thyroid disorder. These tests are discussed in detail in Chapter 2.

Treating Thyrotoxicosis

Treating thyrotoxicosis may be simple or very complex, depending on the cause. If the cause is too high a dosage of thyroid hormone medication, then the dosage is lowered and you may be placed on a beta-blocker (see Chapter 11 on thyroid drugs) to stop the adrenaline rush symptoms that are responsible for a racing heart, panic, and so on. In

---

Will I Become Hyperthyroid?

You are more likely to develop hyperthyroidism if you:

- Are between the ages of twenty and forty
- Had a baby less than six months ago
- Had a thyroid condition in the past or are being treated for hypothyroidism
- Have another autoimmune disease (such as Addison's disease, type 1 diabetes, rheumatoid arthritis, lupus)
- Have vitiligo (pigmentation loss, which Michael Jackson claims to suffer from)
- Have other family members with thyroid disease

such cases, it is critical to have your thyroid hormone dose readjusted to make sure that the TSH is normal when checked at least eight weeks later. If you are taking T3 in addition to T4, then T3 should probably be stopped and your TSH levels should be rechecked.

If the cause of thyrotoxicosis is hyperthyroidism, then the exact cause has to be found in order to determine treatment options, and you may be placed on a beta-blocker and antithyroid medication until you can be treated with radioactive iodine or surgery. In some cases of thyroiditis, the thyrotoxicosis resolves on its own and runs its course. So you may just need to "hang out" on a beta-blocker.

Treating Hyperthyroidism

Treatment for hyperthyroidism depends on the cause and can involve decreasing the function of the thyroid gland using radioactive iodine, surgery in the case of large goiters that may be multinodular, or just alleviating the symptoms of thyrotoxicosis in cases where thyroiditis is the cause, which frequently resolves on its own. Details of treatment and management of these conditions can be found in Chapter 5, on Hashimoto's disease (for treating Hashitoxicosis) and thyroiditis; Chapter 6, on Graves' disease; and Chapter 7, on goiters.

5 Hashimoto's Thyroiditis and Other Types of Thyroiditis

The most common autoimmune thyroid disease is Hashimoto's thyroiditis, also known as Hashimoto's disease. It is important to note, however, that there are other types of thyroiditis that are not autoimmune disorders (discussed further on). In medical circles, Hashimoto's disease is referred to as *chronic lymphocytic thyroiditis* because the thyroid gland contains lymphocytes that are attacking it. The disease is named after Hakaru Hashimoto, the Japanese physician who first described the condition in 1912. This chapter outlines autoimmune disease in general, and then discusses symptoms, diagnosis, and treatment of Hashimoto's disease. We also discuss other forms of thyroiditis as well as other autoimmune diseases that are commonly seen with autoimmune thyroid disease.

What Is an Autoimmune Disorder?

The word *autoimmune* means "self-immune" or "self-attacking." But before you can really grasp what this means, it's important to understand how your body normally fights off infection or disease.

Whenever an invading virus or bacterial cell is detected, your body produces specific armies called *antibodies*, which attack these foreign intruders, known as *antigens*. Antibodies are special proteins made from a type of white blood cell (called *lymphocytes*), and each antibody is designed for a specific antigen in the same way that a key is designed for a specific lock. The antibody serves as the key, while the antigen, or intruder, is the lock. For example, if you contracted the chicken pox as a child, despite being exposed to the virus again, you do not contract it again; your body is armed with the antibody that kills the chicken pox virus. But the specific chicken pox antibody is useless against all other viruses, such as mumps or measles. The importance of this can be seen when the immune system is impaired, such as in AIDS from HIV; impaired antibody production permits many of these diseases to come back. Also, an impaired immune system leaves the body vulnerable to additional opportunistic infections.

Vaccines prevent the development of a particular virus, such as polio, for example. Vaccines work like this: the vaccine serum contains a small amount of a particular virus in a deadened, noncontagious form—an antigen. Essentially, the vaccine shows your body a sample of the virus. This stimulates your immune system to produce a specific antibody to combat the unwanted virus. Later, if you catch the virus, your body will have sufficient specific antibodies, as well as "primed" lymphocytes ready to make more, to destroy it before it can do any damage. That's why you don't necessarily need to get chicken pox to be protected from it; you can be vaccinated against it instead. However, creating a vaccine is a painstaking, complicated process, and it can take years for scientists to develop vaccines to combat specific viruses. Polio struck at epidemic proportions throughout the 1940s and 1950s until a vaccine was discovered.

With an autoimmune disorder, your body's immune system makes some mistakes when it tries to distinguish foreign antigens, such as viruses and bacteria, from normal parts of your body. It confuses the two and perceives specific healthy body parts as foreign. Your immune system then winds up attacking parts of your own body. Some doctors describe it as a sort of allergy, where your body is in fact allergic to itself. So in the same way that the body develops specific antibodies to fight specific infections, the body develops specific antibodies to attack specific organs. These are known as *autoantibodies*, meaning "self" antibodies. Many kinds of illnesses are autoimmune disorders; Hashimoto's disease and Graves' disease (see next chapter) are two types of thyroid autoimmune diseases. In other examples, antibodies against joints cause rheumatoid arthritis, antibodies against muscles cause myasthenia gravis, while antibodies against DNA cause lupus erythematosus.

Who Is Vulnerable to Autoimmune Disease?

Generally, anyone can develop an autoimmune disorder. Some diseases are hereditary, while other diseases, although not directly hereditary, run strongly in families. This is referred to as a *genetic tendency* or *inherited predisposition*. Most autoimmune diseases seem to have a genetic tendency with several members of the family showing the same or similar types of autoimmune diseases. Autoimmune thyroid disease is no exception. Often, multiple family members and generations of family members, particularly in female members, will have one or more types of autoimmune thyroid disease. This suggests that there are significant genetic changes related to this disease, but it is far more complex than would be seen in simple directly hereditary situations.

There is some evidence to suggest that stress is one factor that may contribute toward triggering an autoimmune disorder. Clearly, when you are under unusual or extreme stress, many hormonal changes occur in the body, particularly between the brain and the adrenal glands, which affect your immune system. What is labeled "unusual" or "extreme"? A death or a tragedy in the family is considered to be extremely stressful. Starting a new job, moving, or relocating is also very stressful; getting married or having a new baby is stressful. This psychological stress produces stress hormone responses in the body that may be similar to some of the physical stress responses seen when you have a severe illness or are in a traumatic accident, such as an automobile wreck. It is not clear exactly how this could cause an activation of autoimmune disease, but it seems to be a factor. (See Chapter 22 for stress-reduction strategies.)

Many scientists believe that environmental factors contribute to starting autoimmune thyroid disease. These factors include infections, trauma, drugs, smoking, poor nutrition, pregnancy, and aging. Iodine is one type of nutritional factor that seems to be important. In countries with iodine deficiency, autoimmune disease is less common, although hypothyroidism is very common because of this deficiency. When these countries supply sufficient iodine to their people, hypothyroidism from lack of iodine goes away, but autoimmune thyroid diseases go way up. Smoking is well known to increase the chance of getting Graves' disease and intensify its symptoms if smoking is continued; however, no one knows the exact way this affects the immune system. The reason for the predominance of autoimmune thyroid disease in women likely relates to the differences in hormones between men and women; but again, no one knows the precise reason why this happens. There is some evidence suggesting that certain viruses may infect people and stimulate the immune system in some way that causes the development of autoimmune thyroid disease. Likewise, certain bacteria seem to stimulate the immune system in ways that may generate antibodies that cross-react with parts of the thyroid gland. All of these factors, or none of these factors, may be part of the cause of such thyroid conditions as Hashimoto's thyroiditis or Graves' disease; however, this remains a fertile topic of research for scientists around the world.

Infectious Diseases and Hashimoto's Disease

As already discussed, over the years, some studies have found that people with autoimmune diseases, such as Hashimoto's thyroiditis or Graves' disease, have antibodies that cross-react to various viruses or bacteria more commonly than seen in the general population. The theory is that when fighting other infections, the immune system may turn on autoantibodies, which triggers autoimmune diseases. This theory remains unconfirmed and is only one of many theories regarding the causes of autoimmune diseases. That said, there is no way one can avoid Hashimoto's disease by deciding to be vaccinated against a particular virus or bacteria or by taking antibiotics to ward off particular infections.

Unfortunately, sometimes news that Hashimoto's patients have antibodies to another infectious agent is sensationalized and mischaracterized as something that is new. This is actually old news, and each additional study in this area contributes more suspect infectious agents we can add to the list. What would be news is to define how the immune system attacks a person's own body, once it creates antibodies to other infections; this has not yet been revealed. There are a variety of additional theories regarding the cause of autoimmune diseases that have nothing to do with infectious agents. Time will tell which of these theories proves to be correct.

Pregnancy and Autoimmune Disease

Autoimmune thyroid disorders such as Graves' disease or Hashimoto's thyroiditis are most likely to strike during the first trimester of a pregnancy and within the first six months after delivery, or in the postpartum (right after childbirth) phase. It's normal for the thyroid gland to enlarge slightly during pregnancy because the placenta makes a hormone, human chorionic gonadotropin (HCG), that stimulates the mother's thyroid gland. Researchers have found that HCG has portions that share a very similar molecular structure to TSH (thyroid stimulating hormone). Situations that increase TSH levels often stimulate the enlargement of the thyroid gland (goiter). Likewise, the great increase in HCG seen in pregnancy affects the thyroid gland in a similar fashion, working like TSH to cause some enlargement of the thyroid gland. It is possible that this is part of the complex assortment of factors that help induce autoimmune thyroid problems.

During pregnancy, the immune system is naturally suppressed in some ways to prevent the body from rejecting the fetus. After pregnancy, the immune system "turns on" again. But this may have a rebound effect in that it may result in the production of antibodies that attack normal thyroid tissue, which is what occurs in autoimmune thyroid disease. This may be one reason why women are more prone to autoimmune disorders after pregnancy. Thyroid disease in pregnancy is discussed more in Chapter 13.

Hashimoto's Thyroiditis

Like other autoimmune diseases, a tendency for Hashimoto's disease is also inherited, but much of the time Hashimoto's disease strikes adults over age thirty (though many younger women have also been diagnosed with it), and it is much more frequently diagnosed in women. Statistically, one in five women will likely develop Hashimoto's disease in her lifetime.

Hashimoto's disease is caused by abnormal autoantibodies and white blood cells attacking and damaging thyroid cells. Eventually, this constant attack destroys many of the thyroid cells; the absence of sufficient functional thyroid cells causes hypothyroidism. In most cases a goiter develops because of the inflammation and overstimulation of the residual thyroid cells by TSH from the pituitary gland, though sometimes the thyroid gland can actually shrink. Classically, the diagnosis of Hashimoto's thyroiditis was limited to people who had enlarged thyroid gland (goiters) that contained invading white blood cells (specifically lymphocytes) and some scar tissue. In common practice, most situations of thyroid inflammation (thyroiditis) caused by autoimmune invasion of lymphocytes are called Hashimoto's thyroiditis, even if the thyroid is not enlarged. Some of the differences between these different forms of thyroiditis will be discussed later in this chapter. Also, in keeping with common practices, we sometimes use the name *Hashimoto's disease*.

If you develop Hashimoto's disease, you probably will not notice any symptoms at first. Sometimes there is a mild pressure in the thyroid gland and fatigue can set in, but unless you are on the lookout for thyroid disease, usually because some other family member may have had it, Hashimoto's disease can go undetected for years. Only when the thyroid cells are damaged to the point that the thyroid gland functions inadequately will you begin to experience the symptoms of hypothyroidism, described in Chapter 3.

In rare instances, thyroid eye disease can set in as well (see Chapter 23). In many ways, Hashimoto's disease is the same as Graves' disease (see next chapter) except that the antibodies don't stimulate the thyroid to make excessive thyroid hormone. In fact, the same antibodies, which destroy the function of the thyroid gland, as seen in Hashimoto's disease are usually produced in Graves' disease. As discussed further on, the thyroid-stimulating antibodies produced in Graves' disease most likely also attack the proteins in the eye muscles, causing them to swell. For unclear reasons, sometimes these antibodies are more effective in attacking eye muscles than stimulating thyroid cells, producing a situation in which Graves' disease causes thyroid destruction (as in Hashimoto's thyroiditis) with protruding eyeballs (Graves' ophthalmopathy). This could seem confusing unless you remember that both Graves' disease and Hashimoto's thyroiditis are just different expressions of a wide spectrum of autoimmune thyroid diseases. Treating eye problems associated with Hashimoto's disease involves treating the initial hypothyroidism first. If eye problems persist, the same treatment pattern outlined for Graves' disease will be necessary.

Also rarely, some people with Hashimoto's disease experience thyrotoxicosis as well as hypothyroidism. This occurs because of two phases of the disease. First, the attack of the antibodies causes the stores of thyroid hormone within the follicles of the thyroid gland (see Chapter 1) to suddenly leak out and raises the thyroid hormone level in the blood too high. This condition, as mentioned in the previous chapter, is coined *Hashitoxicosis*. Anyone suffering from this somewhat paradoxical condition would first experience all the symptoms of thyrotoxicosis (see Chapter 4). After a month or two, the antibodies attacking the thyroid cells cause them to stop working, and the leaking stored hormones are depleted, causing the thyrotoxicosis to resolve. Then, as the thyroid-destructive features of Hashimoto's disease progress, you would eventually become hypothyroid and develop the symptoms outlined in Chapter 3, unless replacement thyroid hormone was prescribed.

Diagnosing Hashimoto's Disease

The signs of Hashimoto's disease are not at all obvious. In its early stages, a goiter can develop as a result of inflammation in the thyroid gland. The goiter is usually firm but is not tender. The goiter's presence can suggest Hashimoto's disease, but it is usually suspected because of the sudden recognition of symptoms of hypothyroidism or detection of an elevated TSH level during routine medical evaluations.

Hashimoto's disease is frequently missed as a diagnosis, however. Often, symptoms of hypothyroidism are attributed to age—particularly in women entering menopause. Such a misdiagnosis results in failing to relieve hypothyroid symptoms, otherwise easily treatable with thyroid hormone. This is a good reason to make your family members aware of any family history of autoimmune thyroid disease, prompting them to insist that their physicians monitor their TSH levels and examine their thyroid glands at their regular health checkups.

Hashimoto's disease is easily diagnosed through a blood test that indicates high levels of thyroid autoantibodies in the blood. It used to be diagnosed by evaluating the thyroid gland under a microscope after a surgical biopsy; however, physicians found out that the blood test for thyroid autoantibodies was sufficiently accurate and much easier to evaluate. The specific antibodies are called *TPO* (*thyroid peroxidase*) *autoantibodies* and *antithyroglobulin* (*TG*) *antibodies*. TPO antibody used to be called *antithyroid microsomal antibody* before it was recognized that this antibody actually attacked a special enzyme inside thyroid cells, thyroid peroxidase, responsible for using iodine to form thyroid hormones. TSH levels must also be measured, and high TSH levels indicate hypothyroidism and the need to take thyroid hormone medication. For more on TSH see Chapters 2 and 3.

Another method of confirming diagnosis is through a needle biopsy. As we discussed in Chapter 2, a needle is inserted into the thyroid gland to remove some cells. The cells are then smeared onto a glass slide, which, in the case of Hashimoto's thyroiditis, would reveal abnormal white blood cells and typical changes in the thyroid cells. This procedure is usually not necessary, except when making sure that a thyroid nodule is because of Hashimoto's thyroiditis rather than thyroid cancer.

Hashimoto's Disease and Other Thyroid Diseases

Since Hashimoto's thyroiditis is so common, particularly in women, it is very likely to be present along with other diseases. Later in this chapter, we discuss the various autoimmune diseases of other parts of the body that seem to be more common in people with autoimmune thyroid diseases. Besides them, it is possible that other thyroid diseases may coexist with Hashimoto's thyroiditis. For example, if you had a goiter (enlargement of your thyroid gland) along with elevated TPO antibodies and/or thyroglobulin antibodies, then it would be very likely that you have Hashimoto's thyroiditis. However, should the goiter be significantly larger on one side than the other or have a large, distinct lump (nodule), it is possible that there could be a thyroid cancer inside the gland as well as Hashimoto's thyroiditis. It would be necessary to have a fine needle thyroid biopsy performed on the nodule or larger portion of the goiter to check for this.

Besides having hypothyroidism or hyperthyroidism, the goiter from autoimmune thyroid disease can cause direct problems in your neck. The lower neck is a very important place, serving as the connection between the inside of the chest and the head, the *thoracic inlet*. The esophagus (food tube), trachea (windpipe), and major blood vessels (carotid arteries and jugular veins) pass through it. If the goiter becomes large enough to push on these important connections it might need to be surgically removed to prevent a host of new problems. This will be discussed in greater detail in Chapter 7.

Hashimoto's Disease and Thyroid Lymphoma

Thyroid lymphoma is a very, very rare type of thyroid cancer. You probably have a greater chance of being struck by lightning than getting this disease; however, nearly every person with thyroid lymphoma has preexisting Hashimoto's thyroiditis. This suggests that rare cases of Hashimoto's thyroiditis may evolve into this type of cancer of the lymphocytes in the thyroid. On the other hand, just because you (and millions of other people) have Hashimoto's thyroiditis, you should not have any worries or concerns regarding thyroid lymphoma. The particular circumstance that tells you and your physician to think of thyroid lymphoma is when your gland suddenly and rapidly enlarges over the course of a few weeks or days. When this happens, your physician should arrange for you to have a fine needle biopsy performed with the addition of an unusual procedure called *flow cytometry* to assess the type of lymphocytes in your thyroid gland. In nearly all thyroid cancers, surgical removal of the thyroid gland is mandatory; however, in thyroid lymphoma the usual appropriate treatment uses chemotherapy and external beam radiation treatments. The fine needle biopsy enables you to avoid surgery that is often unnecessary. Again, it is important for you to know that thyroid lymphoma is so very rare and distinctive in its growth that you should not routinely worry about it just because you have Hashimoto's thyroiditis.

Treating Hashimoto's Disease

The treatment for Hashimoto's disease is simple: thyroid hormone is prescribed as soon as the diagnosis is made if there is an elevated TSH—even if there are no symptoms. This is done for three reasons. First, the thyroid hormone suppresses production of excessive TSH (thyroid stimulating hormone) by the pituitary gland, which, in turn, shrinks any goiter that may have developed or is about to develop. Second, because Hashimoto's disease often progresses to the point where clinical symptoms of hypothyroidism set in, the thyroid hormone nips hypothyroidism in the bud and prevents the Hashimoto's patient from suffering the unpleasant symptoms of hypothyroidism. Finally, for some reason, synthetic thyroid hormone may interfere with the autoimmune response by reducing TSH-stimulated release of thyroid antigens.

If you have developed a goiter as a result of Hashimoto's disease, the goiter usually persists unless thyroid hormone is prescribed. There might be so much scarring in the thyroid gland that the goiter never diminishes; however, occasionally, the goiter shrinks on its own. On average, it takes anywhere from six to eighteen months for the goiter to shrink, and, if it does shrink, you will most likely be hypothyroid. However, sometimes Hashimoto's disease is present in a gland that is small and shrunken without ever having been enlarged. In many instances, goiters can persist—despite synthetic thyroxine—indefinitely. If a large goiter persists, you may require a thyroidectomy, in which case the entire enlarged thyroid gland is removed. Of course, you would require thyroid hormone replacement, just as you would if you did not have the gland removed.

Treating Hashitoxicosis

Hashitoxicosis, as discussed earlier and in the previous chapter, might occur at the beginning stages of Hashimoto's disease, when the thyroid gland begins to leak out its thyroid hormone stores, before failing completely. The symptoms of Hashitoxicosis are the same as thyrotoxicosis, discussed in the previous chapter. As the stored thyroid hormone is depleted, you would begin to become slowly hypothyroid because the afflicted thyroid gland is too ill to make more thyroid hormone. Some physicians may misdiagnose you with early Graves' disease. In fact, as discussed earlier, most of the antibodies seen in Hashimoto's disease are also present in Graves' disease; however, in Hashitoxicosis the level of free T4 will spontaneously become lower each week, while this doesn't happen in Graves' disease. Also, the radioactive iodine uptake test (see Chapter 2) will be very low in Hashitoxicosis and high in Graves' disease.

While you're in the throes of symptoms related to too much thyroid hormone, it makes no sense to prescribe thyroid hormone replacement (the usual treatment for Hashimoto's disease with hypothyroidism) until this stage has passed or *burned out*. In this case, treating the symptoms of too much thyroid hormone (thyrotoxicosis) involves using a beta-blocker (see Chapters 11 and 25) to slow the heart as well as block the adrenaline rush symptoms we discussed in the previous chapter. Free T4 testing, as well as TSH testing, at regular intervals will reveal when you are beginning to become hypothyroid, and that is when thyroid hormone ought to be prescribed.

Treating Hashimoto's Disease in Pregnancy

If you are diagnosed with Hashimoto's disease during pregnancy, it is critical that you are prescribed thyroid hormone replacement as soon as possible to avoid complications in pregnancy as a result of hypothyroidism and to avoid problems with fetal development as a result of insufficient thyroid hormone. We discuss this in much more detail in Chapter 13.

Hashimoto's Disease and Miscarriage

There is a statistical association of having TPO antibodies and having a higher risk of miscarriage. Nobody knows why this is so. Any purported explanations are just theories as of this writing. Since there is nothing that you can do to alter whether you have TPO antibodies or not, there isn't much value to having this information. It's akin to knowing you have a gene for a potential disease but there is nothing you can do to prevent the disease. Similarly, there is no way you can prevent a miscarriage just because you know you have TPO antibodies. And we still don't know if TPO antibodies are even linked to miscarriage.

What is important to note is that studies indicate a 32 percent risk of miscarriage in women with antithyroid antibodies, compared to a 16 percent risk in the general pregnant population without them. In women who are under thirty-five, in good health, with no history of miscarriage, the rate of miscarriage is one in six, and that number rises with maternal age. For more information, see Chapter 13.

Other Common Autoimmune Disorders

If you have one autoimmune disease, you are more likely to start a collection of them. Hashimoto's disease is associated with other conditions, particularly myasthenia gravis. The following is a list of other autoimmune disorders, listed alphabetically, that may accompany Hashimoto's disease or Graves' disease (discussed in Chapter 6). Sometimes, multiple autoimmune diseases coexist in the same person. This is called *polyglandular autoimmune disease.*

Addison's Disease

Addison's disease is caused by your adrenal glands failing to make cortisol and other steroid hormones—the adrenal products your body needs to function properly. This is rare among thyroid patients, but it tends to occur more frequently in a person with pernicious anemia, discussed later, which is commonly found in thyroid patients. Addison's disease is an autoimmune destruction of the adrenal glands; however, loss of adrenal function can be consequent to trouble with the pituitary gland.

Anemia

When you're anemic, there's a decrease in the number of red blood cells carrying oxygen to various body tissues. Often, people who are hypothyroid are mildly anemic because of the body's tendency to slow its functions and a decrease in its need for oxygen. There are usually no specific symptoms associated with mild anemia, and it corrects itself when hypothyroidism is treated. A more serious type of anemia—pernicious anemia—tends to occur more frequently in older people diagnosed with Graves' disease or Hashimoto's disease. Pernicious anemia is caused by a deficiency of vitamin B_{12}, which is essential for producing red blood cells. When your body is functioning normally, cells lining the stomach produce *intrinsic factor*, which enables the body to absorb vitamin B_{12} from food. Self-attacking antibodies to intrinsic factor occur in this disorder. Thus, they can be considered an associated autoimmune disease genetically related to Graves' disease or Hashimoto's thyroiditis (like the eye disease). The antibody interference can prevent the body from absorbing the vitamin B_{12} it needs to manufacture sufficient quantities of red blood cells and make the nervous system work normally. When vitamin B_{12} levels drop, anemia can set in.

Symptoms of pernicious anemia include numbness and tingling in the hands and feet (this happens because vitamin B_{12} also nourishes the nervous system), loss of balance, and leg weakness. Studies suggest that up to one-sixth of people with autoimmune thyroid disease may develop pernicious anemia. However, because this type of anemia usually develops in older people, younger people with either Graves' disease or Hashimoto's thyroiditis are probably not at as high a risk. But if you have anemia (particularly if the red blood cells seem large, called *macrocytosis*) and have ever been diagnosed with autoimmune thyroid disease, ask your doctor to specifically measure vitamin B_{12} levels in your blood. If the levels are low or borderline, request an additional test, known as the *Schilling test*, which can detect if you're having difficulty absorbing vitamin B_{12} from food. If you do have pernicious anemia, it is easily corrected with an intramuscular injection of vitamin B_{12}. Usually the treatment is once monthly but, depending on the severity, can vary.

Besides pernicious anemia, some younger and menstruating women with Hashimoto's thyroiditis are found to have anemia from iron deficiency. This is because their menstrual periods may have been exceedingly heavy for the months they were unknowingly hypothyroid. Blood tests for iron levels, transferrin saturation, and ferritin levels will usually show if this is the case. Although the treatment for this uses iron supplementation pills, it is important to avoid taking these pills within five hours of taking the thyroid hormone replacement tablet, because the iron will prevent the absorption of the thyroid hormone, making both problems worse (see Chapter 10).

Arthritis

Some people with Graves' disease or Hashimoto's thyroiditis experience tendon and joint inflammation. Painful tendonitis and bursitis of the shoulder, for example, was reported in a greater number of Graves' disease and Hashimoto's thyroiditis patients, compared to the general population. This is likely to be consequent to untreated hypothyroidism, present in many Hashimoto's patients before thyroid hormone therapy and in Graves' disease patients after surgery, radioactive iodine, or the natural process of the disease has destroyed their thyroid gland. Hypothyroidism may cause fluid to accumulate around the joints, and its effects on muscle pain and stiffness add to the joint symptoms. Accumulation of fluid or thickening of tissues around tendons may compress nerves at critical places, particularly in the wrists, causing carpal tunnel syndrome.

On the other hand, rheumatoid arthritis, a more serious autoimmune joint disease, appears to be only slightly more common among thyroid patients than the general population. Nevertheless, it can cause inflammation of many joints in the body including knuckles, wrists, and elbows. Stiffness tends to be more severe in the morning. If you are either hyper- or hypothyroid and have noticed this kind of pain or stiffness, ask your doctor to recommend appropriate medication for arthritic symptoms. Sometimes, pain and stiffness will improve when the thyroid condition is corrected.

Diabetes

There is an increased incidence of type 1 diabetes mellitus (formerly known as juvenile diabetes or insulin-dependent diabetes) in families where Graves' disease or Hashimoto's thyroiditis has been diagnosed. Antibodies and lymphocytes attacking the special cells in the pancreas responsible for making insulin cause this autoimmune type of diabetes.

If you do happen to have both conditions, an overactive thyroid will often make the diabetes worse and more difficult to control with insulin. Once your thyroid condition is treated, though, you will find it easier to regain control over the diabetes. On the other hand, there are not usually any problems of glucose control directly related to hypothyroidism. If true hypoglycemia is documented by low blood sugar levels (often this is inappropriately diagnosed; see Chapter 4) in people with hypothyroidism, it is important to see if the pituitary gland is abnormal, causing both hypothyroidism and loss of adrenal function (causing the low blood sugar). Autoimmune destruction of the pituitary gland, as well as pituitary tumors, might be responsible.

Inflammatory Bowel Disease (IBD)

This is an umbrella term that comprises Crohn's disease as well as ulcerative colitis. IBD is a miserable condition where the lower intestine becomes inflamed, causing abdominal cramping, pain, fever, and mucus-laden, bloody diarrhea. IBD is not known to occur more often in thyroid disease patients, although the effects of too much or too little thyroid hormone may worsen its symptoms. If you have IBD, it's best to ask to be referred to a gastroenterologist (also know as a *GI specialist*), who is the specialist to manage it. This is not to be confused with irritable bowel syndrome (IBS), a stress-related disorder that often masks hyperthyroid symptoms.

Hypothyroidism slows down the rate at which food travels through the stomach and intestines. This can result in gastroesophageal reflux disease (heartburn) and constipation. On the other hand, thyrotoxicosis from untreated Graves' disease causes more frequent bowel movements consequent to an increased rate of movement of food through the intestines. These functional differences may be mistaken for primary intestinal diseases, including IBD.

Lupus

Lupus is a condition that imitates many other diseases. For years, lupus patients went undiagnosed, similar to many thyroid patients. This is an autoimmune condition that affects many body tissues causing arthritic symptoms, skin rashes, and kidney, lung, and heart problems. Lupus patients often test positive for antithyroid antibodies. What's interesting about lupus is that it is rare among thyroid sufferers even though lupus sufferers often have thyroid problems. For these reasons, anyone with lupus should have his or her thyroid checked regularly, particularly since hypothyroidism and thyrotoxicosis can badly aggravate a lupus flare.

Myasthenia Gravis

Myasthenia gravis is a rare autoimmune disorder of the muscles that is much more common in people with autoimmune thyroid disease. Symptoms include muscle weakness, double vision, and difficulty swallowing—symptoms that can be present in both Graves' disease and Graves' eye disease (see next chapter). Ask to be tested for myasthenia gravis when you have these symptoms. Graves' disease may not be the sole cause of them.

Other Forms of Thyroiditis

This section explains other kinds of thyroid inflammation in more detail and discusses the three common forms and two uncommon forms thyroiditis can take. Sometimes inflammation can be caused by the autoimmune process, as described earlier in this chapter for Hashimoto's thyroiditis. In rare cases, bacterial infections (abscesses; infectious or suppurative thyroiditis) may cause a severely painful and swollen thyroid gland, along with fever and increases in the white blood count. These situations require hospitalization and intravenous antibiotic therapy. In other rare cases, painful inflammation of the thyroid gland may be associated with inflammatory nodules (granulomas) in the gland, possibly because of viral infection and known as *subacute thyroiditis*.

Subacute Thyroiditis: A Pain in the Neck

Subacute thyroiditis is also known as *painful thyroiditis* and *de Quervain's thyroiditis*, after the Swiss physician who first described it. This form of thyroiditis seems to be particularly prevalent in North America although still quite uncommon. It's suspected that subacute thyroiditis has a viral cause, but there is not yet sufficient real proof that this condition is viral in origin.

The condition ranges from extremely mild to severe and runs its own course the way a normal flu virus would. Usually, most people with a very mild case of subacute thyroiditis would not bother to see a doctor, because they wouldn't notice any unusual symptoms other than a sore throat perhaps. But in more severe cases, you can be extremely uncomfortable. The illness usually imitates the flu. This means you'll be tired and have muscular aches and pains, a headache, and fever. As the illness progresses, your thyroid gland will swell or enlarge from the infection and become very tender. It will hurt to swallow, and you might feel stabs of pain in your neck.

To make matters worse, you can also become thyrotoxic. When the gland gets inflamed, thyroid hormones leak out as they do in Hashitoxicosis. Then, of course, your system has too much thyroid hormone in it, and you experience all the classic thyrotoxicosis symptoms outlined in Chapter 4. The good news is that subacute thyroiditis is quite temporary, and even the more severe case tends to run its course in about six weeks; however, it can be a miserable six weeks, particularly if you don't know what's wrong. Although the condition can take longer to clear up, it's very unusual for it to linger beyond six months.

Subacute viral thyroiditis is diagnosed in part through the process of elimination. Because your thyroid gland is tender, the doctor should know it isn't Graves' disease. Hashimoto's thyroiditis is often suspected; however, it is not associated with such a tender, painful thyroid gland. The radioactive iodine uptake test (see Chapter 2) shows almost no uptake of radioactive iodine in the gland. The thyroid hormone levels and the thyroglobulin levels are very high because of the hormones leaking out of the inflamed thyroid gland. Nonspecific tests of inflammation in the body, the erythrocyte sedimentation rate (ESR) and the C-reactive protein (CRP), are usually both quite high in this condition. Sometimes, particularly if the thyroid gland is irregular and needs to be checked for a possible cancer, a fine needle aspiration biopsy (see Chapter 2) can diagnose de Quervain's thyroiditis.

For mild cases the treatment is aspirin to alleviate the swelling and inflammation. If the thyrotoxicosis is more severe, sometimes a beta-blocker is given to slow your heart. In more severe forms, cortisone analogs are given, such as prednisone. Sometimes, the inflammation causes temporary damage to the thyroid cells and hypothyroidism can set in. If this happens, a temporary dosage of thyroid hormone is prescribed until the hypothyroidism corrects itself. Only 10 percent of de Quervain's thyroiditis cases result in permanent hypothyroidism. Basically, as the inflammation clears up, the thyroid gland resumes normal, healthy function.

Silent Thyroiditis

This silent form of thyroiditis is so named because it's tricky to diagnose and often avoids detection until symptoms become sufficiently severe. It is debatable whether this is a unique type of thyroiditis or merely a type of Hashimoto's thyroiditis that is not associated with a goiter. Since it is common to call most forms of autoimmune thyroiditis that have lymphocytes invading the thyroid gland (lymphocytic thyroiditis) Hashimoto's thyroiditis, the differences between these two labels might be insignificant. Silent thyroiditis runs a painless course and is essentially the same as Hashitoxicosis. With this version, there are no symptoms or outward signs of inflammation, but thyrotoxicosis is present because of the same stored hormone leakage reasons. Usually silent thyroiditis sufferers are women, and it's common in the postpartum period. Actually, postpartum thyroiditis, discussed in Chapter 13, is silent thyroiditis after delivery.

This kind of thyroiditis was not discussed until the 1970s and was possibly mistaken for transient Graves' disease before then because of thyrotoxicosis. Again, the thyroiditis runs its course and the thyrotoxicosis clears up. In the course of the diagnosis, a silent thyroiditis sufferer may be given a radioactive iodine uptake test, showing almost no uptake, to distinguish it from Graves' disease with high uptake. Often, no treatment is necessary, and the condition clears up by itself. At other times, beta-blockers provide relief from some thyrotoxic symptoms. If a period of hypothyroidism follows the transient episode of thyrotoxicosis, it may require thyroid hormone treatment unless it is very brief. Some people with this thyroiditis become permanently hypothyroid, requiring lifelong thyroid hormone replacement therapy.

Postpartum Thyroiditis

Women with TPO antibodies are more likely to experience postpartum thyroiditis. This is a general label referring to silent thyroiditis occurring after delivery, causing mild hyperthyroidism, and a short-lived Hashimoto's type of thyroiditis, causing mild hypothyroidism. Until quite recently, the mild hypothyroid and mild thyrotoxicosis symptoms were simply attributed to the symptoms of postpartum depression, those notorious postpartum blues, thought to be caused by the dramatic hormonal and emotional changes women experience after pregnancy. But recent studies indicate that as many as 20 percent of all pregnant women experience transient thyroid problems and subsequent mild forms of thyrotoxicosis or hypothyroidism. See Chapter 13 for more information on postpartum thyroiditis.

Acute Suppurative Thyroiditis

Also known as simply *bacterial thyroiditis*, acute suppurative thyroiditis is a very rare condition. The term *suppurative* refers to the presence of bacteria and pus. Here, the thyroid gland suffers a dramatic pus-forming bacterial infection similar to the ones that cause abscesses. The thyroid gland becomes painful and inflamed, and a high fever and chills accompany the infection. Sometimes there is an abscess within the gland containing pus. Usually, the tenderness to the thyroid gland is obvious, so it's difficult to miss the symptoms. Sometimes, a fine needle biopsy can provide abscess material to examine for bacteria. Antibiotics, incision, and drainage are the treatment, with a beneficial response to this treatment confirming the diagnosis.

Riedel's Thyroiditis

Riedel's thyroiditis is the rarest form of thyroiditis. Here, the thyroid gland is invaded by scar tissue, infiltrating throughout the gland and binding it to surrounding portions of the neck. The thyroid will feel very hard like wood. Hence, the term *ligneous* (meaning woody) or *fibrous* (meaning scar tissue) thyroiditis is used to describe this peculiar condition. Because the gland attaches itself here to overlying skin and deeper structures in the neck, your windpipe might feel constricted, and your vocal cords could be affected as well. Your voice might become husky, and swallowing would be difficult. The diagnosis for this disorder usually involves a biopsy to rule out cancer, and usually the only treatment is surgical removal of the front part of the gland itself. The cause is unknown, but, luckily, it is an extremely rare condition. Since it is so rare, portions of the thyroid, removed during surgery, must be evaluated by specialist pathologists with expertise in thyroid pathology.

6 Graves' Disease

Graves' disease is the next most common autoimmune thyroid disease after Hashimoto's thyroiditis. It is named after Robert James Graves, the nineteenth-century Irish physician who published a description of three patients with this condition in 1835 in the *London Medical and Surgical Journal*. Caleb Parry was the first physician to identify this disease, collecting eight cases, but unfortunately, they were published after his death in 1825 without the accolade or fame. Carl Adolph von Basedow described four more such patients in 1840, providing the Germans and the French the opportunity to avoid the English eponym by calling it Basedow's disease.

Graves' disease occurs in both sexes and at all ages, but tends to affect younger and middle-aged women—usually between ages twenty to forty. It is also not uncommon for people in their fifties or sixties to develop Graves' disease or for young children to get it. Similar to Hashimoto's disease, Graves' disease occurs much more frequently in women than men. Even so, roughly 1 percent of the population has Graves' disease, which includes former U.S. President George Bush, former First Lady Barbara Bush, and even their dog! The late John F. Kennedy, Jr., suffered from Graves' disease as well as Addison's disease (another autoimmune disease) like his father, the late President John F. Kennedy. As mentioned in Chapter 5, people with one autoimmune disease are more likely to develop another, and autoimmune disorders tend to be familial, although no distinct mode of inheritance has been identified.

What Happens in Graves' Disease?

In Chapter 5, we described what happens in autoimmune disease and how the autoimmune response is triggered. With Graves' disease, an abnormal antibody is produced, called TSA (thyroid stimulating antibody), also known as TSI (thyroid stimulating immunoglobulin). TSA stimulates the thyroid gland to vastly overproduce thyroid hormone. Normally controlled by the pituitary gland, the thyroid's triggers are tricked into being stimulated by abnormal antibodies. This particular trigger is the thyroid follicular cell's receptor for TSH, stimulated by TSI instead of TSH. The result is hyperthyroidism, and a goiter frequently develops. Yet sometimes the goiter is so minimal that your doctor cannot feel it.

The symptoms of Graves' disease are those of thyrotoxicosis, discussed in Chapter 4. But there are some additional, unique complications.

Thyroid Eye Disease (TED)

Thyroid eye disease (TED), also known as Graves' ophthalmopathy (GO) or Graves' orbitopathy, can be quite severe in people with Graves' disease. The majority of thyrotoxic Graves' disease patients suffer from measurable TED. At one time, only those with noticeable changes to the eyes were considered to have TED, but more sophisticated methods of diagnosis reveal that eye changes are present in almost all Graves' disease patients, even though symptoms may not be noticeable. Some patients develop GO for one or more years before they develop thyrotoxicosis, while in others the thyrotoxicosis precedes GO.

The following symptoms usually appear at least a year before GO is diagnosed, and you may be inclined to think you have an eye infection or another problem:

- Gritty, itching, and watery eyes
- Aching discomfort behind the eyes, especially when you look up or to the side
- Sensitivity to light or sun
- Congestion in the eyelids (this may be mistaken for an infection)
- Dry eyes
- Lid lag (where the upper lids are slow to follow when you look down; resulting from effects of thyrotoxicosis)
- Bulging eyes or a staring look (the first is caused by inflammation; the second caused by lid retraction)
- Double vision, particularly when looking to the side

The most common eye changes are bulginess and double vision. All of these problems, and treatment approaches, are discussed more in Chapter 23.

Risks for Heart Disease

The racing heart that is characteristic of thyrotoxicosis can complicate preexisting heart disease, or worsen risk factors that predispose you to heart disease, even in the absence of Graves' disease. If you have any of these conditions while thyrotoxic, you need to take steps to lower some of these other risk factors as soon as possible. In addition, heart rhythm problems can be induced by thyrotoxicosis in Graves' disease. While most young people with otherwise normal hearts have rapid regular heartbeats (called *sinus tachycardia*), older people or those with some heart problems may have an irregular rapid heart rhythm called *atrial fibrillation*. Atrial fibrillation requires the intervention of a cardiologist, particularly since it can cause blood clots that result in strokes. Thyrotoxicosis is also a risk for these clots, and if it results in atrial fibrillation, blood thinners are usually necessary. (See Chapter 25 for more on heart complications.)

Smoking

Quitting smoking will obviously cut your risk of dying from a heart attack in the absence of Graves' disease, and will reduce heart complications in the presence of Graves' disease. But what you may not realize is that quitting smoking will dramatically improve your eye problems if you have thyroid eye disease. The reasons for this are not known, but the effect is well described. This is discussed more in Chapter 23.

High Blood Sugar

Thyrotoxicosis, as we discussed in Chapter 4, can increase your need for insulin if you have type 1 diabetes or in some cases of type 2 diabetes. If you have type 2 diabetes (as one in four adults over forty-five do), you are already at a much greater risk of heart attack or stroke because of blood vessel complications. It is critical that you have your diabetes medications or insulin and your blood-sugar targets reassessed by your doctor, since they can be thrown off by the symptoms of Graves' disease and thyrotoxicosis. If you have diabetic eye disease, it's important to assess whether new eye symptoms are a result of developing thyroid disease or a worsening of preexisting diabetes eye disease (also worsened by smoking).

Restlessness and Anxiety

The typical person with Graves' disease is chronically restless, to the point where he or she cannot sit still for a minute, and is terribly anxious and worried. As discussed in Chapter 4, this is partly because of the increased sensitivity to adrenergic hormones (adrenaline and related hormones) that comes with thyrotoxicosis. There is often a distinct tremor of the hands, also resulting from the adrenaline sensitivity. In Chapter 4, we discussed how thyrotoxicosis has many crossover symptoms with generalized anxiety disorder and panic disorder. The restlessness and anxiety may dramatically interfere with your ability to relate to others or to perform normally in your workplace.

Mania and Graves' Disease

People with thyrotoxic Graves' disease may have difficulty sleeping, rapidly changing emotions, disjointed thoughts, irritability, and agitation. These symptoms resemble those of mania, except that manic people have a feeling of increased energy levels while thyrotoxic people have decreased energy, complaining of tiredness. People with Graves' disease with high energy levels might actually also have bipolar affective (manic-depressive) disorder.

Rarely will the psychological symptoms of Graves' disease become severe enough to be called psychotic, although sometimes the thought processes are delusional and paranoid. Unless a significant underlying psychiatric illness is present, these behavioral and thought disorders resolve when the thyrotoxicosis is resolved.

Rapid Weight Loss

It's been observed that Graves' disease commonly presents in people (women in particular) after they have begun a rapid weight-loss program. The rapid weight loss from the diet can mask the symptoms of Graves', and even lead some physicians to suspect amphetamine abuse or an eating disorder. A theory (not confirmed) is that sudden changes in the metabolic rate, which can be brought on by starvation or rapid weight loss, may trigger autoimmune thyroid disease in people who have antithyroid antibodies.

Exhaustion

The exhaustion, briefly discussed in Chapter 4, that can accompany Graves' disease is different from the fatigue of hypothyroidism. It may look to some as though you have "burnout." Burnout may be the primary diagnosis, for example, if you are in the role of a caregiver for an elder or person with dementia.

A variety of factors can contribute to exhaustion. Muscles, particularly the thighs and shoulders, are weak and fatigue easily. If an underlying heart dysfunction is present, such as thyrotoxic heart failure, tiredness can be severe. In this way, exhaustion is a combination of physical and psychological features.

Gender Differences in Graves' Disease

It's been observed that men with Graves' disease tend to have more subtle symptoms, which can be confused with stress and heart disease—especially since thyroid disease is more frequently diagnosed in women. Men with thyroid eye disease, however, are likely to be diagnosed earlier with Graves' disease because the signs are more obvious than in men without TED. Women tend to have more severe symptoms than men, which can lead to an early diagnosis. However, because so many women's health problems can be confused with Graves' disease (for example, hot flashes, irregular periods) and women suffer more from double duty–related stress (i.e., the supermom who works both outside and inside the home), depression, and anxiety, Graves' disease can be missed, too.

Diagnosing Graves' Disease

The signs of Graves' disease are often obvious: you may develop a goiter and display all the classic signs of thyrotoxicosis. Or you may just develop thyroid eye disease symptoms, which are usually telltale signs of Graves' disease. When the signs are obvious, your doctor simply confirms the diagnosis with blood tests that check your thyroid hormone levels and sometimes test for the presence of antithyroid antibodies in the blood.

If you're not showing any blatant signs of hyperthyroidism but suspect Graves' disease because it runs in your family or you're experiencing more subtle symptoms, Graves' disease is detected through blood tests that check thyroid function, which include free T4, free T3, and TSH tests (see Chapter 2). If your thyroid function tests confirm hyperthyroidism, your doctor will look for evidence of associated autoimmune symptoms, such as Graves' ophthalmopathy or pretibial myxedema, which suggest the diagnosis. Your physician will also try to establish a historical record of symptoms to see how long you have had symptoms of thyrotoxicosis. Long-term thyrotoxic symptoms make it less likely that a transient thyroiditis is the cause of the thyrotoxicosis. If it is not obvious, a radioactive iodine uptake scan (see Chapter 2) will show increased uptake in Graves' disease and little or no uptake in thyroiditis. Sometimes, a blood test to measure TSA may prove useful. Since Graves' disease is responsible for 80 percent of all cases of thyrotoxicosis without a previous history of thyroid disease, most doctors routinely screen for it when thyrotoxicosis is diagnosed. If the Graves' disease is not obvious, or there is a lumpy gland, a radioactive iodine scan may be needed to make the diagnosis and exclude autonomous nodular disease (see Chapter 8). These scans are discussed in detail in Chapter 2.

Treating Graves' Disease

There is no way to treat the root cause of Graves' disease—the autoimmune disorder itself. Therefore, treating Graves' disease involves treating hyperthyroidism. To treat hyperthyroidism, the thyroid gland is usually rendered inactive and ablated (destroyed). One method of doing this is with radioactive iodine, which will typically make you hypothyroid and easily treated with thyroid hormone replacement for life. Alternatively, you may be treated with antithyroid medication, which in some (usually mild) cases can lead to remission, meaning that you can stop the medication and remain normal with normal thyroid hormone levels. The other method of rendering the thyroid gland inactive is through surgical removal of the thyroid gland, known as *thyroidectomy*. This process is discussed briefly in this chapter and in detail in Chapter 9 on thyroid cancer. Graves' disease treatment in pregnancy is covered in Chapter 13.

Radioactive Iodine (RAI) Therapy for Graves' Disease

Radioactive iodine (RAI) is the most common treatment for Graves' disease in the United States and increasing in popularity in most other parts of the world. In many ways, it is almost an ideal therapy. It has a remarkably long and safe track record with more than a half century of experience. Radioactive iodine is simply an isotope of iodine that releases radiation. The specific isotope used for treatment is iodine-131 (I-131). Since the thyroid naturally and avidly takes in iodine to form thyroid hormones, when a radioactive iodine isotope is used, the thyroid gland greedily sucks it up and, if a high enough dose is given, destroys itself in the process. Sometimes some residual thyroid function is left, perhaps enough to keep your thyroid hormone levels normal, but this result is uncommon and unpredictable, so most physicians aim to destroy all function of the thyroid gland. Although this sounds dramatic, the procedure isn't dangerous, and there are usually no side effects other than some temporary minor swelling or irritation to the base of the neck, discussed more in Chapter 12. (There are several misconceptions and much misinformation surrounding radioactive iodine therapy for Graves' disease, which we deal with in Chapter 19.)

It appears as though some Graves' disease patients with severe thyroid eye disease who receive radioactive iodine treatment tend to have a worsening of these symptoms (see Chapter 23). If you have significant thyroid eye disease, you should discuss going on a steroid medication if you're having RAI. The combination of a steroid drug and RAI has been shown to prevent a worsening of TED. That said, in cases of very severe TED, or when steroid medications present a risk to your health because of other health problems or medications you're taking, you may need to discuss other options.

Aside from the issues with TED, the only other time radioactive iodine cannot be used is when patients are pregnant. RAI is now considered safe to use in children, although it is less commonly used in preadolescents (we will discuss this more in Chapter 15).

If a person indicates a strong preference for antithyroid medication or surgery instead of radioactive iodine, it is unethical of doctors not to offer these options so long as the risks are thoroughly disclosed and the person with Graves' disease has made a genuinely informed decision (see Chapter 21) rather than a decision based on fear of RAI.

In more than fifty-five years of active use, radioactive iodine has not yet proved harmful as a therapy for Graves' disease. Over the years, many studies have been conducted; however, there is no evidence that RAI (as given for Graves' disease) increases the risk for cancer, or that it causes infertility or birth defects. Taken in either capsule form or in water, radioactive iodine can effectively destroy the thyroid gland. This effect takes from several weeks to months. There is usually a waiting period of at least six months after the radioactive iodine treatment is administered to determine if the full effect of the RAI has been seen.

In a third of Graves' patients, a second RAI treatment may be necessary. In rare cases, a third treatment needs to be used. The doctor will wait until you are hypothyroid before prescribing thyroid replacement hormone to replace the thyroid hormone output of a normal functioning thyroid. Occasionally, after radioactive iodine treatment, just enough of the thyroid gland remains to function normally on its own. In this case, thyroid hormone replacement is not necessary. This is not the norm, however. Radioactive iodine therapy is discussed in much greater detail in Chapter 12, including side effects of therapy.

Antithyroid Medication

Sometimes, doctors (or patients) prefer to treat Graves' disease with antithyroid drugs. These drugs prevent the thyroid from manufacturing thyroid hormone and are usually a way of managing Graves' disease in the short term. Propylthiouracil (PTU) and methimazole (Tapazole) are the most commonly used drugs, and they are very useful under specific circumstances, such as:

- Graves' disease in pregnancy
- Patients with severe thyrotoxicosis, to lower their thyroid hormone levels prior to I-131 treatment
- Treatment of mild thyrotoxicosis in Graves' disease with a very small goiter
- Controlling thyrotoxicosis in people with severe Graves' ophthalmopathy and a reluctance to undergo thyroid surgery
- Treatment of thyrotoxicosis in any patient in an unstable clinical condition or in thyroid storm
- Strong fears against RAI

As the production of thyroid hormone decreases, the symptoms of thyrotoxicosis will disappear. The practice is to take you off the drugs after several months of treatment, if the TSH has been normal or elevated, to see if Graves' disease relapses, which occurs about 80 percent of the time, or goes into remission. Some people like to take their chances at remission, which is certainly reasonable, unless Graves' disease is severe. Usually, antithyroid drugs are used if patients are pregnant or refuse to consent to RAI, but some doctors prefer to use them as a first option.

Remission and Antithyroid Medication

The main benefit to going on antithyroid medication is to try your luck at achieving full remission without the need for RAI or surgery. This usually results in either an indefinite period of normal thyroid activity or lifelong hypothyroidism. In general, antithyroid drugs are effective in achieving remission about 20 to 30 percent of the time, but some doctors report even lower success rates. The main effect of antithyroid drugs is to buy time until either a spontaneous remission occurs, in which the immune system stops producing thyroid stimulating antibodies (TSA), or the autoimmune effects destroy enough of the thyroid gland to ablate the gland despite persistent TSA production. This spontaneous remission is most likely to be seen in people with very mild thyrotoxicosis and small goiters. The process can take from six months to a year, if it is going to happen at all.

Although it is possible for remissions to take place after longer periods of time, it is better to avoid open-ended treatment courses; at that point, there is no advantage in postponing more definitive treatment with RAI. Thus, Graves' disease, in virtually all patients who are tolerant of these medications, can be easily controlled with antithyroid medication. However, when patients are taken off the drugs, around 80 percent will experience a recurrence of thyrotoxicosis from their Graves' disease.

Such a percentage begs the question, why even bother with antithyroid medication? Many patients and doctors feel it's worth it to gamble on a full remission initially before more definitive therapies are used. It takes about six to eight weeks on the medication for the thyroid hormone levels to reach a normal range, but patients are usually kept on them for six to twelve months in the hope that a true remission will occur. Signs that antithyroid drugs are failing to provide a remission include TSH levels that remain less than normal, persistently high TSA levels, and a relatively high level of T3 in the blood compared to T4. In the end, many of the patients on antithyroid drugs wind up having either radioactive iodine treatment or thyroidectomy eventually.

There is an upside to antithyroid drugs, however. Patients with eye problems may experience more improvement in their eyes while on antithyroid medication than with other forms of treatment. One downside of antithyroid drugs is a small (around 1 percent) risk of destroying bone marrow (aplastic anemia) or the liver (requiring a liver transplant).

Additionally, some data show that radioactive iodine therapy doesn't work as well on Graves' disease patients who were treated with the antithyroid medication propylthiouracil (PTU) first. If you're having radioactive iodine therapy after pretreatment with antithyroid medication, the current literature suggests using higher doses of radioactive iodine.

If you have Graves' disease, it's far more realistic to assume that after treatment you'll need to be put on thyroid hormone for life. The general recommendation is to avoid antithyroid medication if a doctor knows for certain that you'll be having radioactive iodine therapy and your thyrotoxic symptoms are not too severe. Instead, beta-blockers are used to control some of the symptoms of thyrotoxicosis until the thyroid hormone level is restored to the normal range.

Thyroidectomy or Partial Thyroidectomy

Another treatment is either a partial or near-total thyroidectomy (surgical removal of the thyroid gland). This is reserved for Graves' patients who are pregnant, Graves' patients with a goiter causing obstruction in the neck, patients where there is a concern that a thyroid nodule accompanying Graves' is suspicious for cancer, or patients who refuse RAI therapy. A partial or near-total thyroidectomy means that you deliberately leave behind remnants of the thyroid gland so that thyroid hormone may not be necessary. In a total thyroidectomy, the entire gland is removed.

Generally, more risks are involved with thyroidectomy than with RAI therapy for Graves' disease, which is why this is not the first line of therapy for most Graves' patients. These risks include damage to the nerves that supply the vocal cords (recurrent laryngeal nerves), as well as damage to the parathyroid glands, which control calcium levels. These risks are discussed more in Chapter 9, but it's critical to understand that the risks are not insignificant, even in surgeries performed by the very top thyroid surgeons; they magnify when thyroidectomies are performed by general surgeons who do not have sufficient experience with this surgery or do not perform at least twenty thyroidectomies per year. Unfortunately, the vast majority of Graves' patients who have thyroidectomies will see general surgeons, given current managed care restrictions.

A thyroidectomy is also major surgery that involves a general anesthetic, carries other risks, and requires a postsurgical stay in the hospital of at least one to two days. Some surgeons attempt this surgery with same-day discharges, but thyroid experts consider this to be too risky. Sometimes, even in total thyroidectomy, small pieces of thyroid tissue are left behind that could potentially continue the thyrotoxicosis of Graves' disease. Radioactive iodine is used to kill off the remaining bits of tissue. These small pieces can also leave you euthyroid, without having to be on thyroid hormone. In most people, surgery will leave them hypothyroid, and thyroid hormone will be prescribed.

Spontaneous Remission of Graves' Disease

In rare cases, Graves' disease can go into remission without any treatment, which may explain why some people go into remission on antithyroid medication, too. If a person's thyrotoxicosis is mild enough to be controlled on beta-blockers alone, the rate of remission is similar to people on antithyroid drugs over the same period of time.

Thyroid experts have theorized that removing certain stressors, which may have triggered the autoimmune disease in the first place, could help lead to spontaneous remission. Although unproven, it is helpful to review some of the stress-reduction techniques described in Chapter 22.

Euthyroid Graves' Disease

In some cases of *euthyroid Graves' disease*, no symptoms of thyrotoxicosis are present in spite of Graves' disease. In such cases, the person is noted to have the bulging eyes of Graves' ophthalmopathy, but the thyroid gland is still working normally. Many of these people will ultimately develop thyrotoxicosis; however, some never do. As discussed earlier, this is more common in men than women. With euthyroid Graves' disease, it is critical to provide the appropriate measures to deal with the eye problems, while performing regular monitoring of thyroid hormone levels so as to avoid missing the development of thyrotoxicosis.

Allowing Graves' to Run Its Natural Course

Many with Graves' disease have mild symptoms and wonder whether they should refuse active therapy and allow Graves' disease to run its natural course, which might normally result in the thyroid gland burning out and failing on its own, leaving you hypothyroid anyway. This approach is commonly recommended for the small group of people who have such low degrees of thyrotoxicosis that ablative therapy with RAI, surgery, or risks of drug effects of antithyroid medications seem unnecessary. These people often do well with beta-blockers; however, they must be carefully monitored since thyrotoxicosis may worsen without warning. Also, the risks of worsening of osteoporosis and chronic effects of excess thyroid hormone on the heart should be considered. For these reasons, post-menopausal women with brittle bones (see Chapter 14) and people with irregular heart rhythms (see Chapter 25) are appropriately directed toward RAI treatment.

Screening Family Members for Graves' Disease

Many Graves' disease patients wonder whether their children or other family members will develop it; they may also wonder whether genetic screening is available for Graves' disease. Although it is clear that autoimmune thyroid disease has genetic risk, as of this writing, no specific gene has been identified for screening. Even if this were the case, there is no advantage to genetic screening for Graves' disease or Hashimoto's disease because neither is necessarily life-threatening, both are usually present in mid to late adulthood, and both have good treatment options available. Thus, it makes no sense to ablate or remove healthy thyroid glands simply to prevent the possibility of inheriting thyrotoxicosis or Graves' disease.

However, it is important to be alert to signs of thyrotoxicosis or hypothyroidism so that family members can be treated early before serious symptoms develop. In Graves' disease and Hashimoto's thyroiditis families, all female family members should have regular thyroid function tests in their childbearing years, including before conception, during pregnancy, during the postpartum period, and after forty years of age. In cases where a woman in early pregnancy has antibodies suggestive of Graves' disease, even with no symptoms, she should be carefully monitored to see if antithyroid drugs are needed. The fetus may need to be monitored (by evaluating the fetal heart rate) if the mother has been known to have had previous RAI therapy for Graves' disease, because she may still be making TSA that can cross the placenta and stimulate the fetal thyroid gland. This is discussed more in Chapter 13. Male family members should have annual thyroid function tests by age forty.

Parents with Graves' disease and Hashimoto's disease should be especially watchful of:

- Delayed puberty in their children
- Signs of hypothyroidism or thyrotoxicosis in children
- Goiters in their children

Thyroid disease in children is discussed more in Chapter 15.

Are There Natural Therapies for Graves' Disease?

Some patient literature suggests Graves' disease can be treated using "natural" or alternative means through a goitrogenic diet and herbs that supposedly support thyroid function. Goitrogenic foods, discussed in Chapter 3, are foods that can block thyroid hormone formation (for example, foods from the *Brassica* family), essentially working like antithyroid drugs. Some laypeople wonder whether large quantities of goitrogenic foods can cause hypothyroidism. Unfortunately, this is highly unlikely unless the diet is severely deficient in iodine and massive quantities of these raw foods are eaten.

In the case of hyperthyroidism, such a diet could theoretically work to block the effects of thyroid hormone, but reality is not so obliging. It seems easier to take a methimazole tablet twice a day than to eat twenty pounds of raw cabbage, chew cassava, and follow a strict low-iodine diet (see Chapter 20) each day. Also, a goitrogenic diet cannot cure the autoimmune disease that is causing thyrotoxicosis.

Certain herbs have been touted to inhibit the enzyme responsible for the peripheral conversion of T4 to T3 (various dried roots, flowers, leaves, and seeds). Such effects are possible theoretically but definitely not of clinical significance and, even if of marginal effect, wholly insufficient to safeguard your health.

Some reputable physicians use saturated iodine solutions (SSKI or Lugol's solution) to help control thyrotoxicosis in patients after insufficient response to RAI or to supplement antithyroid drugs to lower thyroid hormone levels and reduce the blood flow to thyroid glands before surgery. The use of such iodine preparations without previous RAI or antithyroid drug therapy can be dangerous, fueling the production of more thyroid hormones and worsening thyrotoxicosis. The suggestion that lay practitioners can treat Graves' disease with these agents alone is alarming.

In general, herbs that are considered good for thyroid health are generally dangerous or useless for Graves' disease patients who may be purchasing them in the belief that they will restore thyroid function. Kelp, sargassum, and bladder wrack are especially noteworthy in this way. Manganese, iron, selenium (touted as "necessary for T4/T3 conversion"), magnesium, zinc, copper, sulfur, and calcium are also all sold as thyroid health supplements but are dangerous or useless for Graves' patients. In general, the notion of natural therapy for Graves' disease is misleading and, in some ways, exploits patients. We discuss the notion of false alternatives in Chapter 19.

7 Goiter: An Enlarged Thyroid Gland

Agoiter is an enlarged thyroid gland. Many years ago, people's thyroid glands were large enough to see at a glance. Goiters were considered signs of beauty, often depicted in paintings of Peter Paul Rubens, the seventeenth-century Flemish painter. In the late 1980s, while traveling through Italy, I (Ken) saw that nearly every Etruscan funeral urn in Sienna depicted a figure with a prominent goiter. Most of these goiters were the result of iodine deficiency, most severe in the Alpine regions of Europe. Iodine deficiency is still endemic in many of the nonindustrialized regions of the world, but it is much less common in more developed countries. There are a number of different causes of goiter. In this chapter, we'll explore the different types of goiter and discuss known and potential causes of them, as well as the consequences and treatment of goiter.

Evaluating a Goiter

The best way to evaluate a goiter is to consider three areas: functional status (how much hormone it makes), anatomical features (how big it is, how it feels, and if it blocks vital structures in your neck), and pathologic features (is it a benign goiter or a cancer?).

Functional Assessment

If you have a goiter, the first thing doctors will assess is whether or not your thyroid hormone levels are normal. This evaluation is discussed in detail in Chapter 2; however, simply stated, you need to know your thyroid stimulating hormone (TSH) level and your free T4 level (your thyroxine level). If your TSH level is normal, particularly if your free T4 is also normal, then your thyroid hormone status is considered normal, a condition known as being *euthyroid*. There are several types of goiters in euthyroid people, generally called *euthyroid goiters*.

The TSH is most sensitive, provided that your pituitary gland is normal. That's why a normal TSH is confirmed by the free T4. If the free T4 is low, despite a normal or low TSH, this could be a sign of a dysfunctional pituitary gland, often from a benign pituitary tumor. On the other hand, if the free T4 is very high, yet the TSH is inappropriately normal or elevated, there are two possible explanations. If you have thyrotoxic symptoms (see Chapter 4), you may have a rare pituitary tumor that makes TSH. If you are clinically euthyroid, with no symptoms of hypothyroidism (see Chapter 3) or thyrotoxicosis, then you may have thyroid hormone resistance (discussed in Chapter 18).

If the TSH is elevated then you're hypothyroid, and it's likely that the elevated TSH itself has contributed to the growth of the goiter. Of course, the TSH is most often elevated because of Hashimoto's thyroiditis (in industrialized countries), discussed in Chapter 5, or iodine deficiency (in much of the underdeveloped world), discussed in Chapters 1 and 3. Adequate thyroid hormone replacement reduces TSH levels to normal and often reduces the size of the goiter. However, sometimes there is so much scar tissue in the thyroid that thyroid hormone treatment doesn't shrink the goiter very much.

When the TSH is suppressed because of thyrotoxicosis, a number of possibilities need to be considered. If the entire gland is generally enlarged, then the most common diagnosis is Graves' disease. (See Chapter 6.) On the other hand, the entire gland may be enlarged, containing individual thyroid nodules, many of which could be autonomous toxic nodules; this condition is called a *toxic multinodular goiter*.

Does the Goiter Take Up Iodine?

A radioactive iodine scan of the thyroid gland (using I-123 or I-131) shows a picture of which areas of the gland suck up the most iodine. This can be quantified by actually measuring the percentage of the radioactive iodine that enters the gland, the *radioactive iodine uptake (RAIU)*. The thyroid gland normally sucks up iodine when it is stimulated by TSH (see Chapter 1) or thyroid-stimulating antibodies (as seen in Graves' disease, discussed in Chapter 6), or if portions of it become independent, or *autonomous* (see Chapter 8).

If the TSH is elevated and the thyroid gland is enlarged, there's no need to measure the RAIU and no need to get a thyroid scan. Likewise, if the TSH is normal, showing the person to be euthyroid, there's no reason to get these tests either. On the other hand, if the TSH is low (suppressed) then the goiter could be a toxic multinodular goiter or a diffuse goiter, as seen in Graves' disease. The radioactive iodine thyroid scan is best suited to identify whether the goiter is a Graves' disease goiter or a toxic multinodular goiter. The scan also lets you see if there may be a cold nodule in a Graves' disease goiter that could be a thyroid cancer (see Chapter 9).

Anatomical Assessment

The following chart outlines how we classify the size of a goiter.

STAGE	DESCRIPTION
0	No goiter is present.
Ia	A goiter is felt on exam but not able to be seen when the neck is fully extended.
Ib	A goiter is felt on exam and also visible only when the neck is fully extended.
II	The goiter is visible when the neck is in a normal position, and exam isn't needed.
III	The goiter is large enough that it can be seen easily at some distance away.

The normal size of a thyroid gland is measured in weight (grams), roughly corresponding to the same volume (milliliters), and is around eighteen to twenty grams. In countries with adequate iodine intake, the gland size averages a smaller volume than in countries with marginal or severe iodine deficiency. A goiter, being an enlarged thyroid gland, is larger than twenty grams. A thyroid is considered a small goiter when it weighs less than thirty grams. Between thirty and fifty grams is a moderate goiter, while a large goiter exceeds these values.

I (Ken) typically assess a person's goiter by examining it from in front of the person. The method is similar to the self-exam technique described in Chapter 1. Standing in front of and slightly to the person's right side, my right hand feels down the middle of the windpipe under the Adam's apple until the soft thin cushion of the thyroid isthmus (middle of the thyroid gland) is felt. This may be quite obvious in large goiters but requires practice with smaller thyroids. Keeping my fingers on the isthmus, I slide them to the left side of the person's windpipe, keeping my fingers in contact with the skin and pushing muscle and fatty tissue to the side while I feel the left thyroid lobe. Sometimes a goiter is raised slightly in the neck so that the bottom edge can be felt. I often have to slide my fingers down to above the collarbone, and I then ask the person to swallow, drawing the gland upward under my fingers. This process is repeated identically (using reverse sides) while I stand in front of the patient to the person's left, to feel the right thyroid lobe with my left hand.

A thyroid exam can help assess the size of the gland, the texture of the gland, whether there are any nodules, and if there is any thoracic inlet obstruction (described in the next section).

The Pemberton's Maneuver

When examining a goiter, it is important to see if it is blocking the vital structures passing between the neck and the chest (the *thoracic inlet*), such as the windpipe, esophagus (gullet), carotid arteries, and jugular veins. The technique, briefly described in Chapter 2, is called a *Pemberton's maneuver*. Here, a doctor will have you stand in front of him or her, looking straight ahead while the doctor looks at your neck. Next, he or she will have you raise your hands straight up in the air, with your arms nearly against your ears. If the doctor sees that your neck has turned red, your neck veins have started to bulge, or you start to have difficulty drawing a breath, this means that your goiter is large enough to block the thoracic inlet (called an *obstructive goiter*); this result is called a positive Pemberton's maneuver.

It's a good idea to have a thyroid surgeon remove obstructive goiters, particularly if very large. Exceptions include moderately obstructive goiters associated with elevated TSH levels (hypothyroid goiters), which may shrink with thyroid hormone treatment; goiters with Graves' disease, which may shrink with radioactive iodine treatment; and very rare thyroid lymphomas, which usually shrink very rapidly with external beam radiation therapy.

Ultrasound Exams and Other Imaging Methods

Sometimes the physical examination does not provide enough information about a goiter, which may be because the gland is situated low in the neck or the person may be too obese to effectively examine it. The ultrasound exam (discussed in Chapter 2) is very useful for determining the shape and size of the thyroid gland. It can show nodules, assessing whether they're solid or cysts. The physician performing the exam with the ultrasound can do a fine needle aspiration biopsy (see Chapters 2 and 8) with the ultrasound guiding the placement of the biopsy needle to be sure that the correct region is biopsied. An ultrasound exam also allows precise measurements of nodules and the entire gland so the doctor can accurately determine if these structures are changing in size over time.

There are other ways to image the thyroid gland. CT scans can show details of the thyroid gland, particularly if the gland is beneath the breastbone, a *substernal goiter*. The only problem with CT scans is that they usually require the use of contrast dye in your veins. This dye contains massive amounts of nonradioactive iodine that can hang around in your body for two to ten months. If a thyroid cancer is found in your thyroid gland, this stable iodine interferes with radioactive iodine scans and treatments.

An alternative to CT scans is magnetic resonance imaging (MRI). The contrast dye used for MRI scans is called *gadolinium* and won't interfere with radioactive iodine. An MRI scan provides much of the same information as a CT scan, but the MRI scanning machine may be a bit more confining and sometimes causes problems for people with claustrophobia.

Types of Goiter

Goiters are classified into three main types: *euthyroid*, *hypothyroid*, and *thyrotoxic*. In other words, does the goiter alter thyroid hormone levels in any way?

Euthyroid Goiters

People with euthyroid goiters have normal thyroid hormone levels and normal TSH levels. Euthyroid goiters should not be evaluated with radioactive iodine scans. Instead, besides physical exams, ultrasounds can be useful, particularly if a fine needle aspiration biopsy is done.

Euthyroid Diffuse Goiters

Euthyroid diffuse goiters are thyroids that are enlarged over their entirety, without any evidence of nodules or cysts. Their cause is not clearly understood. It may be because of a variety of growth factors made by the thyroid gland that stimulate its growth. Some physicians believe that environmental factors, such as waterborne contaminants (see Chapter 3), may cause these goiters, but there aren't any concrete answers regarding the causes. Although some people with euthyroid diffuse goiters are treated with sufficient dosages of thyroid hormone to suppress the TSH levels, there isn't any evidence to support this as an effective treatment to shrink these goiters. Likewise, radioactive iodine therapy is not an effective treatment for these goiters.

The focus of the evaluation of euthyroid diffuse goiters is to make sure that there isn't any thoracic inlet obstruction. Another concern is to be certain that a thyroid cancer isn't missed. This is particularly important if there is asymmetry to the shape of the goiter. Fine-needle biopsies should be done whenever such questions arise. Surgery, to remove half of the gland or the entire gland, is done when there is a question of the gland containing a cancer or when there is any thoracic inlet obstruction. Thyroid surgery is discussed more in Chapter 9.

Euthyroid Multinodular Goiters

Euthyroid multinodular goiters are thyroid glands that are enlarged and contain multiple nodules, much like a bag of marbles. Some physicians believe that euthyroid diffuse goiters can become nodular over time. With these goiters, the ultrasound exam is very important, permitting your physician to find out which nodules are dominant (largest) and perform fine-needle biopsies on them. Sometimes these goiters are called *benign adenomatous goiters*. The same concerns regarding thoracic inlet obstruction as with euthyroid diffuse goiters apply to these goiters also. Treatment methods are also similar.

Hypothyroid Goiters

Hypothyroid goiters are the most common types of goiter in the world. In such goiters, inadequate thyroid hormone levels result in subtle or dramatic elevations of TSH levels, which stimulate the thyroid gland to grow. Two general categories of hypothyroid goiter are endemic goiter, resulting from iodine deficiency, and Hashimoto's thyroiditis (see Chapter 5), caused by destruction of thyroid gland function by antibodies and infiltrating white blood cells.

Endemic Goiter

Endemic goiter arises from iodine deficiency. If this deficiency is mild, the enlarged gland stimulated by TSH is able to sufficiently compensate for the low iodine with only borderline hypothyroidism. On the other hand, hypothyroidism during fetal development to early childhood can cause a condition known as *cretinism*. Individuals with cretinism have mental deficiencies, including defects in hearing, speech, gait, and/or intelligence. This is the most common cause of mental retardation globally. In addition, these individuals may have stunted growth, dry skin, sparse hair, and retarded sexual development. Prevention of cretinism, by providing iodine supplementation to people in regions of iodine deficiency, is a primary concern of the World Health Organization and many public service and charitable groups throughout the world.

Hashimoto's Thyroiditis

Chapter 5 is devoted to the topic of Hashimoto's thyroiditis. In the industrialized world, particularly in regions with high dietary intake of iodine or good levels of iodine supplementation, Hashimoto's thyroiditis has increased in frequency to become the most common cause of goiter. Several coincident factors contribute to the goiter in this condition. First, the immune system generates antibodies that attack the thyroid follicular cells, impairing their ability to make thyroid hormone. Next, lymphocytes (small white blood cells) invade the gland in large quantities, sometimes causing nodules resembling lymph nodes to appear within the thyroid gland. Scar tissue, known as *fibrosis*, makes the thyroid irregular and firm in texture, sometimes feeling *bosselated*, having dimpled depressions like the surface of a golf ball. As the ability of the gland to make thyroid hormone declines, rising TSH levels stimulate the remaining functional regions of the gland to enlarge. The goiter that results from this may be quite large or only slightly larger than normal. It is typically firm and irregular, sometimes with multiple nodules. When these nodules are biopsied, you can see large quantities of lymphocytes and thyroid follicular cells that seem reddish in color when the microscope slides are stained for viewing.

Hashimoto's thyroiditis can be present at the same time as a thyroid cancer. For this reason, despite knowing that Hashimoto's is present, you still need to have the largest of the thyroid nodules examined by fine-needle biopsy. Thyroid hormone therapy (see Chapter 10) is necessary to provide the proper amount of thyroid hormone for good health, although there may be so much scar tissue in the gland that it doesn't shrink much from the treatment.

Thyrotoxic Goiters

In the case of a thyrotoxic goiter, the TSH is suppressed (less than 0.2). Of course, in some cases of Hashimoto's thyroiditis there is a temporary release of stored thyroid hormone (Hashitoxicosis, discussed in Chapter 5) causing a transient thyrotoxicosis. For the purposes of this section, we focus on goiters associated with prolonged thyrotoxicosis (see Chapter 4). There are two major categories: Graves' disease, associated with a diffuse toxic goiter, and toxic multinodular goiter (TMNG), associated with many autonomous nodules within a goiter.

Graves' Disease

Graves' disease is the topic of Chapter 6. It's the most common cause of a thyrotoxic goiter. When I see someone who is thyrotoxic, has bulging eyes, and has an easily seen diffuse goiter, there's no need for me (Ken) to do fancy blood tests to know that the person has Graves' disease. These goiters can be small, barely larger than a normal 18-gram thyroid, to sizes in excess of 140 grams. Once in a while, a Graves' disease goiter can cause thoracic inlet obstruction, which might prompt a surgical removal of the gland, treating both the obstruction and the thyrotoxicosis. Radioactive iodine treatment can be very effective in reducing the size of these goiters, sometimes to normal size.

It is important to do a careful physical examination of this type of goiter. If the gland is diffusely enlarged (without lumps), a thyroid scan is not usually necessary to evaluate the thyroid. On the other hand, if there is marked asymmetry of the gland (one side much larger than the other) or a distinct thyroid nodule or mass, a radioactive iodine thyroid scan is needed. If the enlarged portion or nodule takes up less radioactive iodine than the rest of the thyroid (a cold region or nodule), it needs to be biopsied to make sure that there isn't a coincident thyroid cancer. If the biopsy is positive for cancer or suspicious (see Chapter 8), surgical removal of the goiter treats the thyrotoxicosis as well as allowing doctors to diagnose the suspicious mass or initiate the treatment of the cancer.

Toxic Multinodular Goiter (TMNG)

If you have a suppressed TSH, there might be a detectable goiter or it might be too low in the neck to feel easily. In rare cases, you may be able to feel multiple thyroid nodules; they may feel like a bag of grapes or marbles. Usually, you can feel two or three nodules in your thyroid. Since the thyrotoxicosis is further evaluated with a radioactive iodine scan, this is the test that most commonly shows the goiter to be a toxic multinodular goiter. The scan shows hot nodules (that are brighter on the scan image than surrounding parts of the thyroid) in two or more parts of the gland. These scans can be misleading if the doctor fails to correlate them with a physical examination. For example, if there is a nodule clearly felt in the gland, yet the hot nodule is in a different part of the gland, then the nodule that is felt is *not* a toxic nodule and must be biopsied to make sure that it isn't malignant.

There are two choices for definitive treatment of a TMNG. Antithyroid drugs (see Chapter 11) are not useful, except temporarily, because there is virtually no chance that a TMNG will have a spontaneous remission or cure. A TMNG is most often found in older people (over fifty years), a group that is less tolerant of surgery than younger people; however, surgery to remove the goiter is a reasonable treatment. Frequently, radioactive iodine treatment does an excellent job of eliminating the thyrotoxicosis and helping to shrink the goiter. Beta-blockers are the most important drugs to control many of the thyrotoxicosis symptoms until the radioactive iodine treatment results in lowered thyroid hormone levels.

8 Thyroid Nodules

The word *nodule* means lump. If you're worried about a thyroid lump or nodule, this is the chapter to read. Most thyroid cancers are first found as nodules in the thyroid gland or in other places in the neck. Finding a nodule gives doctors the chance to discover and treat possible thyroid cancer, providing you with the best opportunity to prevent the cancer from getting the upper hand. Most thyroid nodules are benign, and seeing a doctor will allow you to quickly put your fears of cancer to rest should they prove unwarranted.

Some benign thyroid nodules make thyroid hormone in greater than normal amounts without being controlled by the pituitary gland through its TSH secretion. These are called *autonomous toxic nodules (ATN)*. If there are multiple ATNs in your gland, it's called a *toxic multinodular goiter*. Most thyroid nodules are benign *colloid* nodules. Colloid nodules do not produce too much thyroid hormone and usually do not require any particular treatment once identified.

Sometimes a thyroid nodule is shown to be a bag of fluid within the gland, called a *cyst*. Most cysts are benign, but some may contain thyroid cancer in the wall of the cyst. Sometimes the nodule is part fluid and part solid parts. This is called a *complex cyst*. Complex cysts are usually benign but sometimes contain thyroid cancers.

This chapter will walk you through the entire process of discovering and evaluating a thyroid nodule. It will show you exactly how to think about a nodule, and it will outline management according to state-of-the-art standards of care. As we discuss in Chapter 21, there are different standards of care; this chapter will help you navigate nodule management with your doctor and help you avoid wasted time, unnecessary lab tests and scans, and expense.

Finding a Thyroid Nodule

Most thyroid nodules are found as obvious lumps in the lower front of the neck, seen by the person in a mirror or by a friend or family member. Sometimes a physician will find a nodule during a physical examination. This may be prompted by a complaint of a sore throat, usually completely unrelated to the nodule, but serving as a reason to focus on the neck, resulting in the nodule being found by accident. If your neck was exposed to radiation therapy during childhood, you have increased chances of developing thyroid cancer. In this case, you should have regular thyroid exams to detect thyroid nodules that could be cancers. You can also do your own thyroid self-exam, which is discussed in Chapter 1.

Some thyroid cancers first show up as lumps in the neck, outside of the thyroid gland. These are usually lumps of thyroid cancer that have spread to lymph nodes in the neck. The easiest way to evaluate them is with a fine-needle aspiration (FNA) biopsy as discussed in Chapter 2 and later in this chapter. Often, their discovery prompts a careful exam of the thyroid gland, revealing the source of the cancer cells. Alternatively, a surgeon might perform surgery to remove an enlarged lymph node in the neck, revealing it to contain a thyroid cancer.

Although it's tempting to use an ultrasound scan of the thyroid to look for thyroid nodules, unfortunately, as discussed in Chapter 2, these scans are so sensitive they will detect tiny harmless thyroid nodules in nearly everyone examined. For that reason, a nodule with the size of 1 centimeter (0.4 inch) in diameter or less is considered too small to be significant and is usually not further evaluated.

Steps in Evaluating a Thyroid Nodule

The following are the precise steps used in evaluating a thyroid nodule. Different approaches are used for nodules in the neck that are not associated with the thyroid gland itself.

Is the TSH Suppressed?

First, check your TSH level (see Chapter 2). The reason for this is very simple. The nodule *cannot* be an autonomous toxic nodule (ATN) if the TSH is not suppressed (under 0.2). The only type of nodule that can be treated without the need for a biopsy is an ATN because these are very unlikely to be cancers. Every other thyroid nodule that is larger than 1 centimeter (0.4 inch) in diameter requires a biopsy.

This means that the course is made clear by the TSH test. If the TSH is low (less than 0.2), then the next step is a radioactive iodine thyroid scan (see Chapter 2). This scan will show whether the nodule you've discovered is "hot," sucking up most of the radioactive iodine, or not hot. If it is a hot nodule then a biopsy is not needed, and you can be reasonably certain that this is an ATN. If the rest of the thyroid is hot but the nodule is *not* hot, then the nodule should be biopsied. This situation could be seen if a person has Graves' disease as well as a thyroid nodule. In such a case, the nodule could be benign (colloid nodule, inflammatory nodule, or cyst) or it could, in rare cases, be a thyroid cancer. If it were malignant (cancer) then surgical removal of the entire gland would be appropriate for both the Graves' disease and the cancer. The best test to ascertain the nature of the nodule in this situation is an FNA biopsy.

FNA Biopsy: The Critical Procedure

For any thyroid nodule or asymmetrical enlargement of the gland, when the TSH is greater than 0.2, a nuclear thyroid scan is useless. There is no possible scan result that could answer whether the nodule is cancer or not. The only test that can determine this is the FNA biopsy. Although the FNA biopsy is described in detail in Chapter 2, a few key points should be emphasized. First, when performed competently by an experienced physician, the procedure should be relatively painless, often compared favorably to drawing blood from your arm. Next, the FNA can provide information about only the part of the body the needle is placed in. If the physician samples the wrong place or the needle misses the nodule, the information it provides is useless for discerning whether the nodule is a cancer. Last, the biopsy is only as good as the skill of the cytologist interpreting the slides.

A cytologist is a type of pathologist (a doctor who is an expert in examining tissue) who specializes in reviewing cells. The cytologist will assess whether the slides made from the biopsy samples contain sufficient numbers of thyroid cells to provide a diagnosis; in other words, are the slides *adequate*? For example, if only blood cells are seen in the slides, there is no way to figure out whether the nodule is a cancer. Benign nodules are diagnosed not by the absence of cancer cells but rather by the presence of benign thyroid follicular cells. There are three general categories of diagnoses made by the cytologist if the slides are adequate: *benign*, *malignant* (cancerous), or *suspicious*.

The Benign Thyroid Nodule

A benign thyroid nodule is usually a benign colloid nodule. Colloid is the thick pink material normally found inside the thyroid follicles and frequently present in benign nodules. These are usually solid nodules, but sometimes a complex nodule (meaning that it is partly cystic and partly solid) is also partly a colloid nodule. It's imperative that the thyroid nodule, or enlarged portion of the thyroid gland, be accurately measured. I (Ken) often use a tape measure for this purpose. If the nodule is positioned in a way that makes it difficult to measure, a thyroid ultrasound can be used to document its size. In this way, the nodule can be reassessed eight to ten months later, to see if it has grown larger. Many benign colloid nodules will spontaneously shrink in size over that length of time. If this happens, then the diagnosis is confirmed, because the absence of progressive growth (meaning that the nodule doesn't get larger) is one of the key features of a benign nodule. Nodules like these, which are described as benign by a cytologist and also shrink by themselves over time, need no further evaluation or concern.

On the other hand, a large thyroid nodule (more than 3 centimeters) that stays the same size over eight to ten months, or a nodule of any size that grows larger, needs to be biopsied again. Sometimes, despite several benign biopsies, continuous enlargement of a nodule necessitates thyroid surgery because of two potential problems: the nodule could push on vital structures in the neck (windpipe, esophagus, arteries) causing thoracic inlet obstruction, and the continued growth of the nodule could suggest the presence of a thyroid cancer, despite the results of the biopsy. Because of this, the surgeon should remove the half of the thyroid gland involved by the nodule, permitting the pathologist to make a definitive diagnosis. If cancer is confirmed, the rest of the thyroid gland is removed. (This is known as a *total thyroidectomy*, discussed in Chapter 9.)

These days, there is no need to use thyroid hormone (levothyroxine) in slightly higher than normal amounts to keep the TSH low to suppress these thyroid nodules. This practice was originally intended to discriminate between benign nodules (which were expected to shrink with this treatment) and potentially malignant nodules (which would continue to grow). Unfortunately, a large number of studies over the years have clearly shown that benign nodules will spontaneously shrink or grow regardless of whether thyroid hormone is given. For this reason, the treatment plan should be based upon the results of the biopsy, not upon a plan of thyroid hormone suppression therapy.

The Malignant Thyroid Nodule

It's extremely rare for a skilled cytologist to interpret a thyroid nodule FNA biopsy as cancer unless a cancer is truly present. The types of thyroid cancer that could be seen include papillary cancer, anaplastic thyroid cancer, or medullary thyroid cancer (see Chapter 9). Follicular cancers are usually seen as follicular neoplasia (discussed in the next section). If the nodule is more than 1.0 centimeter (0.4 inch) in diameter, the surgeon will perform a total thyroidectomy (see Chapter 9). If the nodule is smaller, then the surgeon will remove half of the thyroid gland, pending the results of the final pathology exam. If the cancer is found to be anything larger or more extensive than a spot of papillary cancer (called a *single focus*) that is 1.0 centimeter (0.4 inch), or any other type of thyroid cancer, then the surgeon will remove the rest of the gland during a second surgery.

Please note that you must never permit a surgeon to perform only a nodulectomy (surgical removal of the thyroid nodule without removing the complete half of the gland with the nodule). This would be considered substandard surgical care. Treating thyroid cancer (see Chapter 9) requires that the entire thyroid gland be surgically removed before any additional treatment can be given. Additionally, many thyroid cancers are *multifocal*, meaning that many individual tumors are present at different places in the thyroid gland, but frequently the surgeon cannot see this solely based on the obviously visible, or *gross*, physical appearance of the thyroid gland. Also, it's always safest for a surgeon to operate on a "virgin" side of the neck so that scarring from previous surgery has not obscured key landmarks inside the neck that help the surgeon to avoid complications. By performing a total thyroid lobectomy (removal of a complete side of the thyroid) instead of a nodulectomy, the surgeon avoids the need to return to the previous operative site in subsequent surgery.

The Indeterminate or Suspicious Thyroid Nodule

In the case of an indeterminate or suspicious thyroid nodule, the cytologist can't find enough proof to suggest a thyroid cancer, yet the nodule does not have the characteristics that could prove it is a benign nodule either. Ultimately, at least one-fifth of such nodules are proved to be thyroid cancer when a pathologist evaluates the thyroid gland after it's surgically removed. When a nodule is defined as suspicious or indeterminate, no known test, short of surgery, will answer the "is it cancer?" question. Thyroid scans, blood tests, and x-rays cannot provide any additional answers. For this reason, the most appropriate approach to a nodule with this classification is to have a surgeon remove the half of the gland containing the nodule. If the surgeon finds definitive evidence of cancer (lymph nodes with tumor, obvious signs of grossly invasive tumor) then it's appropriate to remove the entire thyroid gland at this time. Otherwise, if the pathologist finds that the indeterminate nodule is actually a thyroid cancer after later review of the pathology slides, a second surgery is needed to remove the rest of the thyroid gland.

If the surgery reveals that the nodule is benign, then there is no need for further thyroid surgery and you can be assured that all pertinent questions have been answered and issues addressed. Even though the remaining half of the thyroid gland is usually capable of making enough thyroid hormone to maintain normal levels, it seems that the remaining half of the gland sometimes enlarges. To prevent this, I (Ken) often advise people to take thyroid hormone (levothyroxine) in a dose sufficient to keep the TSH level in the lower portion of the normal range.

Some of the thyroid nodules that are classified as indeterminate or suspicious fall into a category of *follicular neoplasia*. These nodules could be either benign follicular adenomas or follicular thyroid cancers. The only way for a doctor to distinguish the benign adenoma from the cancer is by removing the half of the thyroid gland containing the nodule and having it analyzed very carefully by a pathologist. As mentioned in Chapter 2, a doctor can't always rely on the pathology report that distinguishes the benign from malignant follicular neoplasm. It requires a compulsive and painstaking evaluation of multiple microscopic slides to tell these conditions apart. For this reason, it's usually a good practice to request a second opinion from an outside expert thyroid pathologist, particularly when a benign follicular adenoma is diagnosed.

The Thyroid Cyst

Thyroid cysts present a special challenge for your physician. As in the case of solid thyroid nodules, you don't need to worry about small cysts of 1.0 centimeter (0.4 inch) or less in diameter. When the cyst is larger than this, you'll need to have it evaluated properly for two reasons. First, it might contain a thyroid cancer growing from the wall of the cyst or from the solid portions of a complex nodule. Second, the cyst might grow quite large and cause pain or discomfort, sometimes enlarging rapidly. For this reason, the FNA biopsy is performed *after* placing a thin needle into the cyst and sucking out the cyst fluid with a syringe. The cyst fluid might be a straw-colored liquid or chocolate brown in color. It can be watery and thin or thick with blood. Sometimes its color appears greenish. Once the cyst is completely drained, an FNA biopsy is performed on the cyst's walls or solid components. This biopsy is evaluated using the method discussed earlier in this chapter.

After the cyst is drained of fluid, it might seem to disappear completely. More often, the fluid gradually accumulates back into the cyst, sometimes making the cyst even larger than before. I (Ken) often drain the cyst again; however, should it again accumulate fluid, a procedure called *cyst sclerosis* might be done. This is a technique in which a mildly irritating liquid is injected into the cyst, intending to make the inside of the cyst walls sticky so that they adhere to each other, eliminating the cyst space. Alternatively, a surgeon may remove that half of the gland (a thyroid lobectomy), although this is usually done if there is a complex cyst that contains a relatively large solid portion.

Hot Nodules

Following the assessment plan described in the beginning of this chapter, this section deals with the hot nodule. This means that your TSH is suppressed (under 0.2) and you have a nodule in your thyroid gland. In addition, you have had a radioactive iodine thyroid scan (using I-131 or I-123) or a radioactive technetium thyroid scan. This scan should reveal that the nodule that is felt in the gland directly corresponds to a "hot" focus of radioactive tracer concentration seen in the thyroid scan. Ideally, the rest of the thyroid gland is suppressed, meaning that it doesn't light up very well on the scan. This is because the hot nodule is a portion of the thyroid gland that is independent (autonomous) from needing the pituitary's TSH to turn it on. As the nodule grows larger and larger, it produces thyroid hormone in larger and larger amounts until it produces so much thyroid hormone that the pituitary senses the toxic levels and shuts off its TSH production. Thus, the nodule is called an *autonomous toxic nodule (ATN)*. Without TSH, the remaining normal portions of the thyroid gland "sleep" and don't suck up the radioactive iodine or technetium on the thyroid scan.

It's useful to note common mistakes nuclear medicine physicians make when interpreting thyroid scans. First, you *cannot* have an ATN, by definition, unless the TSH level is lower than 0.2. Sometimes, particularly if the thyroid gland has Hashimoto's thyroiditis, there are normal areas of the gland between areas of scarring, making it look like there are hot nodules. In this case, the "hot nodules" seen on the scan do not correspond to any nodule that can be felt on examination, and the TSH is not suppressed. Such a scan should not cause your doctor to avoid doing the proper evaluation with an FNA biopsy of your nodule.

What Causes Autonomous Toxic Nodules (ATNs)?

As discussed in Chapter 1, each thyroid cell (called a *follicular cell*) has specialized proteins in its cell membrane ("skin") that are receptors for TSH. When TSH is released by the pituitary gland because thyroid hormone levels are too low, it travels around in the bloodstream until it finds these TSH receptors in the thyroid follicular cell membrane and sticks there. When TSH is bound to the TSH receptor, the receptor is activated. The activated TSH receptor turns on the thyroid follicular cell, compelling it to suck up iodine, make thyroid hormone, make thyroglobulin, and grow (divide into daughter cells, making the gland larger).

Sometimes, a thyroid follicular cell has a change in its gene for its TSH receptor. This mutation in the TSH receptor gene causes the TSH receptor to become permanently turned on, even when there is no TSH bound to it. This particular thyroid follicular cell has an advantage over its neighboring normal thyroid follicular cells. Because it's always turned on, it makes more thyroid hormone and grows (by dividing into two new cells) faster than its neighbors. Over time, a nodule of these cells, with the same mutated TSH receptors, grows in the thyroid gland. As it becomes larger, this nodule makes more and more thyroid hormone until you become sufficiently thyrotoxic to suppress your pituitary's TSH production. This can make you feel thyrotoxic with many of the symptoms described in Chapter 4. This nodule is an ATN (autonomous toxic nodule).

How Do We Treat ATNs?

In verifying that your TSH level is suppressed and the nodule in your thyroid corresponds exactly to the position of a hot nodule seen on the thyroid scan, the doctor can diagnose an ATN. Sometimes few or no symptoms of thyrotoxicosis are present, and the nodule is very tiny. In this situation, beta-blockers (see Chapter 11) can give you some time before you get definitive treatment. Otherwise, there are two appropriate choices of definitive therapy: radioactive iodine or thyroid surgery. It is not a good idea to use antithyroid drugs, such as propylthiouracil (PTU) or methimazole (Tapazole), because these nodules will continue to grow and do not have remissions (spontaneous cures, such as seen in Graves' disease, discussed in Chapter 6).

Radioactive iodine (RAI) treatment, which will be discussed thoroughly in Chapter 12, can be used to treat ATNs. In many respects, RAI can work as "surgery without a knife," selectively destroying the "hot" ATN without much effect on the normal suppressed thyroid gland surrounding the ATN. The dosages of RAI that are needed are usually a little higher than used in Graves' disease, but much lower than used to treat thyroid cancer. Because the surrounding normal thyroid gland is "sleeping," due to lack of TSH, the radioactive iodine (I-131) is selectively taken up by the ATN. If sufficient radioactive iodine is given, the usual result is that the thyroid hormone levels in the blood gradually decline after three to six weeks and the TSH starts to rise. The TSH may even rise slightly above the normal range since it may take a few weeks for the remaining normal thyroid gland to "wake up." Eventually, you are likely to end up with a significantly smaller remnant of the nodule, no longer producing thyroid hormone, within a normally functioning thyroid gland. Rarely, the radioactive iodine may cause the entire gland to stop working, or unmask a dysfunctional thyroid gland, necessitating thyroid hormone replacement medication thereafter.

If the ATN is very large, 5 centimeters (2 inches) or more in diameter, you are pregnant, radioactive iodine treatment has not worked sufficiently, or you are reluctant to use radioactive iodine, it's reasonable to have a skilled surgeon remove the ATN. Again, as for other types of thyroid surgery, it is preferable to remove the entire thyroid lobe rather than just the part of the lobe containing the ATN. In this case, thyrotoxicosis would clear up faster, usually within a week or two. Again, there may be a brief period of hypothyroidism as the pituitary gland "wakes up" to make TSH and the remaining thyroid gland "wakes up" to respond to TSH. As in thyroid surgery of other types of benign nodules, it may be reasonable to take thyroid hormone medication indefinitely after surgery to decrease the chance that the remaining half of the thyroid gland increases in size.

Some physicians, particularly thyroid experts in Italy, have used an injection technique to treat ATNs. First, they are very careful to make the proper diagnosis to ensure that the thyroid nodule is truly an ATN. Next, they carefully inject alcohol directly into the center of the nodule in an effort to destroy the nodule. Even when done properly, there is often some discomfort in your neck and sometimes the injection needs to be repeated. Although the results reported from the physicians who devised this technique suggest this is a reasonable treatment choice, it certainly requires a great deal of expertise to perform. For that reason, you should make sure that your physician has had a lot of experience doing this particular treatment and a good "track record" before you choose the procedure.

Radiation Exposure to the Neck During Childhood

In the 1940s and 1950s, many conditions were treated with external beam radiation therapy (XRT) in the belief that it was therapeutic. For example, some physicians believed that sudden infant death syndrome (SIDS) could be caused by a baby's thymus gland (located in the mid-upper chest) pushing on the airway (clearly a false idea in the light of modern knowledge). They gave x-ray therapy (XRT) to babies to shrink their thymus glands. Other physicians felt that bad acne lesions or recurrent tonsil infections would be helped by XRT. Some immigrant children were given XRT to their scalp to rid them of fungus. There are clearly therapeutic uses of XRT; we use it today to treat Hodgkin's disease and other childhood cancers. But all of these early treatments resulted in exposing the thyroid glands to radiation. We now know that this predisposed the children to the development of thyroid cancers as adults, although the first medical report suggesting this association dated as early as 1950. The risk for development of thyroid cancer seems to be greatest when the child is younger, with the greatest risk in children under five years of age. Even older children are at risk, although this diminishes considerably when the person exposed is older than eighteen. This risk is not evident with the lower exposures seen from diagnostic x-ray tests, such as chest x-rays, simple CAT scans, dental films, or evaluating for broken bones.

Besides XRT, nuclear fallout usually contains radioactive iodine isotopes that carry radiation directly to the thyroid gland if they enter the body. Recent reports from the National Cancer Institute in the United States suggest that thousands of people have been placed at risk for developing thyroid cancer from their exposure to radioactive fallout from aboveground atomic testing in the 1950s and 1960s. The risk is particularly significant in people exposed to fallout from testing in the Marshall Islands during 1954. The association of nuclear fallout with thyroid cancer was first recognized in the survivors of the atomic bombs dropped on Hiroshima and Nagasaki in World War II.

Unfortunately, in times of peace, there has been exposure through accidents at nuclear power plants. The most dramatic example was the explosion of the Chernobyl reactor in Belarus in 1986. A precipitous rise in thyroid cancer among children exposed to radioactive fallout (some were exposed while in their mother's womb) removed any shred of doubt concerning this risk. Even more notable was the *absence* of thyroid cancer in nearby Polish children who had been given potassium iodide pills to keep them from absorbing the radioactive iodine fallout that fell upon them in an otherwise similar exposure.

Were You Exposed to Radiation?

Knowing whether you have been exposed to radiation as a child should be your first concern. Clearly, you won't know about exposure as an infant unless you ask your parents or have access to all of your medical records. Although inappropriate uses of XRT should have ended by the 1960s, I know of several cases in which patients were given such treatment as recently as 1978.

Additionally, there are maps documenting the estimated sites and dates of radioactive fallout exposure in the United States during the 1950s. However, other factors are also relevant. For example, the only significant exposures in many regions are thought to have occurred in people drinking milk from their own dairy cows eating contaminated grass. Milk from local dairies in the same region was not likely to be contaminated because the extra time it took for this milk to be collected, processed, packaged, and sold resulted in loss of most of the short-lived radioactive iodine isotopes.

It is interesting to note that exposure to radioactive iodine, given as a diagnostic dose to perform a thyroid scan, or given as a larger dose to treat Graves' disease or an ATN, does *not* put you at risk for the development of thyroid cancer. It's been observed (and theorized) that the radiation dose to the thyroid from a radioactive iodine scan is too low to cause this risk; conversely, in the case of radioactive iodine treatment doses, they are too high to cause the risk because they are high enough to kill thyroid cells outright. The perceived and actual risks from radioactive iodine are often very different. This is discussed in more detail in Chapter 12.

If you find that your thyroid gland was exposed to radiation at any time, particularly when you were a child, it's crucial to perform a thyroid self-examination (see Chapter 1) on a regular basis—just as women should be doing breast self-exam or men should be doing testicular self-exam. If your thyroid gland is difficult to feel, request a baseline thyroid ultrasound examination. As we discussed earlier, the only difficulty with this is that the ultrasound frequently finds tiny nodules that are too small to be of significance, yet may arouse some anxiety (see Chapter 2). Nonetheless, thyroid nodules, which usually have a 10 percent chance of being a thyroid cancer, have a threefold higher risk of being cancerous if you have a history of radiation exposure. Should any nodule exceeding 1.0 centimeter (0.4 inch) in diameter be discovered by any technique, an FNA biopsy should be performed. If the nodule is suspicious, for example, a nodule that keeps growing in spite of benign or indeterminate biopsy results, you should seek out a surgeon to remove the half of the thyroid with the nodule so it can be analyzed more thoroughly.

Some physicians advise people with a history of radiation exposure to take thyroid hormone medication in high enough amounts to suppress the TSH levels. This does not reduce the risk of thyroid cancer; however, it seems to reduce the number of nodules that develop. This may provide some advantage in reducing the number of times that nodules need to be assessed, but it is not clear whether it's useful for everyone in this situation. Certainly, it should be considered as a treatment if benign nodules are found.

Preventing Thyroid Exposure from Radioactive Fallout

By using potassium iodide, we can prevent thyroid cancer from radioactive iodine fallout. Potassium iodide blocks radioactive iodine from being absorbed by the thyroid gland by providing so much iodine that it overwhelms the ability of the gland to take up radioactive iodine. This is the only specific way to protect against thyroid cancer triggered by radioactive iodine fallout; potassium iodide has no protective effect against any other kind of radiation. Potassium iodide is available through pharmacies. In the event that there is an alert about a potential nuclear attack (such as a terrorist threat), ask your doctor about the best way to obtain potassium iodide.

To be effective, potassium iodide must be dispensed just prior to being exposed to radioactive iodine, and then continued for the duration of the exposure. This is pretty difficult to do unless an accident or incident is predicted in advance, or the air path of a specific accident is tracked and therefore anticipated. And potassium iodide is not designed as a long-term therapy because of side effects that occur with prolonged use. Complications include serious allergic reactions, skin rashes, and thyroid disorders (aggravating Hashimoto's thyroiditis or worsening hyperthyroidism). In pregnant women, long-term use of potassium iodide can also cause the fetus to develop a goiter; however, the short-term use would protect the fetus against radioactive iodine isotopes.

For the past forty years, various government agencies around the world have monitored the amount of radioactive iodine in the air. And for many years, they've detected low levels of radioactive iodine fallout as a result of nuclear testing or reactor problems. Emergency plans for potassium iodide distribution in European countries require pills or tablets to be predistributed to households within three miles of nuclear plants, and possibly to households within six miles. Tablets also are stored at central locations, such as schools, factories, and town halls for quick distribution within 15.5 miles of plants. Since 1982, households within about 9 miles of four nuclear plants have received tablets. Every five years, regional authorities repeat the distribution, to approximately fifty thousand households, through the mail.

Distribution of potassium iodide in the United States remains controversial, but is being revisited in light of 9/11. To date, the Three Mile Island accident was the most serious nuclear reactor accident to have occurred in North America. Twenty-five years later, state and federal officials are still debating potassium iodide's costs and benefits. In view of the proven benefit demonstrated by potassium iodide use in Poland during the Chernobyl accident, it is surprising the United States has not yet enacted the same level of protection.

9 Thyroid Cancer

As we discussed in the previous chapter, thyroid cancer is typically discovered in a thyroid nodule. In some cases, however, it is found after a tumor is discovered somewhere else in the body, such as in the lungs or in a bone, with the biopsy of this tumor eventually leading to the thyroid as the source of the cancer.

This chapter serves as a detailed introduction to thyroid cancer and its treatments. Chapters 2, 3, 10, and 12 are also critical to read if you have thyroid cancer, as these provide additional details about follow-up tests and scans, hypothyroidism, thyroid hormone treatment, and radioactive therapy for thyroid cancer. Appendix A lists additional patient resources on thyroid cancer.

Thyroid cancer is actually a general term referring to a group of different types of cancer with different treatments and outcomes. In general, there are two major types of thyroid cells that tend to turn into cancers: follicular thyroid cells (responsible for making thyroid hormone) and parafollicular thyroid cells (located near the thyroid follicles, these make calcitonin).

When you have thyroid cancer, you need to seek out the proper physician to provide your care because this is usually outside of the expertise or ability of a general internist or family physician. Most endocrinologists (hormone specialists) are likely to have received some training in the management of thyroid cancer, although not all of them specialize in this area. Although the field of oncology (the study of cancer) would seem to be appropriate, most oncologists receive little or no training in helping people with thyroid cancers. Sometimes nuclear medicine physicians, particularly if they are trained in both endocrinology and nuclear medicine, take care of people with these diseases; however, very few physicians have enough expertise and training to call themselves thyroid oncologists. Fortunately, most people with thyroid cancer can obtain reasonable care from an endocrinologist, although in the case of unusual problems or recalcitrant tumors, you should enlist the aid of a thyroid oncologist, even if you must travel significant distances for your care.

There has always been a wide diversity of approaches in the management of thyroid cancers. Although the majority of thyroid cancer patients live for many decades after their diagnosis, tumor recurrences and problems can be seen for years after the initial thyroid surgery. This makes it difficult for physicians to know the full effects of different treatment methods. Nonetheless, there is more agreement on treatment approaches between thyroid cancer specialists than between physicians with less experience in treating this disease.

Who Gets Thyroid Cancer?

Thyroid cancer still remains a rare cancer, accounting for just about 2 percent of all cancers in people of all ages and 4 percent of cancers in children. Nevertheless, thyroid cancer is now ranked as the fastest rising cancer in women, topping the rate of increase in lung and breast cancers. Women outnumber men in developing thyroid cancer by three to one. Put another way, women account for 75 percent of all new cases of thyroid cancer, and 58 percent of all deaths from thyroid cancer occur in women. In 2004 in the United States, an estimated 5,900 men developed thyroid cancer, compared to 17,700 women; around 620 deaths from thyroid cancer occurred in men, and 850 deaths occurred in women. This statistical imbalance may have something to do with the fact that thyroid cancers are seen much more frequently in women but seem to be more lethal in men. It is currently not known why these sex differences are seen.

What Causes Thyroid Cancer?

As discussed in the previous chapter, it is well known that radiation exposure to the thyroid gland, particularly a young child's thyroid gland, predisposes the child to develop thyroid cancer in later years. Papillary thyroid cancer is the most common type. (Types of thyroid cancer will be explored later in this chapter.) Research is revealing that the chromosomes of thyroid cells are organized in a particular structural pattern in the nucleus (or center) of thyroid follicular cells. When radiation inside the cell strikes the nucleus, it causes particular breaks and rearrangements in the chromosomes that result in a greater chance that the cells will eventually become cancers. Unfortunately, known exposures to radiation seem to account for only a small portion of the thyroid cancers seen every year.

The Genetic Link

There is good evidence that some papillary and follicular thyroid cancers run in families, although such thyroid cancers are still exceedingly rare among the far larger number of non-inherited papillary thyroid cancers. Since there is not yet enough knowledge about the specific genes responsible for the few inherited cases, there is not yet a role for genetic testing. In addition, there are a few unusual genetic syndromes, such as Gardner's syndrome, Carney's complex, and Alagille syndrome, that seem to carry a greater risk of thyroid cancers.

Medullary thyroid cancer is a type of cancer of the thyroid parafollicular cell. Twenty percent of people with this cancer have inherited it from their mother or father. It's been well established that there is a special portion of the tenth chromosome, the RET proto-oncogene, that carries mutations causing this type of thyroid cancer. Both males and females inherit this mutation equally from either parent. Nearly everyone with the mutated gene is virtually guaranteed to get this cancer at some time in their life. In genetic-speak, this is known as an *autosomal dominant disorder* (meaning it takes only one parent with this mutation to give you the cancer) with 100 percent penetrance (meaning you are 100 percent likely to get the disease if you have this mutated gene).

Families with the inherited form of medullary thyroid cancer have one of three different patterns of inherited disease. The first type, *multiple endocrine neoplasia type 2a (MEN2a)*, is medullary thyroid cancer that is inherited along with a tumor of the adrenal gland that makes adrenaline (*pheochromocytoma*) and a tumor of the parathyroid gland that results in high calcium levels (*hyperparathyroidism*). The second type, *multiple endocrine neoplasia (MEN2b)*, is medullary thyroid cancer that is inherited along with pheochromocytoma and unusual body features, such as elongated fingers and toes or bumps on the tongue. The third type is just inherited medullary thyroid cancer without the other associated problems.

If you have a medullary thyroid cancer, it is critical for your physician to send your blood sample to a genetics testing laboratory to see if you have the mutated gene associated with this cancer. If you do (meaning that you test positive for the gene), you need to have your family members tested for the same gene mutation. If other family members have this mutation, they could prevent getting the thyroid cancer by having their thyroid gland completely removed by a surgeon as soon as possible. This procedure is known as a *prophylactic* (preventive) *thyroidectomy*. Removing the thyroid gland is necessary because medullary thyroid cancer has no effective treatments once it has spread throughout your body. So a prophylactic thyroidectomy could stop this cancer before it starts, or remove it in an early stage, which could be lifesaving for those affected by this mutation.

For the majority of people with other types of thyroid cancer, there is no evidence of any particular pattern of inheritance, no evidence for previous exposure to cancer-causing radiation, and no known agents that are likely to cause this cancer. Considering the increasing rates of thyroid cancer, however, it seems likely that additional environmental factors, such as some type of pollution or chemical exposure, are responsible for some of these cases.

Types of Thyroid Cancers and Their Behavior

Thyroid cancer runs the gamut from the least aggressive tiny papillary thyroid cancer to the most aggressive type of tumors known in humans, anaplastic thyroid cancer. So the first order of business is to find out which type of thyroid cancer you have. There are three major groupings of thyroid cancers: *papillary*, *follicular*, and *anaplastic*. Within each major group are subtypes that have different clinical consequences.

In several studies over the last fifty years, pathologists (doctors who specialize in analyzing tissue) examined people who died from a variety of causes. They found that up to two-thirds of these deceased people had small, single microscopic papillary thyroid cancers that were less than 1.0 centimeter (0.4 inch) in size. These small cancers had not contributed to any health disorder; in other words, these people had all died from something else despite these tiny cancers. These small cancers are called *occult* (hidden) or *subclinical* thyroid carcinomas and do not warrant any therapy beyond the initial surgery that discovered them. An exception is when thyroid cancer is first found spread to some portion of the body outside the thyroid gland and removal of the thyroid gland reveals only a microscopic focus of tumor. In such cases, the cancer is *clinical* rather than occult disease.

Pathology and Prognosis

Determining the classification, or pathology, of your thyroid cancer provides important information regarding your treatment and your risk of later problems (known as the *prognosis*). Besides the pathology, other features provide information that affects prognosis. Your age at the time your thyroid cancer is discovered is an important feature. Children under seventeen seem to have mostly papillary thyroid cancers; however, their cancers tend to be more aggressive with higher rates of spread outside of the thyroid gland to distant sites, such as lung, bones, and liver. People over forty-five tend to have tumors that behave more aggressively and are less likely to respond to treatment. Age does not affect the prognosis for people first diagnosed between ages seventeen and forty-five.

Gender is another important feature. As mentioned earlier, thyroid cancer is three times more prevalent in women than in men. On the other hand, men appear to have a greater chance that their cancer will recur or kill them, not accounted for by other tumor features. No one yet has an explanation for this observation.

Size is a third crucial feature in prognosis. In all thyroid cancers, just as in any type of cancer, the larger the size of the thyroid tumors, the more aggressive the cancer and the more difficult the prognosis. As mentioned earlier, very small papillary cancers that present as a single tumor (as opposed to several tumors) measuring 1.0 centimeter (0.4 inch) or less in diameter behave so well (meaning that they do not tend to recur or spread) that nothing more is necessary than the surgical removal of the half of the thyroid gland containing the tumor. For all other types of thyroid cancer, tumors of any size are significant and warrant thorough treatment and follow-up. In addition to size, tumors that invade through the thyroid gland and into the surrounding body tissues are very likely to spread (metastasize) to distant regions of the body, such as the lungs, liver, bones, or brain. This is known as *metastatic* disease. Tumors that have spread to those regions are very aggressive and equally dangerous.

Differentiated Versus Undifferentiated

No matter how old you are, how big the tumor is, or how far it has spread, the defining and most critical feature is whether the cancer is differentiated or undifferentiated. Differentiated cancer cells retain the functional features of normal thyroid follicular cells. These features include functional TSH receptors so that TSH stimulates these cells to grow and lack of TSH causes them to "sleep," the ability to respond to TSH and produce iodine pump proteins that cause the cells to suck up iodine, the ability to produce thyroglobulin, and a generally slow rate of growth (in comparison to many other types of cancers). Thyroid cancer cells that are well or moderately differentiated tend to respond well to treatment with surgery and radioactive iodine.

Cancer cells that are either poorly differentiated or undifferentiated do not have the functional features of a normal thyroid follicular cell. This means that you cannot use radioactive iodine scans to find them or treat them. When these cancer cells spread beyond the neck to other parts of the body, they become difficult or impossible to treat. New treatments are needed for these poorly differentiated thyroid cancers, and this has been the main mission of my (Ken's) research laboratory and clinical research trials.

Papillary Carcinomas

Around 80 percent of thyroid cancers are papillary carcinomas. They originally earned this name by their fingerlike appearance (papillae) under the microscope, although modern diagnostic techniques rely more upon distinct features visible in the nucleus (or center) of these cancer cells. The usual type of papillary cancer constitutes around 85 percent of papillary cancers. The remaining papillary cancers can be divided into several subtypes with particular significance in regards to prognosis.

Around 5 percent of papillary cancers are tall cell variant cancers, named because of the shape of these cancer cells. (We believe Sara was diagnosed with this in 1983 at age twenty, before this type of thyroid cancer was described.) Tall cell cancers are frequently very large and invasive. They have a greater chance of spreading (metastasizing) to body parts outside of the neck than most other types of thyroid cancers. It also seems that this type of thyroid cancer has a greater chance to lose the ability to suck up iodine, making it unable to be detected with radioactive iodine scans or respond to treatment with I-131. I've (Ken) noticed that these types of thyroid cancer also have greater chances of further mutations to become anaplastic cancers (see later in this chapter).

Another 5 percent of papillary carcinomas are called *Hurthle cell variants*. These are papillary cancer cells with a reddish appearance when viewed under the microscope (slides have to be prepared using particular methods for the red to be visible). These cancers seem to have a greater chance of losing the ability to suck up radioiodine than typical papillary cancers, but do not seem as aggressive as tall cell variant cancers. Thyroid cancers that are called *Hurthle cell* thyroid cancers (as opposed to *Hurthle cell variants of papillary cancer*) are usually variants of follicular thyroid cancer (discussed later in this chapter).

Survival Rates

It is impossible to give statistics regarding the rates and lengths of survival from papillary thyroid cancer because papillary cancers range from tiny occult (meaning hidden) cancers, which have no effect on your life span if left untreated, to distantly metastatic tall cell variant papillary cancers that can dramatically affect your life span if left untreated. In general, most people with papillary thyroid cancer have a typical papillary cancer with excellent long-term survival, provided that reasonable medical care and follow-up evaluations are done. Survival statistics are altered by many variables, including your age at the time you were diagnosed, your sex, the size of your thyroid tumor, the extent of your tumor, whether you have metastases to other parts of your body, and whether your cancer cells are able to suck up radioactive iodine. These statistics are most useful to doctors trying to predict the outcome of large groups of people with similar cancer features. Essentially, you need to be aware of each of these prognostic features to ensure that you obtain optimal treatment and follow-up care by your health-care providers.

Follicular Thyroid Carcinomas

Follicular thyroid cancers comprise roughly 10 percent of all thyroid cancers. They are often difficult to distinguish from benign follicular adenomas (see Chapter 8), and we strongly suggest that a second pathologist verify the diagnosis by analyzing the thyroid gland removed during surgery. These types of thyroid cancer are more likely to spread via the bloodstream to distant sites, such as the lung, bones, and liver. They tend to be more aggressive than typical papillary thyroid cancers, but less aggressive than tall cell variant papillary cancers. Hurthle cell thyroid cancers (also known as *oxyphilic variant follicular cancers*), like their papillary counterparts, may lose the ability to take up radioactive iodine, making them difficult to treat if they recur after surgery.

A much less common type of follicular thyroid cancer is known as *insular thyroid cancer*. More than a decade ago, insular carcinomas were thought to be types of anaplastic thyroid cancer, suggesting that they could not be treated with radioactive iodine and were likely to be lethal. Since then, physicians have learned that insular carcinomas are a subtype of follicular thyroid cancer that sometimes takes up radioactive iodine. They are usually much more aggressive than follicular cancers and require special attention.

Additional Rare Types of Thyroid Cancer

Among the other types of thyroid cancers are medullary thyroid cancers, which we've discussed briefly already, anaplastic thyroid cancers, and thyroid lymphomas. There are extremely rare additional types that are beyond the scope of this chapter. (For more information on these rare types of cancer, consult the Appendix A at the back of this book.)

Medullary Thyroid Carcinomas

Medullary thyroid cancers are very different from papillary or follicular cancers and account for 5 to 10 percent of thyroid cancers. Papillary and follicular cancers arise from a cancerous transformation of the thyroid follicular cells that respond to TSH, suck up iodine, and make thyroglobulin. Medullary thyroid cancers arise from a cancerous transformation of the thyroid *parafollicular* cells that do not share any of these functional features. Instead, both parafollicular cells and medullary cancer cells make a hormone, calcitonin, instead of thyroxine. Medullary cancer cells also make another protein called carcinoembryonic antigen (CEA). Calcitonin and CEA can be measured in the blood, serving as markers for the presence of persistent or recurrent medullary cancer after surgical removal of the primary tumor with the thyroid gland.

As discussed in the beginning of this chapter, 20 percent of medullary thyroid cancers arise because of a mutation in the RET proto-oncogene. Some of these are just medullary cancers while others are part of a combination of inherited tumors, MEN2a and MEN2b (see earlier in this chapter for detailed descriptions). Genetic screening of family members is the only way to find out whether they are at risk of developing inherited medullary thyroid cancer. As discussed earlier, family members who test positive for the mutation will develop the cancer, but prophylactic thyroidectomy can stop the cancer before it starts, or at least before it has spread outside the thyroid gland. This preventative surgery is done in children as young as three years of age. If your family is affected by the MEN-type medullary thyroid cancers, it is also important to do blood and urine tests for adrenaline and related hormones that are made by pheochromocytomas, which could put you at risk for severely elevated blood pressure and cardiovascular disease.

The main treatment for all types of medullary thyroid cancer is to have a surgeon perform as complete a removal of the thyroid gland and the lymph nodes in the neck as can be safely done. As discussed later in this chapter, this requires a specialized surgeon with particular training. No known effective chemotherapies can destroy metastatic medullary thyroid cancers. Radioactive iodine has no effect on this cancer since the cells involved do not suck up iodine. Fortunately, even when spread widely in the body, this cancer may be sufficiently slow-growing, with years passing before the tumor causes significant symptoms or death.

Anaplastic Thyroid Cancer

Thyroid cancer represents the best and worst of cancer types. Occult papillary thyroid cancers are considered among the "best" cancers to get because they are easy to treat and grow pretty slowly in a predictable pattern. The result is almost a 100 percent cure rate in these small "easy" cancers. Anaplastic thyroid cancer, however, is one of the worst types of cancer to get, as it is considered one of the most aggressive cancers in existence. The good news is that anaplastic thyroid cancer is very rare, with fewer than four hundred cases in the United States each year, representing roughly 1.6 percent of thyroid cancers. Current evidence suggests that it arises from a mutation in an existing papillary or follicular thyroid cancer. It is important to have the diagnosis of anaplastic thyroid cancer confirmed by a second pathologist because it requires a particularly aggressive treatment plan. Although the prognosis for this cancer is usually less than one year after it is discovered, appropriate treatments can extend life beyond this time.

Anaplastic thyroid cancer usually shows itself as a rapidly growing tumor in the thyroid gland. I (Ken) have seen some such tumors double in size every two days. Sometimes, after surgery for a papillary thyroid cancer, the pathologist finds that one of the lymph nodes in the neck that contains a papillary cancer metastasis has transformed into an anaplastic cancer. If this is found, despite the presence of the papillary cancer, the doctor will focus all of the therapy on the more aggressive anaplastic cancer. Although this is extremely rare, I (Ken) have several patients who have survived their anaplastic thyroid cancer and then have their treatments focused upon the papillary thyroid cancer that had been left alone until that point.

The basic principles of treating this cancer are outlined here. First, despite frequent surgical bias to the contrary, it is important to find a surgeon who will go the extra mile to remove as much of the thyroid gland and the cancer as possible because, despite possible spread of tumor outside of the neck, control of the tumor in the neck is critical to prolong health and survival. After the surgeon has done the best job possible, the radiation therapist should provide aggressive external radiation therapy to the neck, decreasing the chance that the tumor will block breathing, eating, or the blood supply to the head. All the while, CAT scans should be used to check for distant spread of this cancer to the lungs and bones, if it hasn't already spread.

Although there are no chemotherapy drugs that are definitely curative for this cancer, some drugs (particularly paclitaxel) can temporarily diminish the tumor and extend your health and survival. There are very few physicians with enough experience with this cancer to have a clear understanding how to proceed. Make sure that your doctor is motivated to ask questions of other physicians and research available treatment options. Treatment options for anaplastic thyroid cancer are limited enough to make any person with anaplastic thyroid cancer an appropriate candidate for reasonable experimental clinical trials.

Thyroid Lymphoma

Thyroid lymphoma accounts for less than 3 percent of thyroid cancers and shows itself as a rapidly enlarging nodule in the gland that may seem to involve half or more of the entire thyroid. This is almost always seen in elderly people. Instead of growing gradually over months, increases in size are seen every week or so. In fact, your physician might be worried that you have anaplastic thyroid cancer, which can also grow as fast. Nearly everyone with thyroid lymphoma has Hashimoto's thyroiditis (see Chapter 5), either preceding the discovery of the lymphoma or discovered at the same time. On the other hand, Hashimoto's thyroiditis is so common that having it does not make you at risk for getting thyroid lymphoma.

If your doctor thinks you have thyroid lymphoma, the first test you will take should be an FNA biopsy. Usually, the cytologist evaluating the slides will order a second FNA be done using a technique called *flow cytometry*. If you have this type of tumor and the FNA is used to diagnose it, the next step is to quickly begin chemotherapy (usually using a regimen called CHOP: cyclophosphamide, doxorubicin, vincristine, and prednisolone). Halfway through the chemotherapy schedule you should receive external beam radiotherapy (XRT) to your neck and then continue with the chemotherapy. This approach has been shown to have a very high cure rate without needing any surgery. Alternatively, sometimes the surgeon has already removed some or all of the thyroid gland and finds out that the tumor is a thyroid lymphoma. Unless the surgeon has completely removed all trace of this tumor (perhaps making the XRT unnecessary), the same treatment course already outlined should be followed. The chemotherapy is necessary because a thyroid lymphoma involves much more than just the thyroid gland and chemotherapy provides a systemic (complete body) treatment.

Treatment for Papillary and Follicular Thyroid Cancers

Many people, upon discovering that they have thyroid cancer, become very anxious and are quick to follow the first treatment plan presented to them. Some may be frightened of their diagnosis, avoiding physicians and procrastinating, preventing necessary care. Others may be distrustful of "establishment medicine" and might seek out alternative medicine that does not cure cancer, such as herbs, vitamins, or energy healing in place of curative therapies. It is most important is to seek out physicians within reach who have the greatest expertise in this disease. Chapter 21 will discuss how you can be a well-informed consumer and full participant in your medical care.

The majority of thyroid cancer patients will require treatment for differentiated papillary and follicular thyroid cancers. Appropriate treatment starts with as complete a thyroidectomy as can be accomplished, along with surgical removal of any metastatic tumor in the neck, taking care to avoid unnecessary complications. From six to eight weeks later, after an appropriate preparation, radioactive iodine scans will tell you and your doctor the extent of spread of your tumor. Radioactive iodine therapy is given to eliminate residual disease and the thyroid surgical remnant. Blood tests for thyroglobulin provide additional evidence for persistent disease, independent of the radioactive iodine scans. Tumors sometimes lose the ability to concentrate iodine, making sole reliance on radioactive iodine scans unwise. Additional tests, such as CT scans (without the use of iodinated contrast dyes that compromise the use of radioactive iodine) and PET scans have their place in the follow-up of people with thyroid cancers (all discussed in Chapter 2).

Follow-up of thyroid cancer is *lifelong* because disease recurrences may be seen ten, twenty, or even thirty years later. I (Ken) often tell my patients that I only know if they are effectively cured if they die of old age. Since I'm increasingly older than many of my new patients, I assure them that someday they will need to break in another thyroid cancer physician.

Many people with thyroid cancer obtain appropriate surgery and radioiodine treatment with long-term follow-up, never showing any evidence of recurrent tumor from thyroid cancer cells that persisted and later grew. On the other hand, some people have aggressive tumors that don't respond well to treatment or have recurrent disease that may threaten their life. I'm reminded of one eighteen-year-old patient treated by thyroid surgery in 1954 for a papillary thyroid cancer who was then apparently free of disease (according to her physician) because she had no evidence of tumor after twenty years of follow-up. At that point, her thyroid cancer care ended. Five years ago, she was found to have recurrent tumor that had invaded her spine, and three years later, despite aggressive treatment, she died from her thyroid cancer. Since there is no way to discern whether you will ever again have trouble from your thyroid cancer, until future discoveries create tests that are sensitive enough to prove you free of any cancer cells, it is best to continue to monitor your cancer status indefinitely.

Thyroid Surgery

One of the most important aspects of your treatment for thyroid cancer is your thyroid surgery. If the surgery is done properly, it places you in the best position to eliminate your disease and begin the lifelong process of follow-up monitoring for recurrent disease.

Minimal thyroid surgery for a nodule that is suspicious or indeterminate is a total removal of the thyroid lobe containing the nodule and removal of the central portion of the thyroid gland, called the isthmus. In medical-speak, this is called a *total ipsilateral lobectomy and isthmusectomy*. This type of surgery gives the pathologist enough thyroid tissue to examine to provide an accurate diagnosis of whether the nodule is a cancer. In addition, if the nodule turns out to be cancer, the rest of the thyroid must be removed, usually done in a second surgery (although the surgeon may have enough evidence to do the complete surgery the first time). If the nodule is a single papillary thyroid cancer that measures 1.0 centimeter (0.4 inch) or less and has no evidence of tumor spread outside of the thyroid gland, or if the nodule proves to be benign, then there is no reason to remove the remaining thyroid lobe.

If the FNA biopsy reveals that the nodule is a papillary cancer that exceeds 1.0 centimeter in size, or is any other type of thyroid cancer of *any* size, then the initial surgery should be a total or near-total removal of the thyroid gland (called a *total thyroidectomy* or *near-total thyroidectomy*). The adequacy of this surgery depends upon the skill of the surgeon. Nearly every surgeon leaves a small remnant of thyroid tissue behind, usually less than 2 grams, but larger amounts of residual thyroid tissue can compromise further care and may complicate later radioactive iodine treatments.

It is important for the surgeon to remove any obvious (gross) tumor that has spread (metastasized) to lymph nodes in the neck. The extent of this procedure (called a *neck dissection*) varies depending upon the type of thyroid cancer and the knowledge and skill of the surgeon. For example, if the cancer is a medullary thyroid cancer or a tumor that is known to be unlikely to take up radioactive iodine (such as an aggressive tall cell variant papillary cancer, an insular carcinoma, or an anaplastic cancer), then a painstaking neck dissection, sometimes removing more than fifty lymph nodes, is appropriate. On the other hand, bulky metastatic tumor deposits should always be removed, if possible, even if the tumor is a typical papillary cancer. In this case, I (Ken) generally prefer that the surgeon consider removing the lymph nodes in the central region of the neck and on the same side of the neck as the thyroid cancer because radioactive iodine is much less effective when pieces of tumor deposits are in the way. The node resection better eliminates this, or what we call "bulky" disease.

Picking a Thyroid Surgeon

Nearly every general surgeon and ENT (ear, nose, and throat) surgeon claims competence to perform thyroid surgery for thyroid cancer. Unfortunately, not every surgeon willing to perform this surgery has the specialized training and judgment, as well as sufficient regular experience, to be the best surgeon for the job. If you are fortunate enough to have access to a medical center known for providing care for thyroid cancer patients, there are likely to be one or more thyroid surgeons available to care for you. Some patients without this proximity spend some effort to seek out such surgeons, even if they need to travel. Otherwise, it is useful to ask certain questions of your surgeon to decide if you choose his or her care. Complication rates from this surgery are least with the most experienced surgeons. Generally, it is best to choose a surgeon who performs at least twenty thyroid cancer surgeries each year. If you are able to find an

---

Questions to Ask Your Thyroid Surgeon

1. How many thyroid cancer surgeries do you perform annually? (A good number would be more than thirty per year.)
2. Do you do total thyroidectomy or do you leave sections of the thyroid behind? (It's a bad sign if your surgeon leaves sections of the thyroid behind.)
3. How many patients do you have with hypoparathyroidism? (The answer should be "once in a while" not "many" or "most.")
4. How many patients have paralyzed vocal cords? (Again, this should be an uncommon occurrence, rather than "normal" or "usual.")

---

endocrinologist with experience in managing thyroid cancer care, you might also obtain advice as to an appropriate surgeon.

Risks and Complications from Thyroid Surgery

The major factors that determine whether you will have any significant problems from your surgery are the size and extent of your cancer (particularly if it is invading into the neck tissues or has spread to other parts of your body) and the skill and experience of your surgeon.

Hypoparathyroidism: Problems with Low Calcium Levels

Damage to the parathyroid glands is the most common risk of thyroid surgery. It is especially common when dealing with invasive or locally metastatic tumors. As discussed in Chapter 1, the parathyroid glands are four tiny nodules located near the thyroid gland that release parathyroid hormone (PTH). This hormone controls the calcium level in your body, telling the kidneys to keep calcium from going out in the urine and enhancing the activation of vitamin D to absorb more calcium from the intestines. If all four parathyroid glands are damaged, the loss of PTH (hypoparathyroidism) causes the kidneys to lose calcium in the urine and decreases the ability to absorb more calcium. The result is that calcium levels plummet. This causes numbness or tingling sensations around the lips, numbness or tingling of the hands or feet, muscle cramps, twitching, and sometimes seizures. If the parathyroid glands are merely bruised from the surgery, the low calcium (hypocalcemia) will be temporary, lasting from days to weeks. If the parathyroid glands have been accidentally removed or their blood supply disrupted during the surgery, the loss of PTH can be permanent. Although severe PTH disturbances could be detected by obtaining a calcium level, an *ionized calcium* level is the most sensitive test for this.

Treatment of hypoparathyroidism entails taking high doses of vitamin D, along with sufficient calcium pills to maintain the ionized calcium within the low end of the normal range. Vitamin D analogs (calcitriol, dihydrotachysterol, or vitamin D_2) cause the intestines to absorb sufficient amounts of the calcium pills to offset the calcium losses through the kidney. A reasonable analogy is to imagine the normal calcium level as the level of water in a bathtub. Since there is no PTH, the bathtub drain is wide open, as the kidneys permit unrestrained calcium losses through the urine. By taking vitamin D analogs and calcium tablets, the "faucet" is kept wide open as well, keeping the ionized calcium level normal, just as the running faucet would keep the water level normal in the bathtub in spite of the open drain.

Nerve Damage: Problems with Your Voice, Muscles, or Sensation

The nerves that supply the vocal cords, telling them to move appropriately during speech, are the *recurrent laryngeal nerves*. Sometimes they are very close to the thyroid gland and can get damaged during the surgery. At other times the cancer may directly invade these nerves. If only one nerve is damaged, it results in hoarseness that gradually may improve as your body adjusts to the loss. On the other hand, if both nerves are damaged, neither of the two vocal cords can move properly, preventing speech and interfering with proper breathing. This usually results in a *tracheotomy* (a hole made in your windpipe below your Adam's apple to help you breathe). Although aggressive and invasive tumors might damage these nerves before the surgery is performed, they are most often damaged during the course of the surgery. The likelihood of this complication occurring is less than 1 percent with the most highly skilled and experienced surgeons, but much higher if the surgeon lacks such skill.

Other complications are sometimes unavoidable. For example, if extensive surgery is needed to remove cancer that has spread to the lymph nodes in the neck, then some nerves may get cut. This can leave parts of your neck and shoulder area numb, taking years for the nerves to grow back, if at all. Since these nerves grow slowly, some people must endure a few decades with this numbness. Very rarely, your shoulder muscles may become weak because the nerves that stimulate them have been cut. In addition, if a surgeon needs to remove thyroid cancer deposits that have spread (metastasized) to other parts of your body, such as your pelvis, spine, rib, liver, or brain, then each particular type of surgery has its own kinds of risks.

Radioactive Iodine Therapy

Although radioactive iodine therapy for thyroid cancer is discussed in Chapter 12, it's worth summarizing some key aspects here. The first time that you receive this treatment is called the *ablation dose*. Its purpose is to destroy the remnant of the thyroid gland left by the surgeon, as well as any residual (remaining) thyroid cancer in the neck or elsewhere in the body. Radioactive iodine (I-131) is given, sipped in water or swallowed in a capsule; preparation for this therapy involves going off of your thyroid hormone and being on a low-iodine diet. (See the radioactive iodine scan preparation information in Chapter 2.) The ablation dose follows the thyroid surgery (after the thyroid is completely removed) by six to eight weeks, and the size of the radioactive iodine dose depends upon the extent of the tumor during the surgery and the results of a radioactive iodine scan, often done before the ablation dose. The smallest radioactive iodine dose for the ablation dose is 100 mCi (millicuries) or 3.7 GBq (billion Becquerels), and it can range up to 200 mCi if there is evidence of a great deal of residual cancer. Some physicians give I-131 doses smaller than 100 mCi; however, I (Ken) don't consider such doses to be sufficient. You may wish to show your doctor this chapter if you are concerned that you're not being treated with a high enough dose. You can consult the resource list in Appendix A for more information.

Different physicians have a variety of approaches to the dosing and timing of subsequent radioactive iodine scans. Whenever such scans show any evidence of thyroid cancer, it's customary to provide a radioactive iodine treatment, provided that the preparation is sufficient and it fits in with your physical condition and treatment plan. Chapter 12 contains much more detail and discussion regarding I-131 therapy.

Thyroid Hormone Suppression Therapy

Thyroid hormone treatment in the form of levothyroxine is absolutely necessary after the thyroid is removed. In people who have never had thyroid cancer but are merely hypothyroid, sufficient levothyroxine is given to make the TSH normal (0.5 to 3.0; see Chapter 2). People with thyroid cancer should keep their TSH levels less than 0.1. This is because TSH stimulates the growth of thyroid cancer cells. When you are preparing for radioactive iodine scans or therapies, or when you need to assess the level of thyroglobulin, you want to stop your levothyroxine to make the TSH greater than 30, stimulating thyroid cancer cells to suck up iodine and make thyroglobulin. On the other hand, it's necessary to keep the TSH suppressed (less than 0.1) at all other times, so that any thyroid cancer cells still in your body are not stimulated to grow and reproduce. Chapter 10 gives all of the details on thyroid hormone medication.

Levothyroxine is the only type of thyroid hormone able to keep the TSH suppressed around the clock. The average daily levothyroxine dose needed to suppress TSH is 2.0 micrograms per kilogram of body weight. For example, a person weighing 75 kilograms (165 pounds) would be expected to need a 150-microgram (0.15 milligram) dosage of levothyroxine to suppress TSH. There is such a wide variation from person to person that this average is useful only as a starting point for choosing a levothyroxine dose. The dose is gradually adjusted to appropriately suppress the TSH.

External Beam Radiotherapy (XRT)

When thyroid cancer is no longer able to take up radioactive iodine, it's necessary to use external beam radiotherapy to kill tumor cells that cannot be completely removed by the surgeon. Some thyroid cancers, particularly anaplastic cancer and thyroid lymphoma, require XRT as part of their standard treatment plan. On the other hand, should you have a differentiated thyroid cancer that is well able to suck up iodine, it is nearly always preferable to use radioactive iodine instead of XRT because you can more effectively deliver larger doses of radiation to the tumor with greater safety.

Sometimes, XRT is used to treat thyroid cancer metastases that no longer suck up radioactive iodine and have spread to bone. It is usually best to have a surgeon remove these tumor deposits if possible, before the XRT is given, to gain the maximal benefit. Generally, you can get the best therapy response if a surgeon cuts away obvious tumor, from any part of the body, before you receive XRT.

There are special forms of XRT for thyroid cancers spread to certain parts of the body. If thyroid cancer spreads to the brain, particularly if it is in a place that cannot be approached safely by a surgeon, you can receive *stereotactic radiosurgery* (one form is called the *gamma knife*). This technique focuses the radiation beams so that they avoid damaging delicate normal body tissues surrounding the tumor.

Diagnostic Evaluation: Long-Term Follow-Up

I follow a general pattern of thyroid cancer follow-up evaluation, modifying it to fit each patient's particular needs and disease features. After the thyroid surgery, removing the entire thyroid gland and all detectable tumor in the neck, the first radioactive iodine scan is usually done from six to eight weeks later. This timing is based upon the time that it takes for the TSH level to rise to greater than 30 after the thyroid gland is gone. I don't use recombinant human TSH (Thyrogen) at this point, as is explained in detail in Chapter 2, because it is not approved by the FDA for radioactive iodine treatments (for appropriate reasons). This first radioactive iodine whole body scan (WBS) provides information regarding whether and where the thyroid cancer is still present in the body and also if it takes up iodine (provided that another type of test can show that the tumor is still present). Provided that we're treating a differentiated thyroid cancer, it's hoped that the radioactive iodine ablation dose (see earlier discussion) eliminates this evidence of thyroid cancer.

The next radioactive iodine WBS is performed six months later. If no evidence of residual thyroid cancer is found, the next interval is one year, then two years, three years, four years, and finally five years between WBSs. I usually tell my patients that, at that point, they'll have such scans with me every five years thereafter, until one of us dies of old age or we discover a better way to follow up on this disease. Provided that there have been several preceding clean scans and no evidence of persistent thyroid cancer by any other means, it is reasonable to use Thyrogen for some of these WBSs.

Anytime that the WBS is found to show persistent thyroid cancer and additional radioactive iodine treatment is given, the interval between WBSs decreases back to six months. In addition to radioactive iodine scans, other diagnostic imaging tests are done, as described in Chapter 2. These include CT scans (performed without intravenous contrast dye because it contains nonradioactive iodine), MRI scans, ultrasounds, nuclear PET scans, and other tests. These are used to confirm the absence of tumor when the scans are clean, as well as to look for disease when there is evidence that the cancer no longer takes up radioactive iodine.

Monitoring Thyroglobulin Levels

Thyroglobulin measurements in the blood are very important tests for differentiated thyroid cancer. When you're taking thyroid hormone, suppressing the TSH level, thyroglobulin release from any residual thyroid cancer cells is also suppressed, meaning the thyroglobulin test might not reveal the presence of thyroid cancer if you're still taking your thyroid hormone.

Whenever you are made hypothyroid to prepare you for a radioactive iodine scan, besides stimulating any residual thyroid cancer cells to take up radioactive iodine, the cells are stimulated to make more thyroglobulin also. For this reason, the thyroglobulin blood test is most sensitive during this hypothyroid preparation. Thyrogen will do much the same, stimulating the release of thyroglobulin from any thyroid cancer cells.

It's important to remember that when differentiated thyroid cancer cells become undifferentiated, some features change and some don't. Usually, thyroid cancers lose the ability to suck up iodine long before they lose the ability to make thyroglobulin, meaning some people have thyroglobulin levels showing persistent thyroid cancer, despite the radioactive iodine scan being clean. Less common, but sometimes seen, are people with thyroid cancers that don't make thyroglobulin while still taking up radioactive iodine. Because over 20 percent of thyroid cancer patients have interfering antibodies against thyroglobulin, making the blood test measuring thyroglobulin nearly useless, this test is not definitive in such patients. This emphasizes the need to use a variety of tests to check for thyroid cancer and not to rely on only a single type of scan or a blood test, placing all your eggs in one basket.

10 Thyroid Hormone: The Inside Scoop

Thyroid hormone is the common thread to most thyroid problems. Most people with thyroid conditions end up taking thyroid hormone. People with hypothyroidism (see Chapter 3) require thyroid hormone. Those with thyrotoxicosis from hyperthyroidism (see Chapter 4), after surgery or radioactive iodine treatment (see Chapter 12), eventually need thyroid hormone because they eventually become hypothyroid. And thyroid cancer therapy (see Chapter 9) starts with surgical removal of the thyroid gland (which leaves the person without a thyroid gland and, therefore, hypothyroid), necessitating thyroid hormone suppression therapy. As explained in Chapter 9, suppression therapy means that thyroid cancer patients require higher doses of thyroid hormone to keep their TSH levels suppressed, which suppresses any remnant thyroid cancer cells as well. Except for short-lived transient hypothyroidism from thyroiditis (see Chapter 5), treatment with thyroid hormone is lifelong.

Clinical experience and medical research tells us that the best form of thyroid hormone therapy is a pure preparation of levothyroxine sodium, chemically synthesized, purified, and mixed with inert ingredients to make it into a tablet. This chapter discusses all aspects of thyroid hormone therapy, including the history of this treatment, the types of thyroid hormone preparations available and the reasons for their use, and, finally, all the useful information you need while on this therapy.

How It All Started

Until the end of the nineteenth century, the medical conditions identified as cachexia strumipriva, myxedema, and cretinism (all types of hypothyroidism) were not known to have anything to do with the thyroid gland. Imagine the uproar caused by physician Sir Felix Semon in November 1883, when he announced to the Clinical Society of London that these conditions were all caused by a loss of function of the thyroid gland. The proof came in 1891 when George Redmayne Murray first reported that needle injections of an extract of sheep's thyroid were able to successfully treat myxedema in a forty-six-year-old woman who later lived an additional twenty-eight years. This was such fantastic news to physicians of that time that the treatment took off like wildfire. One year later, physicians Hector Mackenzie and Edward Lawrence Fox independently reported effective treatment of this condition using oral doses of the sheep thyroid extract.

As a result, desiccated (dried) thyroid extract was used for many decades. Even though synthetic levothyroxine (called *L-T4* by physicians, and *T4* in this book) was made as early as 1927, it was so costly to produce that it was rarely used until the 1960s. By then, both T4 and triiodothyronine (called *L-T3* by physicians, and *T3* in this book) were readily available, both as separate tablet preparations and as mixtures. Considering that both T4 and T3 are produced by the thyroid gland, it seemed logical to provide both thyroid hormones together in a tablet. This concept lost favor in the 1970s when researchers learned that most of the body's T3 was produced in the body's tissues by converting T4 to T3. Over the past three decades, T4 therapy has emerged as the state of the art.

T4: The Details

T4, generically known as levothyroxine, can provide all of the thyroid hormone needs for your health and happiness. Life with too little T4 is uncomfortable at best, afflicting all parts of the body (see Chapter 3), while life without any T4 is impossible for more than a few months. This section discusses all the intimate details of this critical hormone pill, so you can take full advantage of its benefits.

The T4 Pill: The Right Stuff

Levothyroxine pills (T4) are the second most frequently prescribed medication in North America. Taking T4 is not as simple as taking aspirin, nor is it as complex as chemotherapy. The following information will ensure that you are getting the most out of your T4 treatment. Unfortunately, you can't assume that the pills provided by the pharmacist best meet your needs unless you understand these details.

Which One to Take: Name Brands Versus Generics

A generic drug is a pill made to contain the same chemical form of the medication as a branded pill. Ideally, it should be identical to the name-brand version. With some types of medicine, it is close enough so that the generic form can be used just as well, which usually translates into less expense and is sometimes preferred by health insurance plans. The essential differences between some name-brand medications and their respective generic forms have to do with the quality control of the manufacturer, as well as the way that the tablet is put together (containing filler substances and dyes). These standards determine whether you end up with the proper amount of T4 in your blood and whether you can count on the same accurate dose the next time you go to the pharmacy and purchase a new batch of medication.

Thyroid hormone has a narrow *therapeutic index*. This means that very small differences in the amount of active T4 taken will result in significant differences in how it works in your body. This is very easy to measure for T4, because a TSH level is so sensitive in revealing the effect of T4 in your body (see Chapter 2). Such TSH measurements may reveal differences between various brands of the same amount of T4. For this reason, it is usually best to choose a reputable brand of T4 and, once adjusted to the correct dosage, stick with the same brand for each refill of your prescription. Although the government organizations entrusted with monitoring our pharmaceutical industry—the Food and Drug Administration (FDA) in the United States and Health Canada in Canada—have required tests to show that the same dosages of different T4 brands are pharmacologically equivalent, they do not use TSH levels to show that different brands cause the same *biologically* equivalent response in people. These potential differences between various T4 brands are usually not very important for people who are taking the pills because they are hypothyroid. On the other hand, thyroid cancer patients (see Chapter 9) must keep their TSH level tightly controlled and suppressed to a level of 0.1 or less, without having any symptoms of thyrotoxicosis. Very small differences in T4 pills can easily shift them from being "just right" to being too much or too little.

The Wise T4 Shopper

Some rulings by the FDA have allowed pharmacists to substitute different brands of T4 for the particular one that your physician requested (called *generic substitution*) without permission from the physician. Sometimes this translates into a cost savings to your insurance company. Sometimes this practice results in a greater profit margin for the pharmacy. Sometimes the co-payments on your insurance-subsidized prescription end up costing you more than the retail price if you chose not to use your insurance. Less frequently, the cost savings are passed on to you through lower prices.

Although many drugs are far more expensive than T4, chances are that you will be buying T4 for the rest of your life. I (Ken) sometimes joke with my patients that they'll be taking T4 forever, except that they are permitted to stop taking it when they die. In this respect, small differences in prescription prices add up to many dollars over the long haul. For example, in the United States, one particular brand of T4 has a retail price of around $45 for one hundred pills. One of my patients has an insurance plan that charges her a $20 co-payment per prescription but limits her to getting only thirty pills for a single month's supply. This means that one hundred pills cost her $66.67 using her insurance plan. That's $21.67 more than the wiser course of not using her insurance plan, for a savings of nearly $80 per year and thousands of dollars over her lifetime. In addition, use of the insurance plan compels her to go to the pharmacy each month, while paying the retail price permits her to get one hundred days of pills at a time. The financial concerns are different in Canada.

I (Ken) spent much of my childhood working in my dad's pharmacy, dusting shelves, filling inventory, waiting on customers, and ringing up sales. Later, on summer breaks from college, I worked for a pharmacy wholesaler in the warehouse, packing drug orders into crates. As a result, I know a lot about drugstores. I also know that the same drugs have very different retail prices in different pharmacies in the same community. It amazes me that some patients will travel miles between supermarkets, buying chicken for the best price at one store and milk for the best price at another store, yet never compare the prices of their prescription medications between pharmacies. This is of greatest value when you intend to purchase your T4 with the best retail price, rather than using your insurance plan's co-payment. Some insurance plans provide greater cost savings when you send away for your T4 through their mail-order pharmacy, purchasing ninety-day supplies at a time. Although this is an attractive option, there are a few negative features. As discussed under "Storage and Heat Sensitivity," pills shipped by mail, particularly in the summer, are exposed to conditions that partially destroy their effectiveness. In addition, you may have little control over having the mail-order pharmacy substitute an unwanted T4 brand for the one you want.

For many people taking T4 to treat hypothyroidism, the differences between brands of T4 do not cause much change in their effect because differences in their TSH levels from, for example, 0.5 to 1.8, do not cause any perceptible change in the way they feel or their health. On the other hand, as mentioned already, people with thyroid cancer taking T4 need to have the amounts closely regulated. Good research studies show that changes in the level of TSH, for example, from 0.03 to 0.4, increase the chances that there will be a recurrence or spread of a thyroid cancer years later. This knife-edge of control is very difficult to achieve if the pharmacist substitutes different brands of T4 on each monthly refill, based on the latest preferences of his store manager or the insurance plan. I (Ken) recommend that any change in T4 brand be checked with blood tests, measuring a free T4 level and a TSH level after at least six weeks of continuous treatment with the new T4 brand. The cost of these blood tests is usually higher than the total cost of the T4 prescription. People with thyroid cancer can choose which brand of T4 they want, but they need to be vigilant about not letting pharmacists make changes in their selected T4 brand.

Pill Sizes: Strengths of T4

Levothyroxine (T4) pills now come in a wide range of strengths. All of them, within the same brand, are the same physical size and shape, but there is considerable difference in the amount of T4 contained in each strength of pill. They range from 25 micrograms (0.025 milligrams) to 300 micrograms (0.3 milligrams). Because of the wide variety of pill strengths, your doctor should not need you to cut pills in half or take different size pills on different days. Sometimes, I need to put my patients on dosages that don't come in the available pill strengths, and I will combine pills to get the right dosages, such as 162 micrograms (112 micrograms + 50 micrograms), for example.

Although the pharmacist is supposed to write the strength (or dosage) of the pill on the bottle, it's best to know your pills from their appearance. Each strength usually has a characteristic color and identification numbers written on each tablet. This is particularly important, considering the tens of thousands of pharmacist errors made every year.

While the average dose of T4 for a hypothyroid person is 1.6 micrograms of T4 per kilogram of body weight per day, there is a wide variation. The best way to find out the proper dose for you is to take a reasonable dosage T4 tablet (near to the average amount), to be determined by your doctor, every day for at least six weeks, then have your physician check your TSH level. If the TSH is between 0.5 and 2.0, then you are on the correct T4 dose. If the TSH is higher, your dose needs to be increased and the TSH rechecked in six more weeks. If the TSH level is lower, then a slight reduction in the T4 dose would be appropriate and also verified with a TSH level after at least six weeks.

Thyroid cancer patients, who need to keep their TSH levels just around 0.1, average 2.0 micrograms T4 per kilogram body weight per day. Dose adjustments are made in the same way as already discussed.

Storage and Heat Sensitivity

Although this is not common knowledge to pharmacists or doctors, T4 is very sensitive to heat. A good rule of thumb is to use the "chocolate bar" rule. If the temperature is warm enough to soften a milk chocolate bar, then it will cause the T4 pill to go bad fairly quickly. Although the pill will look OK, it will not work, providing far less T4 to you than a fresh pill would. I've had patients who kept their T4 pills on a shelf above the stove, insisting that they were taking their T4 pills, yet ending up severely hypothyroid with TSH levels greater than 50. I've seen some people leave their pills on the seat of their car, parked for a few hours in a Kentucky July afternoon, then find their tablets providing inadequate T4 levels. Many women carry their pill bottle in their purse, yet wouldn't keep a chocolate bar there, knowing it would melt. Some people, living without air-conditioning in hot climates, need to keep their pills in the refrigerator. This problem can also occur in the drugstore. Some pharmacy chains have been known to transport their inventory in unrefrigerated trucks during summer, likely degrading their T4 stock. Additionally, in the summer, postal workers may travel in open delivery vans and deliver the packages to mailboxes that sit in hot sunlight. I've seen TSH levels rise in the summer and fall in the winter, in step with the outdoor temperatures.

Even with optimal storage conditions, T4 pills lose 5 percent of their potency each year. Consider asking your pharmacist to check the expiration date on the stock bottle in the pharmacy. You don't want pills at the end of their shelf life. The retail prices of some T4 pills, purchased in one-hundred-pill quantities, are less than, or equal to, the insurance co-payments for some people. If this is so, it makes great sense to pay the retail price in order to get the full one hundred–pill package, freshly sealed at the factory, rather than a monthly dispersal from a large T4 container of uncertain age.

The Best Way to Take T4

T4 is best taken first thing in the morning on an empty stomach. Consistency is important. If you forget to take the morning dose, then take it as soon as you are able. Even if you miss the dose for the entire day, the next day you should take two doses to make it up. If you miss multiple days, even up to a week, it is far safer to take all of the missed pills at once than to miss the doses. Food in your stomach causes a slight decrease in the amount of T4 that is absorbed into your body. Even the slight delay between waking up and breakfast time is often sufficient to provide enough time for best absorption. Certain foods are more likely to interfere with T4 absorption; notable among them are liquid soy preparations.

Problems in Taking T4: Compliance

Remembering to take a pill every day, and/or taking it correctly, is known as *compliance* in pharmacy-speak. Some people take their daily T4 medication like clockwork; but most people (including Sara) are a bit forgetful. A useful device is a day-of-week pill container. These can be filled up once a week and used to remind you to take your pill. Forgetfulness in regularly taking T4 seems to be the most common reason for people to become hypothyroid while taking the same T4 dosages that were previously sufficient to make their TSH levels normal.

A small number of people with psychological problems seem to purposely miss taking their T4 pill, somehow gaining some satisfaction by being sick, even if self-induced. If this happens, counseling may be helpful. In severe cases, psychiatric help is needed.

Children are a special case in this regard. One thirteen-year-old girl, with papillary thyroid cancer spread throughout her lungs, wakes up each morning with her T4 and other medications placed in a little dish by her mother, ready for her to take. On a routine clinic visit, I was horrified to see that her TSH level was 85. It turned out that she had been throwing away her medication as a manifestation of adolescent rebellion. I routinely caution parents to directly observe their children taking their T4, sometimes even checking their mouths to make sure it was swallowed. A caretaker may also need these precautions for elderly people who may be debilitated and require strict supervision (see Chapter 17).

Problems in Taking T4: Other Drugs or Supplements That Interfere

T4 pills are completely absorbed within five hours from the time they are swallowed. Certainly, most of this takes place within the first three hours. Some medications will prevent the T4 pill from becoming completely absorbed. Iron, either as a supplemental medicine to treat iron deficiency or as part of a vitamin pill, will prevent T4 pills from being fully absorbed. If iron is needed, take the first daily dose at least four hours after the T4 is taken. If you take vitamin pills that contain iron, take them at bedtime so that the T4 can be taken in the morning without interference.

Some people need to take large daily doses of calcium. People with thyroid cancer who have suffered damage to their parathyroid glands frequently need this. If several calcium pills are taken at the same time as T4, then there might be some interference in absorption of the T4. Usually, as long as the T4 is taken immediately upon waking in the morning, the first calcium dose can be taken an hour or so later without much problem. (You can read more about calcium treatment in Chapter 11.)

A few medications are infamous for interfering with your T4 treatment. Sucralfate is used to coat your stomach to treat irritation or ulcers, and it can keep T4 from being absorbed into your body. Cholestyramine and colestipol (used to treat high cholesterol levels) and high doses of antacids (aluminum and magnesium hydroxides) also keep T4 from getting absorbed properly. Liquid soy preparations, often used as milk substitutes or for baby formulas, can also bind to T4 if taken in moderately large amounts within four hours of taking your T4 dose.

T3: Specific and Limited Uses

T3, also known as triiodothyronine, is the active form of thyroid hormone. It is available in pill form as liothyronine sodium (L-T3) or Cytomel (the only brand in North America). As discussed in Chapter 1, only 20 percent of the thyroid hormone made by the thyroid gland is T3, the rest being T4. Most of the T3 in each cell of the body comes from T4 that has been converted into T3 while inside that cell. This T3, inside of each cell, does essentially all of the things that thyroid hormone is known to do. When your thyroid hormone is provided as a T4 pill, each cell in your body is able to make its own T3, exercising some control over this by controlling the enzymes inside the cells that change T4 to T3. In some situations, you can substitute a pill providing T3 for your T4 pill. There are particular reasons why you would want to do this in special circumstances, but there are also reasons why you shouldn't do this.

When to Use T3

Most people who need to take T3 are those with papillary or follicular thyroid cancers. People with hypothyroidism may hear of using T3, either instead of, or in combination with, T4; however, as discussed later, this isn't advised. For people with thyroid cancer who are preparing for a withdrawal whole body scan or thyroglobulin test (see Chapters 2 and 9), a short course of T3 treatment is used when there is a need to make them hypothyroid (to raise the TSH to a level greater than 30) while minimizing hypothyroid symptoms. After they're through with being hypothyroid (having finished their radioactive iodine scan or therapy or after measuring the thyroglobulin level), another short course of T3 treatment can be used to restore their thyroid hormone levels faster, relieving hypothyroid symptoms and allowing these people to go back to work and drive sooner.

All drugs and hormones have limited times that they last inside the body. If you have been taking T4, for example, each day for several months, there will be a steady (baseline) level of this hormone in your body. The half-life of T4 is the length of time it would take for the T4 level to decrease to one-half of that steady level if you suddenly stop taking your T4 pill. The half-life of T4 is one week. This means that one week after stopping T4, the T4 level is 50 percent of the baseline level, after two weeks it's 25 percent of the baseline (half of 50 percent), after three weeks it's 12.5 percent of the baseline, after four weeks it's 6 percent, after five weeks it's 3 percent, and after six weeks it's just over 1 percent of the T4 level measured before stopping the T4 pill. While the half-life of T4 is one week, the half-life of T3 is only one day. This provides some advantages and disadvantages.

The advantage of T4 is that the levels of T4 remain rock-steady when it's taken daily and that people with thyroid cancer, who need their TSH suppressed to less than 0.1 all of the time, can be adjusted to a regular daily T4 dose that does what is needed without any significant ups or downs. The disadvantage of T4 is that stopping it takes around six weeks of gradually worsening hypothyroidism before enough T4 is gone to make the TSH rise high enough (to at least 30) for radioactive iodine scans or treatments.

The advantage for T3 is that its short half-life lets you stop it for only a short time to get your T3 levels low enough to permit the TSH levels to rise. This lets you use T3 as a "filler hormone" when you stop T4. Typically, T4 is stopped six weeks before a radioactive iodine whole body scan for checking on a person with thyroid cancer. For the first four weeks, T3 is taken twice daily (usually around 25 micrograms each dose for the average-sized adult), preventing any symptoms of hypothyroidism during this time. During the two weeks off of T3 (the fifth and sixth weeks off T4), symptoms of hypothyroidism begin quickly and the pituitary gland is able to make high enough TSH levels. This stimulates any thyroid cancer cells still around to reveal themselves, by sucking up radioactive iodine during the scan or by producing thyroglobulin that can be measured in the blood.

In much the same way, but in reverse, the weeklong half-life of T4 means that it takes six weeks of daily T4 pills before hypothyroid people with thyroid cancer can restore their T4 level to their usual baseline. I use T3, in gradually decreasing dosages, to help these people feel better faster, in combination with the T4 for the first three weeks. After the radioactive iodine scan or treatment is done, I have them start their usually daily T4 dose. For the first week they supplement this with a twice-daily T3 pill (usually a 25-microgram pill for the average adult), for the second week they take half a T3 pill twice daily, and for the third week they take half a T3 pill to get started each morning. By the end of the third week of resuming their thyroid hormone, the T4 level (although not yet at the final level) is high enough to prevent them from having more than minimal hypothyroid symptoms and no further T3 is taken.

T3 for Myxedema
A myxedema coma is a very rare complication of severe, unrecognized hypothyroidism. It usually occurs when someone has longstanding hypothyroidism that has evaded a doctor's notice and is suddenly made worse by the addition of another serious medical illness, such as a bad bacterial or viral infection. A physician suspects this if he or she sees a scar in the neck of an unconscious person in the intensive care unit suggesting previous thyroid surgery, if the person's body temperature is low despite an infection, if the respiratory rate is unusually diminished, or if the bowels are severely constipated. Although it is usual to start treatment with T4, as well as other supportive measures, sometimes T3 is given also, using liquid preparations made for injection into the veins.

When Not to Use T3
The disadvantage of T3 alone, as the treatment for hypothyroid people, is that the peak-and-valley effects of T3 (because of its short half-life) cause people to spend part of the day slightly hypothyroid and part of the day slightly thyrotoxic. Ideally, a timed-release pill that releases a steady amount of T3 into your body would seem to be helpful; however, to date, there is no such pill available. Another disadvantage of T3 is that it bypasses the natural body processes that regulate and customize the amount of T3 produced in each cell from T4. There is good evidence that T4 is more easily transported from the blood into the brain than T3, and that brain cells (neurons) are best suited to respond to T3 made from T4 entering their support (glial) cells or entering the neurons directly.

A variety of medical and nonmedical people have suggested that there is a need for T3 pills instead of, or in addition to, T4 pills to treat hypothyroidism (see Chapter 19). Most of these ideas are clearly false based on known facts of human physiology. Certainly, a few ideas warrant further investigation. Maybe we'll eventually be able to see properly done studies that provide answers. Until these answers are available, the best medical and physiological knowledge shows pure T4 pills as the appropriate way to treat hypothyroid people.

People with thyroid cancer have special needs that cannot be provided by long-term T3 treatment. They must keep their thyroid hormone levels high enough to suppress TSH levels under 0.1, while simultaneously avoiding such high levels that cause symptoms and complications of thyrotoxicosis. The steady levels of T4 work very nicely to make this possible. On the other hand, the peaks and valleys of T3 levels, during daily T3 treatment, result in either a large portion of the day spent with TSH levels that are not low enough to suppress thyroid cancer, or such high levels of T3 that thyrotoxic troubles result. Sometimes, both problems happen in the same person at a different time each day. The only role of T3 for people with thyroid cancer is for the temporary preparation and recovery from hypothyroidism for radioiodine treatment, thyroglobulin tests, and scans (see Chapters 2 and 9).

Mixtures of T3 and T4

Since the thyroid gland normally releases 80 percent of its thyroid hormone as T4 and 20 percent as T3, it seems logical to make a tablet that combines both T4 and T3 together in a similar ratio. Some pills manufactured do just that. Unfortunately, this type of pill cannot do the same thing as a normal thyroid gland that releases a constant, steady stream of both hormones all day and night. Instead, the pill releases both the T4 and T3 completely over one to three hours. Careful consideration of the points raised in the previous section on T3 shows that the short half-life of T3 would cause a peak of T3 followed by little T3 for much of the day. This is far from the natural state of affairs and causes unnatural ups and downs of thyroid hormone. Nonetheless, some physicians prescribe these pills for hypothyroid people and some people seem to do reasonably well with them. On the other hand, these pill mixtures are definitely inappropriate for long-term treatment of people with thyroid cancer.

Thyroid Extracts, or Natural Thyroid Hormone

More than half a century ago, the state-of-the-art thyroid hormone therapy used "Thyroid, U.S.P. (United States Pharmacopoeia)," a preparation of dried, cleaned, powdered thyroid glands from cows or pigs. One brand of this type of thyroid extract that came from pigs is called Armour Thyroid Tablets. These extracts contain a wide variety of hormones and chemicals from thyroid glands that are nearly impossible to accurately standardize from batch to batch. These hormones include T4, T3, thyroglobulin, and products of T3 with fewer iodine atoms on each molecule. Originally, the only way to measure the potency of thyroid extracts was by measuring the amount of iodine in the pills, a method that was extremely poor at determining the amount of effective thyroid hormone. Eventually, additional biological tests were used, but none of them are able to approach the accuracy of methods currently employed to test pure T4 pills. This inaccurate and variable-potency thyroid extract pill is superimposed upon the problems inherent in using synthetic T4 and T3 mixtures, discussed in the previous section.

There are absolutely no advantages of any thyroid extract preparation over synthetic T4 pills. Their continued availability and use is an artifact of antiquated medical habits or ill-informed expectations of consumers (see Chapter 19). These extracts contain no special substances that provide any benefit to people needing thyroid hormone, and most doctors would be happy to see them disappear from use.

11 Other Drugs Used in Thyroid Disease

I n addition to thyroid hormone, discussed in Chapter 10, and radioactive iodine, discussed in Chapter 12, several medications are used to treat thyroid disease. Other medications used to treat hyperthyroidism include propylthiouracil (PTU), methimazole (Tapazole), beta-blockers, and stable (nonradioactive) iodine. Stable iodine is also valuable as a protection against thyroid radiation from radioactive fallout. Potassium perchlorate is sometimes used to diagnose thyroid gland enzyme deficiency; recent reports of groundwater contamination with perchlorate in the western United States have renewed interest in it (see Chapter 3). Lastly, lithium carbonate, normally used to treat manic-depressive illness (bipolar affective disorder) can also be used in thyroid treatment; I (Ken) have found it to be useful in enhancing the treatment of thyroid carcinomas with radioactive iodine under certain circumstances.

In the last part of this chapter, we'll discuss the medications used to treat hypoparathyroidism, an unfortunate complication of thyroid surgery. We'll cover the different types of vitamin D and the way it's used to prevent calcium levels in the blood from dropping (hypocalcemia).

Drugs Used to Treat Hyperthyroidism

Two main approaches are used to manage hyperthyroidism (see Chapters 4 and 6). First, you need to block the effect of thyrotoxicosis on the heart (see Chapter 4), preventing the high thyroid hormone levels from overstimulating the heart rate and risking cardiovascular disease (see Chapter 25). This is accomplished with beta-blockers. Then it's important to make a decision regarding additional therapy. For example, if you had an overactive thyroid gland from Graves' disease, and if it's appropriate to treat the overactive thyroid with radioactive iodine (see Chapter 12), this can be done immediately if you're otherwise stable and in reasonable health. The beta-blockers can diminish thyrotoxic symptoms until the radioactive iodine has reduced the thyroid hormone levels, usually several weeks later. Alternatively, antithyroid drugs (thionamides) can be used to block your thyroid from making more thyroid hormone, allowing thyroid hormone levels to diminish over the course of a couple of weeks. This is useful if your thyrotoxicosis is causing severe symptoms or if there is some reason beta-blockers can't be used. Thionamides can be used as the only treatment or they can be used to quiet things down prior to radioactive iodine treatment.

Antithyroid Drugs (Thionamides)

Antithyroid drugs, a class of drugs known as *thionamides*, block the formation of thyroid hormone by thyroid cells. If hyperthyroidism is caused by single or multiple autonomous toxic nodules (ATNs, see Chapter 8), antithyroid drugs can be used to temporarily lower thyroid hormone levels but are not useful for long-term management since ATNs don't spontaneously get better over time. On the other hand, they're often used to treat hyperthyroidism in Graves' disease, since roughly one-quarter of people with Graves' disease will see a permanent end to Graves' thyrotoxicosis after a year of treatment with thionamides (known as a *remission* or *resolution*). Although some people take thionamides for many years, I (Ken) don't advise taking them longer than one year because of potential toxicity (explained later) and because these spontaneous remissions of Graves' disease are much less likely to occur if they do not happen within the first year of thionamide treatment.

You'll find regional differences in the methods physicians use to treat Graves' disease. In the United States physicians including myself (Ken) prefer to treat Graves' disease patients with radioactive iodine (see Chapter 12), with the exception of patients who are pregnant (see Chapter 13) or young children (see Chapter 15). On the other hand, physicians in Japan and Europe tend to use thionamides more often, and radioactive iodine less often, than their American counterparts.

Thionamides are the only safe and effective form of treatment to control hyperthyroidism during pregnancy, aside from surgery to remove the thyroid gland. This is because radioactive iodine can't be given to a pregnant woman without causing harm to the fetus within her. Surgery is an option for treatment; however, this can be a problem during pregnancy and usually can be avoided. Also, if hyperthyroidism is caused by Graves' disease (see Chapter 6) the thyroid-stimulating antibodies causing stimulation of the mother's thyroid will cross through the placenta into the blood supply of the fetus, stimulating the fetal thyroid gland. Thionamides, given to the mother, will also cross through the placenta into the fetal blood supply, treating both the mother and the fetus to prevent overproduction of thyroid hormone.

The two thionamide drugs used today are propylthiouracil (PTU) and methimazole (Tapazole). These drugs were developed in the 1940s when they were found to cause goiters in laboratory animals. They work similarly to block the formation of thyroid hormone within the thyroid cells. It is possible that they may also have effects on suppressing the immune system, decreasing the autoimmune effects of Graves' disease.

PTU seems to have an additional effect, not shared by methimazole, of decreasing the conversion of T4 to T3.

Propylthiouracil (PTU)

PTU comes in 50-milligram pills. When thyrotoxicosis is fairly severe, PTU is usually started at a dosage of 100 to 150 milligrams, taken every six to eight hours. Less severe thyrotoxicosis is treated with lower initial dosages. Eventually, PTU can be adjusted to a lower total dosage taken twice daily. PTU is most commonly used to treat women during pregnancy. In pregnancy, dosages are slightly reduced because the fetus may be more sensitive to its effects than its mother is. On the other hand, it seems that PTU treatment, even if stopped at least four days before radioactive iodine (RAI) treatment, will interfere with the effectiveness of RAI and necessitate higher doses. In such situations, methimazole is preferred.

Methimazole (Tapazole)

Methimazole, dose for dose, is at least ten times as potent as PTU and lasts much longer. Initial dosages for severe thyrotoxicosis range from 10 to 20 milligrams taken twice daily. Lower doses may be used for milder disease and, eventually, a 10- to 20-milligram dosage given once daily can maintain thyroid hormone levels within the normal range. This once-per-day dosing schedule is easier to remember than the multiple daily doses required by PTU and may be easier for people to take reliably.

Side Effects of Thionamides

Both PTU and methimazole are well tolerated by most people; however, it's important to note that these drugs can be responsible for major, potentially life-threatening side effects or toxicities. The major concern is a condition known as *agranulocytosis*, when the bone marrow stops producing the specialized white blood cells responsible for fighting bacterial infections. This happens in fewer than one out of two hundred people taking thionamides. If you are on PTU or methimazole and you develop a sudden sore throat or fever, it's critical to contact your doctor and request that your white blood cell count be measured right away to rule out this problem. Failure to stop the thionamide and take the appropriate antibiotics can result in a life-threatening infection. A rarer side effect of these drugs is for the bone marrow to stop producing all types of blood cells, which is known as *aplastic anemia*. This is an even more dangerous situation than agranulocytosis. Treatment for aplastic anemia requires emergency care with a hematologist (blood specialist).

Both of the thionamides can also cause liver problems. Methimazole can cause blockage of bile in the liver (a product the liver makes to emulsify fats), resulting in a yellowing of your skin and eyes called *jaundice*. PTU can cause far more dangerous liver damage, very rarely resulting in destruction of large areas of the liver necessitating a liver transplant for survival.

The most common side effects of these drugs, each occurring in fewer than one out of twenty people, include rash, itching, joint pains (arthritis), fever, nausea or vomiting, and transient lowering of the white blood cell count. Taken together, there is more than a one in eight chance that at least one of these side effects will be noticed. If a problem occurs with PTU, methimazole could be tried (as well as the opposite); however, at least half of people develop the same reaction to one thionamide as to the other.

Beta-Blockers

As discussed in Chapter 4, thyrotoxicosis increases the body's sensitivity to adrenaline by increasing the number of beta-adrenergic receptors (also called beta-receptors) in many of the cells of the body. This results in many of the symptoms associated with thyrotoxicosis, particularly symptoms of rapid heart rate, palpitations, and anxiety. In fact, blocking these beta-receptors can alleviate these symptoms and can prevent severe effects on the heart (see Chapter 25). Beta-blockers are drugs that block the effect of the body's own adrenaline on activating these receptors. Beta-receptors come in two types, beta-1-receptors (increasing the heart rate) and beta-2-receptors (opening up airways). If you are asthmatic or have emphysema, you may need special beta-blockers that only block the beta-1-receptor, because blockage of beta-2-receptors would make you severely short of breath. If you're a severe asthmatic, such as myself (Ken), you may not be able to tolerate any type of beta-blocker.

Types of Beta-Blockers

One of the first beta-blockers was propranolol. It blocks both kinds of beta-receptors and must be given every six hours (four times daily), a dosing schedule that has pros and cons. Because this drug has a short time of action in the body, it is easy to adjust the dosage fairly quickly to slow the pulse to a safe and reasonable rate. In severe thyrotoxicosis, propranolol is given as 10 to 20 milligrams every six hours, adjusted every two or three days by adding 10 milligrams per dose (40 milligrams each day) until the propranolol is able to reliably keep the pulse less than eighty beats per minute. In more severe cases, when a person is sick enough to be in the hospital, propranolol can be given as a continuous drip through a needle into a vein.

Now, many varieties of beta-blockers are available, some with longer durations of action permitting once or twice a day dosing, and some that are selective for the beta-1-receptor with less potential for aggravating the breathing of people with asthma or emphysema. Severe thyrotoxicosis, sometimes called *thyroid storm*, used to be a dangerous condition with a significant risk of death. Aggressive use of beta-blockers, as well as other supportive measures, such as better intensive care, the use of steroids, stable iodide, and attention to other illnesses complicating the condition, has made thyroid storm less likely to develop, and less likely to be fatal. The following is a table of some common beta-blockers and their pertinent features. Some of them come in long-acting forms that are not listed here. All of them have the suffix *-olol*.

Generic Name	Time of Dosing	Type of Beta-Receptor Blocked
Propranolol	Four times daily	Both receptors
Metoprolol	Three times daily	Beta-1-selective
Atenolol	Once daily	Beta-1-selective
Nadolol	Once daily	Both receptors
Sotalol	Twice daily	Both receptors
Bisoprolol	Once daily	Beta-1-selective
Timolol	Twice daily	Both receptors
Acebutolol	Twice daily	Beta-1-selective
Esmolol	Continuous drip into a vein	Short-acting beta-1-selective

Other Valuable Uses for Beta-Blockers

Besides managing obvious thyrotoxicosis, beta-blockers have additional benefits in people with thyroid cancer. Unlike people with hypothyroidism, taking sufficient thyroid hormone to provide normal TSH levels (see Chapter 2), those with thyroid cancer take a slightly higher daily levothyroxine dosage, sufficient to suppress the TSH to levels less than 0.1 (see Chapter 9). In most, this doesn't cause any thyrotoxic symptoms, but in around one-third of such people (including Sara), this causes a rapid resting pulse rate (greater than 80 beats per minute), a sensation of palpitations, or some difficulty getting to sleep. If this happens, a once daily beta-blocker (particularly one that is beta-1-selective) makes these symptoms disappear. It also prevents any potential effects of this dosage of thyroid hormone on thickening the left ventricle heart muscle. (See Chapter 25.)

Beta-blockers are also effective medications to treat high blood pressure, prevent angina or heart attacks in people with cardiovascular disease, reduce the frequency of migraine headaches, and prevent panic attacks. This makes their appropriate use, in thyroid cancer patients, multifunctional. Sara has told me that her beta-blocker has also eliminated her panic attacks and feelings of jitteriness after eating (which she had wrongly attributed to hypoglycemia). In this context, the beta-blocker nicely balances the thyroid hormone suppression therapy (to keep TSH low) that is a mainstay of thyroid cancer treatment.

Stable Iodide

Stable iodine (or, more accurately, as its salt, *iodide*) means nonradioactive iodine, which is added to salt and vitamins as a dietary supplement; the addition of iodine to salt in developed countries has virtually eliminated the problem of iodine deficiency. (Chapter 12 will explain the meaning of the term *stable* in greater detail.) Iodine has multiple uses. It's an important part of the treatment of severe thyrotoxicosis caused by hyperthyroidism, helping to lower the release of thyroid hormone. It's a critical part of the diet for anyone with a functional thyroid gland, providing the raw material for the thyroid to manufacture thyroid hormones. Stable iodine has also become an important tool of radiation protection in the event of a nuclear disaster, already proven to prevent thyroid cancer from exposure to radioactive fallout. Each of these uses of stable iodide is explored here.

Use of Stable Iodide to Treat Hyperthyroidism

Although, on one hand, thyroid hormone is made with iodine, very high doses of iodine will block the formation of thyroid hormone by the thyroid. This is an important use of iodine, as a saturated solution of potassium iodide (SSKI), blocking both the incorporation of iodide into thyroid hormone and the release of thyroid hormone already produced. To prevent the chance that it might serve to make more thyroid hormone, SSKI is usually not used until a thionamide (see earlier in this chapter) has already been given.

SSKI is also used before surgical treatment of Graves' disease to decrease the flow of blood through the thyroid gland, making it easier to remove. Iodine-containing contrast dyes used for CAT scans, known as *ipodate* and *iopanoic acid*, have been used to prevent the conversion of T4 to T3, although they are not as effective as thionamides.

Prevention of Hypothyroidism Because of Iodine Deficiency

Iodine deficiency, as discussed in Chapter 3, is the leading cause of hypothyroidism in the world. The daily amount of iodine that is appropriate for proper thyroid function is around 150 micrograms daily. This is the amount contained in most vitamins. Much of the population in the developing world has much lower levels of iodine in their diet. Supplementation, via iodized salt or through iodine added to the water supply, has proven effective in alleviating iodine deficiencies in specific regions. Unfortunately, a small number of older people in these regions have autonomous nodular thyroid glands (see Chapter 8). Iodine supplementation in these people permits them to show symptoms of thyrotoxicosis that were unable to develop in the absence of sufficient iodine.

Stable Iodide for Protection Against Nuclear Accidents

Radioactive fallout from a nuclear accident contains an assortment of radioactive iodine isotopes. These are taken into the thyroid gland and provide sufficient radiation to the gland to increase the chance of thyroid cancer, particularly in a young infant or child. A dose of 30 milligrams or more of stable potassium iodide will reduce the amount of radioactive iodine taken into the thyroid gland by more than 95 percent. For this reason, public health measures dispersing potassium iodide pills (145 milligrams each) or liquid to the public prior to any impending exposure to fallout will prevent this cause of thyroid cancer. This remarkable benefit was demonstrated during the disaster at Chernobyl in 1986, exposing children of Belarus and neighboring Poland to similar radioactive fallout. Stable potassium iodide supplementation to Polish children prevented the epidemic of thyroid cancer that developed in the children of Belarus.

Potassium Perchlorate

Potassium perchlorate has been used in a test to see if the thyroid is able to *organify* iodine, meaning to combine the iodide with proteins in the thyroid cells as the first step in making thyroid hormone. When a small amount of radioactive iodine is given, and the amount taken into the thyroid gland measured, a dose of potassium perchlorate will cause the release of any radioactive iodine that has not been organified. This test is rarely used, except to evaluate unusual conditions in which there are defects in organification, such as Pendred syndrome (see Chapter 18).

Potassium perchlorate has also been used to treat Graves' disease. Generally, it's not as easily used as thionamides and is not considered a standard treatment, but it may be an option for someone with severe allergies to thionamide drugs.

Lithium Carbonate

Most people are familiar with lithium as a drug used to treat manic-depressive illness (also known as *bipolar depression* or *affective disorder*). Thyroidologists have discovered a totally different use for this drug. It has been shown to be quite useful in enhancing the effect of radioactive iodine to treat some aggressive thyroid cancers. Some thyroid cancers that have spread to parts of the body outside of the neck, such as the lungs, may be able to take up radioactive iodine; however, they may fail to respond to the RAI because they expel it before the RAI has had a chance to release much of its radiation to the tumor cells. If lithium carbonate is given to a person with this type of problem a day or two before the RAI treatment dose is given and for five days after, it prolongs the time that RAI is retained within the tumor cells and enhances its effects. This may result in successful treatment of aggressive thyroid cancers that failed previous efforts with RAI.

Treatment of Hypoparathyroidism: Low Calcium

Thyroid cancer surgery, which entails removing the thyroid gland and enlarged lymph nodes in the neck, runs a risk of damaging the parathyroid glands near the thyroid (see Chapter 1). This would cause a low calcium level in the blood, which can be severe, resulting in muscle spasms, anxiety, and abnormal numbness or tingling sensations. Most often this is temporary, caused by bruising of the parathyroid glands during surgery that resolves on its own within a few days or weeks. But sometimes this is a permanent situation that requires lifelong treatment. Low calcium caused by one or more damaged parathyroid glands is called *hypoparathyroidism*. To understand the treatment for hypoparathyroidism, it's important to first explain how parathyroid glands normally function; otherwise, medications used to treat hypoparathyroidism will not make sense to you.

Parathyroid Hormone and Calcium Regulation

Here's a glimpse of "a day in the life" of normal parathyroid glands. The parathyroid glands make parathyroid hormone (PTH). PTH works on two major body organs: the kidneys and the bones. PTH tells the kidneys to keep calcium in the blood and, at the same time, instructs the kidneys to release phosphorus into the urine. This raises calcium while lowering phosphorus in the blood. PTH also converts vitamin D from less active to more active forms. Activated vitamin D works on the intestines, helping them to absorb calcium and phosphorus from your food into your blood. In the bones, PTH mobilizes calcium deposits by turning on the osteoclasts, bone cells that "eat" the calcium phosphate in the bone, releasing calcium into the blood. The parathyroid glands are sensitive to blood calcium levels, making more PTH if the calcium is low and less PTH when calcium levels are high.

When the parathyroid glands are accidentally removed during thyroid surgery, or, more frequently, damaged by bruising or disrupting their blood supply, the PTH levels plummet. This loss of PTH causes the kidneys to lose calcium into the urine and keep the phosphorus in the blood. In short, calcium levels drop and phosphorus levels rise. The low calcium is worsened by the decrease in vitamin D activation, with less calcium entering the blood from the intestines. I (Ken) have explained this to my patients using a bathtub analogy.

Imagine that the calcium level in the blood is like the water level in a bathtub. The water needs to be kept at a precise level to avoid any symptoms. The tub's drain represents the kidneys; the calcium "drains" into the urine through the kidneys. The faucet replaces the water lost down the drain; it represents the calcium entering the blood from the intestines with the help of vitamin D. Extra activated vitamin D functions to turn the faucet knob to increase the water flow. Likewise, PTH, by keeping calcium out of the urine, serves as the plug or stopper, keeping the calcium from leaving the bloodstream the way a plug stops water from leaving a bathtub.

Treating Low or No PTH

In the bathtub model, low or no levels of PTH opens up the drain fully. Water drains from the tub at a furious rate. Unless something is done to stop the calcium from draining out, the "tub" will be empty, which can be disastrous. Since the medical community doesn't yet have suitable ways to administer PTH as a medication, which would "close the drain," the only thing left to do is to turn the faucet on high, replacing the calcium lost down the "drain." This means that your doctor must increase the amount of calcium getting into your body by giving you high enough doses of oral calcium and enough activated vitamin D to absorb it into the blood.

Treating hypoparathyroidism means two things: (1) taking enough vitamin D, and (2) taking enough oral calcium medication. The vitamin D is given in far higher doses than those recommended for the general population. The calcium pills are also given in higher dosages than just the regular supplements recommended for women with osteoporosis (see Chapter 14). Also, it is necessary to take the calcium pills at two or more times daily so that there is always some calcium in the intestine to be absorbed.

Many people with this problem wonder whether they can top up their calcium levels with diet alone. Calcium-containing foods will help only if they do not contain phosphorus. Many dairy products, for example, are high in phosphorus. Any dietician can help you find low-phosphorus, high-calcium foods. Calcium-fortified orange juice is a good example of such a food. That said, it is impossible to supplement your calcium levels enough in this case, using diet alone, because you will need to ensure that you have exactly the same amount of calcium per day, which would mean you'd have to eat the same things each day. That's why taking a pill is your calcium insurance. But by all means, use a low-phosphorus, high-calcium diet as a backup!

Vitamin D Preparations

Three major types of vitamin D are typically used to treat hypoparathyroidism. Your doctor should discuss the pros and cons of each form with you, and help you select the best one for your situation. Each type of vitamin D available has a different potency, takes a different length of time to become active, stays active for a different length of time, and, perhaps most important (depending on your health insurance status), has a different price tag. The formulations discussed here are in order of potency (least to greatest).

- **Vitamin D_2 (Ergocalciferol).** The typical daily dosage is 50,000 international units (the same as 1,250 micrograms). This is usually the least expensive pill and has the advantage of lasting a long time (two to four months) once a steady dose has been taken for several months. The disadvantage is that it takes one to two months before it starts to normalize calcium levels and, if the calcium levels become too high, it may take two months before the calcium levels decrease.

- **DHT (Dihydrotachysterol).** DHT is three times as potent as vitamin D_2. It comes in both a 0.125-milligram and 0.25-milligram pill size, and the typical daily dose ranges from 0.25 to 1.0 milligram daily. DHT begins to work one to two weeks after you start it, reaching its maximum effect by two to four weeks. If too much is given and DHT is decreased, calcium levels will decrease in one to three weeks.
- **Calcitriol.** This is the most potent form of vitamin D (1,500 times more potent than vitamin D_2) and also the preparation used most often to treat hypoparathyroidism. Its great advantage is that it starts working quickly, raising the calcium within three days of starting it, and responding just as soon to changes in dosage. Most people need 0.5 microgram each day with daily requirements ranging from 0.25 microgram to 1.0 microgram. It tends to be a bit more expensive than the other forms of vitamin D. It's crucial to note, however, that the 0.5-microgram pill size has red dye #3 (erythrosine), containing large amounts of iodine that can interfere with a low-iodine diet (see Chapters 9 and 20).

Calcium Preparations

Typically, hypoparathyroid people need roughly 2 grams of elemental calcium each day, divided into two to three doses. It's important to distinguish between the sizes of the different calcium pills and the amount of elemental calcium they contain. For example, calcium carbonate is 40 percent elemental calcium, meaning that a 500-milligram calcium carbonate pill contains 200 milligrams of elemental calcium. So in this case, to get 2 grams of elemental calcium, it takes 5 grams of calcium carbonate, 8 grams of calcium acetate, 11 grams of hydrated calcium chloride, 16 grams of calcium lactate, or 22 grams of calcium gluconate. Some people require much less calcium and some require more.

Monitoring Treatment

I (Ken) measure the ionized calcium rather than the total calcium to check that the amount of calcium and vitamin D preparation are right. It's best to aim for a level of ionized calcium at the bottom of the normal range. You have to be careful not to let the phosphorus level get too high or it may cause kidney problems. Because dairy products are high in phosphorus, as well as calcium, it's best to use calcium pills instead of dairy, to prevent the phosphorus level from getting too high.

12 Radioactive Iodine Therapy

The thyroid gland is unique because it's the only part of the body that makes special use of iodine to do its job, namely, the production of thyroid hormone. Most of the iodine in the body is stored in the thyroid gland, except for the iodine contained in the thyroid hormones T4 and T3 (thyroxine and triiodothyronine) and the thyroglobulin released into the bloodstream. A healthy thyroid gland can take up around a quarter of the total iodine taken into your body each day from food and beverages. This is possible because each thyroid follicular cell makes special proteins that are found in its membrane (see Chapter 1) that pump iodine from the blood into the cell. These iodine pumps (officially known as the *sodium-iodide symporters*) are found in much smaller amounts in salivary glands, female breasts, and the lining of the stomach.

The dawn of the atomic age fostered great interest among physicians who treated thyroid disease. Since thyroid glands took up iodine, it seemed reasonable that they might take up radioactive forms of iodine (known as *isotopes*). Thyroid glands take up radioactive iodine the same way that they take up nonradioactive, or stable, iodine. This permits radioactive iodine to be used as a form of targeted radiation treatment of hyperthyroid glands and toxic thyroid nodules, particularly since it avoids damaging most other parts of the body. Fortunately, many thyroid cancers are also able to take up iodine, permitting radioactive iodine to be used for scans and treatments. In fact, the entire field of nuclear medicine originated with endocrinologists using radioactive iodine isotopes to investigate the thyroid gland.

Radioactive iodine, frequently called by its isotope name as either I-131 or I-123 (the *I* stands for *iodine*), is used in small doses ranging from 5 to 200 microcuries, to make scan images of the thyroid gland or measure the quantity of radioactive iodine taken up by the gland (see Chapter 2). Slightly larger doses of I-131, ranging from 1 to 5 millicuries (same as 1,000 to 5,000 microcuries), are used to perform scans of the entire body after a cancer-containing thyroid gland is removed, looking for thyroid cancer deposits. The doses of I-131 used to treat Graves' disease range from 4 to 30 millicuries. Thyroid cancer treatments use the highest doses of I-131, ranging from 30 to 200 millicuries for most situations and much higher doses (200 to 800 millicuries) for special situations with widespread tumors. Chapter 2 discusses using radioactive iodine for thyroid scans and whole body scans. This chapter focuses on the use of radioactive iodine, specifically I-131, in the treatment of thyroid disorders.

What Is Radioactivity?

This section will give you a simple view of a complex topic. Since only a small portion of our readers can actually boast a degree in nuclear physics, we have tried to make this lay-reader friendly without leaving out important details. This chapter is designed to help you understand radioactive iodine. We anticipate that this section will probably be the most difficult, but promise that you will be able to understand a lot of other sections in this chapter even if this first bit is challenging. So don't get too frustrated! It's extremely difficult stuff for even most primary care doctors.

Understanding What an Atom Is

To understand radioactive iodine, we have to explain atoms. Atoms have a nucleus, containing protons and neutrons clustered together, surrounded by electrons that orbit the nucleus like planets around the sun. An atom of each distinct element, such as iodine, has a particular number of protons in the nucleus, called its atomic number. Although all the atoms of each element have the same atomic number, they may differ from each other by having different numbers of neutrons in their nucleus.

What Makes an Isotope?

When atoms of a particular element, which all have the same number of protons, have different numbers of neutrons, they are called *isotopes* of that element. Some isotopes are stable, meaning that they don't undergo radioactive decay by releasing radiation. Others are unstable, releasing several different types of radiation.

There are a number of types of radioactive decay; to explain it well would entail a long description about radiation physics—something that is far beyond the scope of this book. But the following are more simple explanations, which are still helpful. When atoms of radioactive isotopes decay, sometimes the number of protons changes, turning these atoms into different elements. This type of radioactive decay is called *particulate radiation* because the radiation is composed of particles. Other types of radioactive decay are called *electromagnetic radiation* and are known as *x-rays*.

Particulate Radiation: Alpha and Beta

Some radioactive isotopes release alpha particles, which are made of two protons and two electrons (the same as the nucleus of helium, used to fill balloons). These particles travel only very tiny distances if released inside the body; however, they release the largest amount of energy of all of the radioactive decay particles and can be very destructive. Isotopes that release alpha particles are not used for scans or other diagnostic tests. It seems likely that, in the future, they may be coupled to some chemicals or antibodies that could be taken into cancer cells so that the cells are destroyed by the alpha particles.

Beta Particles: How RAI Works

Beta particles are a different type of radioactive decay product. The typical type of beta particle is an electron with a negative charge that is released when a neutron turns into a proton. These beta particles also travel very short distances when they are released into a person's body. When they are released inside a cell, they may collide with atoms of critical parts of the cell, imparting their energy to these atoms (and pushing off electrons from these atoms, a process called *ionization*) and killing the cell. This is how radioactive iodine (specifically, the I-131 isotope of iodine) works to kill thyroid or thyroid cancer cells that take it in.

A different type of beta particle is released when a proton turns into a neutron. This is an electron with a positive charge (actually an antimatter electron) called a *positron*. (*Antimatter* and *positrons* are terms you may have heard on "Star Trek" episodes, but they're for real!) Isotopes that release positrons are often coupled to chemicals and used to take images or scans in special machines that are able to detect positrons. This is called *positron emission tomography*, also known as *PET* scanning (see Chapter 2). Usually, sugar (glucose) is coupled to an isotope of fluorine (F-18), which releases positrons, and injected into your blood when you are in a PET scanner. Since thyroid cancer cells may suck up sugar faster than other cells in your body, this type of PET scan may find thyroid cancer deposits in your body that were otherwise hidden.

All beta particles are made with energy levels that are characteristic of the particular isotope that released them. When beta particles of I-131 are released inside thyroid cells or thyroid cancer cells, they travel an average of 2.2 millimeters before their energy is completely absorbed by the thyroid or thyroid cancer deposit. This permits the I-131 treatment to specifically target thyroid cancer cells without bothering other nearby body cells.

Electromagnetic Radiation: Gamma Rays (X-Rays)

The terminology used here is more reminiscent of 1950s sci-fi movies, but now's your chance to really understand this.

Gamma rays, also known as x-rays (or gamma ray photons), are not particles and can travel large distances through the body before they release their energy by ionizing a part of a cell. Radioactive isotopes can release x-rays using different methods (in terminology you've probably never heard before): electron capture, isomeric transition, internal conversion, stimulation of Auger electrons, or release of characteristic x-rays. No matter which method makes them, x-rays are not very useful for killing thyroid cells or thyroid cancer cells. Instead, they provide a useful way to produce images (scans) of the thyroid or of thyroid cancer, wherever it may have spread in the body. I-123 produces only x-rays and is used only for making thyroid scans. On the other hand, I-131 produces both x-rays and beta particles. For this reason, it has dual use, both for making scans and for treating Graves' disease and thyroid cancer.

Types of Treatment with Radioactive Iodine

Radioactive iodine, specifically I-131, has been used for treating thyroid disorders for more than half a century. It's used to treat cases of hyperthyroidism, when the thyroid is overproducing thyroid hormone (see Chapter 4). It's also the mainstay of thyroid cancer treatment, after the thyroid gland and the main thyroid cancer is removed by the surgeon. This is a remarkably easy treatment to take. I-131 is dissolved in water. Sometimes this is added to gelatin capsules and swallowed. My (Ken) preference is to give it in its liquid form, so that patients can sip it through a straw. The actual amount of iodine that is swallowed is rarely more than a couple of milligrams, although it's usually quite radioactive. In fact, an average cup of milk contains severalfold more iodine (nonradioactive) than is contained in a treatment dose of radioactive iodine. This is why people who are allergic to iodine or seafood can usually tolerate radioactive iodine treatment without activating an allergic reaction.

Radioactive iodine (RAI) cannot be given to a pregnant woman or one who is breast-feeding. If RAI is given to a pregnant woman, it will be taken into her fetus, destroying its thyroid gland and exposing it to unwanted radiation. Likewise, if RAI is given to a woman who is breast-feeding, it will get into her breast milk. If you're breast-feeding, it will take nearly two months for your breast milk to be sufficiently clear of RAI to be considered safe for your child, making it unreasonable to give you radioactive iodine until you've completely weaned your baby.

Different doses of I-131 are given for different thyroid disorders. The following sections describe how this treatment is used, its benefits and risks, as well as the methods used to determine the dose.

Radioactive Iodine for Graves' Disease

When you are hyperthyroid from Graves' disease (see Chapter 6), your gland is usually quite "hungry" for iodine. This hunger can be measured as the *radioactive iodine uptake* or *RAIU*. The normal RAIU is 15 to 25 percent; meaning that, on average, 20 percent of a dose of radioactive iodine (after being swallowed) will find itself taken up by your thyroid gland. This amount will be lower if you like to eat foods with a large amount of nonradioactive iodine, such as sushi or food with red dye #3. A Graves' thyroid gland can have RAIU values from 25 to 80 percent, depending upon how "hungry" the gland is and how much thyroid-stimulating antibodies turn it on.

There are two ways that someone with Graves' disease can be prepared for RAI treatment. If you are young or in a reasonably healthy state, aside from your hyperthyroidism, it is often easiest to treat you immediately with radioactive iodine, avoiding using antithyroid drugs (see Chapter 11). Beta-blockers (see Chapters 11 and 25) can be used as needed. Alternatively, if you have heart disease (see Chapter 25) or are sufficiently ill or unstable from your thyrotoxicosis (see Chapter 4), it's often a good idea to lower your thyroid hormone levels with antithyroid drugs before giving you RAI. The antithyroid drug (methimazole or propylthiouracil) should be stopped three or four days before giving the I-131 dose so that it doesn't interfere with the treatment.

RAI is an excellent treatment for Graves' disease and physicians in North America most frequently use it. In Europe and Japan, antithyroid drugs are used more often than RAI. It seems that this reflects regional differences in how physicians treat this disease, rather than any unique knowledge about disadvantages of RAI with respect to its safety or effectiveness. This is an example of how the prejudices (right or wrong) may influence how people are treated and the recommendations they receive from their physicians.

How Much RAI Is Used for Graves' Disease?

Different methods are used to decide upon the dosage of RAI. Some physicians give arbitrary doses of I-131, knowing that most people will have some good results as long as the dose is reasonable (often around 10 millicuries). I (Ken) prefer to make measurements that permit the dose to be individually adjusted. It is nearly impossible to reliably give such a precise dose of RAI that a person ends up with normal thyroid gland function and, ultimately, the ongoing autoimmune processes of Graves' disease usually cause the thyroid gland to eventually fail anyway, resulting in hypothyroidism. For this reason, I feel that it's better to aim to give enough RAI to make a person hypothyroid reasonably soon, so that thyroid hormone replacement therapy can be started, which will allow that person to resume his or her usual quality of life faster. First, I estimate the size of a person's thyroid in grams, knowing that a normal-sized thyroid weighs around eighteen to twenty grams. Then I obtain the RAIU, using a small tracer dose of RAI to make this measurement. I use these numbers to calculate the amount of I-131 needed that would deliver at least 150 microcuries of I-131 per gram of the thyroid (with the entire result divided by the RAIU). It takes from one to four months before the RAI has had sufficient time to do all that it will do. Thyroid hormone levels should be monitored every three to five weeks until it is clear that a person needs thyroid hormone treatment (see Chapter 10). About one-third of the time a second treatment with I-131 is needed to provide sufficient treatment. It's very rare to need a third treatment.

Side Effects and Risks of RAI for Graves' Disease

It's pretty accurate to say that the only long-term side effect of RAI for Graves' disease is hypothyroidism. As we also explain in Chapter 19, this is actually the intention of the treatment because once you're hypothyroid, you can be treated with the proper dose of thyroid hormone, which makes you feel balanced and well again. This is preferable to the roller coaster of thyrotoxicosis from Graves' disease (see Chapter 6), which wreaks havoc on your body (and life). So, to most Graves' patients, hypothyroidism is not so much a side effect but a side benefit as it is truly a desired outcome.

Some people express worry about a risk of RAI causing cancer. This should not be of concern; after five decades of RAI use, despite many studies over the years, it has not shown itself to be a significant risk factor for any future cancers to develop. It seems odd that radioactive iodine fallout from atomic testing or nuclear reactor accidents would be a cause of thyroid cancer and RAI treatment of Graves' disease would not be. This may be because low-level radioactive iodine exposure, the type seen from fallout or accidents, is too low to kill thyroid cells outright, as do the higher RAI doses used for Graves' disease treatment. So instead, this low-level radioactive iodine causes minor breaks in chromosomes that contribute to thyroid cancer risk. That is why RAI exposure from fallout can lead to cancer risk, but high-level treatment doses kill thyroid cells and, thus, their potential to be dangerous to you. A lot of clinical evidence reassures us of the safety of RAI for scans and treatment.

This theoretical concern regarding cancer risk is part of the reason why young children with Graves' disease have been less frequently offered RAI for treatment. In fact, there is a growing trend among physicians to treat younger and younger children with RAI, particularly since there haven't been any particular problems seen from it and it's a very effective and easy-to-give treatment. Antithyroid drugs are still the mainstay of Graves' disease treatment for most young children, but RAI is a reasonable option for some.

RAI does not have any effect on the future fertility of women, and there hasn't been any evidence of increases in birth defects of children born to women who had been treated with RAI in the past, despite multiple studies. Of course, RAI should not be given to a pregnant or breast-feeding woman. Men do not experience any harmful effect on their fertility from this treatment, either.

There are some minor and temporary effects of RAI. Some people notice a slight tenderness of their thyroid gland for a day or two after they swallow the I-131. Sometimes, the thyroid hormone levels get higher for a couple of weeks as the thyroid hormone stored in the gland is released into the blood. A more worrisome side effect is a risk of worsening of thyroid eye disease, but this occurs only if it is already severe prior to the RAI treatment. A short course of steroids (usually prednisone) can prevent this particular problem.

Radioactive Iodine for Toxic Thyroid Nodules

Autonomous toxic nodules (ATNs), either single or as part of a toxic multinodular goiter (TMNG), are appropriate for RAI treatment because these nodules produce enough thyroid hormone to suppress the TSH level. The TSH suppression causes the normal thyroid tissue surrounding the nodules to become suppressed also and not take up RAI.

This results in protection of the normal thyroid from the RAI and specifically directs the I-131 to enter the toxic nodules that don't require TSH for their stimulation. The doses of RAI used for these nodules are slightly higher than doses used for Graves' disease, but far lower than doses used for thyroid cancer. Most of the stipulations concerning use of RAI, discussed previously, apply to ATNs and TMNGs. Toxic nodules larger than 5 centimeters are usually best treated with surgery.

Radioactive Iodine for Thyroid Cancer

RAI treatment is the only useful treatment of papillary and follicular thyroid cancers once they have spread beyond the thyroid gland. It is the only known effective systemic thyroid cancer treatment; that is, it can kill thyroid cancer cells in the entire body system, wherever they may be hiding. This is necessary because many thyroid cancers have spread to multiple sites in the neck, or distantly to the lungs or bones, long before they are discovered in your thyroid gland. Also, the smallest tumor deposit that can be seen by a human eye contains more than a million cancer cells. While the surgeon may be able to see and remove some of these during your surgery, the surgeon is incapable of finding and removing tumor deposits of one hundred thousand cells, ten thousand cells, one thousand cells, or even smaller numbers. In theory, it can take only a single cancer cell to start the process of cell division and reproduction that brings back much larger tumor deposits. This means that a surgeon is incapable of reliably providing a cure by surgery alone, making the surgery only the first step of your treatment. I-131 therapy becomes the second step of your treatment because it is an effective systemic treatment for iodine-avid thyroid cancers. In addition, by using nuclear medicine scanning equipment, the same I-131 that is used for treatment provides a way of detecting the sites of these thyroid cancer deposits.

RAI is given in the same way that it is administered for Graves' disease as described in the preceding section, either as a liquid that's sipped through a straw or in capsules that are swallowed. The major difference is in the higher amount of I-131 that's used. Because there are concerns about exposing other people who come in contact with you after your treatment to unnecessary radiation, there are regulations that often require you to spend a day or two in a special hospital room for what is called *radioactive isolation*.

Preparation for RAI Treatment of Thyroid Cancer

A major difference between RAI treatment for Graves' disease or ATNs and RAI treatment for thyroid cancer is the importance of proper preparation for treatment. Radioactive iodine uptake is high in thyrotoxic Graves' disease and autonomous toxic nodules. On the other hand, whereas normal thyroid tissue takes up iodine at 1 percent per gram, papillary and follicular thyroid cancers take up iodine at from 0.01 to 0.1 percent per gram, making it important to use the best preparation to optimize RAI uptake in thyroid cancer treatment. As discussed in Chapter 2, there are three methods of preparing for I-131 whole body scans: hypothyroid preparation (the "gold standard"), the moderate hypothyroid preparation, and recombinant human TSH (Thyrogen). The key to each of these methods is to have the TSH above 30 mIU/mL.

The "gold standard" approach is a six-week withdrawal from thyroid hormone replacement (T4 or levothyroxine). This entails stopping T4 therapy and switching to T3 (Cytomel) for the first four weeks. The final two weeks, you would start a low-iodine diet (see Chapter 20), and then stop T3 and be on no thyroid hormone at all, inducing severe hypothyroidism. This gold standard method is the method against which other preparation methods are compared. At the current time, Thyrogen is not approved for I-131 treatment. It is intended only to be used for I-131 whole body scans. Experimental studies using Thyrogen for RAI therapy show it to be useful or necessary in some unusual situations, but it is not the best method to get the most effective I-131 treatment for most people. No matter how you are prepared for your RAI treatment (hypothyroidism or Thyrogen) it is most important to follow a low-iodine diet (see Chapter 20) to optimize the absorption of the RAI into the tumor cells.

Radioactive iodine treatment is most effective if it is used on the smallest remains of thyroid cancer deposits after surgery has removed all evident tumors. If large (bigger than half an inch) lumps of thyroid cancer are present, radioactive iodine, no matter how high the dose, is often unable to destroy them. The best results are seen when the surgeon has thoroughly removed all obvious thyroid cancer, as well as all portions of the thyroid gland. This should be done before performing I-131 scans or treatments.

Standard Dosing

For a long time, many physicians based their decisions on how much RAI to give for each person's treatment on custom and financial concerns. Rules from the U.S. Nuclear Regulatory Commission (NRC) stated that doses of I-131 less than 30 millicuries could be given as an outpatient dose, without the need to admit the patient to the hospital. Insurance companies and physicians jumped on the bandwagon, making the 29.9-millicurie dose the most common dose used. Physicians went to great lengths to avoid higher doses that required their patient to be admitted to a radiation isolation room in the hospital for one to three days at greater monetary and logistic expense than outpatient treatment. Unfortunately, this low-dose therapy was insufficient to eliminate evidence of persistent thyroid remnant or metastatic thyroid cancer in the majority of patients. Repetitive low-dose treatment is likely to increase the chance that surviving thyroid cancer cells are less and less likely to be responsive to later RAI treatments until they are considered to be unable to take up RAI. This situation is akin to bacteria becoming resistant to antibiotics. For example, if you take too low a dose of penicillin for your strep throat, the infection is only partially treated and the surviving bacteria are less responsive to penicillin. With each low, ineffective dose, the surviving bacteria eventually learn to "like" penicillin, and even high doses won't work. In science-speak, this is known as "Darwinian selection for treatment failure."

Standard RAI doses for thyroid cancer have evolved *empirically*, that is, by analyz-ing the experiences of treating patients over the years. They are effective for the major-ity of people with thyroid cancer, but it is important to know when higher, more aggressive treatments are appropriate. With standard RAI dosing, 100 millicuries are given when the thyroid cancer does not extend beyond the limits of the thyroid gland, there is no evidence of any metastases (spread of the cancer to body regions beyond the thyroid gland), and the type of thyroid cancer is not particularly aggressive (such as tall cell variant or insular thyroid cancer). If the original thyroid surgery shows that cancer cells have spread to lymph nodes in the neck or the RAI whole body scan (per-formed immediately before the RAI therapy) shows spots of I-131 in the neck, out-side of the place where the thyroid gland used to be (the *thyroid bed*), a condition called *locally metastatic tumor*, the typical RAI dose is 150 millicuries. If the scans reveal thyroid cancer spread outside of the neck, such as in the lungs, liver, or bones, stan-dard doses are usually inadequate to deal with these tumors, although some physi-cians give 200-millicurie doses for such situations. I (Ken) do not use these standard doses of I-131 for such aggressive disease. Instead, these situations are best dealt with by using the maximum doses of I-131 that can be safely given without causing intol-erable side effects. A method of giving safe maximal-dose therapy is described in the following section.

A variety of different I-131 dosing schemes are used by various physicians. Although some people with thyroid cancer will do well with these other treatment methods, I (Ken) feel that lowering the I-131 dose decreases the chance that the treatment will be effective. Also, despite the best efforts with I-131 treatments, some thyroid cancers fail to respond, often by losing the ability to take in the radioactive iodine.

High-Dose Treatments for Aggressive Cancers

People with papillary or follicular thyroid cancers that have spread to regions of their body beyond their neck, either above to their head or below to their chest or abdomen, as well as to vital parts of their body, including their spine or trachea (windpipe), can expect their cancers to be very difficult to treat as well as potentially deadly. One good general principle is that the surgeon, if possible, should remove such tumors, then high-dose radioactive iodine treatment should be used for the tiny remaining cancer cells after such surgery. In particular, metastases (tumor spread within the body) to bones are nearly impossible to eliminate without first using surgery to remove these metasta-tic deposits. Sometimes, many metastases throughout the lungs are unable to be removed by the surgeon and high-dose RAI is the only useful option for treatment.

I-131 dosimetry is the method used to figure out the maximum safe I-131 dose, beyond which there are unacceptable effects on the bone marrow. Only a handful of academic medical centers have the expertise and ability to perform this method and give such treatments. Using dosimetry, I've (Ken) been able to safely give my patients high doses of I-131, from 300 to 800 millicuries in a single dose, when the extent of their tumor showed this to be necessary. If you have such aggressive thyroid cancer, ask your physician to refer you to a physician skilled in this method.

Some physicians tell their patients that there is a "lifetime limit" to the cumulative amount of I-131 that they can safely tolerate (sometimes as low as 600 millicuries). This is an example of a doctor's "old wives' tale." Unfortunately, I've (Ken) seen too many references to this fictitious "lifetime limit" of I-131. There is absolutely no basis in reality for such a limit. Although you may find references to such a limit in some medical articles, careful research of this claim reveals that there is no data anywhere to support such a concept. In fact, I have treated patients to total cumulative doses of 2,000 to 3,000 millicuries without any significant ill effect from the treatment, aside from dysfunctional salivary glands. If the thyroid cancer is distantly spread and still is able to respond to radioiodine, then there is no reason to withhold therapy if it can be helpful. As long as dosimetry shows that each single I-131 dose is within the safety margins of 200 REM (a measure of radiation exposure) marrow exposure and less than 80 millicuries I-131 retained in the lung at 48 hours (this may permit single doses up to 800 millicuries in some patients), there should be no permanent ill consequences from necessary thyroid cancer treatment. The biggest problem is the use of repetitive low-dose (less than 200 millicuries) treatments for aggressive distant disease. This may result in the use of many doses, with each particular dose too low to destroy the thyroid cancer cells.

Side Effects of Treatment
One of the potential nuisances (as opposed to dangers) of radioiodine therapy is permanent damage to the salivary glands, which may result in diminished flow rates of saliva. There are a few medical consequences and solutions:

- Decreased saliva may make eating certain foods difficult. Use frequent small sips of water while eating to help this.
- Decreased salivary flow produces increased risk of tooth decay because saliva is critical to wash food particles off of teeth after eating. Patients can carry a small travel toothbrush kit in their pocket or purse and should brush their teeth after *every* meal. Sometimes this produces an added benefit by reducing between meal snacking.
- Decreased salivary flow predisposes to salivary stones, which refers to the swelling of one or more salivary glands located under the ears and under the lower jaw. The salivary stones are caused by partial blockage of the salivary ducts by dried saliva. (This is a problem that Sara has, which baffled many of her doctors who were unfamiliar with this phenomenon.) This can be startling and worrisome if not recognized for what it is. Immediate use of antibiotics is not advised unless there is fever and elevated white blood cell counts. Instead, this problem usually responds to swishing warm water (or tea, coffee, broth, and so forth) in the mouth while gently massaging the swollen salivary gland. Usually, there is a sudden sour taste as the stale saliva is released and the swelling goes away. If this does not work or if it is rapidly and frequently recurrent,

then it is important to go to your physician. Usually this problem happens several times within a few weeks and then doesn't happen again for a long time.

Rarely, thyroid cancer patients develop a constant watering of the eyes. This seems to be related to a blockage of the tear duct that drains tears into the nose. A physician can often repair this by opening up this duct. Also, some people get a little nauseous several hours after swallowing their radioactive iodine dose. Most often, this is just a case of a nervous apprehension regarding the treatment. In some cases, it may be related to the RAI dose. It's important to take appropriate medication to relieve these feelings so that you feel comfortable and so that vomiting doesn't compromise the RAI treatment.

Most of the time, physicians (inappropriately) warn their patients of the risk of the RAI causing leukemia (cancer of the white blood cells) or bladder cancer. These problems are extremely rare from RAI and almost never seen. It's questionable whether they are truly related to the treatment. High-dose RAI treatment isn't used unless the thyroid cancer is aggressive enough to need it, making unlikely risks of leukemia irrelevant in the presence of such dangerous disease.

Radiation Safety Precautions

Government regulations provide guidelines for dealing with radioactive iodine treatments, to make sure that other people are not unnecessarily exposed to any radiation that doesn't benefit their health. In recent years, these regulations have been made more liberal, permitting many people the opportunity to receive I-131 doses of 120 millicuries or more without hospitalization. On the other hand, most RAI doses of 150 millicuries or more are given in a radiation isolation room in the hospital. This is to limit the exposure of other people to your RAI dose. In my (Ken's) hospital, we rarely keep these patients in the hospital longer than one day, unless the RAI dose is larger than 500 millicuries. Such precautions are good public policy but are not done because you could harm anybody. The policy is to keep the radiation that other people receive to as low a level as possible.

When my patients go home, I (Ken) give them the following instructions, or "rules to live by" for the next fourteen days. There is no need for the following precautions after fourteen days.

- Do not exchange bodily fluids with anyone (no sex, wet kissing, sharing utensils, and so forth). (Your bodily fluids are slightly radioactive and you do not want to expose other people unnecessarily.)
- Please urinate while sitting (instead of standing). (Your urine is still slightly "hot" and you don't want it to splash on the seat or the floor.)
- You may use normal eating utensils, dishes, and cups, but rinse them before anyone else handles them. Dispose of your toothbrush after fourteen days. (Again, you don't want to expose anyone to your bodily fluids unnecessarily. Your toothbrush ought to be replaced since it was in a lot of contact with you while you were "hot.")

- Try to place a little bit of distance between yourself and others to avoid exposing them unnecessarily to radiation. One useful technique is to imagine that you have a minor contagious illness such as strep throat; the distance that others should keep from you would be similar.
- Do not sleep in the same bed as others for this time to avoid unnecessary exposure to radiation.
- Do not operate a motor vehicle for at least ten days (because the thyroid hormone that was restarted on discharge takes a while to start working; this driving rule does not have anything to do with radioactivity).

P A R T

2

People in Special Circumstances

THYROID DISORDERS CAN affect certain populations differently and complicate other conditions. This section addresses our readers who are in special circumstances, such as those who are pregnant, those who are going through menopause, or those who are children (or parents of infants with thyroid problems). This section covers thyroid disease in older persons, people who are obese, and people who have rare genetic disorders that interfere with thyroid function.

13 Thyroid Disease in Pregnancy and After Delivery

This chapter discusses issues for distinct groups of women: pregnant women with unrecognized or subclinical thyroid disease, pregnant women with preexisting thyroid disease, women who only first discover (or develop) a thyroid problem during pregnancy, and women who only first discover (or develop) a thyroid problem within the first six months of delivery. In the latter situation, this frequently takes the form of postpartum thyroiditis, classically misdiagnosed as postpartum depression.

Autoimmune thyroid diseases, such as Hashimoto's disease (see Chapter 5) or Graves' disease (see Chapter 6), frequently strike during the first trimester of a pregnancy or within the first six months after delivery. That said, you should note that preexisting autoimmune thyroid disease as well as other autoimmune diseases tend to improve during a pregnancy but can worsen after delivery. Although the reasons for this are not known, these changes parallel the changes in estrogen levels in the pregnant woman; high levels of estrogen are associated with improvement in the thyroid problem. Thyroid nodules and thyroid cancer can also be first discovered during a pregnancy, and in those cases, there are particular management strategies we'll discuss.

One of the aims of this chapter is to educate you and your doctor on the potential dangers of untreated thyroid disease during pregnancy. All women planning pregnancy and their prenatal health-care team should be aware of the following facts:

- Pregnant women with hypothyroidism (overt or subclinical) are at an increased risk for premature delivery.
- Pregnant women who have antibodies for autoimmune thyroid disease are at an increased risk for miscarriage, postpartum thyroiditis, Graves' disease, and hypothyroidism.
- Children born to mothers with hypothyroidism or high TSH levels are at higher risk of intellectual or motor impairment.

For these reasons, all women should be screened for thyroid disease prior to pregnancy and at regular intervals throughout their pregnancy as appropriate. This translates into TSH tests and thyroid antibody tests upon the discovery of the pregnancy, and monthly TSH tests if the thyroid antibody tests are positive. (See Chapter 2 for details on these tests.) Although not yet common practice, routine thyroid function tests, meaning TSH tests, ought to be done at regular intervals on all fertile women who could become pregnant, because they might not seek medical care until well into their pregnancy.

The Normal Thyroid in Pregnancy

It was customary in ancient Egypt to tie a fine thread around the neck of a young bride; when it broke, it meant she was pregnant. It's normal for the thyroid gland to enlarge slightly during pregnancy because the placenta makes a hormone, human chorionic gonadotropin (HCG), that stimulates the mother's thyroid gland. Researchers have found that HCG has a very similar molecular structure to thyroid stimulating hormone (TSH). Increased TSH causes enlarged thyroid glands (goiters), such as with an iodine-deficient woman (usually one who lives in an iodine-deficient area) who is hypothyroid. Likewise, large increases of human chorionic gonadotropin (HCG) seen in normal pregnancy affect the thyroid as if it were TSH, activating the TSH receptor and causing the gland to grow larger. The thyroid usually increases in volume by 30 percent between eighteen and thirty-six weeks into pregnancy. (As a precaution, however, even a modestly enlarged thyroid gland or goiter should be checked. And, of course, iodine deficiency should be treated with iodine immediately.)

Normal, healthy pregnant women often develop symptoms and signs that suggest thyrotoxicosis or hyperthyroidism, such as a rapid pulse or palpitations, sweating, and heat intolerance because the metabolic rate increases during pregnancy. Despite this, hyperthyroidism occurs only in about one in a thousand pregnancies. Total thyroid hormone levels also increase during pregnancy because of the high levels of estrogen made by the ovaries. This estrogen causes an increase in a binding protein (thyroxine binding globulin, made by the liver and released into the blood) that carries thyroxine and releases it so it can enter the body's cells. The amount of the free thyroxine available to the tissues, however, is not increased, and the *free* T4 level is not affected (see Chapter 2). Many doctors mistakenly order *total* T4 levels and become alarmed, thinking that their pregnant patient has thyrotoxicosis. This can cause much anxiety and can be avoided if the doctor checks your TSH level and *free* T4 level.

Normal Pregnancy Discomforts

This section looks at some common pregnancy discomforts that mimic, or mask, hypothyroidism. In cases of unrecognized or subclinical hypothyroidism, these symptoms might suggest doing a TSH test, but the confusing changes in pregnancy might throw a doctor off the scent of thyroid disease. Subclinical hypothyroidism could aggravate or magnify these discomforts, too.

Backaches

The most common back pain in early pregnancy is lower back pain; your expanding uterus might put pressure on your sciatic nerve, which runs from your buttocks down through the back of your legs. This may worsen as the pregnancy progresses. Muscular aches and pains are also common in hypothyroidism, and backaches could be exacerbated by it. On the other hand, if you complain of muscular aches during pregnancy, few doctors will think it's related to hypothyroidism.

Constipation

During pregnancy, your bowel function slows down to ensure absorption of vitamins and nutrients from food. Progesterone also relaxes the smooth muscles of your small and large intestines. This slows down the entire digestive process, and the result is constipation, which may get worse as the pregnancy progresses. Constipation is typical in hypothyroidism, too, so complaints about it during pregnancy may not point to hypothyroidism in your doctor's mind.

Edema (Water Retention)

Classic edema symptoms are swollen feet, ankles, and fingers, which occur because the growing uterus puts pressure on your lower extremities. The pressure then forces water into the tissue around your feet and ankles. Additionally, increased amounts of progesterone in your body cause you to retain more water—the reason why many women will become bloated just before their periods. In later pregnancy, severe water retention can also be a symptom of preeclampsia, discussed later in this chapter. Similarly, in hypothyroidism, edema is also quite common; complaints of edema during pregnancy will have your doctor thinking it's all because of pregnancy, rather than hypothyroidism.

Emotional Symptoms

It's normal to feel weepy, irritable, nervous, sad, or anxious during pregnancy. Some of these feelings have to do with the social impact of the pregnancy; some of these feelings are attributed to major hormonal shifts in your body. Most women begin to feel their "happy hormones" by the second trimester. Both hypothyroidism and thyrotoxicosis can also cause emotional symptoms (see Chapters 3 and 4).

Fatigue

Fatigue is a major symptom in pregnancy. This begins after the first missed period and persists until the fourteenth to twentieth week of pregnancy. About ten hours of sleep per night is suggested during the first trimester. Fatigue is also a classic hypothyroid symptom, yet during pregnancy, most fatigue will be chalked up to the pregnancy.

Heartburn

As your uterus expands, it pushes the stomach up. Combine this with a slower digestive system, and your stomach doesn't empty as fast as it used to. The result: heartburn. And it just gets worse until the third trimester when the baby's head finally drops down. Add the digestive slowdown from hypothyroidism, and the heartburn is magnified.

Numbness

Your expanding uterus can put pressure on your nerves, which sometimes causes numbness and tingling in hands, legs or feet, or lower back. In the second and third trimester, water retention can put pressure on the median nerve in your wrist, cutting off feeling in your hand and fingers resulting in carpal tunnel syndrome, as discussed in Chapter 3. In hypothyroidism, edema can result in the same type of numbness.

Morning Sickness and Sufficient Iodine

Morning sickness refers to the infamous nausea and vomiting women tend to experience during early pregnancy. Between 60 and 80 percent of all women suffer from morning sickness in their first trimester, and a significant number have severe morning sickness that can last the duration of pregnancy, also known as *hyperemesis gravidarum*. Morning sickness may interfere with sufficient iodine intake during pregnancy. It's critical that adequate amounts of iodine are in the maternal diet for normal fetal development; in fact, maternal iodine deficiency is one of the leading causes of mental impairment and cretinism in underdeveloped countries. If you live in the United States or Canada, or other developed countries, this is usually not a problem. But if you can't keep anything down, you may be nutrient-deprived. The recommended total daily iodine intake for pregnant women should be 220 micrograms per day and 290 micrograms per day for lactating women.

Dairy products are very high in iodine content; while the iodine in milk varies greatly (depending upon the season, the cow's feed, and the location), it averages around 250 micrograms per liter (60 micrograms per cup), which is more than sufficient. Prenatal vitamins, which most North American pregnant women take, contain at least 150 micrograms of iodine per day. If you take these vitamins with a glass of milk, you should be fine. But, if you're unable to keep any liquids down, your physician should pay careful attention to all of your nutritional needs, including iodine, in an effort to prevent malnutrition.

If you are suffering from severe morning sickness in early pregnancy, this may be a sign of gestational thyrotoxicosis, a transient form of thyrotoxicosis, discussed further on. It's believed that morning sickness can become increasingly severe because of the overproduction of thyroid hormone. Morning sickness also presents other problems for women who take thyroid hormone (for preexisting or newly diagnosed thyroid diseases), discussed further on.

Being Pregnant with Preexisting Thyroid Disease

If you are hypothyroid or are taking thyroid hormone for a thyroid condition diagnosed prior to this pregnancy, it's important to have your thyroid levels assessed monthly with a target TSH of between 0.5 and 3.0 (see Chapter 2) so that your dosages of thyroid hormone can be appropriately adjusted, which is necessary for the growing fetus. Total T4 (or TT4) assessments are useless, since T4 naturally rises because of increased thyroxine binding globulin (see earlier in this chapter). Although very little thyroid hormone will cross over from you to the fetus, the little that does is very important, since normal thyroid hormone levels in you are critical for proper fetal development until the fetus develops its own thyroid gland. Sometimes a change in dosage is needed because requirements for thyroid hormone can increase during pregnancy. It's normal to require as much as a 30 to 50 percent increase in your dosage. In this case, doctors should generally monitor the TSH level monthly and should increase your dosage as necessary. Since prenatal vitamins often contain iron, it's important to take them at night so that the iron doesn't interfere with the absorption of your morning thyroid pill.

First trimester body changes, discussed earlier, can mimic several hypothyroid symptoms. If you're uncertain as to whether you're hypothyroid, request a TSH test. Hypothyroidism is not only risky for fetal development but can also worsen normal pregnancy symptoms, such as fatigue.

Pregnancy and Graves' Disease

If you're taking antithyroid medication (see Chapter 11) for Graves' disease and are pregnant, this is perfectly safe, and you should continue on this medication so long as you're under the supervision of a doctor. In fact, this may protect the baby in your womb from the effects of thyroid-stimulating antibody, which crosses from you into the baby's circulation. When you're pregnant, however, the dosage of the antithyroid medication usually needs to be decreased by your doctor for two reasons: your baby's thyroid is more sensitive to these drugs than your own, and Graves' disease activity changes during the course of your pregnancy.

If you're pregnant with active Graves' disease that was newly discovered, you must start antithyroid drugs as soon as possible, and you should remain slightly hyperthyroid so the baby can be properly suppressed. This is discussed more in the section on gestational thyrotoxicosis.

If you are pregnant with a history of previously treated Graves' disease, there is still a risk that you could have a hyperthyroid baby because you may still be making thyroid stimulating immunoglobulin (TSI). Since you don't have a working thyroid anymore you won't have any symptoms, but TSI could still cross the placenta into the baby. In the case of previously treated Graves', you should request that your prenatal healthcare provider monitor the fetal heart rate during the pregnancy to look for signs that suggest fetal thyrotoxicosis; under rare circumstances your health-care provider may need a blood sample from the placenta to check thyroid hormone levels. If you've had a remission of Graves' disease, fetal thyrotoxicosis from your Graves' history should not be a risk.

If You Had Radioactive Iodine Therapy

If you were treated for hyperthyroidism or thyroid cancer with radioactive iodine, a reasonable recommendation is that you shouldn't plan to get pregnant for about six months. If you're pregnant after you had RAI, but did not wait this six-month period, you shouldn't be worried since there isn't any definite evidence that there's any harm to your child. Pregnancies should proceed normally so long as you're taking sufficient doses of your thyroid hormone replacement and the TSH is monitored monthly.

Morning Sickness and Thyroid Hormone Replacement

Morning sickness may be mild, moderate, or severe. For more severe cases, the nausea and vomiting begin between six and eight weeks after your last menstrual period, persists strongly until about fourteen weeks after your last menstrual period, and then either disappears or gets much better. But it can persist well into the second trimester too and can even last the duration of the pregnancy. Generally, while most doctors and pregnancy books tell you that morning sickness lasts for about twelve weeks, the average length is just over seventeen weeks.

Numerous other symptoms accompany morning sickness, including an aversion to certain tastes or smells that never bothered you before, such as coffee or meat. Some women find it difficult to even prepare any foods and may be turned off by every food except one in particular, such as grapefruit, yogurt, crackers, and so on.

The nausea is caused by changes in hormone levels that somehow affect your stomach lining and stomach acids, so an empty stomach aggravates the nausea. Giving your stomach something to digest is the way to combat it. Consult a nutritionist or ask your doctor to recommend a pregnancy book for more information.

The problem with nonstop nausea and vomiting is that your thyroid hormone pill could be poorly absorbed, leaving you hypothyroid, which is dangerous to fetal health. If you think your thyroid hormone pill came out with your breakfast, with your doctor's permission, it's probably all right to take an additional tablet as long as this isn't a frequent event. In extreme situations, your physician could give you thyroid hormone medication as an intramuscular (IM) or subcutaneous (SC) injection, but this is rarely necessary.

It has been shown that taking a vitamin B_6 supplement is effective in reducing severe morning sickness in pregnancy, but it doesn't seem to have any effect on mild and moderate nausea.

Gestational Thyroid Disease (Thyroid Disease During Pregnancy)

With two rare exceptions, discussed further on, the causes of thyroid disease during pregnancy are the same as in the general population. The most common thyroid diseases in pregnancy mirror the most common thyroid diseases in the general population. As in the general population, Hashimoto's disease (see Chapter 5) is the most common thyroid disease in pregnancy, followed by Graves' disease (see Chapter 6). In both cases, the risk spikes during the first three months of pregnancy, and then spikes again in the first six months after delivery. Many women will first develop Hashimoto's or Graves' disease within a year of their pregnancies. After delivery, up to 20 percent of all women (particularly those with thyroid antibodies or insulin-dependent diabetes) will develop postpartum thyroiditis, which usually resolves on its own but 25 percent of the time can leave women permanently hypothyroid.

Just as in the general population, pregnant women can develop hypothyroidism or thyrotoxicosis for other reasons, discussed in Chapters 3 and 4. But what does seem clear (at least to thyroid researchers) is that pregnancy increases your body's thyroid hormone requirements. Pregnancy may lead to relative iodine deficiency, which can increase the severity of preexisting hypothyroidism, and worsen preexisting Hashimoto's or Graves' disease. Finally, it can unveil overt hypothyroidism in women who had subclinical hypothyroidism prior to pregnancy. In some rare cases, if there is a great deal of bleeding during delivery, the pituitary may be damaged (Sheehan's syndrome) and result in hypothyroidism, loss of cortisol from the adrenal gland, and infertility.

Gestational Hypothyroidism

If hypothyroidism is suspected while you're pregnant, your doctor will give you a TSH test. Just as in nonpregnant women, your TSH levels will be increased if you're hypothyroid, and you'll be treated with thyroid hormone replacement. As discussed earlier, sometimes pregnancy itself can mask hypothyroid symptoms. For example, constipation, puffiness, and fatigue are all traits of pregnancy as well. These symptoms will likely persist after delivery if your hypothyroidism remains untreated, and they can seriously interfere with pregnancy and your postpartum health.

Gestational hypertension, preeclampsia, and eclampsia are more common in women with overt or subclinical hypothyroidism. These pregnancy complications may warrant early delivery or lead to premature delivery.

More on Gestational Hypertension (High Blood Pressure During Pregnancy)

During early pregnancy, blood pressure levels normally decrease, but during the second and third trimesters, they begin to steadily rise. If your blood pressure was high prior to your pregnancy, you have what's known as *chronic hypertension*; if you first develop hypertension only after the first twenty weeks of pregnancy, you have *gestational hypertension*. You're more likely to develop gestational hypertension if you:

- Are hypothyroid
- Are experiencing a first pregnancy
- Have a kidney disease
- Have diabetes (chronic or gestational)
- Are not eating well

If you develop gestational hypertension because of hypothyroidism, it's crucial to begin thyroid hormone supplementation at a dosage that is at least 100 micrograms daily. After a month, if your TSH levels are still high, the dosage may need to be increased. Gestational hypertension usually clears up after delivery, in the absence of other causes.

Women with chronic hypertension (which may be first unveiled during pregnancy) tend to have a family history of hypertension. Chronic hypertension is more common in women over thirty-five and is aggravated by smoking, obesity, or kidney problems.

Whether you have chronic or gestational hypertension, high blood pressure in pregnancy could lead to preeclampsia (a serious condition discussed next), placental problems, or oxygen problems. If your diastolic blood pressure (the bottom half of the fraction) is higher than 90, you may need antihypertensive medications to control the problem.

More on Preeclampsia and Eclampsia

Preeclampsia comprises three conditions that trigger one another in a domino effect: water retention, high blood pressure, and protein in your urine (called *proteinuria*), which can lead to (or be symptomatic of) kidney damage. If you have only one or two of these symptoms, you don't have preeclampsia. All three of the symptoms must be present to be diagnosed with preeclampsia.

Eclampsia is a more severe form of preeclampsia, where in addition to the three symptoms listed, you may suffer from epileptic-like seizures. Usually, preeclampsia is caught and treated early enough to prevent eclampsia. But if you do progress to this, hospitalization and possibly early delivery by Cesarean section may be necessary.

Premature Labor

Untreated hypothyroidism can lead to premature labor. This is characterized by contractions, accompanied by vaginal bleeding, vaginal discharge, or even a vaginal pressure anywhere from the twentieth week to the thirty-seventh week. Premature rupture of the amniotic sac occurs in 20 to 30 percent of all premature deliveries and is a sign that something is wrong as well. Other symptoms of premature labor are menstrual-like cramps, with possible diarrhea, nausea, or indigestion; lower back pain; and other symptoms of labor.

Between 5 and 8 percent of all deliveries are premature in the absence of any health problem. In addition to untreated hypothyroidism, other known causes of premature labor include poor general health, uncontrolled diabetes, cocaine use, syphilis, placental problems, and physical trauma. The health of the premature newborn greatly depends on exactly how premature the delivery is, what kind of neonatal care is available, the weight of the newborn, and how developed the baby is.

Premature labor can be treated with medications that postpone the labor. In the worst-case scenario, the baby is delivered prematurely and treated in a neonatal intensive care unit.

Gestational Thyrotoxicosis

Gestational thyrotoxicosis is a transient form of thyrotoxicosis caused by rising levels of human chorionic gonadotropin (HCG), which stimulate the thyroid gland to make thyroid hormone. This is usually found in women with severe morning sickness and is typically diagnosed toward the end of the first trimester. It usually resolves on its own after pregnancy. Temporary treatment with propranolol, a beta-blocker (see Chapter 11), may be used as long as it is definitely necessary and not used for more than a few weeks—using it for more than a few weeks can sometimes result in a smaller baby. If the thyrotoxicosis is very severe, antithyroid drugs, such as propylthiouracil (PTU), may be used in smaller than usual dosages.

Thyrotoxicosis Because of Molar Pregnancy

Roughly one in every fifteen hundred to two thousand pregnancies in North America will develop into a *molar pregnancy*, also known as a *hydatidiform mole* or *gestational trophoblastic neoplasia*. Here the placenta, in a cruel and bizarre twist of biology, becomes precancerous. This condition is most frequently reported among Asian women in the South Pacific and in Mexico.

A molar pregnancy will usually start out like any normal pregnancy, but for some unknown reason, the placental tissue transforms into small cysts that overtake the womb, destroying the fetus within the first few months of pregnancy. The cysts grow in a grapevine fashion and begin to fill up the uterine cavity. Once a molar pregnancy develops, it will usually consume the contents of the womb, but sometimes, a partial molar pregnancy will occur (where the womb remains fairly undamaged), in which the fetus actually survives, and a normal vaginal delivery can occur. However, as rare as a molar pregnancy is in North America, a partial molar pregnancy is even rarer.

The cysts that characterize a molar pregnancy will usually be benign but can develop into a type of cancer called *choriocarcinoma*, cancer of the chorion, which secretes the vital hormone human chorionic gonadotropin (HCG). Since HCG can stimulate thyroid hormone production, molar pregnancy can result in thyrotoxicosis (see Chapter 4). It's imperative that a molar pregnancy be terminated upon discovery, unless the fetus is healthy. (Healthy fetuses in this situation are rare, but treatment of the molar pregnancy will vary depending on the duration of the pregnancy and fetal health.)

Symptoms of molar pregnancies can begin in the first trimester, but the molar pregnancy is often not diagnosed until the second trimester. The first sign is continuous staining. The molar pregnancy can even damage the placenta to the point of miscarriage, and you might experience what you think is a normal first or second trimester miscarriage until you're examined via ultrasound—which will always confirm a molar pregnancy. In this case, bleeding will usually become heavy and a dilation and curettage (D & C) will be performed to prevent any molar tissue from being left behind.

In other cases, the bleeding can be light and the fetus may die, but not expel itself. In this case, a suction procedure followed by a D & C is performed.

Another sign of a molar pregnancy is thyrotoxicosis, because of very high levels of HCG, which drop only slightly over time after the pregnancy ends. If the HCG levels don't drop, it means that the danger of choriocarcinoma is still present, and you'll need to consult a gynecological oncologist, a type of cancer specialist.

Gestational Hyperthyroidism

Diagnosis and treatment of hyperthyroidism during pregnancy presents some unique fetal and maternal considerations. First, the risk of miscarriage and stillbirth is increased if hyperthyroidism goes untreated. Second, the overall risks to you and the baby increase if the disease persists or is first recognized late in pregnancy. As in non-pregnant women, specific hyperthyroid symptoms usually indicate a problem, but here again, some of the classic symptoms, such as heat intolerance or palpitations, can mirror classic pregnancy traits. Usually, symptoms such as bulgy eyes or a pronounced goiter give Graves' disease away. But because radioactive iodine scans or treatment are never performed during pregnancy, gestational hyperthyroidism can be confirmed only through a blood test. (If, by some fluke, you are exposed to radioactive iodine during pregnancy because the pregnancy was not suspected, you may want to discuss the risks and the possibility of a therapeutic abortion with your practitioner as there may be serious damage because of exposure of a developing fetus to radioactivity.) In fact, it's a good practice to always take a pregnancy test on a fertile woman before giving her any radioactive substance, either for scans or for treatments.

The treatment for hyperthyroidism in pregnancy is antithyroid medication. Propylthiouracil (PTU) or methimazole are most commonly used, but PTU is the one usually used during pregnancy. The antithyroid medication in pregnancy is used first to control the hyperthyroidism. Then, the aim is to administer the lowest dose possible to maintain the thyroid hormone levels in the high-normal or maximum-without-risk range. Because thyroid-stimulating antibodies (TSI) cross the placenta, they can cause fetal hyperthyroidism, which is very dangerous and may even cause fetal death. Therefore, the PTU, by suppressing the fetal thyroid, actually benefits the fetus. Since the fetal thyroid is slightly more sensitive to PTU than the mother's thyroid, the dose is slightly less than would completely normalize the mother's thyroid hormone levels.

Sometimes women discover they are allergic to PTU. In this case, methimazole is used instead. When there is a problem with both drugs, sometimes a thyroidectomy is performed during the second trimester. This is rare, though; in general, surgery is avoided during pregnancy because it can trigger a miscarriage.

Many times, hyperthyroidism becomes milder as the pregnancy progresses. When this happens, antithyroid medication can be tapered off slowly as the pregnancy reaches full term and, often, normal thyroid function resumes after delivery. Careful thought should be made about breast-feeding, since radioactive iodine treatments should not be given while breast-feeding and not until at least one month after weaning.

Sometimes, beta-blockers such as propranolol are added to PTU, which can be continued safely during pregnancy if absolutely necessary (although, as discussed, there is a potential risk of having a smaller than normal baby if used too long).

The Risk of Miscarriage

Studies indicate a 32 percent risk of miscarriage in women with antithyroid antibodies, or subclinical Hashimoto's disease or Graves' disease, compared to a 16 percent risk in women without them. The risk of miscarriage also rises because of age. In the general population of healthy pregnant women under thirty-five, one in six pregnancies ends in miscarriage with risk at its highest point during the first trimester. Given these statistics, it's important to be alert to signs of miscarriage.

Symptoms of Miscarriage

Heavy bleeding and cramping anywhere between the end of the second month to the end of the third month are classic signs that you're in the process of miscarrying. The bleeding can be heavy enough to saturate several pads within an hour or may be manageable and more like a heavy period. Cramps without bleeding are also a danger sign that you're miscarrying. You may also experience unbearable cramping that renders you incapacitated. Sometimes, you can pass clots, which are dark red clumps, or you may even pass gray or pink tissue. A miscarriage can also be occurring if you have persistent, light bleeding and milder cramping at this stage.

When you miscarry prior to twenty weeks, it's called a *spontaneous abortion*.

Discovering Thyroid Nodules in Pregnancy

If you discover a lump (nodule) on your thyroid gland during pregnancy, investigation and treatment will vary depending on what stage you are in.

At any time, a fine-needle biopsy (see Chapter 8) should be done to determine whether the nodule is benign or likely to be malignant (cancer). If it is malignant, surgery will probably be performed during the second trimester, which is considered the safest time for surgery. If a cancerous nodule is confirmed in the second trimester, surgery may still be performed if there is time. Otherwise, you might simply have to wait until after you deliver.

If, however, a cancerous nodule is discovered well into the second trimester or in the third trimester, surgical treatment can usually wait until you deliver. Then, you will be able to have the appropriate thyroid surgery, discussed in Chapter 9.

After the Baby Is Born

During pregnancy, your immune system is naturally suppressed to prevent your body from rejecting the fetus. After pregnancy, your immune system "turns on" again. But this has a rebound effect in that the immune system is so alert that it is almost too powerful and can develop autoantibodies that attack normal tissue. This is what's known as an *autoimmune disorder* (see Chapter 5) and may be one reason why women are more prone to thyroid autoimmune disorders after pregnancy. I (Sara) liken the scenario to having a guard dog tied up for nine months (during the pregnancy) and then let out. The dog will be feistier and may even attack his owner.

If you first develop an autoimmune thyroid disease such as Graves' disease or Hashimoto's disease after you deliver, you would undergo normal treatment for either disease, as outlined in Chapters 5 and 6. If you developed Graves' disease after delivery and are breast-feeding, you may continue breast-feeding while on antithyroid medication but must not breast-feed if you're having radioactive iodine therapy or scans.

If you develop Graves' disease during pregnancy, the condition can get worse after delivery unless antithyroid drugs are continued.

If you were diagnosed and successfully treated for Graves' disease prior to pregnancy, you can sometimes suffer a relapse after delivery. But depending on the severity of Graves' disease after delivery, some women can opt to postpone treatment until they're finished breast-feeding.

Postpartum Thyroiditis

Postpartum thyroiditis means "inflammation of the thyroid gland after delivery" and is often the culprit behind the so-called postpartum blues. Postpartum thyroiditis occurs in 5 to 18 percent of all postpartum women and usually lasts six to nine months before it resolves on its own.

Postpartum thyroiditis is a general label referring to silent thyroiditis (see Chapter 5) occurring after delivery and causing mild thyrotoxicosis and/or a short-lived Hashimoto's-type of thyroiditis (see Chapter 5), resulting in mild hypothyroidism. Until quite recently, the mild hypothyroid and thyrotoxic symptoms were attributed simply to symptoms of postpartum depression (PPD), or those notorious "postpartum blues" thought to be caused by the dramatic hormonal changes women experience after pregnancy. But recent studies indicate that as many as 18 percent of all pregnant women experience transient thyroid problems and subsequent mild forms of thyrotoxicosis, hyperthyroidism, or hypothyroidism. This statistic does not account for the many women who develop Graves' disease either during or after pregnancy.

Usually, the silent thyroiditis or short-lived Hashimoto's thyroiditis lasts for only a few weeks. Often, women don't even realize what's wrong with them, because the symptoms are mild and usually associated with the natural fatigue that accompanies taking care of a newborn.

These conditions usually clear up by themselves. Short-lived Hashimoto's thyroiditis is usually more common than silent thyroiditis after delivery (although the difference is not significant), and, in more severe cases, thyroid hormone is administered temporarily to alleviate the hypothyroid symptoms.

If you have thyrotoxic symptoms and they are severe, you may be placed on beta-blockers until the excess thyroid hormone is depleted. Regardless of whether you are given thyroid hormone or beta-blockers, you can usually still breast-feed safely. Women who experience this sudden thyroid flare-up tend to reexperience it with each pregnancy, however. Obviously, women who do experience postpartum thyroiditis are predisposed to thyroid disorders and seem to be vulnerable in that particular area.

Today, it ought to be standard practice for all pregnant women in North America to have thyroid function tests after delivery. If you have not been offered this test after delivery, request it. If your thyroid test is normal yet you still have symptoms of PPD or maternal blues, then you can rule out an underlying thyroid problem.

Postpartum Thyroiditis, Blues, or Postpartum Depression?

If you look at the symptoms of hypothyroidism in Chapter 3, it's easy to see how they can be confused with symptoms of postpartum depression or the "maternal blues," which affect as many as 70 percent of all women after delivery.

Symptoms of maternal blues are frequent crying episodes, mood swings, and feelings of sadness, low energy, anxiety, insomnia, restlessness, and irritability. Women who experience these should find comfort in knowing that they are normal and will pass on their own in a couple of weeks. It's akin to a whopper PMS phase. Maternal blues are most likely caused by enormous hormonal shifts in your body. An enormous lifestyle shift may also trigger these feelings because of an increase in stress and responsibility, worry about your newborn, physical discomfort associated with your postpartum physique, and possible exhaustion following labor and delivery.

Postpartum Depression (PPD)

Postpartum depression is more serious and persistent and it affects 10 to 15 percent of the postpartum population. Depression can begin at any time after delivery—from the first few hours afterward to a few weeks after. These symptoms include sadness, mood changes, lack of energy, loss of interest, change in appetite, fatigue, guilt, self-loathing, suicidal thoughts, and poor concentration and memory. When these feelings last for more than a couple of weeks, the consequences can be truly negative, leading to problems with bonding and relationship trouble. However, women don't go from the maternal blues to depression. In fact, you can feel well after delivery and then suddenly develop postpartum depression.

The causes of postpartum depression are possibly similar to those cited as causes for the milder maternal blues. But women at risk for this more serious depression are those with a family history of depression and women who have a poor support system at home (spouseless, bad relationship with partner, teenage mothers, and so on).

If you do begin to notice these feelings, treatment is available through counseling or therapy (see Chapter 24). Some women may require antidepressant medication combined with talk therapy. Above all, make sure that your TSH level has been checked by your doctor to make sure that you get the correct diagnosis and treatment.

14 Thyroid Disease During Menopause

When it comes to menopause, women with thyroid disease have a little more to be concerned about than women without thyroid disease. First, all women postmenopause are at an increased risk of heart disease, which is the major cause of death for this population. But in postmenopausal women with untreated hypothyroidism or hyperthyroidism (or thyrotoxicosis), cardiovascular changes with possible damage to the heart can result, magnifying the normal risk of heart disease that exists in the general female population. Hyperthyroidism or thyrotoxicosis can also speed the process of osteoporosis, another risk for women after menopause.

In women with normal thyroid function prior to menopause, the signs of thyroid disease can be masked by perimenopausal symptoms. Thus, thyroid disease can be missed, which can aggravate menopause and postmenopause risks of other diseases, such as osteoporosis or heart disease. Or, you may be mistakenly told you are perimenopausal when you are not. It's important to note that mild or subclinical hypothyroidism (meaning that symptoms may not be obvious but still contribute to general malaise) steadily rises with age, increasing from 10 percent in the premenopausal age group to 20 percent in the postmenopausal age group.

Finally, in light of the 2002 studies on hormone replacement therapy (HRT) and heart disease, managing menopause for all women presents a challenge. But we also know that the roughly 5 percent of postmenopausal women on thyroid hormone also taking HRT typically need to increase their thyroid hormone dosages, similar to the scenario during pregnancy.

Natural Menopause

When menopause occurs naturally, it tends to take place anywhere between the ages of forty-eight and fifty-two, but it can occur as early as your late thirties or as late as your

Menopause or Thyroid?

The following menopausal symptoms may also be signs of hypo- or hyperthyroidism:

- Erratic periods
- Hot flashes (women who are hyperthyroid will feel hot all the time)
- Vaginal dryness and/or changes in libido
- Muscle aches and pains (could be signs of bone loss)
- Skin changes
- Irritability
- Mood swings

mid-fifties. When menopause occurs before age forty-five, it is technically considered early menopause, but just as menarche is genetically predetermined, so is menopause. For an average woman with an unremarkable medical history, what she eats or the activities she engages in will not influence the timing of her menopause. However, women who have had chemotherapy or who have been exposed to high levels of radiation (such as radiation therapy in their pelvic area for cancer treatment) may go into earlier menopause. In any event, the average age of menopause is fifty to fifty-one.

Other causes that have been cited to trigger an early menopause include mumps (in small groups of women, the infection causing the mumps has been known to spread to the ovaries, prematurely shutting them down) and specific autoimmune diseases, such as lupus or rheumatoid arthritis (some women with these diseases find that their bodies develop antibodies to their own ovaries and attack the ovaries).

The term *perimenopause* refers to women who are in the thick of menopause—their cycles are wildly erratic, and they experience hot flashes and vaginal dryness. This label is applicable for about four years, covering the first two years prior to the official last period to the next two years following the last menstrual period. Women who are perimenopausal will be in the age groups discussed previously, averaging to about fifty-one.

The term *menopause* refers to your final menstrual period. You will not be able to pinpoint your final period until you've been completely free from periods for one year. Then you count back to the last period you charted, and that is the date of your menopause. The term *postmenopause* refers to the last third of most women's lives and includes those who have been free of menstrual periods for at least four years to women celebrating their one hundredth birthdays and beyond.

Signs of Natural Menopause

The three classic short-term symptoms of menopause—erratic periods, hot flashes, and vaginal dryness—are caused by a decrease in estrogen. The emotional symptoms of menopause, such as irritability, mood swings, melancholy, and so on, are actually caused by a rise in follicle-stimulating hormone (FSH). As the cycle changes and the ovaries' egg supply dwindles, FSH is secreted in very high amounts and reaches a lifetime peak—as much as fifteen times higher; it's the body's way of trying to "jump-start" the ovarian engine.

Decreased levels of estrogen can make you more vulnerable to stress, depression, and anxiety because estrogen loss affects REM sleep. When we're less rested, we're less able to cope with stresses that normally may not affect us. Stress can also increase blood sugar.

Every woman entering menopause will experience a change in her menstrual cycle, discussed later. However, not all women will experience hot flashes or even notice vaginal changes, particularly true if a woman is overweight. Estrogen is stored in fat cells, which is why overweight women also tend to be more at risk for estrogen-dependent cancers. What happens is that the fat cells convert circulating male sex hormones into estrogen, creating a type of estrogen reserve that the body will use during menopause and that can reduce the severity of estrogen loss symptoms.

Cycles may become longer or shorter with long bouts of time without periods (amenorrhea). There will also be flow changes, where periods may suddenly become light and scanty, or very heavy and crampy. Of course, all of this could be masking thyroid disease; or, thyroid disease may be the cause of your menopausal symptoms and you may be misdiagnosed as being menopausal when you are not.

Roughly 85 percent of all pre- and perimenopausal women experience hot flashes. They can begin when periods are either still regular or have just started to become irregular. The hot flashes usually stop between one and two years after your final menstrual period. A hot flash can feel different for each woman. Some women experience a feeling of warmth in their face and upper body; some experience hot flashes as a simultaneous sweating with chills. Some women feel anxious, tense, dizzy, or nauseous just before the hot flash; some feel tingling in their fingers or heart palpitations just before. Some women will experience their hot flashes during the day; others will experience them at night and may wake up so wet from perspiration that they need to change their sheets and/or nightclothes.

Other Changes

Estrogen loss will also cause vaginal changes. Since it is the production of estrogen that causes the vagina to stay moist and elastic through its natural secretions, the loss of estrogen will cause the vagina to become drier, thinner, and less elastic. This may also cause the vagina to shrink slightly in terms of width and length. In addition, the reduction in vaginal secretions causes the vagina to be less acidic. This can put you at risk for more vaginal infections. As a result of these vaginal changes, you'll notice a change in your sexual activity. Your vagina may take longer to become lubricated, or you may have to depend on lubricants to have comfortable intercourse. Some of these changes may be intensified if you are also unknowingly hypothyroid.

Estrogen loss can affect other parts of your sex life as well. Your libido may actually increase because testosterone levels can rise when estrogen levels drop. (The general rule is that your levels of testosterone will either stay the same or increase.) However, women who do experience an increase in sexual desire will also be frustrated that their vaginas are not accommodating their needs. First, there is the lubrication problem: more stimulation is required to lubricate the vagina naturally. Second, a decrease in estrogen means that less blood flows to the vagina and clitoris, which means that orgasm may be more difficult to achieve or may not last as long as it normally has in the past. Other changes involve the breasts. Normally, estrogen causes blood to flow into the breasts during arousal, which makes the nipples more erect, sensitive, and responsive. Estrogen loss causes less blood to flow to the breasts, which makes them less sensitive. And finally, since the vagina shrinks as estrogen decreases, it doesn't expand as much during intercourse, which may make intercourse less comfortable, particularly since it is less lubricated.

Mood Swings

Mood swings can be an especially tricky symptom of both menopause and thyroid disease. While irritability and depression can be symptoms of menopause, they may also be signs of thyroid disease.

The following menopausal symptoms can also be confused with symptoms of hypo- or hyperthyroidism:

- Erratic periods
- Hot flashes (women who are hyperthyroid will feel hot all the time)
- Vaginal dryness and/or changes in libido
- Muscle aches and pains (could be signs of bone loss)
- Skin changes
- Irritability
- Mood swings

HRT, Menopause, and Thyroid Disease

The average woman will live until age seventy-eight, meaning that she will live one-third of her life after her menopause. Since thyroid disorders affect women so much more frequently, particularly as they age, balancing thyroid hormone replacement with the confusion surrounding traditional estrogen and progesterone hormone replacement is challenging. Since heart disease can be a major complication of hypothyroidism or thyrotoxicosis, in the 1980s and 1990s, women with thyroid disease were encouraged to seriously consider hormone replacement therapy after menopause, because it was believed that long-term HRT protected women from heart disease. That's all changed.

In July 2002, a study by the U.S. National Heart, Lung, and Blood Institute, part of a huge research program called the Women's Health Initiative (WHI), suggested that HRT should not be recommended for long-term use; in fact, the results were so alarming, the study was halted before its completion date. It was found that Prempro, a combination of estrogen and progestin, which was a "standard issue" HRT formulation for postmenopausal women, increased the risk of invasive breast cancer, heart disease, stroke, and pulmonary embolisms (blood clots). The study participants were informed in a letter that they should stop taking their pills. However, Prempro did reduce the incidence of bone fractures from osteoporosis and colon cancer.

For women in good health without thyroid disease, taking HRT in the short term to relieve menopausal symptoms is still considered a good option, as there is no evidence to suggest that short-term use (one to five years) of HRT is harmful. The study has implications only for women on oral HRT for long-term use (versus the patch)—something that was recommended to millions of women over the past twenty years because of perceived protection against heart disease.

In 1998, an earlier trial known as the Heart and Estrogen/Progestin Replacement Study (HERS) looked at whether HRT reduced risk in women who already had heart disease. HRT was not found to have any beneficial effect. Women who were at risk for breast cancer were never advised to go on HRT; similarly, women who had suffered a stroke or were considered at risk for blood clots were also never considered good candidates for HRT. It had long been known that breast cancer was a risk of long-term HRT, as well as stroke and blood clots. However, many women made the HRT decision based on the perceived heart disease protection. Today, the only thing the experts can agree on is that the HRT decision is highly individual and must be an informed decision, where all of the possible risks and benefits of taking—or not taking—HRT are disclosed.

More recent analyses point to the fact that all problems with HRT identified to date stem from the use of oral HRT dosing. When estrogen pills are swallowed, they must be absorbed from the intestines into the blood that flows directly to the liver. This exposes the liver to much higher levels of estrogen than the rest of the body. Since the liver is the manufacturing site of clotting factors and cholesterol, oral HRT causes changes in the liver that are likely to be responsible for most of the HRT problems. The solution may be to use HRT patches. Putting the estrogen into the bloodstream by directly absorbing it through the skin avoids the liver problem and may prove to be safe and effective. This needs to be explored further in future clinical trials.

If you are suffering from great discomfort during perimenopause, and your thyroid hormone levels are normal (again, hypothyroid women in perimenopause may need to increase their thyroid hormone dosage), discuss with your health-care provider whether short-term HRT is an option. If you suffered from cardiovascular effects as a result of untreated hypothyroidism or thyrotoxicosis, oral HRT may be more risky for you, in light of the 2002 study results. So, ask about HRT patches.

Numerous natural methods are available to help control symptoms. For example, many women use soy, a plant estrogen (or phytoestrogen), in place of conventional HRT. It's critical to note that if you're on thyroid hormone, soy supplements taken within five hours of your thyroid hormone pill can decrease the absorption of thyroid hormone. Rather than increasing your dosages while on soy, it's better to pay attention to the timing of your pills. Sometimes taking your soy at night and your thyroid hormone pill in the morning may lessen the absorption problem, but it's important to monitor thyroid function with tests (see Chapter 2) while you're on soy.

Osteoporosis

Postmenopausal women are at highest risk of developing osteoporosis (bone loss), which can be aggravated by thyrotoxicosis (see further). Eighty percent of all osteoporosis sufferers are women—as a direct result of estrogen loss. Maintaining bone mass and good bone health is your best defense against osteoporosis. Although osteoporosis can be disfiguring, it is a relatively silent disease in that there are often no immediate symptoms, pain, or suffering that occur with it. The problem is not osteoporosis itself but the risk of fractures. One out of two women over fifty will have an osteoporosis-related fracture in her lifetime. If you have osteoporosis and fall down, a fracture can dramatically affect the current and future quality of life. If you've ever experienced reduced mobility, or you've been dependent on someone else to prepare meals, shop, or run errands, you may have some idea as to how debilitating being bedridden and immobile can be. A full 70 percent of all hip fractures are a direct result of osteoporosis. Twenty percent of those suffering hip fractures will die of complications related to their injuries; 50 percent will be disabled. In fact, more women die each year as a result of osteoporosis-related fractures than from breast and ovarian cancer combined.

Secondary osteoporosis means that an underlying condition has caused bone loss. These conditions include chronic renal disease, hypogonadism (a loss of hormone from the sex glands, or gonads), thyrotoxicosis (see Chapter 4), some forms of cancer, gastrectomy (removal of parts of the stomach, which interferes with calcium absorption), and the use of anticonvulsants.

Calcitonin

As discussed in Chapter 1, your thyroid gland "rents" space to additional thyroid cells called C cells, which make the hormone calcitonin and do not make thyroid hormone. Calcitonin helps to regulate calcium and helps to prevent osteoporosis. It is also used to treat Paget's disease, a bone disease that affects mostly men. But to your *bones*, calcitonin is kind of like a tonsil; it serves a useful purpose, but when the hormone is not manufactured because of the absence of a thyroid gland (if the thyroid is removed or ablated for treatment of a thyroid condition), you won't really notice any effects, just as you don't miss your tonsils. Calcium levels are really controlled by the parathyroid glands, as explained in Chapter 1.

What Causes Bone Loss Anyway?

Our bones are always regenerating (known as *remodeling*). This process helps to maintain a constant level of calcium in the blood, essential for a healthy heart, blood circulation, and blood clotting. About 99 percent of all the body's calcium is in the bones and teeth; when blood calcium drops below a certain level, the body will take calcium from the bones to replenish it. But by the time we reach our late thirties, our bones lose calcium faster than it can be replaced. The pace of bone calcium loss speeds up for freshly postmenopausal women (three to seven years beyond menopause). One of the most influential factors on bone loss is estrogen; it slows the loss of bone mass by directly affecting cells that make bone (osteoblasts) and cells that digest bone (osteoclasts). In men, testosterone does the same thing, but unlike women, men never reach a particular age when their testes stop producing testosterone. If they did, they might be just as prone to osteoporosis as women.

Thyroid Disease and Osteoporosis

Women who take thyroid hormone commonly ask about the link between thyroid disease and osteoporosis. (As mentioned earlier, contrary to what most women think, the link has nothing to do with calcitonin, which the thyroid also produces, as discussed in Chapter 1.)

Again, thyroid hormone is something our body uses literally from head to toe. In general, anyone with too much thyroid hormone in her system is vulnerable to bone loss, because thyroid hormone will speed up or slow down bone cells just as it will speed or slow other processes in our bodies, such as our metabolism. Osteoblasts are the cells responsible for building bone, while osteoclasts are cells that remove old bone so that the new bone can be replaced. When you are thyrotoxic, osteoclasts get overstimulated; in short, they go nuts. They begin to remove bone faster than it can be replaced by the osteoblasts, which are not affected by too much thyroid hormone. The result? You wind up with too much bone removed and subsequent bone loss.

Once your thyroid hormone levels are restored to normal, the risk is gone. But, as discussed in Chapter 10, finding the right dosage can be tricky. Women who have had a thyroidectomy to treat thyroid cancer or for other reasons need to be on a slightly higher dosage of thyroid hormone to suppress all thyroid stimulating hormone (TSH) activity. So they may live in a state of mild thyrotoxicosis. Essentially, postmenopausal women on thyroid hormone should have their thyroid hormone levels checked every year so that they can adjust their dosage accordingly. (See Chapter 2.)

A long list of other factors affect bone loss. One of the most obvious contributing factors is calcium in our diet. Calcium is regularly lost to urine, feces, and dead skin. We need to continuously account for this loss in our diet. In fact, the less calcium we ingest, the more we force our body into taking it out of our bones. Exercise also greatly affects bone density; the more we exercise, the stronger we make our bones. In fact, the bone mass we have in our late twenties and early thirties will affect our bone mass at menopause.

A particular risk for people with thyroid cancer is loss of parathyroid hormone from accidentally damaging the parathyroid glands during thyroid surgery (see Chapter 11). There are further complications with osteoporosis discussed in Chapter 11, which explains treatment for *hypoparathyroidism* or low-functioning parathyroid glands.

How Much Calcium Do You Need?

According to the National Institutes of Health Consensus Panel on Osteoporosis, pre-menopausal women require roughly 1,000 milligrams of calcium a day; for peri-menopausal or postmenopausal women already on HRT or ERT, 1,000 milligrams; and for peri- and postmenopausal women not taking estrogen, roughly 1,500 milligrams per day. For women who have already been diagnosed with osteoporosis, the Panel recommends 2,500 milligrams of calcium a day. Foods that are rich in calcium include all dairy products (an eight-ounce glass of milk contains 300 milligrams calcium), fish, shellfish, oysters, shrimp, sardines, salmon, soybeans, tofu, broccoli, and dark green vegetables (except spinach, which contains oxalic acid, preventing calcium absorption). It's crucial to determine how much calcium you're getting in your diet before you start any calcium supplements; too much calcium can cause kidney stones in people who are at risk for them. In addition, not all supplements have been tested for absorbency. It's crucial to remember that a calcium supplement is in fact a supplement and should not replace a high-calcium diet. So the dosage of your supplement would only need to be roughly 400 to 600 milligrams per day, while your diet should account for the remainder of your 1,000- to 1,500-milligram daily intake of calcium. Calcium supplements, in large quantities, can also affect the absorption of thyroid hormone, so you should discuss with your doctor whether you need to adjust your thyroid hormone dosage accordingly or time your calcium and thyroid hormone at different intervals to maximize the absorbency of your thyroid hormone.

Selective Estrogen Receptor Modulators (SERMs)

SERMs are a new class of drugs originally designed to help treat estrogen-dependent breast cancers but were instead shown to help prevent bone loss—particularly around the spine and hip—and even increase bone mass. The first drug from this family, approved for use in 1998, is raloxifene (Evista). Women who took raloxifene for three years reduced their risk of fractures by about 50 percent. Even better, raloxifene may help protect you from heart disease, as it helps lower bad cholesterol. Some studies suggest that raloxifene may also reduce the incidence of breast cancer in some women. Raloxifene and HRT are equally effective in protecting your bones. And of course, you can continue to take calcium and/or vitamin D with raloxifene. As bone loss is a concern for women who are taking thyroid hormone, and particularly for women who have low calcium levels because of damaged parathyroid glands (see Chapter 11), raloxifene is an important therapy for many women with thyroid disease.

Bisphosphonates: Bone-Forming Drugs

As discussed earlier, osteoblasts are the cells responsible for building bone, while osteoclasts are cells that remove old bone so the new bone can be replaced. Bisphosphonates stop or slow down the osteoclasts, without interfering with osteoblasts, the bone-forming cells. So you wind up with greater bone density. In the past, these drugs were approved only for treating severe bone diseases, such as Paget's disease. Two bisphosphonates—etidronate (Didrocal/Didronel) and alendronate (Fosamax)—have been approved for use in women who are not on HRT but who are at risk of osteoporosis. Although bisphosphonates do not relieve any menopausal signs, such as hot flashes, and offer no protection against heart disease, as discussed, women on thyroid hormone, or who are thyrotoxic for other reasons, are particularly at risk for bone loss, and this is a good option for many.

Parathyroid Hormone (PTH)

The new drug parathyroid hormone (PTH), in the form of recombinant parathyroid hormone, can build bone density back to its original peak and sometimes can even surpass it; the FDA approved one form of PTH, PTH-(1-34), known as Forteo, in 2003. As of this writing, Forteo is the only approved brand of PTH, which your doctor can advise you about, but it is not of use to women who have hypoparathyroidism because you need to have balanced calcium levels to take Forteo.

Staying Alert About Heart Disease

If you are past menopause, you must educate yourself about the signs and symptoms of heart disease, since you are at higher risk. Other risk factors, such as smoking, obesity, high blood pressure, and high cholesterol, can be reduced with lifestyle changes. For example, women who are physically active have a 60 to 75 percent lower risk of heart disease than inactive women.

Heart disease is currently the number-one cause of death in postmenopausal women; more women die of heart disease than lung cancer or breast cancer. Half of all North Americans who die from heart attacks each year are women.

One of the reasons for such high death rates from heart attacks among women is medical ignorance. Most studies examining heart disease excluded women, which led to a myth that more men than women die of heart disease. In reality, more men die of heart attacks before age fifty, while more women die of heart attacks after age fifty. It remains unclear whether estrogen loss increases the risk, or whether the risk is more broadly linked to aging. We do know that women are under unique stresses because of their social "location." Another problem is that women have different symptoms from men when it comes to heart disease, and so the "typical" warning signs we know about in men—angina, or chest pains—are often never present in women. In fact, chest pains in women are almost never related to heart disease. For women, the symptoms of heart disease, and even an actual heart attack, can be much more vague and seemingly unrelated to heart problems. Thyroid disease, both hypothyroidism and thyrotoxicosis, can aggravate these problems. This is explored further in Chapter 25.

15 Thyroid Disease in Infants and Children

Although children can have nearly all of the same thyroid problems as adults, the consequences are far more severe and the solutions more difficult. An infant's brain still has much further to grow and develop, requiring sufficient amounts of thyroid hormone for this to happen normally. Thyrotoxicosis can affect the heart, bones, behavior, and school achievement. Thyroid cancer in children has a greater chance of spreading to the lungs and bones than the same type of cancer in adults. In addition, infants and young children are unable to vocalize their symptoms, making it necessary for parents and physicians to be alert to signs of thyroid disease.

In this chapter, we'll begin explaining thyroid diseases in the newborn and then deal with thyroid disease in young children. We'll discuss the remarkable benefits of newborn screening programs for hypothyroidism, which are now active in nearly all industrialized nations. Newborn infants are also susceptible to factors from their mothers that cause thyroid problems, and they respond to medications differently from adults. Both infants and young children exposed to radiation to their thyroid glands are far more susceptible to later developing thyroid cancer, when they are older children or adults, than those first exposed to this radiation as adults.

Children also have special problems complying with medications, particularly thyroid hormone. This results from a child's lack of truly comprehending the importance of thyroid medication or even refusing to take it as an act of rebellion in teenage years (a common problem also seen in insulin-requiring teens, for example). In this chapter, we'll focus on the special circumstances of infants and children with respect to thyroid diseases, referring you to the appropriate chapters for those thyroid problems that are the same as in adults.

Thyroid Disease in Newborns and Infants

Newborn screening programs provide a clear picture of the incidence of thyroid problems in industrialized countries. These problems are dwarfed by the incidence of hypothyroidism in developing countries with iodine deficiency and poor access to health care. Table 15.1 shows all causes of newborn thyroid disease in industrialized countries, with the exception of thyroid hormone resistance (discussed in Chapter 18).

Hypothyroidism

In adults, hypothyroidism can range from a minor annoyance, easily remedied, to a major medical problem with important, yet temporary, consequences. On the other hand, hypothyroid newborns and infants risk permanent mental retardation if thyroid hormone therapy is not started right away. To combat the effects of iodine deficiency on causing hypothyroidism in the developing countries, the World Health Organization and a number of social service organizations have made iodine supplementation an international priority. To detect and treat hypothyroidism in newborns early enough to prevent developmental problems, industrialized nations have instituted neonatal hypothyroidism screening programs.

TABLE 15.1 Thyroid Disease in Newborns

Thyroid Problem	Incidence (Cases per Births)
Hypothyroidism	1 in 3,800

Permanent (90% of hypothyroidism)
Thyroid dysgenesis
    Athyreotic (25% of dysgenesis)
    Hypoplastic (10%)
    Ectopic (65%)
	1 in 4,500

Dyshormonogenesis	1 in 30,000
Pituitary or hypothalamus disease Transient (10% of hypothyroidism)	1 in 100,000
Blocking antibodies from the mother	1 in 180,000
Excess iodine or drugs from the mother	Not known
Hyperthyroidism (2% of mothers with Graves' disease)	1 in 50,000
Thyroid hormone resistance	Very rare
Deficiency of thyroxine-binding globulin	1 in 7,500

Newborn screening programs to detect hypothyroidism became practical in the 1970s and have become standard practice throughout the United States, Canada, and most industrialized countries. They use drops of blood, obtained by pricking the newborn's heel, spotted on filter paper. Special tests have been developed to measure T4 levels and TSH levels on the same dried blood spot.

Some programs first measure the T4 level, then measure the TSH level in the samples with low T4 levels. If the TSH level is high, then the baby should start levothyroxine treatment. If the TSH is normal, the thyroxine-binding globulin (TBG) level is measured (see Chapter 2) to see if absent TBG accounts for the low T4 level in an otherwise normal infant. If the TBG level is normal, then further endocrine evaluation of the infant is advised, as this suggests pituitary or hypothalamic disease. Other programs first measure the TSH. Slightly high TSH levels are retested with a T4 level. Definitely high TSH levels will lead to the doctor contacting the parents to begin thyroid hormone treatment with their child. These screening techniques have nearly eliminated the severe mental retardation resulting from untreated congenital hypothyroidism in countries fortunate enough to have such programs.

It's important to start treatment with levothyroxine as soon as the hypothyroidism is discovered. Infants are started on a dosage between 37 and 50 micrograms daily, adjusting the dosage according to the baby's response, the free T4 level, and the TSH. It seems that the TSH may stay slightly high despite appropriate levothyroxine treatment; however, this may be a sign that the baby is missing doses of T4.

Symptoms of Hypothyroidism in Newborns

Signs of hypothyroidism in newborn infants are unique to this age group. Classic features include a large tongue, umbilical hernia, enlarged fontanels (the soft spots on a newborn's skull), low muscular tone, goiter (unless the baby has thyroid dysgenesis), low body temperature (less than 36°C or 96.8°F), slow reflexes, and respiratory distress. Symptoms of hypothyroidism include constipation, lethargy, poor feeding, and prolonged newborn jaundice (yellowing of the skin). Newborn screening programs are effective enough so that more than a third of infants diagnosed with hypothyroidism have no abnormal signs or symptoms. Taking advantage of early laboratory testing, rather than waiting for infants to appear ill, is the best way of preventing permanent brain damage from hypothyroidism.

Permanent Hypothyroidism

The majority of hypothyroidism cases detected by newborn screening are permanent, most resulting from abnormal formation of the thyroid gland (called *thyroid dysgenesis*). Two-thirds of newborns with thyroid dysgenesis have thyroid glands in different body locations from the usual location, called an *ectopic* thyroid. Since the thyroid gland descends from the base of the tongue downward to the base of the neck during development of the embryo (see Chapter 1), the most common location for an ectopic thyroid is either at the tongue base or anywhere in the midline of the neck above the breast-bone. Less commonly, thyroid glands may be found in the middle of the chest, sometimes even inside the heart or lower in the body. Ectopic thyroid glands are usually defective and unable to make much thyroid hormone, accounting for the infant's hypothyroidism; however, sometimes they work well enough, making the discovery of a thyroid gland, appearing as a strawberry-like lump at the base of the tongue, a strange surprise during a dental examination.

A quarter of the time the baby hasn't any thyroid gland at all (*athyreotic*). This is likely because of a mutation in the embryo, where the genetic sequence involved with turning on other genes responsible for forming the thyroid gland was flawed. Less common are thyroids that are much smaller than normal (*hypoplastic*) and unable to make sufficient thyroid hormone.

*Thyroid dyshormonogene*sis is a term encompassing a variety of conditions in which the thyroid gland is unable to manufacture thyroid hormone. These conditions include an inability to make iodine join onto proteins or amino acids, inability to join together the components that make T3 and T4, inability of the thyroid to respond to TSH, or failure to take up iodine. Another condition resulting in thyroid dyshormonogenesis is called *Pendred syndrome*, characterized by deafness (caused by nerve dysfunction), goiter, and hypothyroidism from a mutation in the pendrin protein, responsible for some of the movement of iodine out of thyroid cells.

It's rare for newborns to have pituitary or hypothalamic problems as a cause of hypothyroidism. They usually occur together with malformations of facial and brain structures. In these conditions, blood tests show low total T4 levels with normal or low TSH levels. The same blood test results are seen when thyroxine-binding globulin (TBG) is deficient and the thyroid is actually normal, a condition seen much more frequently than pituitary or hypothalamic disease. This is because the screening tests measure only the total T4, which is low when TBG is absent, rather than the free T4, which is normal in TBG deficiency.

Transient Hypothyroidism

A variety of iodine-containing cleansing agents or contrast dyes used in x-ray imaging tests can be given to the mother during pregnancy or to the baby after birth. Excess iodine can inhibit the production of thyroid hormone by the baby's thyroid. This is more likely to happen in small or premature babies. Likewise, medications given to the mother for Graves' disease, such as methimazole or PTU (see Chapters 11 and 13), can block the baby's thyroid from making thyroid hormone. Since the effects of excess iodine and antithyroid drugs disappear when they're no longer around, they cause only transient hypothyroidism.

Antibodies from the mother that block the effects of TSH on its receptor (see Chapter 1) can cause a very rare case of hypothyroidism in her baby. These antibodies are similar to the antibodies that cause Graves' disease by stimulating the TSH receptor, except that they have the opposite effect on the receptor. Since they've been present through much of the pregnancy, they may cause permanent deficiencies in brain development even though they gradually dissipate after birth.

Hyperthyroidism

Almost all of the time, hyperthyroidism in newborns is a temporary problem. Thyroid-stimulating antibodies cause it, transferred through the placenta from a mother with Graves' disease (see Chapter 13). This is suspected when the newborn has an unexplained rapid heartbeat, a goiter, prominent eyes, irritability, poor weight gain, and a mother with active Graves' disease or a past history of Graves' disease. As in adults, PTU or methimazole, as well as propranolol, are used to treat the baby since the antibodies may take a couple of months to go away.

Thyroid Disease in Children and Adolescents

The causes of thyroid disease in children and adolescents are the same as in adults. However, children present challenges in managing thyroid problems that are different from those of adults. Also, symptoms may be subtle or insidious, delaying recognition of thyroid disease. Sometimes, the only initial signs of a problem are changes in growth rate or school performance.

Hypothyroidism

Hypothyroid children may show a decrease in their rate of growth. Although they may gain some weight, the decreased height magnifies the effect of this weight gain. If the hypothyroidism isn't detected for a few years, bone and tooth development is delayed. This can be seen when the pediatrician charts the child's growth curves and when the dentist checks for tooth development milestones. Sometimes, in a chubby child, a goiter (see Chapter 7) isn't easily seen. And while the typical features of hypothyroidism in adults are usually present, often they're not recognized as hypothyroidism early on. Hypothyroid children may be lethargic, constipated, have dry skin and hair, and swelling around their eyes. Puberty is likely to be delayed, but sometimes it can start prematurely (called *precocious puberty*).

Treatment with thyroid hormone (levothyroxine) should be started as soon as possible. The goal is to make the TSH normal (unless the cause is pituitary or hypothalamic disease).

Compliance Issues: When They Won't Take Their Medicine

Compliance is a big problem with children. Even a "spoonful of sugar" won't help some children's medicine go down! Some parents swear that they give their child a levothyroxine pill every morning, yet the child remains hypothyroid. Sometimes a month's supply of pills is found hidden under the refrigerator where they've been spit out. This is not unusual with other pills, such as vitamin pills or antibiotics, but in those cases, they're not as critical. It's a good idea to watch your child swallow the pill, then have the child open his or her mouth to demonstrate that it was actually swallowed. These problems become worse during adolescence, sometimes as an expression of rebellion. I've found compliance issues equally difficult in boys and girls.

Dosages for Children and Teens

The dosage of levothyroxine depends upon the age of the child. For children between one and five years of age, the usual dosage is 4 to 6 micrograms per kilogram body weight each day. By six to ten years of age the dosage is 3 to 4 micrograms per kilogram body weight each day. This same average treatment dosage is reduced in eleven-year-olds or older children to around 2 micrograms per kilogram body weight daily. Eventually, the dosage approaches the average daily adult amount of 1.6 micrograms per kilogram body weight, as discussed in Chapter 10.

Causes of Hypothyroidism in Children and Teens

Just as in adults, Hashimoto's thyroiditis is the most common cause of hypothyroidism in industrialized countries. Antithyroid antibodies in the blood, particularly antithyroid peroxidase and antithyroglobulin antibodies, are present in more than 95 percent of children with Hashimoto's thyroiditis (also known as *chronic lymphocytic thyroiditis*). Although occasional children with mild Hashimoto's thyroiditis might regain full normal thyroid function, most become more severely hypothyroid over time unless given appropriate thyroid hormone treatment with levothyroxine.

Additional causes of hypothyroidism are less common. Unusual partial defects in forming thyroid hormone (dyshormonogenesis), mild enough to evade detection as a newborn, rarely reveal themselves as they worsen in childhood. Pituitary tumors or unusual tumors in the part of the brain controlling the pituitary, the hypothalamus, may result in hypothyroidism because it interferes with TSH production. The most common type of tumor is a *craniopharyngioma*, a benign growth of skin-type cells within the hypothalamus that often contain fluid and disrupt normal function of this portion of the brain. Sometimes previous radiation treatments, particularly radiation given for childhood brain tumors, causes decreased function of the hypothalamus or pituitary. Likewise, radiation to the thyroid gland from radiation treatments of Hodgkin's disease can cause hypothyroidism.

Goiter

Almost one in twenty school-age children in North America have an enlarged thyroid gland (goiter). Most children with goiters are female and most of them are euthyroid (because of colloid goiters, discussed in Chapter 7). Of course, hypothyroid children with Hashimoto's thyroiditis often have goiters, as do thyrotoxic children with Graves' disease. The diversity of causes of goiters, described in Chapter 7, also applies to children with goiters.

Treatment of hypothyroid children with levothyroxine is necessary and noncontroversial, and it may also reduce the size of their goiter. On the other hand, there is no evidence that giving thyroid hormone to euthyroid children with goiters will be effective in reducing their goiter safely. As will be discussed, treatment of hyperthyroid goiters, particularly with radioactive iodine, may shrink them to normal sizes or even smaller.

Thyroiditis

Irritation of the thyroid, *thyroiditis*, because of viruses, bacteria, or autoimmune (self-immune) factors can happen in children as well as in adults. All of the types of thyroiditis described in Chapter 5 apply similarly to this age group, with the exception of postpartum thyroiditis.

Hyperthyroidism and Thyrotoxicosis

The most common cause of thyrotoxicosis in children is Graves' disease, fully discussed in Chapter 6. Graves' disease is not as common in children as in adults. Adolescent girls are most likely to develop it. All of the features seen in adults are seen in children. Children usually have a definite goiter, rapid pulse, irritable behavior, and difficulty sleeping. They frequently lose weight despite a voracious appetite. All of this, coupled with a shortened attention span, contributes to behavioral problems and decreased school performance. Additionally, Graves' ophthalmopathy (orbitopathy) can present considerable challenges in this age group, and similar treatments as given to adults (see Chapter 23) are advised.

Treating Graves' Disease in Children

Treating Graves' disease in children remains an area of controversy. Most often, thionamides (antithyroid drugs) are the first line of therapy (see Chapter 11), while beta-blockers (see Chapter 11) are used to control thyrotoxic symptoms. Compliance with these medications is also a special problem in children. Although methimazole is preferred, because it can be effective given only once or twice a day, around 10 percent of these children develop some significant reactions to thionamides, forcing them to go off of this drug. The rate of remission (disappearance of thyrotoxicosis after stopping six to twelve months of thionamides therapy) is a bit higher than in adults; however, most children eventually need definitive treatment, either surgery or radioactive iodine. American physicians have been more likely to use radioactive iodine for children than physicians in Europe or Japan. Although there is reasonable concern that children may be susceptible to developing thyroid cancers from radioactive iodine exposure, these fears have not proven well founded after many decades of experience.

Concerns regarding future fertility of these children and the risk of birth defects have also proven unfounded with no such ill effects seen at all.

Some aspects of Graves' disease in children suggest different treatment approaches. Children with smaller goiters and less thyrotoxicosis seem to do better with thionamides and have the greatest chance that they could obtain a remission. Children with severe thyroid eye disease and large, potentially obstructive, or nodular goiters may do best with thyroid surgery—provided that the surgeon has sufficient experience to lessen the surgical risks of hypoparathyroidism and damage to the nerves leading to the vocal cords. I (Ken) tend to use radioactive iodine with most other children because it is usually quite effective and simple, with no evidence of long-term ill consequences. Radioactive iodine (Chapter 12) is usually the easiest treatment for children because, after taking sufficient radioactive iodine to make them permanently hypothyroid, it is easier to teach the child to take a single levothyroxine tablet each morning than to take multiple doses of antithyroid pills for an indefinite period of time with their potential side effects and need for frequent blood tests and physician's office visits.

Autonomous Toxic Nodules in Children

Autonomous toxic thyroid nodules (ATNs) are quite rare in young children but sometimes are seen in children after puberty. As discussed in Chapter 8, ATNs are caused by mutations in the TSH receptor in a thyroid cell that turn it on without needing TSH. This cell eventually divides and grows into many such cells, forming a nodule. When the nodule becomes large enough to make thyroid hormone levels too high, it can cause all of the symptoms seen in Graves' disease, except that there is no associated eye disease. Usually, the child develops thyrotoxicosis much more gradually than children with Graves' disease. Aside from the nodule in the thyroid gland, the rest of the gland tends to be smaller than normal, because the TSH levels are low and not present to stimulate the normal surrounding thyroid cells. When a radioactive iodine thyroid scan is performed, you can see that the nodule sucks up all of the radioactive iodine, appearing "hot" on the scan image, while the rest of the thyroid gland takes up little, if any, radioactive iodine.

There is no reason to give children with ATNs any thionamide drugs, except as a temporary measure to lower thyroid hormone levels because these nodules, unlike hyperthyroid goiters in some children with Graves' disease, will never undergo a spontaneous cure or remission. Thionamides would need to be taken lifelong in ever-increasing dosages with greater and greater chances of dangerous side effects. The two treatment options are surgery, removing the entire side of the gland containing the ATN, or radioactive iodine. Generally, radioactive iodine is most effective for small ATNs, under an inch (2.5 centimeters) in diameter, with the normal parts of the thyroid protected from some of the radioactive iodine effects because the suppressed TSH levels prevent much radioactive iodine from being taken into normal parts of the thyroid. Larger ATNs do best with surgery, provided that an experienced thyroid surgeon is available.

In the McCune-Albright syndrome (also known as polyostotic fibrous dysplasia), an exceedingly rare disorder in children, affected children have mutations in the cells of their endocrine organs that make them overresponsive to some hormonal signals. This causes a wide range of problems, including precocious (too early) puberty, characteristic large brown birthmarks, and bone problems. As part of this syndrome, children may develop multiple ATNs. Treatment is similar to that of other children with ATNs.

Thyroid Nodules

Children with thyroid nodules or nodules in their neck have the same need for effective evaluation as adults. They also have additional problems. Since young children may have frequent ear infections and often have enlarged lymph nodes in their necks from these (or other) infections, pediatricians appropriately reassure parents that these enlarged nodes are of little concern. Sometimes they give the child a course of antibiotic treatment, which may lead to false reassurance and the enlarged lymph nodes being ignored. Likewise, thyroid nodules can be mistakenly treated in a similar fashion, even though they're not lymph nodes. Any enlarged lymph nodes in the neck that persist or grow for more than a few weeks need to be biopsied to see if they contain cancer. Likewise, it is important to assess thyroid nodules, using the same approach as used in adults (see Chapter 8).

After checking the TSH level to verify that the child is not thyrotoxic (suggesting the possibility of Graves' disease or ATN), the next step is to perform a fine needle aspiration biopsy (see Chapter 2). I've been able to do fine-needle thyroid biopsies on children as young as eighteen months of age, with excellent cooperation and no need for any anesthesia (using very skinny 27-gauge needles). Not all physicians are comfortable performing biopsies on young children; however, it should not be an excuse for delaying this procedure nor subjecting the child to unnecessary invasive surgery in lieu of a simple biopsy. Any biopsy results that document or suggest malignancy, including indeterminate or suspicious results (see Chapter 8), should lead to the scheduling of thyroid surgery.

Thyroid Cancer in Children

Thyroid cancer is a lifelong illness, in that it requires lifelong follow-up and monitoring for recurrent disease. When thyroid cancer is first discovered in a child, there are unique features to the cancer and unique problems in managing it. This section is divided into three parts. The first part will discuss the special problems of thyroid surgery in children. The second part will discuss papillary and follicular thyroid cancers, usually found consequent to an evaluation of a thyroid nodule or enlarged lymph node as discussed in the preceding section. The third part will deal with medullary thyroid cancers, usually found in children as part of an inherited genetic syndrome and often treated by preventative surgical removal of the thyroid after finding the responsible gene mutation with genetic screening.

Thyroid Surgery in Children

Children have special problems when it comes to thyroid surgery. First, it's important to find the right surgeon. Although pediatric surgery is a distinct surgical specialty, very few pediatric surgeons obtain sufficient experience to become excellent thyroid surgeons. In Chapter 9, we talked about the need for a surgeon to have specialized training and enough surgical thyroid cases each year to maintain his or her skills and lower the rate of complications. Since it's not very common that young children need thyroid surgery for Graves' disease, and thyroid cancers are much less common than in adults, pediatric surgeons rarely see more than several such patients each year. Thyroid surgery is rarely needed before three years of age. Pediatric surgeons (often ear, nose, and throat specialists, also known as *otolaryngologists*) may better serve children less than ten years of age; however, adult thyroid surgeons are often a better choice for children over ten years of age.

Major surgery of any sort is a significant trauma to a young child, and it's best to avoid unnecessarily repeated surgeries. For that reason, particularly since thyroid cancers can grow more aggressively in children and radioactive iodine treatments work best on microscopic (rather than large) residual disease, it's important for the surgeon to do a total thyroidectomy, instead of leaving substantial amounts of thyroid tissue behind. For this same reason, careful removal of enlarged lymph nodes in the neck is a necessary part of this surgery. All of the risks of this surgery, particularly loss of the parathyroid glands or damage to the nerves of the vocal cords, become multiplied by the need for repeated surgeries when the initial surgery was not sufficiently complete. These risks of surgery seem to be higher in young children. Much of this may be the result of surgeons being inexperienced in thyroid surgery. Some may result from the initial invasive growth of the most common thyroid cancers in this age group. For these reasons, it may be wiser to use recognized thyroid surgeons at regional medical centers, rather than local surgeons chosen more for convenience.

Papillary and Follicular Thyroid Cancers in Children

Most thyroid cancers in children are papillary cancers. Follicular thyroid cancers are less common than in adults. In children exposed to radioactive fallout (as was the case in the Chernobyl accident), an unusual type of papillary thyroid cancer, known as *diffuse sclerosing variant*, seems to be more common. There are important differences in the way these cancers grow in children compared to adults. The cancer is more likely to invade through the covering of the thyroid gland into the soft tissues, muscles, and vital structures in the neck (including the windpipe, esophagus, and voice box). Often, a large number of lymph nodes in the neck contain thyroid cancer. Also, compared to adults, the thyroid cancer is more likely to spread to the lungs, bones, and other parts of the body. The tumor seems to be more aggressive in its spread and growth rate than the same type of thyroid cancer appearing first in adults.

There is good news about treating these types of cancers, however; they seem more responsive to radioactive iodine therapy than in adults. This suggests the need to use appropriate and assertive treatment after the thyroid surgery, making sure that the physician is intent on giving radioactive iodine treatment with effective methods of preparation as outlined in Chapters 2, 9, and 12. Children with distant spread of their thyroid cancer to body regions outside of their necks, such as the lungs, may need specialized care using maximal safe dose radioactive iodine (a technique known as *dosimetry*, discussed in Chapter 12). Follow-up, as in adults, is lifelong. Radioactive iodine scans (and appropriate treatments when needed) should be performed at regular intervals, and the dose of thyroid hormone (levothyroxine) should be carefully adjusted to suppress TSH (to levels less than 0.1) without causing thyrotoxic symptoms. Follow-up includes using blood tests for thyroglobulin to check for recurrent tumor and performing regular neck self-exams. Children need to be educated so that they can fully participate in their long-term care. Physician follow-up should involve using appropriate subspecialists (thyroid oncologists, endocrinologists, unusually well-trained oncologists) rather than only general pediatricians.

Medullary Thyroid Cancer in Children

Rarely, thyroid nodules in children turn out to be medullary thyroid cancers, a type of cancer we discuss in Chapter 9. More often, a family is already known to have at least one member diagnosed with medullary thyroid cancer (called an *index patient*), and the child's blood tests have shown that he or she has a mutation in the RET proto-oncogene responsible for causing this cancer. In this case, it takes only one parent with the mutation to pass it on to a child (called an *autosomal dominant* mutation). Furthermore, the likelihood that the mutation will cause cancer (known as *penetrance*) is nearly 100 percent. That means that if an individual has this mutation he or she is expected to develop this cancer at some time in his or her life. Usually, the blood relatives of the index patient should have their blood tested to see if they also have this specific gene mutation. Children in the family should be tested as early as possible. Should these tests show the presence of this mutation, to prevent the development of this cancer or to treat it at an early stage, an experienced surgeon should remove the person's entire thyroid gland. Children as young as three years of age should have their thyroid removed if their genetic tests are confirmed positive. This is because metastatic (spreading) inherited medullary thyroid cancers have been documented in very young children. Some of these children are also at risk for developing tumors of their adrenal glands making too much adrenaline, called *pheochromocytomas*, and need to be checked at regular intervals.

Only around 20 percent of medullary thyroid cancers of all age groups are inherited in this fashion. On the other hand, most childhood medullary thyroid cancers are likely to have been inherited from a gene mutation, since nongenetic medullary thyroid cancers are more common in older adults.

16 Thyroid Disease and Obesity

he most important fact we wish to emphasize when it comes to thyroid disease and obesity is that it is extremely common for all obese persons to wonder whether their thyroid is "making them fat." This chapter will help you sort out whether your obesity predates your thyroid problem, is aggravated by a thyroid problem, or is the result of one. Obesity refers to a body size that is too overweight for good health. Obese people have greater incidences of type 2 diabetes, heart attacks, strokes, peripheral vascular disease (circulation problems, leading to many other health problems), and certain types of cancers. Hypothyroidism can aggravate obesity and complications from obesity. Hyperthyroidism or thyrotoxicosis, however, may cause an unhealthy type of weight loss, aggravating other conditions that may be linked to obesity, such as heart disease (see Chapter 25) or type 2 diabetes.

It is not known how many people with thyroid disease are obese; but it is clear that the majority of obese people do not have thyroid disease. It is important to check for thyroid disease if you are obese, but keep in mind that there are many different causes for obesity, and your thyroid tests may be normal. Nevertheless, many who are overweight may indeed be suffering from unrecognized or untreated hypothyroidism. If you're reading this chapter and wondering whether your weight problem is the result of a thyroid problem, request a thyroid function test from your physician (see Chapter 2).

When obesity is a result of hypothyroidism, most people will find that they start to return to their normal weight once their hypothyroidism is treated. Of course, anything that causes you to gain additional body fat, such as pregnancy or hypothyroidism, may contribute to long-term obesity even after the initial cause is gone or treated. This is why you need to pay careful attention to diet and exercise, even though you are taking the proper amount of thyroid hormone to have normal thyroid hormone levels and a normal TSH.

Feelings of tiredness and low energy, which are symptoms of hypothyroidism, may cause you to crave carbohydrates and quick-energy foods, which are higher in fat and calories. When you are hypothyroid, your activity level will decrease as a result of your fatigue, which can also lead to weight gain or aggravate preexisting obesity. The craving for carbohydrates is caused by a desire for energy. Consuming carbohydrates produces an initial "rush" of energy, but then it is followed by a crash, which is sometimes known as *postprandial depression* (or postmeal depression), exacerbating or contributing to hypothyroid-induced depression. Even in those with normal thyroid function, depression can cause cravings for simple carbohydrates such as sugars and sweets. In the absence of overeating, some of the weight gain in hypothyroidism is bloating from constipation. Increasing fluid intake and fiber will help the problem, which we discuss more in Chapter 20.

The problem for most people who are battling both obesity and hypothyroidism is that their obesity often predates their thyroid problem, indicating that there are other factors involved in their weight gain. Stack a thyroid problem on top of that, and it may exacerbate all kinds of other behaviors that led to the initial weight gain, as well as aggravate risks associated with obesity in general.

Defining Obesity

At one time, anyone who weighed 20 percent more than the ideal weight for his or her age and height was defined as clinically obese. But this is not as accurate an indicator as the body mass index (BMI), which is now the best measurement of obesity. The BMI is calculated by dividing your weight (in kilograms) by your height (in meters) squared. (The formula used is BMI = kg/m^2 if you're doing this on your calculator.) BMI charts abound on the Internet, on the backs of cereal boxes, and in numerous health magazines. Most people can now easily find BMI converters on the Internet, where you simply type in your weight in pounds and your height to arrive at your BMI. A good chart will calculate BMI by gender and sometimes age ranges.

Currently, a BMI of 18.5 or less indicates that you are underweight. A BMI between 18.5 and 24.9 is normal. The most recent clinical guidelines define people with a BMI between 25 and 29.9 as overweight, and those with a BMI between 30 and 34.9 as obese (mild to moderate). A BMI between 35.0 and 39.9 would indicate severe obesity; people with a BMI of 40 or greater are considered morbidly obese. These are the clinical guidelines for defining obesity as of 1998. Changes in the average weight of people in North America since then means that at least 75 million more North Americans are now considered obese who were not considered obese in 1998.

Obesity rates in children and teens are calculated through BMIs that are at or above sex- and age-specific weights within the 95th percentiles. This is a more conservative approach to account for growth spurts.

Obesity experts consider the North American lifestyle to be the single largest contributing factor to obesity. Although social, behavioral, metabolic, cellular, and genetic factors all contribute to obesity, some obesity genes are "turned on" only when they are exposed to an environment conducive to weight gain, such as a sedentary and food-rich environment.

North Americans have the highest obesity rates in the world. More than half of North American adults and about 25 percent of North American children are now obese. These figures reflect a doubling of adult obesity rates since the 1960s and a doubling of the childhood obesity rate since the late 1970s—a staggering increase when you think about it in raw numbers. Obese children will most likely grow up to become obese adults, according to the most recent research.

Waist circumference is another factor in calculating obesity—particularly abdominal obesity. Men with a waist circumference of 40 inches or more are at increased risk of obesity-related health problems, while women with a waist circumference of 35 inches or more are at an increased risk of obesity-related health problems.

Morbid Obesity

Morbid obesity is extreme obesity. People with BMIs in the upper 30s or higher than 40 are classified as morbidly obese. Another method to calculate morbid obesity is through ideal body weight. When people exceed their ideal weight by more than 100 pounds, they are considered morbidly obese. People who are morbidly obese are at the highest risk of health complications. For example, morbidly obese men between the ages of twenty-five and thirty-five have twelve times the risk of dying prematurely than their peers of normal weights. Morbid obesity also causes a range of medical problems, such as breathing difficulties, gastrointestinal ailments, endocrine problems (especially diabetes), musculoskeletal problems, hygiene problems, sexual problems, and so on. Many people now undergo bariatric surgery (the "stomach stapling" procedure or an intestinal bypass) to lower their risk of dying from their fat. It's important to clarify that surgery for morbid obesity is not plastic surgery; it is serious gastrointestinal surgery that carries significant risks, offered only to those people whose weight poses an immediate health risk and who have not been able to find any other way to lose weight. For more information, see Appendix B for resources related to obesity and gastrointestinal surgery.

Biological Causes of Obesity

The physiological cause of obesity is eating more calories than you burn. People gain weight for two reasons: they may eat excessively (often excessive amounts of nutritious foods), which results in daily consumption of just too many calories; or they may eat moderately, but simply be too inactive for the calories they do ingest. Genetic makeup can predispose some body types to obesity earlier in life because of "thrifty genes." But, in general, experts in nutrition agree that genetics plays only a small role in the sharp increase in obesity. Since genetic changes take place over centuries, and our obesity rate has at least doubled since the 1960s, it's fairly obvious that lifestyle factors are the chief culprit. Furthermore, as we age, our metabolism slows down. This means that unless we decrease our calorie intake or increase activity levels to compensate, we will probably gain weight. Clearly, thyroid problems, such as hypothyroidism, can contribute to obesity. Rarely is the appetite of someone with thyrotoxicosis stimulated so much that he or she can gain weight despite the increased rate of metabolism. A number of additional factors contribute to obesity.

Thrifty Genes

Genetics play a role in obesity, particularly in some aboriginal and other minority groups, because of what some researchers call the *thrifty genes*. The body of literature published by anthropologists, medical sociologists, epidemiologists, endocrinologists, and other medical researchers on health in aboriginal people (particularly the Pima Indians, Pacific Islanders, and aboriginal people of Canada and Australia) tell the story. Thrifty genes are thought to be responsible for the higher rates of obesity and obesity-related conditions in the aboriginal and non-European populations. This means that the more recently your ethnic group has lived in an indigenous environment (that is, living off the scarce natural resources found on the land you came from and having different amounts of food seasonally), the more efficient your metabolism tends to be. Unfortunately, it is also more sensitive to nutrient excess. If you're an aboriginal North American, only about one hundred years have passed since your ancestors lived indigenously. This is an exceedingly short amount of time to ask thousands of years of hunter-gatherer genes to adjust to the terrible convenience-food diet that prevails in North America. If you're of African descent, you haven't lived here any longer than about four hundred years. Prior to that, your ancestors were living a tribal, nomadic lifestyle. Again, four hundred years is not a long time with respect to your genes. Many immigrant populations come from families who have spent generations in poverty. Their metabolisms adjusted to long periods of famine, and are often overloaded by our abundance of high-caloric foods. Asian populations generally have the lowest rates of obesity, but that could be because they are frequently able to maintain their dietary habits when they immigrate to North America. In fact, European North Americans tend to benefit when they adopt an Asian diet.

Thrifty genes are evident when you look at obesity patterns in the United States, where obesity is more prevalent among African Americans, Latinos, Native Americans and Native Hawaiians, and American Samoans; these groups have higher incidences of diabetes and cardiovascular disease as well. For example, almost 63 percent of Native Hawaiian women are obese, and between 61 and 75 percent of Yaqui Indians are overweight. Among Hispanics, Mexicans have the highest rates of obesity (48.2 percent), followed by Puerto Ricans (40.2 percent).

Diets of poverty may also be a factor in these percentages; these diets typically rely on calories from high-fat, low-nutrient foods instead of fresher foods, fruits, and vegetables. Aboriginal, African, and Hispanic populations tend to have much lower incomes, and therefore eat lower-quality food, which, when combined with the thrifty gene, can lead to obesity and obesity-related health problems. When epidemiologists look at these same thrifty gene groups in higher income levels, the obesity rates are lower.

Leptin and Other Hormones

The most promising antiobesity treatment once involved the "anti-fat hormone," leptin; its discovery led to a surge of obesity drug research. Leptin, discovered in 1994, seemed promising because it is produced by fat cells and was the first antiobesity hormone that surfaced.

The leptin hormone receptor was discovered in 1997 when a mutant strain of extremely obese mice (lacking the gene to make leptin) were able to shed their weight when given leptin. With injections of leptin, the mice's appetite decreased while their metabolic rates increased. Although researchers wondered whether all obese people would lose weight on leptin, this did not occur. It turns out that, like the mutant obese mice, there are only a few rare cases known of human obesity caused by leptin deficiency. Most people seem to become obese by eating too much and being too sedentary. The leptin discovery should provide a successful treatment for rare cases of obesity in leptin-deficient individuals who, in the past, would not have been able to lose weight.

Many people who are obese actually have higher than normal blood levels of leptin and are resistant to its actions. In some leptin trials, the hormone was intended to be given to overweight people, but it was found that they were leptin-resistant and their leptin levels were already very high. In fact, some obesity researchers now believe that leptin has more to do with protecting against weight loss in times of famine, than protecting against weight gain in times of plenty. When fat stores increase, so does leptin; when fat stores shrink, so does leptin. Appetite increases and metabolism decreases when leptin levels shrink, but the opposite does not occur; appetite is not suppressed when leptin increases, nor is metabolism increased. Leptin, it seems, is one of those evolutionary hormones designed to keep our species alive and protect us from starvation. Finding leptin has led obesity researchers into finding out more about how appetite, fat stores, and famine-protection mechanisms work in the body.

On the Horizon

In the wake of leptin research, a host of antiobesity drugs are now in clinical trials. One drug, a form of human variant ciliary neurotrophic factor, Axokine, works by activating a set of brain cells that produce appetite-dampening peptides. Because it works with brain chemistry, endocrinologists are skeptical about long-term effects. Drug research is also revolving around one hormone, ghrelin, which peaks before meals and triggers appetite, as well as a peptide that rises during meals and signals satiety. Stifling one and boosting the other could develop two more drugs to limit calorie intake. Ghrelin is produced in the gastrointestinal tract; researchers describe it as "your stomach's way of telling your brain you're hungry." Drugs can be made to block ghrelin, which would kill hunger. Again, through calorie intake reduction, such a drug could cause weight loss.

Perhaps one of the most exciting finds in obesity research centers is the discovery of a brand-new hormone, known as peptide YY (PYY). While looking at the effects of bariatric surgery on appetite and the hormones secreted that make us feel full or satisfied, a British research team found that levels of the PYY hormone surged in people who had undergone this surgery. Some investigators suspect that it is PYY that is responsible for a person's loss of the desire to eat excessively. Future research with PYY may lead to a truly effective obesity drug. A nasal spray version of PYY is currently in clinical trials.

How Thyroid Disease Impacts Obesity

The typical obese person with thyroid disease frequently has multiple problems going on at once, which are usually complications of obesity that can become magnified with thyroid disease. For example, the majority of obese people with thyroid disease are also managing high cholesterol, hypertension, and, frequently, type 2 diabetes. Worse, many people who are obese also smoke, which aggravates preexisting obesity complications. It's a complex health-care puzzle for most thyroid specialists.

The key to managing thyroid disease in obese people is to treat all problems at once: treat the thyroid problem as well as obesity and other health complications. In this way, many thyroid specialists see themselves as a primary care doctor. It's not unusual for the "thyroid doctor" to initiate prescriptions for thyroid hormone, cholesterol and blood pressure–lowering medications, as well as the most important prescription: going to the type of program that emphasizes calorie-counting (such as Weight Watchers). Essentially, restoring thyroid function to the obese individual may not contribute so much to a sense of well-being without also achieving weight loss.

The Hypothyroid Obese Individual

Hypothyroidism can cause or aggravate hypertension and high cholesterol, which are risk factors for cardiovascular disease and can also lead to atherosclerosis (clogged arteries) and congestive heart failure, discussed in Chapter 25. When type 2 diabetes is in the picture, some individuals may need to be on more intensive diabetes control and may even require insulin, since hypothyroidism can affect blood sugar control, which in turn increases the risk of heart attack and stroke.

Although lifestyle changes, combined with restored thyroid function, can normalize blood pressure and cholesterol levels in many cases, blood pressure and cholesterol–lowering medications may be necessary, discussed in Chapter 25.

Hypothyroidism can also worsen weight gain, because of decreased activity, bloating, and decreased gastrointestinal motility. In a few cases, unrecognized hypothyroidism contributes to obesity, but many more people who wonder whether "my thyroid is making me fat" have garden-variety causes for their obesity: eating more food than they burn off in activity. As we age, our metabolisms slow down, and we frequently discover that we cannot eat as much without weight gain in our forties and fifties as we did in our twenties and thirties. Hashimoto's disease, for example (see Chapter 5), tends to strike in the forties and fifties, which coincides with the metabolic slowdown, making it appear as though it is responsible for weight gain, when in fact, it is only a temporary problem.

In people who are made permanently hypothyroid because of thyroid ablation or thyroidectomy, obesity is usually not caused by hypothyroidism if they are on sufficient doses of thyroid hormone (see Chapter 10). Again, Graves' disease and many types of thyroid cancers first strike in the forties, so the sudden discovery that weight is a problem is usually due, again, to the metabolic slowdown that progresses with age, when we fail to accommodate for our age by eating less and becoming more active.

Thyrotoxicosis and Obesity

In most cases of thyrotoxicosis (see Chapter 4), some weight loss occurs as the body and metabolism speed up. This is why thyroid hormone used to be wrongly prescribed as a diet drug. However, the hidden danger of thyrotoxicosis in obese people is that it overworks the heart in particular, which can be catastrophic for obese individuals with cardiovascular complications. Palpitations (sometimes because of atrial fibrillation) and angina (both discussed more in Chapter 25) can greatly increase the chances of an obese individual with thyrotoxicosis suffering from a sudden heart attack; the risk of this increases if type 2 diabetes or smoking is in the picture. In such individuals, steps can be taken to reduce the risk of heart attack. First, the individual will be put on a beta-blocker (see Chapter 11), which stops the palpitations by blocking adrenaline. Second, a doctor will treat the underlying cause of thyrotoxicosis (for example, reduce the dosage of thyroid hormone or treat any hyperthyroidism). Third, the doctor will try to eliminate or reduce contributing risk factors for cardiovascular complications by prescribing appropriate additional medications (such as antihypertensive or cholesterol-lowering medications) and counsel about lifestyle changes such as quitting smoking, losing weight, and increasing activity.

Inappropriate Drug Treatments for Obesity

Throughout the 1950s, 1960s, and even 1970s, women, in particular, were prescribed thyroid hormone as a weight loss drug. This practice was long abandoned as people became thyrotoxic, but there are currently supplements with active thyroid hormone still being sold in health food stores as weight-loss supplements—these supplements can cause people to become thyrotoxic.

Many obese thyroid patients are attracted to other types of diet pills. Doctors often prescribed amphetamines or "speed," but these drugs, too, are dangerous, and can put your health at risk—especially if you are obese and at risk for cardiovascular problems.

One of the most controversial antiobesity therapies that some thyroid patients may have been prescribed in the past was fenfluramine and phentermine (fen-phen). Both drugs were approved for use individually more than twenty years ago, and, in the early 1990s, doctors tended to prescribe them together for long-term management of obesity. In July 1997, the United States Food and Drug Administration and researchers at the Mayo Clinic and the Mayo Foundation made a joint announcement warning doctors that fen-phen can cause heart disease. By that September, it was pulled from the market.

Other Antiobesity Pills

In 2000, an antiobesity pill that blocks the absorption of almost one-third of the fat people eat was approved. Unfortunately, this prescription drug, called orlistat (Xenical), can cause diarrhea when the fat content in your meal exceeds 20 percent. In the absence of thyrotoxicosis, to avoid the drug's side effects, simply avoid fat! In the presence of thyrotoxicosis it is likely that usual problems with frequent bowel movements will become much worse. Critics of this medication are concerned that it can decrease absorption of vitamin D and other important nutrients.

Another antiobesity drug, sibutramine, was approved for use in 2001. Sibutramine is meant for people whose body mass index (BMI) registers at 27 or higher. But if you're on thyroid hormone, as well as medications for depression, seizures, glaucoma, osteoporosis, gallbladder disease, liver disease, heart disease or stroke prevention, kidney disease, migraines, or Parkinson's disease, you should discuss whether sibutramine is appropriate.

Lowering Fat and Healthy Eating

Dietary guidelines from nutrition experts, government nutrition advisories and panels, and registered dieticians have not changed in fifty years. A good diet is *a balanced diet* representing all food groups, based largely on plant foods, such as fruits, vegetables, legumes, and grains (also known as carbohydrates), with a balance of calories from animal-based foods, such as meats (red meat, poultry), fish, and dairy (also known as protein and fat). Nutrition research spanning the last fifty years has only confirmed these facts. What has changed in fifty years is the terminology used to define "good diet," and the bombardment of information we receive about which foods affect which physiological processes in the body, such as cholesterol levels, triglycerides, blood sugar levels, and insulin. There are also different kinds of fats and carbohydrates, which has made eating so technical and scientific, ordinary North Americans feel more like chemists when trying to plan for healthy meals and diets.

Confusing information about "low fat" versus "low carb" has further distorted our perceptions about diet. But no matter how many properties in foods are dissected or which diet program you buy into, healthy eating comes down to a "balanced diet"— something that actually means "balanced way of life" because the root word of *diet*— *diatta*—literally means "way of life."

The Right Antiobesity Diet

A diet is considered low fat when it restricts calories from fat to below 30 percent daily. Dozens of established low-fat diets are on the market, but they vary from extremely low-fat diets, which restrict calories from fat to about 10 percent, to more moderate low-fat diets, which restrict calories from fat to 15 to 30 percent. Very low-fat diets (restricting calories from fat to 7 to 10 percent) are modeled after the originators of the very low-fat diet as we know it today—Nathan Pritikin, who popularized low-fat eating in the 1950s, and Dean Ornish, who reframed the original Pritikin diet in the late 1970s. Ornish- and Pritikin-styled diets remain the most well-known and most effective diets for people who are extremely obese and at high risk of dying from an obesity-related health problem. The Center for Science in the Public Interest rated a number of diets for the masses in 2000. Very low-fat diets such as Pritikin's and Ornish's were found to be acceptable but were found to restrict some healthy foods, such as seafood, low-fat poultry, and calcium.

The main problem with very low-fat diets is that they are too restrictive for the general public because they are extremely difficult to stick to unless you are very knowledgeable about low-fat cuisine and a creative chef. Also, new information about the benefits of monounsaturated fats and omega-3 fatty acids (the "good fats") has caused nutritionists to rethink the rules governing fat in the diet. In the 1970s and 1980s, the limitations of the very low-fat diet (never intended for the masses, but rather as a heart disease therapy), led people to gorge on "bad carbs" (meaning that they are high on the glycemic index, or considered simply sugars and starches) because they were led to believe that so long as a food was fat free, it was healthy. Also, too few calories from fat left people hungry and craving food. Unfortunately, the gorging on carbs that peaked in the 1980s and early 1990s led to a sharp increase in insulin resistance from carbohydrate overload in the diet.

Then came the diet backlash: the low-carb or Atkins diet. Low-carbohydrate diets are the opposite of low-fat diets; they restrict carbohydrates (which a healthy diet ought to be based on) to about 5 percent and encourage mostly high-fat foods—the more saturated fat, the better. These diets are also known as high-protein diets and ketogenic diets in clinical circles because they trigger ketosis, a condition in which insulin production is shut down, forcing the liver to produce ketone bodies. The brain switches its nutritional status from using sugar as a primary fuel and starts to consume ketones.

People can certainly lose weight while in ketosis, but living in a state of ketosis does not seem to be exactly what nature intended for a healthy human body. Hyperthyroidism tends to worsen ketosis, possibly by decreasing the effect of insulin. In hypothyroidism, the liver function is impaired, possibly reducing the ability to safely tolerate a diet high in fat. Much is unknown concerning the metabolic interactions of an Atkins diet on people with thyroid disease.

In addition to potential dangers of ketosis, the Atkins diet can cause terrible constipation in the first phase, badly aggravating intestinal problems with hypothyroidism. Additionally, consuming high levels of saturated fat spells disaster for people with hypothyroidism, especially for those with high levels of LDL, by exacerbating their cholesterol status. In addition, many people have a genetic condition that causes high triglycerides, which cannot be controlled through diet alone; in these people, the Atkins diet can be life-threatening, causing pancreatitis (while a very low-fat diet has been shown, since the 1950s, to be lifesaving). Other groups who are warned against the Atkins diet are those who suffer from any disease that puts a strain on the kidneys: hypertension, cardiovascular disease, bladder infections or conditions. Of course, anyone who is pregnant should absolutely stay away from this diet because of kidney strain.

Sound nutritional experts maintain that carbohydrates do not make us fat; it is overindulgence in carbohydrates or protein or fat that makes us fat. Eating fewer carbs, and less protein and fat—in other words, eating everything in moderation and expending more energy than is eaten—is the key to weight loss. The proper diet for living well with thyroid disease, as well as special diets for certain thyroid patients, is discussed in more detail in Chapter 20.

17 Thyroid Disease in Older Individuals

I n this chapter, we explore how thyroid disease manifests in people older than sixty, when people can be managing a number of conditions, including heart disease, arthritis, osteoporosis, as well as neurological diseases, such as Alzheimer's.

In 1886, the physician Victor Horsley put forth the theory that the "aged face" was actually a hypothyroid face, leading many physicians of his day to conclude that thyroid disease was a disease of the aged. The fact is that about 4 to 7 percent of people older than sixty are definitely hypothyroid, but it's suspected that a much greater percentage of people have subclinical hypothyroidism after age sixty that frequently goes unrecognized and untreated. Meanwhile, less than 1 percent of people older than sixty suffer from hyperthyroidism. In either case, the symptoms of hypothyroidism and hyperthyroidism are different in older people, and do not manifest in the same ways as they do in a younger person.

Hypothyroidism in Older Persons

In older people, the signs of hypothyroidism are not obvious, and often few symptoms point to hypothyroidism, particularly when so many of the symptoms can be attributed to aging. For these reasons, it is recommended that anyone older than sixty be screened for hypothyroidism annually with a TSH test. Older thyroid patients report that they feel better once treated with thyroid hormone, and a lot of vague health problems will get better or even disappear.

Most causes of primary hypothyroidism in older people are the result of Hashimoto's disease (see Chapter 5). Hashimoto's disease in younger people frequently causes an enlarged thyroid or goiter (see Chapter 7). In older people, Hashimoto's disease tends to be more insidious and quietly damages the thyroid gland until it shrivels up (or atrophies). Older people could walk around for years with unrecognized Hashimoto's disease unless a thyroid function test was done. Unlike younger people with Hashimoto's disease, thyroid antibody testing in older people is very unreliable as well; many older people with these antibodies are not hypothyroid.

Effects of Hypothyroidism on the Older Body

Hypothyroidism in older people can increase cholesterol levels, which could exacerbate heart disease (see Chapter 25). Hypothyroidism can also worsen depression, cognitive function, arthritis and muscular aches, memory, respiratory problems, and sleep apnea (see Chapter 26). It can also aggravate preexisting dementia.

Treating Hypothyroidism in Older Persons

In people with a TSH of greater than 10, there is a clear benefit to treatment with thyroid hormone. In people with a TSH of 5 to 10, treatment is also likely to be helpful, although the benefits in symptoms are much less obvious. "Normal" ranges for TSH values in older people are generally set higher. It is not completely clear whether this is a normal and expected aspect of aging or, rather, an improper resetting of the normal range. The difference may be because some "normal" older people, whose blood tests were included as part of the "normal" samples to determine the normal range, were actually hypothyroid with elevated TSH levels, making the "normal" range higher than it should be.

The risk of thyrotoxicosis from excessive dosages of thyroid hormone in an older person with either heart problems and/or osteoporosis means that thyroid hormone dosing is often a "start low, go very slow" approach. This is the advice that internists and family physicians are given; however, experienced endocrinologists are often able to better choose appropriate dosages that are not excessive without having to delay treatment by starting too low. Older people also require less thyroid hormone than younger people, which is why starting doses of thyroid hormone are advised to be conservative. It is in this group, especially, that T3 in combination with T4 has not been properly evaluated and could have adverse effects (see Chapter 10). Similarly, "natural" thyroid hormone or thyroid extract (see Chapters 3, 10, and 19) is not recommended in this group.

Once thyroid hormone therapy is started in an older person, it's appropriate for the doctor to test TSH levels and free T4 six to eight weeks later, to make sure the dosage is correct.

The dose ought to be raised in 25- to 50-microgram increments. In some cases, the TSH targets for "normal" are unable to be reached because the thyroid hormone treatment has uncovered previously unrecognized heart disease. If this happens, seeking treatment with a heart specialist is the next step, before taking a sufficient dose of prescribed thyroid hormone for a normal TSH level.

Growing Old with Hypothyroidism and Thyroid Hormone

A lot of people are like me (Sara); they became hypothyroid as younger adults and expect to grow old with thyroid hormone therapy. In this case, your dosage will likely be adjusted as you age; you may graduate to a lower dose, even if you are taking a TSH suppression dose (if you had thyroid cancer). It is not known if this is because you have developed more reliable habits of taking your thyroid hormone medication or if there is truly a reduced need for it. If you are older than sixty and are taking the same thyroid hormone dosage prescribed to you in your forties or fifties, as long as you still have a normal TSH your dosage does not need to be changed. On the other hand, if you are taking a TSH-suppression dose because of thyroid cancer, your doctor should make sure that your dosage of thyroid hormone is the lowest it can be to suppress TSH without excessive elevations of the free T4 level (see Chapter 2).

Thyrotoxicosis in Older Persons

Hyperthyroidism from Graves' disease (see Chapters 4 and 6) or a nodule (see Chapter 8) occurs in less than 1 percent of the population over sixty. In fact, it is less than one-tenth as common as hypothyroidism in the same population. When it does occur, the symptoms are not obvious and do not clearly indicate to the doctor that you have Graves' disease in the same way as they do in a younger person. Similar to hypothyroidism, hyperthyroidism can be insidious in the over-sixty crowd; it can manifest as *apathetic hyperthyroidism* (see next section).

Some cases of thyrotoxicosis in older people are a result of too high a dosage of thyroid hormone in people who grew old with hypothyroidism, as well as outdated thyroid hormone prescriptions that have not been adjusted to newer standards of measuring the TSH levels. In these cases, lowering dosages in accordance with TSH testing is the way to manage it.

Apathetic Hyperthyroidism

Apathetic hyperthyroidism refers to hyperthyroidism without clear symptoms of thyrotoxicosis (see Chapter 4). Normally, people who are thyrotoxic as a result of hyperthyroidism have a racing heart, enlarged thyroid gland, tremor, restlessness and anxiety, and signs of thyroid eye disease (see Chapter 23). In apathetic hyperthyroidism, the telltale signs doctors count on to diagnose hyperthyroidism are absent; instead, a person with apathetic hyperthyroidism may even seem calm and mild-mannered. Or, the person could exhibit more hypothyroid symptoms, such as depression and constipation. Typically, the only sign of hyperthyroidism in an older person is weight loss, fatigue, and irritability, which are easily attributed in most cases to normal aging. In other instances, heart rhythm disturbances (usually rapid heartbeats or atrial fibrillation) are the only clues to thyrotoxicosis. In short, many people with apathetic hyperthyroidism are missed, and the hyperthyroidism remains untreated and unrecognized. The only objective indicator of hyperthyroidism is a low TSH test result and a high free T4 test result (see Chapter 2). In people with low TSH tests but normal T4 levels, the term *subclinical hyperthyroidism* is used, which means that they have mild hyperthyroidism that is not yet resulting in obvious symptoms.

Effects of Hyperthyroidism on the Older Body

The effects of hyperthyroidism on the older body depend on whether there is thyrotoxicosis or not. Even in apathetic or subclinical hyperthyroidism, one of the first concerns is increased bone loss (see Chapter 14) and the risk of atrial fibrillation, worsening angina, or congestive heart failure (see Chapter 25). If there is thyrotoxicosis, all of this is magnified further. Memory and cognitive function may improve with hyperthyroidism, although there may be scattered thinking.

Thyrotoxicosis from Thyroid Hormone Overdose

As stated earlier, thyrotoxicosis in people over sixty is sometimes the result of too high a thyroid hormone dose in people who are growing old with hypothyroidism. The effects of thyrotoxicosis are just as concerning, in terms of greater bone loss and heart disease complications, and are easily treated by adjusting thyroid hormone dosages down.

Treating Hyperthyroidism in Older Persons

Most people over sixty with Graves' disease (see Chapter 6) or toxic nodules (see Chapter 8) will be offered the same options for treatment as a younger person. The one exception is surgery, which is sometimes too risky for people in this age group who have other health problems or who may be frail. Radioactive iodine is not dangerous to older persons, although many older people fear it more than younger people do and may be more inclined to refuse it. Generally, radioactive iodine therapy (see Chapter 12) is preferable in this age group because it is reliable, effective, and (aside from hypothyroidism) free of side effects.

Other Thyroid Problems

In older people with goiters (see Chapter 7), nontoxic nodules (see Chapter 8), and thyroid cancer (see Chapter 9), the treatment options are usually the same as they are in younger people, with these considerations:

- **Weighing the value of doing nothing.** In someone with many serious health problems, who may also be frail, treating goiters that are not life-threatening and small, low-risk malignant thyroid tumors confined to the thyroid may do more damage to the older person than just leaving him or her alone. This is a common approach in geriatric health care, especially when it is far more likely that an older person in very poor health will likely die of something else.

- **Weighing the risk of surgery.** In some cases, where surgery would be logical in a younger person, it is too risky in an older person. In these cases, the risk needs to be carefully weighed. A benign nodule or non-life-threatening goiter could be left alone; an aggressive thyroid cancer (frequently the case in an older person) may be too risky to leave alone, and the value of doing surgery outweighs the value of not doing it.

Thyroid Disease in a Person with Alzheimer's Disease

First, thyroid disease is not more or less common in those with Alzheimer's disease. But there are special considerations for longtime thyroid patients who develop Alzheimer's or people who are first diagnosed with thyroid disease while in obvious phases of Alzheimer's disease.

Alzheimer's is a degenerative, progressive disease that affects all areas of the brain by destroying brain cells. It most often occurs in people over sixty-five, but can affect adults at an earlier age, and can sometimes be diagnosed in the forties and fifties. One in thirteen North Americans over the age of sixty-five has Alzheimer's disease or a related dementia.

Alzheimer's disease affects certain areas of the brain that control memory and basic functions or abilities. This results in specific symptoms or changes in behavior, and unlike a stroke, once an ability or function is lost, it can rarely be relearned. With respect to thyroid disease, it is the loss of mental abilities that can dramatically interfere with managing both hypothyroidism and thyrotoxicosis.

In Alzheimer's disease, the ability to understand, think, remember, and communicate can be severely diminished or lost. The ability to make decisions and perform simple tasks is also diminished or lost. Confusion and memory loss (initially short-term memory) occurs, and, in late stages of the disease, the ability to communicate at all can be lost. Clearly, taking medications, particularly thyroid hormone (see Chapter 10) is a risky proposition. Preparing properly for scans (see Chapters 2 and 12) or any complex diagnostic test can no longer be managed by the person with Alzheimer's. These tasks must be taken over by a third person who is a surrogate decision maker (see Chapter 21). Management goals may need to be tailored to suit the realistic quality of life of the affected person.

Behavior may also be radically affected by Alzheimer's disease, and can include repeating the same action or words, hiding possessions, and having physical outbursts. All of this may be badly aggravated by hypothyroidism or thyrotoxicosis. If you suspect a loved one with thyroid disease has Alzheimer's, it's crucial to involve the physician managing the thyroid problem in planning realistic goals in treatment.

A gradual physical decline also occurs, which can impact a person's ability to remain independent. Alzheimer's disease doesn't occur suddenly, but gradually; it takes place in a series of stages. Assessing the stage of Alzheimer's disease allows you to help make caregiving decisions (for yourself or another) based on the predicted course of the disease. But there is no clear line when one stage ends and another begins, and stages can overlap. The type of symptoms the affected person is exhibiting is the best way to gauge the staging. Early stages of Alzheimer's can also be hidden from other family members, but can be exacerbated by untreated hypothyroidism or thyrotoxicosis, because of taking too much medication or not taking it at all.

Signs of Alzheimer's Disease

Many early signs of Alzheimer's disease can mirror the cognitive and memory problems seen in hypothyroidism. The following established early signs of Alzheimer's disease can help you sort out whether problems with memory and cognitive functioning are related to thyroid disease or not.

- **Forgetfulness.** The affected person seems to forget what he is doing all the time. It's beyond forgetting a name or keys, but why he is going somewhere. Often he cannot remember what he did yesterday, or earlier in the day.
- **Forgetting how to do things.** The affected person forgets how to do things she has done for years such as preparing certain dishes.
- **Language problems.** Simple words or sentences seem completely foreign, as though the person has never heard them before. He may forget the names for objects and places and can't seem to communicate basic things.
- **Wandering or getting lost.** The affected person gets lost on the street not knowing where she is or how to get home.
- **Lack of judgment.** The affected person has lost the ability to judge, such as when to seek medical attention or how to dress for hot weather (wearing a coat in ninety-degree heat, for example).
- **Loss of cognitive functioning.** The person is not able to sort out more complex tasks, such as writing a check or making change.
- **Misplacing objects.** He may put an iron in the freezer or a wristwatch in the sugar bowl. Then he may accuse someone of stealing the object.
- **Severe mood swings for no reason.** The person may be calm one minute, and then experience severe agitation or tears the next, without any perceptible change in environment, and no apparent trigger.
- **Personality changes.** The person may experience changes in personality such as suspicion, apathy, fearfulness, or just doing things out of character.
- **No initiative.** The affected person may lose all interest in doing anything, similar to the type of apathy that can occur in depression. In this case, the apathy may stem from not remembering why the task must be done.

18 Thyroid Hormone Resistance and Rare Genetic Disorders of the Thyroid

This chapter is intended to give a brief overview of some rare thyroid disorders that are unlikely to afflict you or your family, yet are important examples of genetic thyroid diseases that have shed some light on understanding basic thyroid function. Some of them, particularly thyroid hormone resistance, may be mistakenly diagnosed in some people. This chapter is designed help set the record straight.

Some of these disorders are caused by *germline* mutations, meaning that they can be inherited; and some of them are caused by *somatic* mutations, meaning that they can affect only the individual and are not inherited through the family. Two genetic thyroid syndromes, inherited medullary thyroid cancer and toxic autonomous thyroid nodules (already discussed in Chapters 9 and 8, respectively), are each examples of germline (inherited medullary thyroid cancer) and somatic (ATN) mutations.

The chapter will start with an overview of the thyroid hormone resistance syndrome and then touch upon four additional areas: pituitary or hypothalamic genetic disorders, genetic abnormalities in thyroid gland development, genetic defects in the production of thyroid hormone, and inherited abnormalities in thyroid hormone binding proteins in the blood.

Resistance to Thyroid Hormone (RTH) or Thyroid Hormone Resistance

The story of resistance to thyroid hormone (RTH) started forty years ago with my (Ken) mentor, Dr. Samuel Refetoff. As an astute medical resident in a Los Angeles emergency room, he examined a six-year-old girl after she'd been in an automobile accident. This child had a goiter, bones that appeared to be those of a younger child (on x-ray exam), and was a deaf-mute. Such findings would typically make a physician suspect the child to have had severe hypothyroidism since birth; however, Dr. Refetoff was surprised to find that the test for thyroid hormone showed nearly four times the normal level in this child. Some other member of this family had similar findings, although the basal metabolic rates (see Chapter 2) in all of the members were normal, suggesting that this elevated thyroid hormone level resulted in a normal thyroid hormone effect. This meant that the child was resistant to the effects of her thyroid hormone, requiring much more of it to do the same job as normal levels in normal individuals. Over the next third of a century, Dr. Refetoff and his colleagues around the world brilliantly uncovered the genetic causes of this disorder. For this reason, RTH is sometimes called *Refetoff syndrome.*

Types of RTH

Most people with RTH are euthyroid (normal thyroid function), have small to moderate goiters, and are otherwise normal in appearance. When they're children, some seem to have a behavior similar to attention deficit disorder with hyperactivity (ADHD). In the mid-1980s, as Dr. Refetoff's fellow (endocrinology trainee), I (Ken) was surprised to see, counterintuitively, that the hyperactivity diminished when the children were given high doses of thyroid hormone.

RTH affects people in a variety of ways; there appears to be no uniform expression of this disorder. Some people initially seem to have a selective effective pituitary, which is resistant to thyroid hormone, yet the rest of their body reacts to the high thyroid hormone levels normally, seeming to be thyrotoxic (see Chapter 4) in spite of normal TSH levels. Some with this disorder show the extreme effects of general resistance to thyroid hormone, like the original girl seen by Dr. Refetoff, appearing to be hypothyroid despite high thyroid hormone levels. Most of the time, the affected people seem normal and are able to make enough thyroid hormone to make their bodies perform normally despite their resistance to the hormone. The hallmark of this condition is an inappropriately normal or elevated TSH despite high levels of free T4 and free T3 (see Chapter 2).

It's important to distinguish people with RTH from those with pituitary tumors making TSH. In both cases, the TSH is inappropriately normal or elevated despite high thyroid hormone levels. In the case of a pituitary tumor the person is clearly thyrotoxic, while in the case of RTH the person appears euthyroid.

The Molecular Cause of RTH

Twenty years after Dr. Refetoff recognized thyroid hormone resistance in a little girl, the means by which thyroid hormones work inside each cell were revealed. There are three different proteins inside cells that function as thyroid hormone receptors (T3-receptors). These receptors are found in the nucleus of each cell, adhering to the "on/off switch" on specific genes. When T4 enters each cell of the body it's converted to T3 (see Chapter 1) that enters the nucleus. Inside the nucleus, T3 sticks to the T3-receptors, turning on or turning off the specific genes that the T3-receptors are adhered to. In this way, thyroid hormone is able to turn particular genes on or off, regulating genetic processes. In RTH, the gene for one of the T3-receptors has mutated so that the T3-receptor it produces won't stick very well to T3. This makes the cells *resistant* to the effects of thyroid hormone, requiring more T3 (which comes from T4) to do the same job that would be done if the T3-receptors were normal.

The three T3-receptors actually work in pairs, sometimes in combination with another type of receptor, the retinoid X receptor, to regulate many different types of genes. Also, since there are many different types of mutations in the genes for each of these T3-receptors, the multiple possible combinations account for the variety of appearances for different types of RTH.

Inheritance of RTH

There are fewer than one thousand people with RTH identified around the world to date, making this a rare disorder. Most cases of RTH are inherited as an autosomal dominant trait, meaning that there is a fifty-fifty chance that each of your children will receive the gene if you have it, regardless of their sex. In some cases, their parents don't seem to have the mutation, suggesting that these cases represent a new germline mutation. A key point is that each person with RTH is born with it, meaning that this is not a condition that you can later develop as an adult.

Do You Have RTH?

As discussed in Chapter 19, RTH has been misunderstood by other authors of thyroid material for patients and is sometimes misconstrued and misinterpreted to explain why thyroid patients feel hypothyroid despite normal TSH levels. Obviously, it's exceedingly unlikely that you have RTH; however, how does this problem get discovered? The diagnosis and evaluation of RTH is very difficult and outside the expertise and abilities of most physicians. Usually, an astute physician (often a pediatrician or endocrinologist) suspects this problem based upon unusual results of thyroid function blood tests. This physician usually contacts a thyroid specialist with published expertise in RTH who suggests or performs additional tests to confirm the suspicion. You should be doubtful of anyone who claims the ability to make this diagnosis without such intensive evaluation—particularly doctors who are not specifically trained as thyroid specialists.

Pituitary and Hypothalamic Genetic Disorders

As discussed in Chapter 1, the thyroid functions normally when the hypothalamus releases thyrotropin-releasing hormone (TRH; also known as TSH-releasing hormone) to stimulate TSH from the pituitary gland. Elevated thyroid hormone levels inhibit TRH release. Likewise, the pituitary releases TSH in response to TRH and also in response to low levels of thyroid hormones. Again, elevated thyroid hormone levels inhibit TSH release by the pituitary and, as already stated, decrease the stimulation of TSH by inhibiting TRH release from the hypothalamus. When disorders of this finely tuned system show up, they have the potential of disrupting thyroid hormone levels as well as the adrenal system, gonadal system, and regulation of fluids in the body.

Hypothalamic-Pituitary Dysgenesis

Hypothalamic-pituitary dysgenesis is a form of congenital (from birth) hypothyroidism caused by a failure in the normal formation or function of the pituitary gland and/or hypothalamus. A number of genetic mutations cause such failures. Mutations in one particular gene, LHX3, cause a loss of the thyroid and gonadal (sex organs) function of the pituitary gland. Mutations in another gene, HESX1, cause something known as *septo-optic dysplasia*. This is characterized by poor growth of the optic nerve, defects of parts of the brain, and deficiencies of pituitary hormones. Mutations in other genes cause failure of growth of specific pituitary cells responsible for making TSH and other pituitary hormones. One case of hypothyroidism has been described in which the pituitary cell TRH receptors fail to work because the gene is mutated.

Mutations of the gene for the TSH receptor in certain cells in the thyroid gland can cause them to be "turned on," even when there isn't any TSH around to stimulate it. These mutations cause autonomous toxic thyroid nodules (ATNs), discussed in Chapter 8. Different mutations to the TSH receptor have caused the opposite problem, in which case the thyroid does not respond normally to TSH. People with these mutations are usually euthyroid, but the TSH levels are much higher than normal in order to properly stimulate the thyroid gland.

Defects in Formation of the Thyroid Gland

A number of genes are responsible for formation of the thyroid gland. It is likely that at least some of the cases of thyroid dysgenesis (see Chapter 15) are caused by mutations in these genes. Most of the genetic defects responsible for congenital hypothyroidism are still not yet known.

Defects in the Production of Thyroid Hormone

As discussed in Chapters 1 and 10, production of thyroid hormone starts with transport of iodide into the thyroid follicular cells. Some people have mutations in the gene for the sodium-iodide symporter (NIS), the iodide pump. These people have large multinodular goiters that are unable to concentrate radioactive iodine and are thus hypothyroid with high TSH levels. There are also people with mutations in the gene for thyroid peroxidase (TPO), the enzyme that is partly responsible for permitting iodide to be combined with portions of the thyroglobulin molecule, a process called *organification*. There are additional steps in organification that are susceptible to flaws or dysfunction from mutations as well (see Chapter 15 for the incidence of organification defects).

New studies find that there are other very rare conditions in which special proteins in the body's cells that take T4 into cells are defective. This causes severe problems with brain development.

Pendred Syndrome

Vaughan Pendred first described Pendred syndrome in 1896. Affected people are deaf and mute, and have large goiters. There is a partial defect in organification, but their thyroid glands are still capable of making sufficient thyroid hormone to be euthyroid. People with Pendred syndrome have dysfunctional inner ears, causing their deafness, as well as a mutation in the gene coding for another iodide transporter called *pendrin*. This condition accounts for 10 percent of the cases of hereditary deafness and may occur in up to one out of ten thousand individuals.

Other Genetic Mutations

Other genetic defects affecting the formation of thyroid hormone include mutations in the genes responsible for generating hydrogen peroxide in the cell (used to help organify iodide), mutations in the gene for thyroglobulin, and mutations in the genes for enzymes responsible for removing iodine from proteins, enabling recycling of iodine in the thyroid gland. It seems that nearly every conceivable biochemical step in the synthesis of thyroid hormones can be associated with some gene mutation that impairs this step and causes thyroid dysfunction.

Abnormalities in Transporting Thyroid Hormones in the Blood

Three major proteins in the blood bind thyroid hormones, transporting them throughout the bloodstream. Defects to these three types of proteins are discussed here.

Defects for Thyroxine-Binding Globulin (TBG)

The TBG gene is located on the X chromosome, and mutations in this gene responsible for loss of TBG are inherited differently in men and women. Since women have two X chromosomes, one mutated gene causes only a partial loss of TBG in women. Men with a mutated X chromosome may have total absence of TBG. Several different mutations have been found. Some TBG mutations cause partial deficiencies of TBG. In some people, extra copies of the TBG gene are present on the X chromosomes, causing higher than normal amounts of TBG in the blood. None of these TBG mutations will affect the free thyroid hormone status, but they can confuse physicians who inappropriately rely on total T4 levels to assess their patients.

Defects for Transthyretin (TTR; Thyroxine-Binding Prealbumin)

TTR defects are not very important in respect to thyroid disease. Many different mutations of the gene for TTR alter the folding of this protein, causing it to accumulate in a wide variety of the body's organs, a condition known as *systemic familial amyloidosis*.

Defects for Albumin

Albumin defects can cause some difficulty interpreting thyroid hormone tests, but do not affect thyroid function. *Familial dysalbuminemic hyperthyroxinemia (FDH)* is a condition caused by an abnormal type of albumin that has enhanced binding of T4. A different albumin mutation has been found that creates an albumin with enhanced binding of T3.

Genetic defects for each of these proteins can alter their quantity or their ability to bind thyroid hormones. Most of the time, there is no effect upon the person's thyroid status, since changes in these transport proteins do not alter the amount of free T4 that is available to enter cells. On the other hand, changes in these transport proteins will alter the total T4 levels.

That said, the existence of a wide array of inherited abnormal thyroid hormone transport proteins provides additional reasons to insist that diagnostic blood tests for thyroid function use free T4 levels rather than total T4 levels, as well as placing greatest importance on the TSH test.

3

Living Well After Treatment

MOST OF YOU will become hypothyroid as a result of thyroid treatment—a necessary reality of treatment. This section discusses ways to maximize your quality of life after treatment, but it also has chapters that will help you sort out thyroid misinformation you may be reading on the Internet or from other sources, which could confuse you. This section also discusses optimal diets in various situations, complementary therapies incorporating other systems of healing, and making informed decisions about your care.

19 Thyroid Misconceptions and Misinformation

As we discussed in the Introduction, thyroid patients are usually forced to self-educate about thyroid disease. In fact, this was certainly my (Sara's) experience when I was diagnosed with thyroid cancer in the early 1980s. Indeed, throughout the 1980s and early 1990s, it was difficult to find information on thyroid disease. By the late 1990s, as the Internet became much more accessible and popular, thyroid patients began surfing for thyroid information; thyroid websites and listservs abounded, as health became the second fastest growing sector on the Web (after pornography!).

For the most part, access to thyroid information and other thyroid patients has been a wonderful turn of events for thyroid patients. But, alas, like any other health information on the Web, some thyroid information is credible and some is not so credible. Some truth and some fiction can be mixed on the same sites—often run by patients themselves, with the best of intentions. There are also those who have agendas, those who have products to sell you (for example, newsletters or supplements) or sponsors to keep happy. Information is often sensationalized to attract browsers. Worse, scientific articles may be completely misconstrued to suit the agenda of the site.

Misconceptions and misinformation about thyroid disease can confuse and even harm vulnerable thyroid sufferers. For example, because of the many diffuse hypothyroid symptoms (see Chapter 3), hypothyroid patients, in particular, can be easy targets for weight-loss products, "energy boosters," and so forth. Busy thyroid specialists often don't appreciate how convincing some material can be when the reader has no medical background or has decreased ability to think clearly, if hypothyroid, about the material he or she is reading. Even I (Sara) have difficulty deciphering fact from fiction after all the years I've spent writing about thyroid disease. But when people are suffering, and feel desperate for answers, they are easy prey for such material.

After a lengthy misinformation search, we found that much of the thyroid misinformation is like a bad rumor; it gets recycled from some book to some website to some listserv—over and over again. And each reader that comes across it for the first time thinks it's something new or the answer to seemingly hypothyroid symptoms, which can be explained by many other conditions. For example, some authors regenerate long dead and debunked theories about thyroid disease origins, symptoms, and appropriate testing and therapies. Some materials successfully create the illusion that these theories are revolutionary and that there is a widespread conspiracy among allopathic or conventional practitioners to keep them hidden from patients. Some materials on the Web and in published books present just plain old wrong information about how the thyroid gland and thyroid hormone work in the body, especially giving rise to misinformation about various thyroid hormone preparations and brands.

Some materials suggest that conventional thyroid specialists don't understand thyroid disease as well as osteopathic, naturopathic, or other alternative practitioners (with no, or questionable training in endocrinology), causing some patients to abandon proven, ironclad, established therapies for bizarre and unsupported treatments. From a sociological perspective, there is an interesting pattern of cultlike mind control on some thyroid listservs and in some organizations. Conventional practitioners who try to educate patients about misinformation, and spend (or waste) time challenging wrong information, frequently get attacked on the Web, or labeled "closed minded" (as if it were a bad thing instead of the ethical thing to do when confronted with false claims by patients). This creates enormous frustration among thyroid specialists and their patients.

There are conventional practitioners who support (or, at least, don't oppose) reasonable complementary therapies, such as massage or aromatherapy (see Chapter 22), but have zero tolerance for therapies that are clearly sham—causing patients to abandon lifesaving therapies for sheer quackery or potentially harmful therapies. For example, physicians frequently encounter horror stories engendered by interactions with a variety of special interest pseudoscience groups.

The purpose of this chapter is not to point fingers but to correct core conceptual myths and misinformation in an effort to help you make the best informed decisions (see Chapter 21). Thus, we will not cite specific sources for the common misconceptions we correct (since they resurface in hundreds of places like gossip), unless we are addressing a specific "syndrome" or fake thyroid disease with its own website or following.

False Statements About Hypothyroidism

Perhaps more than any other thyroid issue, hypothyroidism has been a magnet for myths. This section deals with some of the critical myths that need to be corrected and which dramatically affect ethical patient care.

The "T4/T3 Conversion Problem" Theory

Internet sites and patient books frequently state that in many people, T4 does not convert into T3 properly at the cellular level, which supposedly explains why many patients with normal TSH levels are still hypothyroid. There are even doctors quoted in some materials (with questionable expertise in thyroidology) who explain why T4/T3 conversion fails in many hypothyroid people.

As we discuss in Chapter 3, *it is absolutely imperative that you understand this entire T3/T4 conversion problem theory is false.*

This is how T3/T4 conversion works in the human body, and why normal TSH levels are how we know you have adequate amounts of T3: a normal TSH level means you are making adequate amounts of T3 from the T4 that enters each body cell. We know this because within the pituitary cells, the gene that makes TSH will make *high levels of TSH unless there is sufficient T3 inside the cell to shut off the TSH production.* The normal TSH response from the pituitary cells shows that there is a normal amount of T3 and reflects the same normal T3 level inside the rest of your body's cells. If your pituitary gland is not functioning, or you have any innate defect whatsoever that interferes with this conversion, your TSH levels will be higher than normal. Period. *Normal TSH levels mean you are converting just fine.*

Why Is the Conversion Problem Theory Harmful?

The T4/T3 conversion problem statements are used to support the theory that "natural" thyroid hormone, questionable herbal concoctions that "help" with T4/T3 conversion, or regular and chronic T3 supplementation is preferable to, or healthier than, taking levothyroxine sodium (factory-made T4) at the appropriate dose. Thyroxine (T4) is the major product of the thyroid gland and is essentially a prohormone with minimal (if, debatably, any) activity of its own. It has a long and stable half-life in the blood (one week) and is transported into cells where it is converted into T3, which directly interacts with receptors that bind DNA and regulate genes. All of this has been well studied and constitutes a vast medical and molecular biology literature. Again, when you do not have enough T3, you will have high TSH levels. As discussed in Chapter 3, the targets for TSH have been too high, which have been adjusted in recent years. The high "normal" range is what has led to the concoction of this theory. We discuss why people continue to feel hypothyroid in spite of newer, lower "normal" levels in great detail in Chapter 3.

The "Falsely Suppressed TSH" Theory

Some materials claim that excess T3 generated at the pituitary level can falsely suppress TSH, which is why TSH tests are not reliable in testing for hypothyroidism. *This idea is completely false.* T4 is converted into T3 by an enzyme called *5 deiodinase*. This enzyme can be found in both the pituitary gland and the body cells. There has never yet been any research showing that the enzyme works differently in the pituitary than in the body cells. The enzyme is what makes T3 out of T4, and the TSH level therefore accurately reflects the effect of T4 on the entire body.

The "Reverse T3" Theory

Some materials claim that trauma and stress can create a "fake" normal T3 level, known as "reverse T3." The claim is that many people with so-called normal TSH levels really have "reverse T3" and are actually hypothyroid but can't seem to prove it to anyone. This theory takes some fact and creates fiction.

T4 is converted to T3 by removing a particular specific iodine from the four iodines on each of the T4 molecules. If a different iodine is removed, "reverse T3" is formed. Reverse T3 is inactive; it cannot do the job of T3, and therefore *will not suppress TSH*. It will not affect TSH levels at all. If T4 is converted to reverse T3 without making enough regular T3, *the TSH levels will be high and you will be hypothyroid*. If the TSH levels are normal, so are the levels of regular T3 inside of your cells.

"Euthyroid Sick Syndrome" as a Cause of Low-Grade Hypothyroidism

There is a condition known as *euthyroid sick syndrome (ESS)*. Some books create the false impression that this is the cause of Wilson's syndrome, a fake disease that we discuss further.

ESS is a leftover term from the days when T4 levels were measured using tests that sometimes failed to provide an accurate picture of the free T4 levels. When patients were severely ill, such as in a coma in the intensive care unit or on a ventilator in the burn unit, various body factors were released that made some thyroid tests look strange. In these people, the *free T4 by equilibrium dialysis* test showed that the thyroid hormone levels were usually normal. Unless you're ill enough to be in an intensive care unit or on a ventilator, absolutely none of this applies, and it does not account for any TSH test abnormalities or any other thyroid test abnormalities.

"Thyroid Hormone Resistance" as a Reason for Persistent Hypothyroidism

Refetoff syndrome is a rare genetic condition that causes thyroid hormone resistance. In fact, the man who described and discovered the cause of this condition, Samuel Refetoff, was also Ken's mentor. This very rare disorder has been misinterpreted by many as a T4/T3 conversion syndrome. This is completely false. Thyroid hormone resistance is fully explained in Chapter 18.

"Peripheral Resistance" and "Thyroxine Resistance"

The already incorrect spin on thyroid hormone resistance has unfortunately led to a string of other "resistance" syndromes supposedly responsible for conversion problems, "reverse T3," and a host of other biochemical falsehoods. *Peripheral resistance* is another term for thyroid hormone resistance; as for "thyroxine resistance," this is not a recognized disorder in any medical literature, and it appears to be a distorted and misunderstood interpretation of the literature on thyroid hormone resistance.

"Synthetic T4 Is Not as Good as Natural Thyroid Hormone or T3/T4 Mixtures"

For patients without thyroid glands, or with thyroid glands that fail to produce adequate amounts of thyroid hormone, the ingestion of a pure levothyroxine product provides all of the necessary thyroid hormone products consequent to normal metabolic and enzymatic bodily processes. The term *synthetic T4* is used because this hormone is created by a pharmaceutical manufacturer using chemical reactions, much like how aspirin is made from willow tree bark or penicillin is made from mold. Making a drug or hormone in this way permits a pure, properly measured and reproducible drug that is free of natural contaminants such as viruses, bacteria, or prions.

There is absolutely no conceivable role for taking natural thyroid extract or mixtures of T3 and T4. Thyroid extract is a mixture of T4, T3, thyroglobulin, and many other breakdown products with erratic pharmacokinetics, and it's nearly impossible to accurately dose for stability or, more importantly, suppression of TSH, which is necessary for thyroid cancer patients. These therapies are not new ideas but antiquated ones that were abandoned in favor of better technologies that made hypothyroid patients healthier.

There is no magical advantage to an animal product. The only reasonable medication is pure levothyroxine. T3 (Cytomel) is useful for the first four weeks of the six-week levothyroxine withdrawal period in thyroid cancer patients who are preparing for I-131 (radioactive iodine) scans and/or therapy (see Chapters 2, 9, and 12); it is also useful for the "climbing back" period after withdrawal scans. But it has very limited utility for supplemental treatment of a myxedema coma unresponsive to levothyroxine. The only small study (see Chapter 3) suggesting T3 supplementation of levothyroxine therapy for hypothyroidism was flawed and could not be verified or replicated by several larger studies done thereafter. T3 can make you thyrotoxic, which can be dangerous, as we discuss in Chapter 4. Since all hypothyroid people on T4 will make T3 because of the laws of biology and biochemistry, adding T3 is not helpful and could be harmful. And as discussed in Chapter 21, physicians cannot ethically recommend a therapy that could be potentially harmful when there is no perceived benefit.

"Natural Thyroid Hormone Is Better Because It Contains All Four Thyroid Hormones"

In many materials, natural thyroid hormone is touted for containing "all four thyroid hormones: T1, T2, T3, and T4." T1 and T2 are what T4 *degrades into* and have no activity, offering absolutely no benefit to you. It's analogous to a bicycle having no useful purpose after losing its wheels. Thus, statements that sell T1 and T2 as any sort of added benefit indicate that the source doesn't know what he or she is talking about and has misinterpreted basic facts about thyroid hormone biochemistry.

Such claims bank on the general public's assumption that something is better because it's "all natural." In this case, nothing is gained by choosing medications solely because they are based on "natural" extracts or processes. Such items, frequently found in natural or health-food stores, are often dangerous, impure, untested, and of unproven value. "Natural" does not mean "not harmful" or "better." And, "factory produced" does not mean "unnatural" or "bad." A product's designation as a "natural" product merely protects its manufacturers from having to justify their purity, safety, and efficacy to the FDA (which is empowered to protect us from *pharmaceuticals* only), permitting great financial profits at the expense of the public.

"Blood Tests Are Inaccurate in Determining Hidden Hypothyroidism"

Some material claims that low body temperature is the best way to measure hypothyroidism. These claims are based on unsupported theories about "hidden hypothyroidism" and ways to diagnose and treat it, using either natural thyroid hormone or T3 alone. This belief system has organized into two thyroid groups: Broda O. Barnes followers and "Wilson's thyroid syndrome" followers. We will outline both groups in detail.

Broda O. Barnes Followers

Reams of material, and an entire movement of sorts, support the ideas of late physician Broda O. Barnes, M.D., Ph.D., author of *Hypothyroidism: The Unsuspected Illness* (1976) and *Solved: The Riddle of Heart Attacks* (1976). Barnes also wrote about the alleged connections between hypoglycemia and hypothyroidism. Barnes practiced from the 1930s through the 1970s. His ideas were recycled by Stephen E. Langer, M.D., in a more recent book called *Solved: The Riddle of Illness*, released in its third edition in 2000.

The Barnes-like theories suggest that most people have hypothyroidism and don't know it, which is the underlying cause of almost all ill health in the Western world, from heart disease and diabetes to infections, from emphysema to cancers. But here's the rub: according to Barnes, lab blood tests are completely inaccurate in testing for hypothyroidism. Barnes advises that the best way to diagnose hypothyroidism is by measuring basal body temperature with a home thermometer. The Barnes-based web-sites sell you a kit with home self-testing information. You can also pay for education packets. According to the Barnes method, if your morning temperature is below 97.8 then you are hypothyroid. This is absurd, when you consider that the so-called normal body temperature, 98.6°F, was found to wildly fluctuate in many well-done studies published in medical literature. In one study, the average temperature varied throughout the day. At 8 A.M., the average temperature was 97.6°F, with more than 50 percent of all the measurements less than 98.6°F, and many less than 98.0°F. This study concluded that "thirty-seven degrees centigrade (98.6°F) should be abandoned as a concept relevant to clinical thermometry." Hence, the Barnes assumption is clearly not correct and certainly not more accurate than a sensitive TSH test used today.

Also, synthetic T4, according to the Barnes movement, doesn't work as well as natural thyroid hormone (as discussed earlier). So the "Barnes system" of self-diagnosing hypothyroidism points directly to a naturopathic or osteopathic doctor willing to sell you lots of other tests comprising a full "metabolic workup," involving hair samples, saliva samples, and so on. (Don't expect any of these tests to be covered by health insurance.) Many of these same practitioners will explain why their special versions of natural thyroid hormone, expensively prepared by compounding pharmacists, will be the only effective form of thyroid hormone, giving you pseudoscientific reasons to back up their claims. From ethical, patient-centered, and clinical perspectives, it's easy to see why this presents a problem in the thyroid world.

The Barnes movement is fueled by the frustrated patients who "feel hypo" despite normal TSH levels (see Chapters 2 and 3). It is also fueled by those who fall between the cracks and are unable to find a specific cause for the many autoimmune diseases in existence and hundreds of other symptoms of malaise and ill health linked in many ways to our unhealthy lifestyle and rather toxic world. Many people with arthritis, chronic fatigue, fibromyalgia, sleep disorders, and so on have glommed onto the "Barnes theory," demanding that they be put on natural thyroid hormone to cure everything from bacterial infections to heart disease. (Interestingly, although Barnes blames heart disease and emphysema on undiagnosed hypothyroidism, not a word about tobacco and smoking is mentioned, perhaps reflecting the dearth of research in that area at the time he mostly practiced, which was from the 1930s through the early 1960s.)

Imagine the problems that can occur when you tell a well-trained thyroidologist that you're hypothyroid because of low basal body temperature and want natural thyroid hormone in spite of the fact that you are clearly euthyroid by all valid measures? A lot of doctors in this position will start by trying to educate you about reality versus quackery, taking time away from other sick patients while explaining why this is not valid science. The patience of many overworked thyroidologists (because of the shortage of thyroid specialists) is often minimal when confronted with people whom we call the "Broda Barnes recruits."

Let's introduce some context here. Yes, Barnes was correct in suspecting that hypothyroidism was the root of many ailments. But one has to view Barnes's theories with a historical lens. First, there was no such concept as mild hypothyroidism in Barnes's day. Many patients diagnosed with hypothyroidism on the basis of obvious physical changes would have been discovered years earlier with modern testing.

Second, the lab tests Barnes refers to, in use in the 1930s through the 1970s, were very insensitive and did not include TSH levels. Barnes was correct to question the blood tests in use then. In fact, no one would use the same lab tests that were in vogue in the 1930s through to the 1970s to diagnose much of *anything* today.

Third, Barnes's recommendation of "dessicated thyroid hormone" makes sense when you consider that *that was the only thyroid hormone available* when he was practicing medicine from the 1930s through the 1960s. Like many doctors of his time period, he probably was used to using it and distrusted newer "experimental" T4 formulations that were just being made available in the 1960s.

As for the "vast" research Barnes did on hypothyroidism, which is discussed in Barnes materials and literature, it was all observation based, which is not really considered to have much merit in today's peer-reviewed world. But his research *questions* surrounding how other ailments were connected to hypothyroidism were good ones, which certainly helped to provoke others to investigate these issues using evidence-based, scientific methods. For Barnes's day, he was progressive about connecting hypothyroidism as an underlying cause for many ailments. But his methodologies about testing and treatment have not withstood the test of time; they are antiquated. That's appropriate, and expected, considering the man practiced medicine a very long time ago. So, while we're sure Barnes was a progressive man half a century ago, his views are mostly of historical relevance and should not be considered a medical standard for practicing modern thyroidology.

Believers in "Wilson's Thyroid Syndrome"

"Wilson's syndrome" is not a recognized thyroid disease or condition by any conventional thyroid practitioners or by the American Thyroid Association. Named by Dr. Denis E. Wilson, it borrows from some of Broda Barnes's theories about low body temperature as a sign of unrecognized hypothyroidism in spite of normal thyroid lab tests. In this case, Wilson, too, suggests that a host of nonspecific ill-health symptoms, which can be attributed to hundreds of conditions, combined with low body temperature, means that you have "Wilson's thyroid syndrome," which can be treated only with a special preparation of triiodothyronine (T3). For this reason, some people who say they have "Wilson's syndrome" wrongly insist they have a "T3 deficiency," which is not even the correct definition of "Wilson's thyroid syndrome." What is bizarre about this so-called syndrome is the recommendation of only T3 therapy for unrecognized hypothyroidism. There is simply no basis for this treatment, even if hypothyroidism *were* discovered based on the strange diagnostic methods and criteria proposed here.

In Wilson's syndrome literature such as his book *Wilson's Thyroid Syndrome: A Reversible Thyroid Problem* (1991), published by the Wilson's Syndrome Foundation (which also appears on the Wilson's Syndrome website), more than thirty-seven symptoms as well as "others" are listed as part of the condition. There are few people, healthy or not, who could say that they don't have at least a few of the symptoms on the list. And while some of these symptoms can be due to genuine hypothyroidism, some of the symptoms describe completely unrelated problems, such as asthma. Wilson's list of symptoms also mimic those that you'll find under the following conditions: neurasthenia, chronic fatigue, fibromyalgia, multiple chemical sensitivity, chronic Epstein-Barr disease, and chronic candidiasis. Since these conditions typically describe people with chronic malaise, in search of an answer to their malaise, it is suspicious and convenient that Wilson's syndrome seems to offer an answer—which, however, is unsupported and false. Given that at any time, more than 20 percent of adults report significant fatigue and 30 percent have current musculoskeletal symptoms, while the typical adult has one of the "Wilson's" symptoms every four to six days, and more than 80 percent of the general population has one of these symptoms during any two- to four-week period, most of us could actually say we have "Wilson's syndrome" if we were looking for a disease label that explained our symptoms. People who truly suffer from some of these other conditions are being exploited. It's crucial, too, to consider that many of these symptoms are rooted in psychological or social stress or mood disorders, including depression and anxiety.

Similar to Barnes's followers, devotees of "Wilson's syndrome" with low morning basal body temperature insist that they are hypothyroid in spite of normal lab tests (see Chapters 2 and 3 for normal ranges). The basal body temperature detection method is highly flawed and inaccurate for the reasons we discuss in the Barnes section.

And, as we've discussed, T3 is not the best treatment for hypothyroidism anyway. As explained in Chapters 3 and 10, T3 therapy results in wide fluctuations in T3 concentrations in blood and body tissues, producing symptoms of thyrotoxicosis in some people, especially cardiovascular complications in some patients, making it potentially dangerous.

Where is the evidence that T3 cures "Wilson's syndrome"? Well, you can read testimonials from satisfied customers on the Wilson's syndrome websites. You don't need us to tell you this is not exactly evidence-based medicine. Without double-blind studies (one group with symptoms taking T3 versus another group with symptoms taking a placebo, or fake pill, with neither research participants nor doctors knowing who is receiving what and just recording symptom relief), we have no idea how people actually feel in any unbiased and fair way. Biochemically, if you give people with normal thyroid function T3 when they don't need it, they will become thyrotoxic (see Chapter 4).

Also, even if we assume these testimonials are real, they fail to account for two well-known facts. First, a lot of people will just get better on their own because these symptoms tend to resolve once certain stressors are removed—even in people who have symptoms for months at a time. And second, the *placebo effect* (the power to heal yourself based solely on the *belief* that you're taking effective medicine) often makes people feel better, as discussed further on.

"My Obesity Is Caused by Hypothyroidism, Even Though My TSH Levels Are Normal"

How many euthyroid people are obese? Millions! Why is that? Because they eat more food than they burn off in activity. We are a sedentary society that is aging and out of shape. If your TSH levels are normal, and you are clinically euthyroid, then your obesity is just as manageable as for those obese individuals with no thyroid problem. Coming from both a hypothyroid patient (Sara) and a thyroid specialist (Ken) who sees nothing but hypothyroid people all day long, we bemoan the unfortunate and inappropriate assumption made by patients that all their problems with obesity are consequent to hypothyroidism. If this were the case, all obese patients would be cured with thyroid hormone and no one with normal thyroid function would ever be overweight.

Sadly, being a patient who is being treated for hypothyroidism with thyroid hormone therapy does not automatically disqualify one from the weight-control issues that plague all the other people with normal thyroid glands. During bouts of untreated hypothyroidism, you may gain weight, similar to weight gain after childbirth or after a weeklong cruise with all-you-can-eat buffets. Just as women may have to work at getting rid of their baby fat, you may have to work at getting rid of extra pounds put on before your hypothyroidism was treated. You may have aged a bit and find that it's not as easy to lose pounds after thirty-five as it was during your twenties and early thirties. Chapter 16 discusses obesity and thyroid disease in detail, and also outlines safe and effective weight-loss programs, such as Weight Watchers.

"If I Took T3 with My T4, I Wouldn't Be Obese"

In years past, practitioners of bariatric medicine (the study of obesity) tried, then abandoned, using higher than normal doses of levothyroxine (T4) or liothyronine (Cytomel, or T3) to help people lose weight. History taught us that this was a terrible practice and made people sick from thyrotoxicosis (see Chapter 4). Thankfully, this practice has long been abandoned. That said, several weight-loss products that contain thyroid hormones are still sold through health-food stores. Worse, in recent years, it has come to our attention that T3, sold over the counter in some countries, is being smuggled in by people with healthy thyroid glands and used as a weight-loss product. This can have devastating health consequences, creating heart arrhythmias and other serious effects of thyrotoxicosis. If you've read on the Internet that T3 solves everything from obesity to depression, you're unfortunately being hoodwinked. Frankly, life sure would be a whole lot easier (for us, too) if it were true!

"If I Took T3, I Wouldn't Be Depressed"

Well, that depends on whether: (1) you are truly hypothyroid, (2) your depression preceded your hypothyroidism, and (3) your depression was worsened by hypothyroidism. If you are hypothyroid and depressed, then T4 will do the same job on your depressed brain as taking T3, but its beneficial effects will be more long-lasting, yet not as immediate, since T4 has a longer half-life.

But it's important to consider what happens when you give depressed people a *placebo* and tell them it is T3, assuring them that it will lift depression. At least half of those people will report an improvement because of the *placebo effect*, which is a real pharmacologic effect caused by our natural endorphins and the power of our beliefs. In fact, several medical ethics articles point out that clinical control trials using placebos are actually testing two types of "drugs," since placebo is not the same as "nothing."

Misconceptions About Radioactive Iodine (RAI)

Radioactive iodine (RAI) is used for thyroid scans (see Chapter 2) as well as therapy for Graves' disease and thyroid cancer (see Chapter 12). The purpose and goals of RAI therapy in all these cases are discussed in Part 1. We also discuss RAI in Chapter 6 on Graves' disease and Chapter 9 on thyroid cancer. But since RAI is a rather complex therapy, and most of us can't boast degrees in nuclear physics, it's understandably a "hot" topic in thyroid disease. There are many misconceptions about RAI, which are reinforced by misinformation that appears on the Web, in some patient books, and from primary doctors who are not knowledgeable about RAI and its use in thyroid disease. We've tried to tackle the most common RAI myths that affect Graves' disease and thyroid cancer patients in this section.

Graves' Disease and RAI Myths

Graves' disease patients have a lot of questions about RAI, particularly because many patients are not properly educated or informed about the pros and cons of *other* therapeutic options. Although we've exhaustively covered the Graves' disease treatment options and goals in Chapter 6, here are the commonly held misconceptions you may find when you read other materials on RAI in Graves' disease therapy.

"RAI Therapy for Graves' Disease Is Bad Because It Causes Permanent Hypothyroidism"

It's amazing how many times you see statements like this on the Internet by outraged patients surprised to find out that they are hypothyroid after RAI therapy for Graves' disease—when, in fact, it is the end goal and *raison d'être* of RAI therapy for Graves' disease in the first place. RAI therapy treats hyperthyroidism caused by Graves' disease by destroying or ablating the thyroid gland, which causes it to stop producing thyroid hormone. No one should be advised that the thyroid gland will be "normal" after RAI therapy, although in rare cases hypothyroidism does not immediately occur, and normal thyroid function may resume without thyroid hormone replacement therapy at first. But in those cases, the thyroid gland will likely fail on its own without a repeat RAI dose. In short, people with Graves' disease who are surprised to learn that they are hypothyroid did not have full information about RAI treatment for Graves' disease from their doctors prior to consenting to this therapy. If you're hypothyroid, it's good news. The therapy worked, and you will no longer suffer from the harmful effects of hyperthyroidism and thyrotoxicosis (see Chapter 4). For more information, please see Chapter 6 on Graves' disease and Chapter 12 on RAI.

In addition, if you were able to tolerate Graves' disease without any treatment (a dangerous road for most), over several years you would likely become hypothyroid anyway as the autoimmune process destroys the thyroid gland. This might happen in a slow and insidious way, letting you gradually become more and more hypothyroid. RAI works quickly enough to enable your hypothyroidism to be properly treated with thyroid hormone early on.

"RAI Therapy for Graves' Disease Causes Thyroid Cancer"

Many Graves' disease patients are concerned that RAI therapy will cause thyroid cancer or thyroid nodules later in life. Although this is a reasonable concern, it isn't the case. See Chapter 12 for details.

"RAI Isn't Safe for Children or Women of Childbearing Years"

This is not so, and is discussed in detail in Chapter 12.

"RAI Causes Birth Defects"

This has been thoroughly studied over the more than half century that RAI has been used and, to date, there's no evidence that RAI treatments cause any birth defects in babies of women who've completed RAI therapy before their pregnancy. On the other hand, you must be absolutely certain that you're not pregnant before you're given any dose of RAI, which would go directly to the fetal thyroid gland and cause severe damage to the fetus. This is why all women in childbearing years have pregnancy tests prior to treatment just to make sure. In other words, you'll need to have a pregnancy test even if you're using birth control, you've had a tubal ligation, or you haven't had sex in months. Even nuns have to have pregnancy tests! The pregnancy test detects the hormone HCG, or human chorionic gonadotropin, the hormone the developing embryo makes. I (Ken) usually advise you wait six months after this treatment before trying to conceive. (Of course, pregnancy carries other risks that have nothing to do with radioactive iodine.) For more information on pregnancy and thyroid disease, see Chapter 13.

"RAI Can Worsen Graves' Disease After Treatment"
This is a misconception discussed in Chapter 12.

"Radioactive Iodine Causes Thyroid Eye Disease"
This is not the case for most Graves' patients in light of the use of steroid treatments. See Chapters 6, 12, and 23 for more information.

"RAI Is Used More in the United States Because It's Cheaper, Not Safer"
This is untrue and is discussed more in Chapter 12.

Thyroid Cancer and RAI Myths
As discussed in Chapters 9 and 12, RAI therapy for thyroid cancer requires much higher doses than those used in treating Graves' disease. Some of the same concerns about RAI safety are shared between Graves' patients and thyroid cancer patients (so do have a look at the preceding section). But there are also some unique myths that surface on the thyroid cancer listservs.

RAI Causes Other Cancers
Many people treated for thyroid cancer are concerned that RAI could increase their risks of getting other cancers. The two most common cancers rumored to be linked to RAI are leukemia and breast cancer.

With respect to leukemia, even with a single RAI dose of more than 800 millicuries, fewer than one out of two hundred people would go on to develop leukemia, which matches the risk in the general population.

With respect to breast cancer, a study published in 2000 found an association between women younger than forty who had been diagnosed with thyroid cancer and an increased incidence of breast cancer. The study, conducted by Amy Chen, M.D., M.P.H., of the University of Texas M. D. Anderson Cancer Center in Houston, found that women under forty who have had thyroid cancer are more likely to develop breast cancer later in life, compared to women who have not had thyroid cancer. None of these studies, to date, has identified how thyroid cancer predisposes a woman to have breast cancer. Although it is tempting to speculate that this could be related to RAI treatment, there is no evidence of this link. Nonetheless, it's important to realize that treatment of a known cancer is more important than worries of a greater risk for a second cancer that is still unlikely to occur.

"RAI Therapy for Thyroid Cancer Causes Bone Marrow Problems"

It is uncommon for there to be clinically significant effects on the bone marrow from typical I-131 doses administered to treat Graves' disease or thyroid cancer. When the absorbed bone marrow radiation dose approaches 200 REM (2.0 Sievert), there may be temporary effects on the platelets, red blood cells, and white blood cells that typically become maximal four weeks after radioiodine and resolve after an additional four weeks. In most patients, I-131 doses of 250 to 800 mCi (as determined by dosimetry calculations in each individual patient) are required to reach marrow-suppressive levels; however, older patients may have marrow suppression with doses as low as 100 mCi. It is my (Ken) practice to carefully monitor the blood counts of every patient given sufficiently high doses of radioiodine. This is discussed in Chapter 12.

"RAI Causes Iron Deficiency"

Radioiodine does not cause iron deficiency, nor does it cause B_{12} or folate deficiency, all of which can cause or contribute to an anemia. It is not unusual for these deficiencies to go unnoticed until a physician orders a blood count, by chance. If iron deficiency is treated with iron pills, it is important not to take this within five hours of the levothyroxine dosage to prevent the iron from binding to the levothyroxine, preventing its absorption.

"There Is a Lifetime Limit of RAI, So More than One Treatment Is Dangerous"

Unfortunately, many references to the fictitious "lifetime limit" of RAI have been made. There is absolutely no basis in reality for such a limit. Although you may find references to such a limit in some medical articles, careful research of this claim reveals that there is no data anywhere to support such a concept. It scares both Graves' patients, who may need repeat therapies of RAI, and thyroid cancer patients, who frequently need repeated RAI therapies and sometimes very high doses of RAI to treat their cancer.

I (Ken) have treated patients with metastatic thyroid cancer to total cumulative doses of 2,000 to 3,000 mCi without any significant ill effect from the treatment, aside from dysfunctional salivary glands. If the thyroid cancer is distantly spread and still is able to respond to radioiodine, then there is no reason to withhold therapy if it can be helpful. As long as each single I-131 dose is within the proper safety margins (200 REM marrow exposure and less than 80 mCi I-131 retained in the lung at forty-eight hours—this may permit single doses up to 650 mCi in some patients), there should be no permanent ill consequences from necessary thyroid cancer treatment. The biggest problem is the use of repetitive low-dose (less than 200 mCi) treatments for aggressive distant disease. This may result in the use of many doses, with each particular dose too low to destroy the thyroid cancer cells. Although some physicians may dispute this, there is simply no data that challenge what I (Ken) know from my vast clinical experience and years of research. The bottom line is that there is no true or definite lifetime cumulative radioiodine treatment limit, provided that appropriate parameters are maintained for each dose, therapeutic response and situation warrants treatment, and bone marrow effects are closely monitored.

"RAI Causes Your Hair to Fall Out"

People say this because they're confusing RAI with external radiation therapy, which also doesn't cause hair loss unless the scalp is radiated. People may also be confusing this treatment with chemotherapy, which often causes hair loss. That said, hair loss during and after the hypothyroid preparation for radioiodine scanning or therapy is consequent to the changes in thyroid hormone status. It is completely unrelated to the radioactive iodine or to any radiation effect. All such hair loss is completely replaced by natural growth when the thyroid hormone levels are restored. It is typically minimal or unnoticed in most people, but some people seem to be particularly susceptible.

"If You're Allergic to Iodine, You Can't Have RAI"

This is not true. The amount of radioactive iodine in a treatment or scan dose is less than the amount of nonradioactive iodine in a cup of milk. People allergic to iodine in seafood or iodine contrast used for CT scans almost never have an allergic reaction to the small amounts of iodine present in iodized salt, milk, or radioactive iodine doses.

"My Surgeon Said All My Cancer Was Removed So I Don't Need to Have RAI Therapy"

A single thyroid cancer cell is so tiny that it requires a powerful microscope to see it. The smallest visible tumor tissue (to the unaided human eye) able to be seen by a surgeon is composed of more than a million thyroid cancer cells grouped together in a lump. Where there are lumps of a million cells, there are probably more lumps of a hundred thousand cells and further lumps of ten thousand and more of one thousand cells, and so on. None of these smaller masses of cancer is possibly visible to a human surgeon, yet all are capable of maintaining and progressing the cancer. It is physically inconceivable that any surgeon could possibly confirm to a patient that he or she has "gotten it all." Any surgeon who is "100 percent sure" is practicing the ultimate self-deception. At the most, a surgeon might believe he had removed most of the obvious gross disease.

This is one of the principles behind the use of radioiodine ablation therapy after surgical thyroidectomy, even if the tumor is within the thyroid gland and not grossly associated with metastatic lesions. Current research studies, using powerful techniques of reverse-transcriptase polymerase chain reaction for thyroglobulin messenger RNA in peripheral blood samples, clearly document that there can be thyroid cancer cells traveling freely around the bloodstream in patients with no known residual tumor masses after extensive surgery. I (Ken) do not doubt that some physicians have deeply held, but incorrect, beliefs in the certainty of their surgical approaches. Unfortunately, opinions cannot alter biology or nature, and medical reality is not changeable by democratic vote, no matter how many physicians may share a belief. RAI therapy is covered thoroughly in Chapters 6 and 12.

Other Myths About Thyroid Cancer

Although we discuss thyroid cancer in Chapter 9, there are a few persistent myths about this disease that we'd like to clear up here.

"It's Impossible to Have Thyroid Cancer and Another Thyroid Disease at the Same Time"

That's not true. Autoimmune thyroid disease is, in fact, particularly common among thyroid cancer patients. Hashimoto's thyroiditis is common, afflicting nearly 20 percent of women and 10 percent of men. For that reason, it is very common to have coincidental thyroid carcinoma and Hashimoto's thyroiditis. It is also likely for women, in particular, to have thyroid cancer and Graves' disease.

"Low Thyroglobulin Levels Always Mean That There Isn't Any Thyroid Cancer Left"

This isn't always true, especially if you have a history of Hashimoto's disease. One of the hallmarks of Hashimoto's thyroiditis is the production of antibodies directed against parts of the thyroid, particularly the thyroperoxidase enzyme and thyroglobulin. Antibodies against thyroglobulin interfere with the ability of all currently known blood tests to accurately measure the actual thyroglobulin level. They tend to make the tests register a lower thyroglobulin level than actually exists. As you know, thyroglobulin levels are extremely important to ascertain the presence of thyroid cancer after a person has had a total thyroidectomy and radioactive iodine therapy. For this reason, a low or immeasurable thyroglobulin level, in the presence of antithyroglobulin antibodies, does not provide any confidence for the absence of thyroid cancer. On the other hand, when thyroglobulin levels are elevated in the presence of antithyroglobulin antibodies, particularly when these levels increase in response to hypothyroidism, this is believable evidence of the presence of thyroid cancer.

"Fluoride Caused My Thyroid Cancer"

We discuss environmental factors likely to have caused many thyroid cancers in Chapter 9. However, the fluoride rumor keeps resurfacing. For the record, fluoride does not cause thyroid cancer. There is not one shred of evidence demonstrating this. The diatribe on fluoride has ranged from maniacal ideas regarding Russian agents (such as those found in the famous movie *Dr. Strangelove*) to current attempts to overgeneralize from inapplicable experiments and claim causation for all of the world's ills. It's important to note many countries without fluoridation have thyroid cancer rates as high as North America.

"A Low-Iodine Diet Means No Sodium, So Labels That Say 'Low Sodium' Are Fine"

Sodium (Na) is a metal. If added in its pure form to any water-based liquid, it will explode. If left in the air, it will burst into flames. Otherwise, it can exist as a chemical salt; that means that it has a positive charge and is bound to other negatively charged chemical groups, for example sodium bicarbonate, sodium chloride, or sodium phosphate. Sodium has nothing to do with iodine or iodide. For public health purposes, table salt (sodium chloride) may be combined with sodium iodide to promote higher iodine levels and prevent hypothyroidism and goiter. For people on a low-iodine diet, this adulterated table salt is inappropriate. But anyone on a low-iodine diet can partake of all sources of sodium, and even sodium chloride, provided that sodium iodide has not been added. The sodium content listed on nutritional package guides does not at all indicate the presence of iodine. For more information on the low-iodine diet, see Chapter 20.

20 Special Diets for Thyroid Disease and Healthy Eating

In Chapter 16, we discussed obesity and thyroid disease and the optimal antiobesity diet, including how low-fat diets and low-carb diets measure up in the thyroid world. In this chapter, you'll find information on optimal diets while hypothyroid; information on the low-iodine diet, necessary for thyroid cancer patients preparing for a thyroid scan; as well as the optimal diet while hyperthyroid. Finally, you'll discover how to maintain a normal, healthy weight after you've been treated for a thyroid condition and are likely on thyroid hormone.

The Hypothyroid Diet

This is a general diet I (Sara) have created for people battling the symptoms of hypothyroidism, which can aid with constipation, bloating, and a slower gastrointestinal tract. This is not the diet to follow if you are on a low-iodine diet.

Because everything slows down when you're hypothyroid, you need to know how to eat and what to eat to compensate for your body's slowness during this time, as well as to avoid complications of hypothyroidism. A high-fiber diet low in saturated fat and rich in unsaturated fat (described later in this chapter) can help improve constipation and bloating, fatigue, and weight gain. In essence, this diet will help you feel better while combating periods of hypothyroidism when you're not properly balanced on thyroid hormone, while helping to prevent cardiovascular problems and colon health problems. It will also complement your thyroid medication if you are balanced right now.

And finally, it will help you combat a preexisting weight problem, which may be aggravated by your hypothyroidism.

Battling the Bloat

Feeling bloated and constipated is a classic hypothyroid ailment. Much of the bloat is actually caused by constipation; much is also caused by not drinking enough water. But few people understand that when you increase fiber, you have to increase water intake. So here's what you need to know about fiber and water. You can take fiber supplements and stool softeners while hypothyroid, which will help you when your fiber content is low. But these supplements can be added to a high-fiber diet as well. It's important to note that fiber can interfere with the absorption of your thyroid hormone so you should take them as far apart as possible, for example, fiber at night and your thyroid hormone pill first thing in the morning.

Fiber is the part of a plant your body can't digest, which comes in the form of both water-soluble fiber (which dissolves in water) and water-insoluble fiber (which does not dissolve in water but instead absorbs water); this is what's meant by soluble and insoluble fiber. Soluble and insoluble fiber differ, but they are equally beneficial.

Soluble fiber lowers the bad cholesterol, or low-density lipoproteins (LDL), in your body. Experts aren't entirely sure how soluble fiber works its magic, but one popular theory is that it gets mixed into the bile the liver secretes and forms a type of gel that traps the building blocks of cholesterol, thus lowering your LDL levels. It's akin to a spider web trapping smaller insects.

Insoluble fiber doesn't affect your cholesterol levels at all, but it regulates your bowel movements. How does it do this? As the insoluble fiber moves through your digestive tract, it absorbs water like a sponge and helps to form your waste into a solid form faster, making the stools larger, softer, and easier to pass. Without insoluble fiber, your solid waste just gets pushed down to the colon or lower intestine, where it is stored and dried out until you're ready to have a bowel movement. High-starch foods are associated with drier stools. This is exacerbated when you ignore the urge, as the colon will dehydrate the waste even more until it becomes harder and difficult to pass, a condition known as *constipation*. Insoluble fiber will help to regulate your bowel movements by speeding things along, decreasing the transit time by increasing colon motility and limiting the time dietary toxins hang around the intestinal wall, which is why slower colon motility can dramatically increase your risk of colon cancer.

Good sources of soluble fiber include oats or oat bran, legumes (dried beans and peas), some seeds, carrots, oranges, bananas, and other fruits. Soybeans are also high sources of soluble fiber. Studies show that people with very high cholesterol have the most to gain by eating soybeans. Soybeans are also a *phytoestrogen* (plant estrogen) that is believed to lower the risks of estrogen-related cancers (for example, breast cancer), as well as lower the incidence of estrogen-loss symptoms associated with menopause.

Good sources of insoluble fiber are wheat bran and whole grains, skins from various fruits and vegetables, seeds, leafy greens, and cruciferous vegetables (cauliflower, broccoli, or brussels sprouts). Keep in mind that you need to understand what is truly whole grain. For example, some assume that because bread is dark or brown, it's more nutritious; this isn't so. In fact, many brown breads are simply enriched white breads dyed with molasses. (*Enriched* means that nutrients lost during processing have been replaced.) High-fiber pita breads and bagels are available, but you have to search for them. A good rule is to simply look for the phrase *whole wheat*, which means that the wheat is, indeed, whole.

What's in a Grain?

Most of us will turn to grains and cereals to boost our fiber intake, which experts recommend should be at about 25 to 35 grams per day. Use the following list, which measures the amount of insoluble fiber in various foods, to help gauge whether you're getting enough. If you're a little under par, boost your fiber intake by simply adding wheat bran to your foods. Wheat bran is available in health-food stores or supermarkets in a sort of "sawdust" format. Three tablespoons of wheat bran is equal to 4.4 grams of fiber. Sprinkle one to two tablespoons onto cereals, rice, pasta, or meat dishes. You can also sprinkle it into orange juice or low-fat yogurt. Wheat bran has virtually no calories, but it's important to drink a glass of water with it, to aid passage through your esophagus. Since wheat bran expands, you don't want it to get stuck. This is why there is a warning on most supplements to drink about eight ounces of water with your fiber.

CEREALS	GRAMS OF FIBER (BASED ON ½ CUP UNLESS OTHERWISE SPECIFIED)
Fiber First	15.0
Fiber One	12.8
All-Bran	10.0
Oatmeal (1 cup)	5.0
Raisin Bran (¾ cup)	4.6
Bran Flakes (1 cup)	4.4
Cheerios (1 cup)	2.2
Corn Flakes (1¼ cup)	0.8
Special K (1¼ cup)	0.4
Rice Krispies (1¼ cup)	0.3

BREADS	GRAMS OF FIBER (BASED ON 1 SLICE)
Rye	2.0
Pumpernickel	2.0
12-grain	1.7
100 percent whole wheat	1.3
Raisin	1.0
Cracked-wheat	1.0
White	0

Keep in mind that some of the newer high-fiber breads on the market today have up to 7 grams of fiber per slice. This chart is based on what is normally found in typical grocery stores.

Fruits and Veggies

Another easy way of boosting fiber content is to know how much fiber your fruits and vegetables pack per serving. All fruits, beans (or legumes), and vegetables listed here show measurements for insoluble fiber, which is good not only for colon health but for your heart. Some of these numbers may surprise you!

FRUIT	GRAMS OF FIBER
Raspberries (¾ cup)	6.4
Strawberries (1 cup)	4.0
Blackberries (½ cup)	3.9
Orange (1)	3.0
Apple (1)	2.0
Pear (1)	4.0
Grapefruit (1)	2.2
Kiwi (1)	1.0

BEANS	GRAMS OF FIBER (BASED ON ½ CUP UNLESS OTHERWISE SPECIFIED)
Green beans (1 cup)	4.0
White beans	3.6

Kidney beans	3.3
Pinto beans	3.3
Lima beans	3.2

VEGETABLES	GRAMS OF FIBER (BASED ON ½ CUP UNLESS OTHERWISE SPECIFIED)
Baked potato with skin (1 large)	4.0
Acorn squash	3.8
Peas	3.0
Creamed, canned corn	2.7
Brussels sprouts	2.3
Asparagus (¾ cup)	2.3
Corn kernels	2.1
Zucchini	1.4
Carrots (cooked)	1.2
Broccoli	1.1

Drink Water with Fiber

It's important to drink water with fiber. Water means water. Milk, coffee, tea, soft drinks, or juice are not a substitute for water. Unless you drink water with your fiber, the fiber will not bulk up in your colon to create easy-to-pass bowel movements. Think of fiber as a sponge. Obviously, a dry sponge won't work. You must soak it with water for it to be useful. Same thing here. Fiber without water is as useful as a dry sponge. In the general population, it's advised that you drink roughly eight ounces of water with a fiber supplement. Generally, this is a good rule of thumb, but too much water can be dangerous when you're hypothyroid. Check with your doctor about how much water to drink with your fiber, as it's based on your individual fiber intake and the extent to which you are hypothyroid.

Avoid Alcohol

Alcohol is poorly metabolized in people who are hypothyroid, and puts a strain on the liver. It is also fattening, delivering about 7 calories per gram or 150 calories per drink. A glass of dry red or white wine has calories but no sugar. The same thing goes for cognac, brandy, and dry sherry that contain no sugar.

On the other hand, a sweet wine contains 3 grams of sugar per 100-milliliter or 3.5-ounce portion. Dessert wines or ice wines are really sweet; they contain about 15 percent sugar or 10 grams of sugar for a 2-ounce serving. Sweet liqueurs are 35 percent sugar.

A glass of dry wine with your meal adds about 100 calories. Half soda water and half wine (a spritzer) contains half the calories. When you cook with wine, the alcohol evaporates, leaving only the flavor.

If you're a beer drinker, that's about 150 calories per bottle; a light beer has fewer calories but contains at least 100 calories per bottle.

The stiffer the drink, the more calories it contains. Hard liquors such as scotch, rye, gin, and rum are made out of cereal grains; vodka, the Russian staple, is made out of potatoes. In this case, the grains ferment into alcohol. Hard liquor averages about 40 percent alcohol but has no sugar. Nevertheless, you're looking at about 100 calories per small shot glass, so long as you don't add fruit juice, tomato, or sugary soft drinks. The bottom line: while hypothyroid, avoid or limit alcohol intake as much as possible.

The Low-Iodine Diet (LID)

If you're preparing for a radioactive iodine whole body scan or radioactive iodine treatment for thyroid cancer (discussed in Chapters 2, 9, and 12) you will need to be on a low-iodine diet (LID) for about two weeks prior to your scan or treatment.

Iodine from food can interfere with the sensitivity and accuracy of radioactive iodine (RAI) scans or treatments. By avoiding iodine prior to RAI scanning or treatment, you can maximize the results.

In general, a low-iodine diet consists of very fresh foods prepared from fresh meats, fresh poultry, fresh or frozen vegetables, and fresh fruits. You are not permitted to use any fish or seafood, dairy products, egg yolks, iodized salt, or red food dye #3. While you're at it, you may even slim down if you need to lose weight. (Or, it may prevent weight gain while hypothyroid.) That said, low-iodine diets can be simple to follow and are a very small price to pay to ensure the greatest benefit from RAI scans and therapy.

People make the mistake of assuming iodine means sodium because of iodized salt. *A low-iodine diet isn't the same thing as a low-sodium diet.* When you're on a low-iodine diet, you can have salt as long as it isn't iodized salt. While most canned goods containing salt are not made with iodized salt, there's no reliable way to know which type has been added, and it's safest to get foods without salt, adding your own noniodized salt. You should avoid iodized salt, sea salt, and salted foods. Noniodized salt (such as kosher salt or salt labeled as without iodine) may be used. You may also want to avoid dining out if you want to stick to your LID. It's important to note that a LID doesn't have to be expensive; avoiding fast foods and prepared foods and substituting with simple fresh foods is healthier and cheaper. See Appendix A for resources on LID cookbooks.

Sources of iodine include (listed alphabetically):

- Chocolate (for its milk content).
- Commercial bakery products. It's not hard to bake your own delicious bread using flour, sugar or honey, yeast, noniodized salt, and olive oil.
- Cured and corned foods (ham, corned beef, sauerkraut, bacon, sausage, salami), unless you produce your own using noniodized salt.
- Dairy: milk, butter, cream, cheese. (These products provide us with a large amount of our iodine. The iodine gets into dairy because the animals secrete dietary iodine into their milk, while cows' teats are washed in iodine. Also, commercial milking machines are often washed with iodine cleansers.)
- Egg yolks. (Whites are fine.)
- Fish or seafood. (This includes both fresh and saltwater fish.)
- Food additives: carrageen, agar-agar, algin, alginate.
- Molasses.
- Red dye #3. Check your ingredient labels, and avoid all artificial red food coloring that is not specifically identified.
- Sea salt or iodized salt (found in potato chips, popcorn, nuts, pretzels, restaurant foods). Keep in mind that kosher salt or noniodized salt is fine, and sodium in any form is fine so long as it's not iodized salt.
- Seaweed or kelp. (This is loaded with iodine!)
- Soy products (soy sauce, soymilk, tofu).
- Vitamins and supplements. Many of these contain iodine; check labels. Any red, orange, or brown pills and capsules may have iodine dyes in them. (Ask your pharmacist to check: only red dye #3 needs to be avoided.)

Low-Iodine Diet Versus No-Iodine Diet

Misinformation abounds on the Internet surrounding the LID. We wish to emphasize that the guidelines we've provided are for a low-iodine diet, not a no-iodine diet. In some materials, patients are advised to stay away from drinking water, potato skins, and countless other foods that may have insignificant trace amounts of iodine. The point of the LID is to lower your iodine intake, but it is virtually impossible to eliminate iodine below 20 micrograms each day.

The Hyperthyroid Diet

If you are currently in the throes of hyperthyroidism and are thyrotoxic, it's important to note that your thyroid helps to control gastric emptying, secretion of digestive juices, and motility of the digestive tract. When you're thyrotoxic, despite a voracious appetite, you might lose weight and experience hyperdefecation (frequent bowel movements). While thyrotoxic, increase your calcium intake by having more dairy products. This is more important for women who are at risk for osteoporosis (see Chapter 14), which can be aggravated by thyrotoxicosis. This will also help to keep your weight up. Peanut butter, mayonnaise, and animal fat can help as well. To reduce diarrhea, cut down on fruit juices and fresh fruits. Peanut butter is also good for binding. Sometimes, thyrotoxic people will develop sudden lactose intolerance. This can lead to gas and other unpleasantness. Eliminate all milk products in this case, and take a calcium supplement while getting your fat from the other foods mentioned previously.

Stay away from caffeine, alcohol, and cigarettes, all of which may stimulate your heart. You may want to take vitamin supplements as well. (Vitamins A, D, and E are stored in body fat and can be lost through excretion if you are thyrotoxic or hyperthyroid.) When you are in balance again, you will need to cut down on your fat and calcium intake.

Goitrogens

As we've discussed in Chapters 3 and 6, goitrogens are chemicals that block or interfere with thyroid hormone formation. They do not affect you unless you are iodine-deficient.

Some people with Graves' disease have investigated a goitrogenic diet over conventional treatment, but this is not effective, as discussed in Chapter 6.

What to Eat After Treatment for Thyroid Disease

People who have had thyroid disease make the mistake of thinking they have to be on a special diet to maintain a healthy weight. Unless you're actively hypothyroid, thyrotoxic, or are preparing for a whole body scan (see Chapter 2), you are in the same boat as the rest of the population: your metabolism will slow down with age, which will likely cause weight gain as you approach your forties and fifties, unless you compensate with more activity. Basically, eating healthy means you must distinguish between "good fat" and "bad fat" as well as "good carbs" and "bad carbs."

The following is a brief overview of this information, which, although it exists elsewhere, is presented here to demonstrate how important it is for thyroid patients to understand that most weight and diet-related issues are not related to the thyroid per se, but to the general problem in our society of having too much food and not enough real comprehension surrounding what is in our food that makes us fat.

Understanding Fat

A gram of fat contains twice the calories as the same amount of protein or carbohydrate. Decreasing the fat in your diet and replacing it with more grain products, vegetables, and fruits is the best way to lower your risk of cardiovascular problems and many other diseases. Fat in the diet comes from meats, dairy products, and vegetable oils. Other sources of fat include coconuts (60 percent fat), peanuts (78 percent fat), and avocados (82 percent fat). There are different kinds of fatty acids in these sources of fats: saturated, unsaturated, and trans-fatty acids (also called *trans fat*), which is like a saturated fat in disguise. Some fats are harmful while others are considered beneficial to your health. The terms *good fats* and *bad fats* began to crystallize when research into diets higher in monounsaturated fats were closely observed, and found, in spite of being fats, to raise good cholesterol, or HDL, which protects against heart disease (see Chapter 25).

Saturated Fat

Saturated fat is solid at room temperature and stimulates cholesterol production in your body. Foods high in saturated fat include fatty meats, lard, butter, margarine, solid vegetable shortening, chocolate, and tropical oils (coconut oil is more than 90 percent saturated).

Unsaturated Fat

Unsaturated fats are partially solid or liquid at room temperature. This group of fats includes monounsaturated fats, polyunsaturated fats, and omega-3 oils (fish oils), which protect you against heart disease. Sources of unsaturated fats include vegetable oils (canola, safflower, sunflower, corn) and seeds and nuts. To make it easy to remember, unsaturated fats, with the exception of tropical oils, such as coconut, come from plants. The more liquid the fat, the more polyunsaturated it is, which, in fact, may lower your cholesterol levels. However, if you have familial hyperlipidemia (high cholesterol), it's important to discuss with your doctor whether you are a candidate for a cholesterol-lowering medication rather than relying on dietary changes alone.

In Mediterranean diets, for example, which are considered among the healthiest diets, olive oil, herbs, and spices are routinely used in place of butter as spreads or dips for breads. Olive oil was found to contain a host of protective factors, and catalyst ingredients that allow phytochemicals from plant-based foods to work their magic in the body. The virtues of a Mediterranean diet, with its "good fats," became the basis for a revolution in dietary fat guidelines, which now recognize that healthy diets should have some monounsaturated fats, the best of which is olive oil. Other monounsaturated oils are canola, peanut, sesame, soybean, corn, cottonseed, and safflower, but olive oil is 74 percent monounsaturated, while the next best oil, canola, is only 59 percent monounsaturated.

Trans-Fatty Acids (or Hydrogenated Oils)

Trans-fatty acids are harmful fats that not only raise the level of bad cholesterol (LDL) in your bloodstream, but lower the amount of good cholesterol (HDL) that's already there. Trans-fatty acids are what you get when you make a liquid oil, such as corn oil, into a more solid or spreadable substance, such as margarine. Trans-fatty acids, you might say, are the "road to hell, paved with good intentions." Someone, way back when, thought that if you could take the "good fat"—unsaturated fat—and solidify it so it could double as butter or lard, you could eat the same things without missing the spreadable fat. That sounds like a great idea. Unfortunately, to make an unsaturated liquid fat more solid, you have to add hydrogen to its molecules. This is known as *hydrogenation*, the process that converts liquid fat to semisolid fat. That ever-popular chocolate bar ingredient, hydrogenated palm oil, is a classic example of a trans-fatty acid. Hydrogenation also prolongs the shelf life of a fat, such as a polyunsaturated fat, which can oxidize when exposed to air, causing rancid odors or flavors. Deep-frying oils used in the restaurant trade are generally hydrogenated.

Trans-fatty acids are now listed on most packaged food labels. The magic word you're looking for is *hydrogenated*. If the product lists a variety of unsaturated fats (monounsaturated X oil, polyunsaturated Y oil, and so on), keep reading. If the word *hydrogenated* appears, count that product as a saturated fat; your body will!

Fish Fat (Omega-3 Oils)

The fats naturally present in fish that swim in cold waters, known as *omega-3 fatty acids* or fish oils, are all polyunsaturated. These fats are crucial for brain tissue. They lower your cholesterol levels and protect against heart disease. Mackerel, albacore tuna, salmon, sardines, and lake trout, which have a layer of fat to keep them warm in cold water, are all rich in omega-3 fatty acids. In fact, whale meat and seal meat are enormous sources of omega-3 fatty acids. These foods were once the staples of the Inuit diet, and once protected that population from heart disease.

The Right Carbs

The diet lingo can often confuse what is meant by *carbohydrates*. Carbohydrates can be simple or complex. Simple carbohydrates are found in any food that has natural sugar (honey, fruits, juices, vegetables, milk) and anything that contains table sugar. These simple carbs are high on the glycemic index (see resource list in Appendix B), and should be minimized as they are higher in calories and can increase your blood sugar too rapidly, causing the "sugar crashes."

Complex carbohydrates are more sophisticated foods that are made up of larger molecules, such as grain foods, starches, and foods high in fiber. These are carbs that are low on the glycemic index and should be maximized as they are higher in nutrients and take much longer to convert into glucose.

Normally, all carbs convert into glucose when you eat them. Glucose is the baseline ingredient of all naturally occurring sugars, which include:

- Sucrose: table or white sugar, naturally found in sugar cane and sugar beets
- Fructose: the natural sugar in fruits and vegetables
- Lactose: the natural sugar in all milk products
- Maltose: the natural sugar in grains (flours and cereals)

What you have to watch out for is added sugar; these are sugars that manufacturers add to foods during processing or packaging. The best way to know how much sugar is in a product is to look at the nutritional label under *carbohydrates*.

21 Making an Informed Decision

As a bioethicist, I (Sara) am frequently asked by thyroid patients whether there are steps they can take to be better informed about their thyroid treatment options. This chapter contains what most patients don't know about informed decision making, which includes the concepts of standards of care and informed consent, as well as the guiding ethical principles in Western-based health care for all healthcare providers.

The Standards of Care

A common scenario in thyroid disease treatment involves differing standards of care, which can have dramatically different consequences for thyroid patients.

The Legal Standard of Care

Legally, you are entitled to the community standard of care: how the average doctor in your community would care for your thyroid problem. This is frequently the only standard that your insurance provider will cover. That means that seeking a higher standard of care, outside your community, may result in your paying for some services out-of-pocket. Even if the community standard of care is dramatically lower than other standards of care for the same thyroid problem, it is not considered malpractice or negligence by legal definition.

Let's explore the legal standard of care for the case of John, who has a 1.5-centimeter nodule on his thyroid gland that he discovered while shaving. After bringing the nodule (see Chapter 8) to the attention of his local family doctor, the family doctor recommends a lobectomy (see Chapter 9) with a general surgeon who does only occasional thyroid surgery, where one side of John's thyroid gland is removed (the side with the nodule). John has the surgery. The nodule removed during surgery is described as a papillary tumor (see Chapter 9). Follow-up after John's surgery involves an annual visit to his primary care doctor, who feels John's neck carefully to make sure it has no other lumps that can be felt.

The Specialist Standard of Care

The specialist standard of care is higher than the legal standard. This is the standard of care according to published, peer-reviewed guidelines by a professional association pertaining to the particular specialty. For thyroid specialists, the professional association guidelines are published by a few different groups, including the American Thyroid Association, the American Association of Clinical Endocrinologists, the Endocrine Society, and so on.

According to the specialist standard of care, John's nodule would be handled quite differently. First, John's nodule would be evaluated by a fine-needle aspiration (FNA) biopsy (see Chapter 2) to see whether the nodule was a benign or malignant growth. Based on the results of John's biopsy, even though it is a small tumor, John would have a total thyroidectomy, with a partial neck dissection; this would be done by a head and neck surgeon. This means that the entire thyroid gland would be removed, and during surgery, select lymph nodes on the side of the neck where the nodule was found would be checked for signs of spread. Following surgery, John would also have radioactive iodine (RAI) therapy (see Chapter 12) to ablate any microscopic remnants of papillary cancer cells. John would then be placed on thyroid hormone (see Chapter 10) on a suppression dosage (see Chapters 9 and 10).

John's follow-up care would involve thyroid function tests every six months (see Chapter 2) to make sure his thyroid hormone dosage suppressed his TSH. He would also have a thyroglobulin test every six months (see Chapter 2). His physician would arrange a radioactive iodine whole body scan (see Chapter 2) to check for recurrence, which would involve going off of his thyroid hormone and becoming hypothyroid. Follow-up scans and blood tests would be done to see if there was successful elimination of any perceptible cancer. With one clean scan after his surgery, John would have a withdrawal whole body scan at least once every five years; thereafter, his thyroid function tests and thyroglobulin tests would be checked at least annually.

State-of-the-Art Standard of Care

State-of-the-art standard of care refers to the highest standard of care money can buy; this is the standard of care in the ideal situation of full access to the best equipment, a renowned expert in the field, the very latest research findings and techniques, and no financial restrictions on costs billed to the patient.

In John's case, the state-of-the-art standard of care would involve the following: an FNA biopsy and total thyroidectomy and partial neck dissection as described earlier, with a head and neck or endocrine surgeon who performs at least thirty such surgeries per year. The surgery would be followed with RAI therapy performed after a low-iodine diet (see Chapter 20) had been followed for two weeks. An additional whole body scan, a *post-therapy scan*, would be done within a few days of the radioactive iodine treatment.

Following the RAI therapy, John would be required to have a withdrawal whole-body scan and thyroglobulin test six months later, which would include checking for thyroglobulin antibodies. If he was antibody-positive (meaning that the thyroglobulin test was insensitive), he would have a PET scan or a SESTAMIBI whole body scan (see Chapter 2). As for his whole body scan, to minimize hypothyroid symptoms, he would be placed on T3 (see Chapter 10) for the first four weeks of the six weeks off of T4. As before, he would also be required to follow a low-iodine diet (see Chapter 20) for two weeks prior to his scan. If the scans were clean, he would be scanned with intervals between scans increasing by one year with every successive clean scan until the scan intervals became every five years. This five-year interval would be maintained there-after, unless evidence of recurrent tumor was discovered. Also, he would continue to have a thyroglobulin blood test every six months. Periodically, to maximize his thy-roglobulin test, he might be offered Thyrogen treatment (see Chapter 2), which can make a thyroglobulin test more sensitive. To minimize thyrotoxic symptoms while on a higher-than-normal suppression dosage of thyroid hormone, John might also be offered a beta-blocker.

The Reasonable Standard of Care

A reasonable standard of care refers to a standard of care a reasonable person could expect, given his or her insurance coverage, financial means, and the information he or she needs to make an informed decision. In the case of John, the legal standard of care would be considered unacceptable by a thyroid specialist. But if John were home-less, unable to afford prescription thyroid hormone, and unable to afford health insur-ance, the legal standard of care still saves his life while preserving some natural thyroid function; prevents death from a spreading, acute cancer; and still gets him in to see a doctor once a year. That's a lot better than the health care the majority of people in this world receive. State-of-the-art care is about refinement and fine-tuning, and giving the patient the "best shot" at health with all the current knowledge and resources. For most cases of thyroid disease in people with health insurance, it is reasonable to expect a specialist standard because we all have reasonable access to specialists, and it is a reasonable request to an insurance provider. But the difference between obtaining a reasonable standard of care and a legal standard of care depends on self-education.

For example, if John had access to a book such as this, which contains a detailed chapter on managing thyroid nodules, John could have requested that he be sent to a thyroid specialist outside his community or referral network. This is a reasonable request to an insurance provider, which a primary care doctor would support. How-ever, it might be unreasonable for John to make the request for state-of-the-art care with the best thyroid specialist unless he had a particularly difficult or unusual case, which he might not even be aware of. It is reasonable to reserve state-of-the-art care for people with unusual health problems that require specially trained doctors. Some private insurance plans provide access to state-of-the-art care, but the cost of these plans may be high. Alternatively, there may be some situations where people self-pay by choice and have sufficient finances to defy restrictions of insurance providers. In such cases, self-education can allow them to seek out the very best care money can buy. That is their option, and one reason why some people in the United States oppose national health-care coverage. At the same time, fairness and justice demand that people who will die *without* a state-of-the-art approach be treated regardless of their health insurance status. This doesn't always happen in the United States, which is why some people favor a system of national health care that would ensure a reasonable standard for all.

In essence, where there is a health insurer involved, with policies that restrict access to "out-of-system" specialists, people with difficult or dangerous thyroid conditions may not gain access to state-of-the-art care unless they are willing to pay out-of-pocket.

What You Should Know About Ethical Guidelines in Health Care

Making an informed decision has to do with understanding what you are ethically "owed" as a patient by your health-care provider. It also means understanding how certain barriers can interfere with your getting the information you need to consent to certain treatments, and/or becoming educated about your options.

In a very general way, Western health care revolves around four basic guiding ethical principles known as respect for persons, beneficence, nonmaleficence, and justice.

Respect for Persons (or Patient Autonomy)

Respect for persons means to respect that each person is a human being with full human rights. That means he or she has a right to be fully informed about all things involving his or her care, his or her body, or things being done to his or his body (if you're pregnant, you also have the right to know about everything that affects the fetus you're carrying), and to make his or her own decisions about care based on accurate information.

A health-care provider has a duty to respect your personhood, wishes, bodily integrity, and health-care preferences. So information, counseling, and informed consent (see further on) are all crucial aspects of care, which support this principle. Sometimes your preferences conflict with other ethical duties of health-care practitioners. For example, in cases where you are refusing clearly beneficial therapy and harm will come to you if you refuse treatment, your health-care provider has a duty to intervene so that you are not harmed unnecessarily. Here are some examples of "respect for persons" issues:

- **You are given no information about your thyroid condition, and your doctor refuses to answer or address your questions.** Your doctor ought to make time to answer questions, or else give you an e-mail address to contact him or her with questions. If your doctor is completely swamped, he or she ought to provide you with literature, good websites, or other contacts for further information.
- **You refuse a certain treatment or procedure after being fully informed of all of the risks and benefits of that procedure, but your health-care provider tries to force you or coerce you into having the procedure anyway, which does not respect your choice.** However, if harm will come to you without a particular therapy, your doctor may have an ethical duty to intervene. (Note: this is often the case with radioactive iodine treatment for Graves' disease patients, discussed in Chapter 6.)
- **You request a referral to a specialist (such as a thyroidologist) and your doctor ignores your request.** Frequently, doctors are happy to refer you to a specialist, but the insurance provider will not permit certain referrals outside a certain geographic region. If you cannot get in to see the appropriate specialist, you need to discuss where the roadblock is: your doctor, your insurance provider, and so on.
- **You do not speak English and your doctor refuses to speak to a translator you've appointed.** With your permission, your doctor can speak to anyone you like about your health status; in some cases, however, a doctor may require written permission from you to discuss your case with somebody else.
- **Your confidentiality is breached in some way.** This is getting trickier and trickier, with new privacy laws passed under the Health Insurance Portability and Accountability Act (HIPAA) in 2003. (We'll discuss this more later in the chapter.)

What Is Informed Consent?

You may have heard the term *informed consent* but may not truly understand what it means. To uphold the principle of respect for persons, you have the right to accurate and full information about your health so you can make an informed decision about your health care. You cannot even know to refuse a procedure if you are not given this information first. This is known as informed consent. In order for informed consent to take place, three things have to happen:

- **Disclosure.** Have you been provided with relevant and comprehensive information by your health-care provider? For example, a description of the treatment; its expected effects (duration of hospital stay, expected time to recovery, restrictions on daily activities, scars); information about relevant alternative options and their expected benefits and relevant risks; and an explanation of the consequences of declining or delaying treatment. Have you been given an opportunity to ask questions, and has your health-care provider been available to answer them?

• **Capacity and competency.** Do you understand information relevant to a treatment decision and appreciate the reasonably foreseeable consequences of a decision or lack of decision? Do you understand what's being disclosed and can you decide on your treatment based on this information? In people who are severely hypothyroid, thyrotoxic, or who are suffering from severe depression, for example, their capacity and competency to make a decision may be impaired.

• **Voluntariness.** Are you being allowed to make your health-care choice free of any undue influences? To answer the question, we need to take into consideration factors such as pain and manipulation (when information is being deliberately distorted or omitted).

Other barriers to informed consent include:

• Language barriers
• Literacy
• Wide gaps in knowledge (When you're not a doctor or have no medical background, how informed can you really be about complete therapies unless you go to medical school?)
• Health-care provider bias (When your health-care provider makes assumptions about your intelligence or character and tailors the information to those assumptions.)

What About Confidentiality?

We live online, making privacy more of a problem than ever before. If you live in the United States, you may have heard of the Health Insurance Portability and Accountability Act (HIPAA). This law has made it harder for health-care providers to disclose private health information to third parties; it particularly protects the privacy and security of certain health information that could identify you. These privacy provisions are known as the HIPAA Privacy Rules, which came into effect April 14, 2003. These privacy rules, which pertain to insurance companies, hospitals, clinics, medical providers, and pharmacies, make it illegal for health-care providers to disclose patient information to any other party, including your family members, without your consent. The U.S. Congress also banned certain uses of genetic information by insurance companies to protect insurance eligibility. In some cases, HIPAA may create more ethical problems than it solves, such as in cases where family members need to be warned about genetic risks for certain thyroid diseases (see Chapter 9 or Chapter 18), but overall, it is designed to ensure greater confidentiality. In Canada and other countries, similar privacy legislation regarding medical information is being drafted and/or passed.

With your permission, however, your doctor can disclose or discuss your health information with anyone you like (such as an employer or other family members). In cases where you may need time off work, you may wish to have your doctor explain your thyroid condition to an employer, for example.

HIPAA privacy regulations make it illegal for any protected health information (PHI) to be disclosed. PHI includes your name; address; telephone numbers; fax numbers; e-mail addresses; URLs or IP addresses; birth and death dates; dates relating to admissions or discharges; numbers that identify social security, health records, or beneficiary plans; motor vehicle information; and a host of other identifiers.

Beneficence and Nonmaleficence

Beneficence means that a health-care provider must strive to maintain or promote the well-being of a patient. At the same time, the health-care provider must also strive not to inflict harm or evil on a patient (this is known as *nonmaleficence*). This means that a health-care provider has a duty not to kill a patient, and a duty not to refrain from aiding a patient. In addition, a health-care provider also has a duty to warn a patient of imminent harm or danger.

To promote the well-being of patients and avoid harming them, therapies, treatments, or diagnostic tests that involve risks to your health need to be weighed against potential benefits. Here are some examples of beneficence issues:

- **Your doctor is recommending you try a therapy that has not yet been proven to work better than a standard therapy, and has unknown risks.** In cases where T3 is added to T4 therapy (see Chapters 3, 10, and 19), there is no proven benefit to T3, while there are risks of thyrotoxicosis (see Chapter 4) and complications of thyrotoxicosis. That is why there may be ethical problems with T3 therapy in patients who do not stand to benefit from it.
- **You are given a drug or therapy, and you're not provided with information on side effects or potential risks.** If you're on thyroid hormone, for example (any formulation), and are not given information about the risk of becoming thyrotoxic from too high a dose, or hypothyroid from too low a dose, this is a breech of beneficence.
- **You are in a drug study that involves some people taking a dummy pill (placebo) and some people taking a real pill.** In this case, you may continue to suffer from an ailment needlessly if you are taking the dummy pill and not offered a standard therapy that will help your ailment. In cases where there is a standard therapy, the trial needs to evaluate a new agent based on whether it is better than the standard agent. (This is how the T3/T4 versus T4 alone trials were conducted, which showed that T3/T4 was not better than T4 alone.) However, in cases where there is no treatment for an ailment, it is important to evaluate whether the new agent is "better than nothing." This is frequently used to evaluate herbal therapies.

- **Your health-care provider breaches your confidentiality, which results in harm.** For example, your doctor socialized with your employer and tells him or her that you have a thyroid disorder, which requires you to take lifelong medication (thyroid hormone). The employer decides to alter your health benefits because of this information.
- **Your health-care provider fails to warn you of a potential danger.** For example, your doctor has a duty to warn you about not driving while hypothyroid. If you drive while hypothyroid and get into an accident, and your doctor has failed to warn you, the doctor could be found to be negligent. If you choose to drive, but have been warned not to, your doctor has nevertheless fulfilled his or her duty.

Justice

Justice means that the health-care provider or health insurance provider has to strive toward enabling fair access to reasonable health-care services (such as hospital beds, medicine, treatments, clinical trials, health-care providers, preventive care, and so on) regardless of a patient's ability to pay, gender, ethnicity or race, physical or mental ability, age, or any other factors, such as behavior or lifestyle.

To be fair, all people should have equal access to reasonable health-care services and resources. Being just or fair means all lives and interests are of equal importance and must be given equal weight. As well, a health-care provider has a duty to provide the same standard of care and options to all patients, regardless of income, education, or race. Here are some examples of justice issues:

- When some people have more access to resources than other people because of privilege and wealth
- When your health-care provider places a greater value on some patients than on others
- When a gay or lesbian person is refused health-care service by a health-care provider who does not approve of gay or lesbian lifestyles
- When certain groups of people die of preventable or curable diseases because they don't have the same access to screening for that disease as other groups of people. For example, cases of inherited medullary thyroid cancer (see Chapter 9) could be prevented with access to genetic screening, and in the developing world, many newborn babies are not properly screened for hypothyroidism, which leads to mental and physical disability.
- When vulnerable populations (the elderly, mentally ill, people in developing countries, or certain ethnic groups) are selected for dangerous or risky medical experiments because they are perceived as expendable

Problems with "Doing the Right Thing" for Patients

In many circumstances it isn't always clear what "the right thing" to do is, and it isn't always possible to do the right thing. Here are some examples:

- When people are unconscious, it's impossible to inform them and ask them about their wishes. (In this case, someone close to the unconscious person makes decisions on his or her behalf.)
- When people are not competent to make their own decisions, it's difficult to inform them. (Here, again, someone close to the incompetent patient makes the decision.)
- When the benefits of certain medications or therapies have to be weighed against certain risks, it's difficult to know what to do, and what's in the patient's best interests. In this case, the decision often requires a doctor-patient partnering so that they can discuss the options together.
- When health-care providers are faced with limited resources, or insurance restrictions, it's difficult to make the best decision or offer all the options.

Steps Toward Informed Decision Making

The following steps can help you make more informed decisions about doctors and treatment options.

- **If you have a thyroid problem, request a referral to an endocrinologist or thyroid specialist even if it's outside your community or referral network.** This is a reasonable standard of care you can expect if you have health insurance. Use the resources in Appendix A under "Finding a Thyroid Specialist" to help you find reasonable specialists.
- **Appoint a surrogate decision maker to advocate on your behalf in the event that you are ill or unable to take in all the information you need.** If you are severely ill from an untreated thyroid problem, your surrogate decision maker can help to organize and record the information you need to get better.
- **If you don't speak English well, bring a translator with you to the doctor (your son or daughter, a friend).** It is not reasonable to expect your doctor or clinic to provide a translator for you, unless you have arranged this well ahead of time. In the United States, most people can expect someone in a large urban hospital or clinic to speak Spanish, but any other unofficial language will likely not be spoken. (In Canada, unless you live in Quebec, don't expect anyone to speak French; it's easier to find Mandarin-speaking and Punjabi-speaking people.)
- **Get informed.** Get a book (clearly you have, if you're reading this!), or go online to one of the websites we recommend at the back of this book. If you have no computer, public libraries have computers with Internet access.
- **Keep a thyroid health folder of all information pertaining to your thyroid treatment.** Request a copy of your complete medical records, and after each doctor visit, request a copy of all thyroid function lab test results, correspondence, and so forth. Keep an updated list of all your medications, including the brand names and dosage strength.

- **Get it in writing or on tape.** If your treatment plan is complex (as in Graves' disease or thyroid cancer, for example), bring a tape recorder to your doctor visits and ask permission to tape some of the information so you can retain it better.
- **Get an e-mail address and ask your doctor if you can send questions from time to time (try not to take advantage).** Some health insurance providers now offer reimbursement to doctors for e-mail time spent with patients. This has been shown to create better access for patients and cut down on travel time to doctors. Many specialists routinely manage some of their thyroid patients long-distance with e-mail access.

22 Complementary Therapies for Thyroid Patients

While you're managing your thyroid condition using conventional treatments, you can also incorporate complementary therapies into your treatment, which may improve your sense of well-being and health. I (Sara) have incorporated a number of these therapies into my health routines, but I must emphasize that the information in this chapter should be regarded as the "feel good" therapies that are, at worst, harmless, and at best, therapies that can make you, well . . . *feel good*! Treat this as your "icing" rather than the cake. Potentially harmful therapies are not discussed.

Although in many of my past works I have discussed specific herbal supplements (particularly the "calming herbs"), in this book we have limited herbal therapies to aromatherapy. While many herbs have been shown to have health benefits, many of them conflict in some way with other medications, and can also affect how thyroid hormone may be absorbed. For example, St.-John's-wort, which was very popular in recent years, was shown, on further study, to interfere with certain medications, such as drugs for HIV. Herbs may be quite beneficial, but they should be treated like any other pharmaceutical product: discuss their benefits and any potential risks or side effects with a knowledgeable pharmacist or doctor. Although herbal medicine experts are very knowledgeable about combining various herbs, they are probably not knowledgeable about thyroid health, or they may not understand the possible interactions the herbal medications might have with the conventional pharmaceutical products you're taking.

You may find that your own physicians are not supportive of complementary therapies. Doctors make the mistake of assuming that *complementary* is synonymous with *alternative* and worry that their patients may abandon clearly curative therapies in the hopes that drinking a Chinese tea will cure their thyroid condition. (We discuss this in Chapter 19.) On the other hand, keep in mind that "natural" is not necessarily "not harmful," and many conscientious physicians require a higher standard of scientific evidence before recommending complementary therapies that have not been evaluated in this fashion. What we mean by *complementary* is that you can "have RAI and a massage, too!"

Therapies Involving "Life Force" Energy

All ancient, non-Western cultures, whether in native North America, India, China, Japan, or ancient Greece, believed that there were two fundamental aspects to the human body: the actual physical shell (clinically called the corporeal body) that makes cells, blood, tissue, and so on, and an energy flow that made the physical body come alive. This was known as the *life force* or *life energy*. In fact, it was so central to the view of human function that every non-Western culture has a word for "life force." In China, it's called *qi* (pronounced "chee"); in India it's called *prana*; in Japan it's called *ki*; while the ancient Greeks called it *pneuma* (which has become a prefix in medicine meaning "having to do with breath and lungs").

Today, Western medicine concentrates on the corporeal body and doesn't recognize that we have a life force. However, in non-Western, ancient healing, it's thought that the life force is what heals the corporeal body. One of the most ancient forms of healing is *energy healing*, which can involve therapeutic touch or healing touch. Technically, these techniques are considered forms of *biofield therapy*. An energy healer will use his or her hands to help guide your life force energy. The hands may rest on the body, or just close to the body without actually touching it. Energy healing is used to reduce pain and inflammation, improve sleep patterns and appetite, and reduce stress. Energy healing, supported by the American Holistic Nurses Association, has been incorporated into conventional nursing techniques with good results. Typically, the healer will move loosely cupped hands in a symmetric fashion on your body, sensing cold, heat, or vibration. The healer will then place his or her hands over areas where the life force energy is imbalanced in order to restore and regulate the energy flow. Several thyroid patient–led conferences are now including energy healing sessions.

Hands-on Healing

All forms of hands-on healing work in some way with the life force energy. Therapies that help to move or stimulate the life force energy include:

- Healing or therapeutic touch (Here, a practitioner uses touch to heal, energize, or balance physical, emotional, mental, and spiritual health. A healing touch client would normally remain fully clothed during a session.)
- Tuana massage (Often combined with acupuncture; this involves key areas for very focused massage.)
- Qi gong

- Reiki (A form of healing touch where your energy fields are worked with using light hand placements.)
- Mari-el (This is a form of Reiki, developed by Ethel Lombardi, a Reiki master.)
- SHEN therapy (Similar to Reiki, this is another form of energy healing using light hand placements on the body.)

Massage

Massage therapy can be beneficial whether you're receiving the massage from your spouse or from a massage therapist trained in any one of dozens of techniques from shiatsu to Swedish massage. If you're hypothyroid, massage therapy may help to improve circulation and depression; if you're thyrotoxic, it can help to relieve anxiety and calm you down. In the East, massage was extensively written about in *The Yellow Emperor's Classic of Internal Medicine*, published in 2700 B.C. (the text that frames the entire Chinese medicine tradition). In Chinese medicine, massage is recommended as a treatment for a variety of illnesses; tuana massage, a form of deep tissue massage, combined with acupuncture is very effective. A Swedish doctor and poet, Per Henrik, who borrowed techniques from ancient Egypt, China, and Rome, developed Swedish massage (what most of us Westerners are familiar with) in the nineteenth century. It's out of shiatsu in the East and Swedish massage in the West that all the many forms of massage were developed.

While the philosophies and styles differ in each tradition, the common element is the same: to mobilize the natural healing properties of the body, which will help it maintain or restore optimal health. Shiatsu-inspired massage focuses on balancing the life force energy; Swedish-inspired massage works on more physiological principles. It relaxes muscles to improve blood flow throughout connective tissues, which is reported to strengthen the cardiovascular system. Massage is more technically referred to as *soft tissue manipulation*. But no matter what kind of massage you have, there exist numerous helpful gliding and kneading techniques used along with deep circular movements and vibrations that will relax muscles, improve circulation, and increase mobility. All are known to help relieve stress, which can be aggravated if you're amidst treatment for thyroid disease, or because of other lifestyle factors. Massage also can ease muscle and joint pain, frequently aggravated by bouts of hypothyroidism. In people undergoing treatment for thyroid cancer, massage can help to ease stress, as well as help cancer patients stay grounded or centered while going through the balancing act of thyroid hormone replacement (see Chapter 10). Massage is so beneficial to a person's sense of well-being that a number of employers cover massage therapy in their health plans. Massage is becoming so popular that the number of licensed massage therapists enrolled in the American Massage Therapy Association has grown from 1,200 in 1983 to more than 38,000 today.

Some benefits of massage include:

- Improved circulation
- Improved lymphatic system
- Faster recovery from musculoskeletal injuries
- Soothed aches and pains
- Reduced edema (water retention)
- Reduced anxiety

Types of massage include:

- Deep tissue massage
- Manual lymph drainage
- Neuromuscular massage
- Sports massage
- Swedish massage
- Shiatsu massage

Yoga

Yoga is not just about various stretches or postures, but is actually a way of life for many. It is part of a whole science of living known as the *ayurveda*. The ayurveda is an ancient Indian approach to health and wellness that's stood up quite well to the test of time (it's roughly three thousand years old). Essentially, it divides up the universe into three basic constitutions or "energies," known as *doshas*. The three doshas are based on wind (*vata*), fire (*pitta*), and earth (*kapha*). In ayurvedic terms, these doshas also govern our bodies, personalities, and activities. When our doshas are balanced, all functions well, but when they're not balanced, a state of disease (*dis-ease* as in "not at ease") can set in. Finding the balance involves changing your diet to suit your predominant dosha (foods are classified as kapha, vata, or pitta, and we eat more or less of whatever we need for balance) and practicing yoga, which is a preventative health science that involves certain physical postures, exercises, and meditation. Essentially, yoga is the exercise component of ayurveda and is designed to tone and soothe your mental and physical state. Most people benefit from introductory yoga classes, or even introductory yoga videos. Yoga does a few things for people with thyroid disease:

- Yoga aids with weight loss. (It is an activity that many people enjoy over more conventional forms of exercise; any activity you do frequently will help with weight loss.)
- Yoga aids with improving oxygen flow throughout the body (through the yogic breath), which improves fatigue and sense of well-being, and can reduce stress and other risk factors for hypertension.
- Yoga aids with muscular aches and pains, aggravated by hypothyroidism.
- Yoga aids anxiety and restlessness, aggravated by thyrotoxicosis.

Qi Gong

Every morning, all over China, people of all ages gather at parks to do their daily qi gong exercises. Pronounced "chi kung," these are exercises that help get your life force energy (or *qi*, pronounced "chi") flowing and unblocked. Qi gong exercises are modeled after movements in wildlife (such as birds or animals), movement of trees, and other things in nature. The exercises have a continuous flow, rather than the stillness of a posture seen in yoga.

Using the hands in various positions to gather in the qi, move the qi, or release the qi is one of the most important aspects of qi gong movements.

One of the first groups of qi gong exercises you might learn is the "seasons"—fall, winter, spring, summer, and late summer (there are five seasons here). These exercises look more like a dance with precise, slow movements. The word *qi* means "vitality, energy, and life force"; the word *gong* means "practice, cultivate, refine." The Chinese believe that practicing qi gong balances the body and improves physical and mental well-being. These exercises push the life force energy into the various meridian pathways that correspond to organs, incorporating the same map used in pressure point therapies, discussed next. Qi gong improves oxygen flow and enhances the lymphatic system. Qi gong is similar to tai chi, except it allows for greater flexibility in routine. The best place to learn qi gong is through a qualified instructor. You can generally find qi gong classes through the alternative healing community, but many local YMCAs offer classes these days. Check health food stores and other centers that offer classes such as yoga or tai chi. Qi gong is difficult to learn from a book or video, so an instructor is best.

Pressure Point Therapies

Pressure point therapies involve using the fingertips to apply pressure to pressure points on the body. They're believed to help reduce stress, anxiety, pain, and other physical symptoms. There are different kinds of pressure point therapies; two of the best known are acupuncture and reflexology.

Acupuncture

Acupuncture is an ancient Chinese healing art, which aims to restore the smooth flow of life energy (qi) to the body. Acupuncturists believe that your qi can be accessed from various points on your body, such as your ear. Each point is associated with a specific organ. Depending on your physical health, an acupuncturist will use a fine needle on a very specific point to restore qi to various organs. Each of the roughly two thousand points on your body has a specific therapeutic effect when stimulated. Acupuncture can relieve many of the physical symptoms and ailments caused by stress; it's now believed that acupuncture stimulates the release of endorphins, which is why it's effective in reducing stress, anxiety, pain, and so forth.

Reflexology

Western reflexology was developed by Dr. William Fitzgerald, an American ear, nose, and throat specialist, who described reflexology as *zone therapy*. But in fact reflexology is practiced in several cultures, including Egypt, India, Africa, China, and Japan. In the same way as the ears are a map to the organs in Chinese medicine, with valuable pressure points that stimulate the life force, in reflexology, the hands and feet play the same role. For example, on a reflexology "map" the thyroid gland is associated with the base of the thumbs and big toes. Imagine you had a ring on your big toes or thumbs; this ring is the pressure point for the thyroid gland. By applying pressure to this part, or other parts of the feet, hands, and even ears, reflexologists can ease pain and tension and restore the body's life force energy. Like most Eastern healing arts, reflexology aims to release the flow of energy through the body along its various pathways. When this energy is trapped for some reason, some believe illness can result. When the energy is released, the body, some believe, can begin to heal itself. A reflexologist views the foot as a microcosm of the entire body. Individual reference points or reflex areas on the foot correspond to all major organs, glands, and parts of the body. Applying pressure to a specific area of the foot stimulates the movement of energy to the corresponding body part.

Shiatsu

Shiatsu massage also involves using pressure points. A healer using shiatsu will travel the length of each energy pathway (also called meridian) by applying thumb pressure to successive points along the way. The aim is to stimulate acupressure points while giving you some of the healer's own life energy. Barefoot shiatsu involves the healer using his foot instead of hand to apply pressure. Jin Shin Jyutsu and Jin Shin Do are other pressure point therapies similar to acupuncture.

Working Your Own Pressure Points

You can learn to work your own pressure points, too. Here are some simple pressure point exercises you can try:

- With the thumb of one hand, slowly work your way across the palm of the other hand, from the base of the baby finger to the base of the index finger. Then rub the center of your palm with your thumb. Push on this point. This supposedly will calm your nervous system. Repeat this using the other hand.
- To relieve a headache, pressure point enthusiasts recommend that you grasp the flesh at the base of one thumb with the opposite index finger and thumb. Squeeze gently and massage the tissue in a circular motion. Then, pinch each fingertip. Switch to the other hand.
- For general stress relief, it's suggested that you find sore pressure points on your feet and ankles. Gently press your thumb into them, and work each sore point. The tender

areas are signs of stress in particular parts of your body. By working them, you're relieving the stress and tension in various organs, glands, and tissues. You can also apply pressure with bunched and extended fingers, the knuckles, the heel of the hand, or by using the entire hand in a gripping motion.

- For self-massage of the hands, use the preceding techniques, paying special attention to tender points on the palms and wrists.
- Use the self-massage technique to self-massage the ears. Feel for tender spots on the flesh of the ears and work them with vigorous massage.

Aromatherapy

Essential oils, comprised from plants (mostly herbs and flowers), can help with many thyroid-related symptoms, particularly those associated with hypothyroidism. The easiest way to use essential oils is in a warm bath; you simply put a few drops of the oil into the bath, and sit and relax in it for about ten minutes. The aroma from the oils can also be inhaled (put a few drops in a bowl of hot water, lean over with a towel over your head, and breathe); diffused (using a lamp ring, or a ceramic diffuser—that thing that looks like a fondue pot); or sprayed into the air as a mist. You can also rub the oils onto the soles of your feet (where the largest pores are), which will get them working fast!

The following essential oils are known to have calming, sedative, and/or antidepressant effects for hypothyroid-related depression: ylang-ylang, neroli, jasmine, orange blossom, cedarwood, lavender (a few drops on your pillow will also help you sleep), chamomile, marjoram, geranium, patchouli, rose, sage, clary sage, and sandalwood.

The following scents are considered helpful in combating fatigue: clove, ravensara, rosemary, thyme, and basil. The following scents are stimulating and energizing: lemon, grapefruit, peppermint, rosemary, and pine.

The following scents can improve circulation: birch, cinnamon bark, clary sage, cypress, hyssop, and nutmeg.

For intolerance to cold, try sandalwood in a bath.

To improve concentration, try basil, cedarwood, cypress, eucalyptus, juniper, lavender, lemon, myrrh, orange, peppermint, rosemary, sandalwood, and ylang-ylang.

For muscle aches, try birch, ginger, nutmeg, and rosemary.

To improve fingernails, try eucalyptus, grapefruit, lavender, lemon, tea tree, myrrh, oregano, patchouli, peppermint, ravensara, rosemary, or thyme.

For sluggish digestion, rub a little fennel, nutmeg, sage, or tarragon on your stomach after eating. For constipation, try fennel, ginger, juniper, marjoram, orange, patchouli, rose, rosemary, sandalwood, tangerine, or tarragon.

To improve dry skin, try chamomile, davana, geranium, jasmine, lavender, lemon, patchouli, rosewood, or sandalwood.

To help with thyrotoxicosis (until it is under control), the most important essential oils are the calming oils, listed previously, as well as oil of orange, which calms palpitations.

Meditation

Meditation helps you relax. Particularly important if you're anxious about your thyroid treatments, or you're thyrotoxic, meditation simply requires you to stop thinking (about your life, problems, and so on) and just *be*. Yogic breathing is a tool for meditation often used to get you to focus solely on your breath. Breathing deeply through one nostril and out through your mouth is the classic technique. To do this, people usually find a relaxing spot, or sit quietly and breathe deeply for a few minutes.

But there is also active meditation that can include:

- Taking a walk or hike
- Swimming
- Running or jogging
- Gardening
- Playing golf
- Listening to music
- Dancing
- Reading for pleasure
- Walking your dog
- Practicing breathing exercises (or simply listening to the sounds of your own breathing)
- Practicing stretching exercises
- Practicing yoga or qi gong

The Healing Environment: Feng Shui

Pronounced "fung shway," this is the ancient practice of creating energy and harmony through your environmental surroundings (landscaping, interior design, and architecture). People tend to think of feng shui as something that can bring wealth to you (as in money corners) or romance (as in hanging certain items over the bed), but this is in fact not what authentic feng shui consultants look for. Harmony has many elements to it, and where you live, how you live, and a host of other geographic surroundings can all affect how to arrange your environment. Feng shui consultants will assess the following:

- **Entrance.** How is it lit? What do you have at your entrance (flowers, chimes, or a stack of old newspapers)?
- **Grounds.** Which kinds or colors of flowers are around your home? Are there rocks or sculptures around the grounds of your home?
- **Specific areas inside your home.** These include your work space/home office, chef station or kitchen, bedroom, bathroom, and so on. Placement of mirrors, pictures, plants, lamps, candles, rugs, furniture, bed, or even aquariums are all considered significant. For example, round or octagonal mirrors are powerful.

In general, feng shui tries to optimize your outdoor spaces through the use of curvilinear and rectangular visual contours or edges, wildlife, landscaping/vegetation, aquatic habitat, and minimizing things that interfere with harmony such as signage, power lines, and so on. Inside the home, live plants, colors, lighting, and the positioning of furniture to maximize views of natural scenery are important. Feng shui is said to reduce stress and blood pressure and to lower adrenaline levels. Beginning with a book on feng shui is a good primer—there are dozens of these!

4

Complications of Thyroid Disease

THYROID DISEASE CAN create other
health complications. This section
covers the most common health
complications you may encounter and
suggests ways to manage and cope with
such complications. Information on
thyroid eye disease, depression,
cardiovascular problems, and fatigue
are all discussed here.

23 Coping with Thyroid Eye Disease

This chapter is devoted to a frustrating symptom associated with autoimmune thyroid disorders: thyroid eye disease (TED), which can be disfiguring and demoralizing. Many people may notice eye problems or changes with their eyes, only to realize there is little or no information about what's going on, what it has to do with their thyroid, what they can do to relieve symptoms, or how they can treat the condition. Many times, this eye condition starts so slowly that the physician is the first one to notice it's there. In this chapter, we'll cover symptoms and treatment for TED, as well as present tips for relieving symptoms. This chapter also explores the more general problem of dry eye syndrome, which affects roughly eleven million North Americans, but particularly aggravates TED.

What Is Thyroid Eye Disease?

Thyroid eye disease tends to strike people with Graves'-related hyperthyroidism (see Chapter 6) and sometimes even those suffering from Hashimoto's disease (see Chapter 5). In clinical circles, TED is known by several different names: *Graves' ophthalmopathy (GO)*; *thyroid-associated ophthalmopathy*; and, infrequently, *dysthyroid orbitopathy*. (The prefix *ophthalmo* means "eyes," while *pathy* means "disease.") It is this disease that lends itself to the expression *thyroid eyes*—bulging, watery eyes—a condition known as *exophthalmos* (pronounced "ek-sof-thal-mos").

A common symptom of excessive thyroid hormone is lid retraction. Here, your upper eyelids can retract slightly and expose more of the whites of your eyes. The lid retraction creates a rather dramatic "staring" look and an exaggerated expression. This specific symptom is related to the excessive activation of the adrenaline system in thyrotoxicosis (see Chapter 4), and can be seen in nonautoimmune thyrotoxicosis. It will improve with beta-blockers (see Chapter 11). It's different from the actual bulging of the eyes (called *proptosis*), which occurs only in autoimmune thyroid disease. Usually the lid retraction will improve when the hyperthyroidism is treated. But this is not always the case with proptosis, as many people also have bulging of their eyeballs from underlying TED, which seems to persist long after the hyperthyroidism ends.

When TED is associated with the hyperthyroidism of Graves' disease, the eye problems can be far more severe. At least 50 percent of all Graves' disease patients suffer from obvious TED. At one time, only those with noticeable changes to the eyes were considered to have TED, but more sophisticated methods of diagnosis reveal that eye changes are present in almost all Graves' disease patients, even though symptoms may not be noticeable.

The most common eye changes for people with Graves' disease are bulging and double vision. Generally, the changes to the eyes reach a "burnout" period within a two-year time frame and then stop. There are severe cases that can progress to blindness, even with proper intervention, but this is very rare. Sometimes the eyes get better by themselves, but often, after the burnout period, the eyes remain changed but do not get any worse. The severity of the eye changes can be measured by an ophthalmologist (an eye disease specialist), with an instrument called an *exophthalmometer*. This instrument measures the degree to which the eyes protrude out from the skull.

TED Alert

When you notice one or more of these nine signs of TED, request a thyroid function test. These symptoms may appear a year or more before signs of thyrotoxicosis or hypothyroid symptoms.

- Gritty, itching, and watery eyes
- Aching discomfort behind the eyes, especially when you look up or to the side
- Sensitivity to light or sun
- Congestion in the eyelids (this may be mistaken for an infection)
- Dry eyes
- Lid lag (where the upper lids are slow to follow when you look down)
- Bulging eyes or a staring look (the first is caused by inflammation; the second caused by lid retraction)
- Double vision, particularly when looking to the side
- Bloodshot and red, irritated eyes (called *chemosis*)

The Stages of TED

In 80 percent of cases of Graves'-associated eye disease, symptoms of TED appear about a year or more before the symptoms of Graves' disease. This, of course, can be very frustrating, and may throw your doctor off the scent of thyroid disease altogether. When symptoms first appear, TED is said to be in its active, or initial, phase. This can last anywhere from eighteen to twenty-four months. During the active phase, you will experience the most dramatic eye changes, and it may not be necessary to treat the condition beyond symptom relief until the eyes reach their "burnout" phase. This means the eye problem will reach a maximum change point, where they will probably remain changed but not worsen. On the other hand, a few people have a rapid worsening that requires steroid treatments or surgery or both.

What Causes TED?

TED continues to fascinate thyroid specialists and researchers. Right now, it is believed that the autoimmune antibodies that develop in Graves' disease cause TED. For some strange reason, the same proteins in your thyroid cells and your eye muscle cells react to antithyroid antibodies that occur with Graves' disease. This is known as cross-reactivity. Since the treatment for the hyperthyroidism of Graves' disease involves reducing the ability of the thyroid gland to make thyroid hormone but doesn't alter the production of antibodies, treatment of the thyroid does not usually help the eyes. This continues to frustrate TED sufferers.

The fact that TED can occur in the absence of hyperthyroidism is what makes this a bit confusing. Probably some antibodies stick to eye muscles better than they stick to the thyroid gland. Environment and lifestyle seem to affect TED, however. Smokers are far more likely to suffer from severe TED than nonsmokers, while stress seems to aggravate the condition, too.

What Causes the Bulging?

Our eyeballs are encased in pear-shaped sockets known as *orbits*. The orbits of the eye are lined with pads of protective fat, connective tissue, blood vessels, muscles, nerves, and the lacrimal glands that are responsible for making tears. When the muscles that move the eyes enlarge and the fatty connective tissue within the orbits becomes inflamed, the eyeballs bulge forward, causing the classic bulging eyes for which TED is infamous.

Who Gets TED?

You are more likely to suffer from TED if you are:

- Diagnosed with Graves' disease (see Chapter 6)
- Middle-aged

- Under stress or working in a stressful environment
- A smoker

Smoking and TED

The link between smoking and TED is so strong that thyroid specialists believe smokers with Graves' disease can probably count on developing TED. TED is much less common in nonsmokers. No one knows exactly why smokers are more vulnerable to TED. What we do know is that smokers are more vulnerable to many more diseases and health problems than nonsmokers. Clearly, TED is one of them. However, it is certainly not surprising that an environment where you're surrounded by your own (or others') cigarette smoke would aggravate—or even help trigger—TED. In people with type 2 diabetes, diabetes-related eye disease is also more common and more severe among smokers because smoking constricts the small blood vessels.

In fact, one of the reasons that nonsmokers are so uncomfortable in smoke-filled rooms is because the smoke irritates their eyes, causing them to be watery, itchy, and red! Quitting smoking may help to ease some of the symptoms of TED.

It seems clear that the following things are true about smoking and Graves' disease:

- Smoking worsens the course of Graves' disease and its severity.
- Smoking increases the likelihood that a person with Graves' disease will have significant TED.
- People with such severe TED that they need steroid treatments or radiation treatment to their eyes will not respond as well to this treatment if they smoke.
- Ex-smokers do not have such risk for the development and worsening of their Graves' disease, suggesting a value to stopping any smoking as soon as possible.

True Grit: The Symptoms of TED

Typical TED symptoms are caused by inflammation of the eye tissues: the eyes become painful, red, and watery with a gritty feeling. Sensitivity to light, wind, or sun is also common. The grittiness and light sensitivity worsen with lid retraction: when your eyes are less protected by the eyelids from dust, wind, and infection, you really feel it.

Other symptoms include discomfort when looking up or to the side. And while some Graves' disease patients suffer from excessive watering of the eyes, many will also suffer from excessive dryness. In rare and extreme cases, vision deteriorates as a result of too much pressure being placed on the optic nerve from the protruding eyeball.

The covering of the eye is also inflamed and swollen. The lids and tissues around the eyes are swollen with fluid, and the eyeballs tend to bulge out of their sockets. Because of eye muscle damage or thickening, the eyes cannot move normally, resulting in blurred or double vision.

During what's called the *hot phase*, or initial active phase of TED, inflammation and swelling around and behind the eye are common. This phase lasts about six months, followed by the *cold phase* where the inflammation subsides and you then notice more changes in vision.

In severe cases, swelling may be so bad that you will find it difficult to move your eye, and you will even develop ulcers on the cornea. This comes from constant exposure to the air because the eye is so swollen that the lids can't close to distribute the lubricating tears. In most cases, both eyes are affected, but one may be worse than the other. You may also experience a phenomenon called *lid lag*, when your upper lids are slow to move when you're looking down. Lid lag results from the effects of too much thyroid hormone and will go away if thyroid hormone levels are lowered or you are treated with a beta-blocker medication.

What You See in the Mirror

Not all of the symptoms of TED are visible in the mirror, but some of them are. Your eyes may look puffy, have bags under them, and look bloodshot at the corners. People may wonder why you seem to look stunned or amazed all the time. This will be the result of your lids being retracted, thus giving you a more dramatic appearance. You may also be able to observe that the whites of your eyes are visible between the iris and lower lid and/or between the iris and upper lid.

Getting a Diagnosis

TED is frequently misdiagnosed as an allergy or pinkeye (conjunctivitis). One easy way to confirm TED is to request that your thyroid be checked and also to request a thyroid-stimulating antibody test. If you have noticed vision problems, you should also request screening for type 2 diabetes. Diabetes-related eye disease is also a common problem for people over age forty-five, in particular. Imaging tests such as CT (computerized tomography), ultrasound, or MRI (magnetic resonance imaging) may be used to view the orbit or eye tissues.

Interestingly, some people will notice that TED symptoms worsen when their thyroid hormone levels are lower than normal. Because hypothyroidism causes bloating and fluid retention, this can exacerbate inflammation of the eyes, triggering TED symptoms of dryness and grit. Many thyroid patients have ongoing disputes with their physicians over whether their TED flare-up is related to their thyroid condition. It may be. And since much is unknown about the relationship between TED and thyroid hormone levels, you do not have to accept your doctor's words upon being informed that you are imagining the connection.

Battling the Bulge: Treating TED

Before specific treatments for TED begin, the thyroid condition is treated first. In some cases, when the hyperthyroidism is treated, the eyes tend to get better—even before burnout occurs. For example, TED in the absence of hyperthyroidism tends to be much easier to treat. In this case, you will probably suffer from irritation and some wateriness. Discomfort, redness, and intolerance of light can also be present. Sometimes, if hyperthyroidism is treated with radioactive iodine, it may seem to worsen TED.

Drug Treatments

Often the first step in treating TED is to use artificial tears during the day and lubricating ointment at bedtime. If TED becomes worse, the next step is to offer a steroid drug, prednisone, which will reduce the swelling and inflammation causing the more severe TED symptoms. Steroids have numerous side effects, however, and you'll need to balance the side effects against TED symptoms. The other problem with steroids is that once you go off of them, TED symptoms can resume, and may even get worse.

Side Effects of Prednisone

When you're on prednisone, you'll have a lower resistance to infections and may develop harder-to-treat infections. It is also associated with mood changes and insomnia that can exacerbate symptoms of thyroid disease in general. There is a long list of other less common side effects associated with this drug, which you'll need to discuss with your doctor prior to consenting to this treatment. If you're pregnant, breastfeeding, or planning to get pregnant, you must not be on this drug.

Diuretics

Some doctors will prescribe diuretics that cause you to urinate more frequently, thereby eliminating excess fluid. This can sometimes help to reduce swelling. Unfortunately, this may place you at risk for losing potassium, and there is not any good evidence that diuretics will improve the outcome of TED.

Radiation

If you choose not to go on steroids, external beam radiation therapy is another option. This procedure starts with CT scans or MRIs and a simulation procedure in which careful measurements are taken in order to aim the x-ray beam properly; the x-ray is targeted at the muscles at the back of the eyes behind the lens—which may conceivably reduce the eye inflammation. The measurement is done using three laser light beams. Many of these treatments are successful, and the x-ray treatment is sometimes a way to avoid surgery, although it is often reserved for particularly severe cases.

Corrective Surgery

A procedure known as *orbital decompression surgery* can remove bone from the eye socket and expand the area alongside the eyeball so that swollen tissue can move into it. It's best to wait until the burnout period before attempting surgery so the eyes do not get any worse.

Other plastic surgery procedures can help to reconstruct the eye area and correct the disfigurement. Before you undergo corrective surgery, it's best to consult with a surgeon who specializes in orbital surgery, facial surgery, and neurosurgery (you may need to see three different surgeons). The special ophthalmologist that has experience with orbital decompression surgery is not the same local eye doctor that fits your contact lenses or does cataract surgery. Often, such a specialist is located at a major academic medical center. If you need such surgery, it's far better to travel to see an experienced specialist than to use someone without specialized skills just because it's convenient. An ear, nose, and throat specialist may also need to be consulted.

Generally, depending on your symptoms, surgery for TED can involve any of the following:

- Adjusting the position of your eyelids
- Correcting swelling around the eye
- Realigning eye muscles
- Orbital decompression

Finding Symptom Relief

To relieve irritation and inflammation, eyedrops or artificial tears are recommended, but it's important to ask your doctor for an appropriate brand. Double vision can be remedied by wearing plastic prism lenses that can be inserted inside your regular glasses, or operations that use techniques similar to those that correct squinting in childhood (strabismus) can be done at a later stage. Injecting Botox (botulinum toxin type A) can also help correct double vision. Botulinum toxin type A is a protein produced by the bacterium *Clostridium botulinum*. When used as an injectable form, small doses of the toxin are injected into the affected muscles and block the release of the chemical acetylcholine that would otherwise signal the muscle to contract.

The following self-help tips have been compiled from TED sufferers:

- Stop smoking and/or avoid secondhand smoke.
- Use artificial tears to help moisten the eyes. (See the later section "The Trouble with Eyedrops.")
- Sleep with the head of your bed raised. (Put some books under the legs.) Or prop yourself up on pillows to drain away excess fluid and reduce puffiness and swelling around the eyes.
- Cover your eyes when you sleep.
- Wear wraparound dark glasses outdoors during the day.
- Turn ceiling fans off before you go to bed.
- Avoid strong sunlight.
- Don't wear contact lenses.

- Try to help relieve swelling by drinking more fluids.
- Use cooling eye masks and gels.
- Wear a patch over one eye to help with double vision.

See the next section on dry eyes for more useful self-help tips.

Dry Eyes

Some symptoms of TED are not unique to people suffering from thyroid disease. Dry eyes are so common that a new syndrome has emerged in general medical practice, known as *dry eye syndrome*. It's estimated that roughly eleven million North Americans suffer from dry eyes, meaning that tear production is inadequate or the tears evaporate so quickly that your eyes are left gritty and irritated with every blink. Sometimes, dry eyes are a result of autoimmune disease against the tear glands and salivary glands, known as *Sjögren's syndrome* (also known as *keratoconjunctivitis sicca*). There is some evidence to suggest that the two autoimmune diseases, Graves' disease and Sjögren's disease, are sometimes associated with each other.

What is unique about dry eyes these days is that they are now observed in much younger people. In the past, dry eyes were observed in people over age sixty-five; today they are common in thirty-year-olds.

Common causes of dry eyes (which could aggravate TED) include:

- Waking up (tear production decreases when we sleep)
- Wind, sun, and pollution
- Smoke
- Airplanes
- Hotels (with "canned air")
- Overly dry places or air-conditioning
- Chlorine from pools
- Saltwater from oceans
- Cycling without goggles
- Contact lenses
- Side effects to medications

Dry eyes can also result from focusing too long on display screens such as television or computer screens, which is one reason why experts think it's becoming increasingly common in young people.

Easy-fix solutions include using humidifiers at night and humidifying the air in winter (when furnaces can dry out the air). If your dryness is related to medication that you are taking, switching to a different brand can sometimes solve the problem, too.

Moisturizing Your Eyes

Here are some ways to keep your eyes moist:

- Hold a warm, wet washcloth over your closed lids for five to ten minutes several times a day to unclog glands around the eyes.
- When you're involved in an outdoor sport, choose protective eyewear to preserve moisture and shield you from the wind.
- Always point air vents away from your eyes—especially in cars.
- When you're working on the computer or watching television, don't forget to blink.
- Avoid prolonged use of hair dryers.

The Trouble with Eyedrops

Using the wrong eyedrops can aggravate, rather than relieve, dry eyes because they can contain irritating preservatives. Even antibiotic or antiallergenic drops can cause problems. The best solution (pardon the pun) is to ask your eye doctor to recommend a lubricating eyedrop that is free of such ingredients. Usually the eyedrop will be a methyl cellulose solution.

In severe cases, you can have silicone plugs surgically inserted into the drainage ducts leading out of the eyes, which will help you retain artificial tears or jellies. This will reduce the number of times you need to use eyedrops.

Who Is Most Likely to Suffer from Dry Eyes?

Dry eyes are often a woman's problem since so many autoimmune diseases, which plague women in particular, are associated with dry eyes. Aside from Graves' disease, women can also be plagued with Sjögren's syndrome, which impairs lacrimal gland function and the formation of watery tears (90 percent of Sjögren's syndrome sufferers are women). Hormonal changes during pregnancy and menopause can also cause dry eyes, while in the general population asthma, glaucoma, blepharitis (chronic inflammation of the eyelids), cornea surgery, and corrective surgery for nearsightedness are other causes.

Dry eyes can also develop because of side effects to medications. These include antidepressants, decongestants, antihistamines, blood pressure drugs, hormones, oral contraceptives, diuretics, ulcer medications, and tranquilizers.

Aging, traditionally the reason why dry eyes were most often observed in older people, is also a cause. As we age, there is a decrease in tear production in both men and women.

24 Coping with Depression and Anxiety

If you look at the list of symptoms that comprise hypothyroidism (see Chapter 3) and thyrotoxicosis (see Chapter 4), many of them overlap and collide with symptoms of depression and anxiety. This chapter discusses ways to cope with and manage depression and anxiety, often a consequence of untreated hypothyroidism or thyrotoxicosis.

It's important to understand that depression is a vast topic, and there are many different types of depression. For the purposes of this chapter, we'll be limiting the discussion to the most common type of depression frequently associated with hypothyroidism. Known in clinical circles as either *major depression* or *unipolar depression*, this form is characterized by one low or "flat" mood. This is distinct from *bipolar depression*, characterized by two moods: a high(er) mood and a low(er) mood, which typically cycle. A few symptoms of bipolar depression can sometimes be confused with thyrotoxicosis, but as discussed in Chapters 4 and 6, the exhaustion that accompanies thyrotoxicosis is not present in people with mania associated with bipolar disorder. In fact, people with bipolar disorder who are in a manic phase have boundless energy, which is the opposite of what occurs in thyrotoxicosis. (Such energy is usually a major clue for doctors.) What can be confused with, or aggravate, thyrotoxicosis is anxiety and panic disorders, which can coexist with, unveil, or predate your thyroid disease.

Unipolar Depression and Hypothyroidism

Most cases of unipolar or major depression are caused by life circumstances and/or situations. For this reason, the term *situational depression* is used by mental health experts to describe most cases of mild, moderate, or even severe unipolar depression.

Situational depression can first mean that your depression has been triggered by a life event. Examples of such a life event include:

- Illness (including your thyroid disease)
- Loss of a loved one (the relationship may have ended, or a loved one may have died)
- Major life change
- Job loss or change
- Moving

Situational depression can also be triggered by the absence of change in your life, meaning that you are living in a state of continuous struggle, unhappiness, or stress in which no "light" appears at the end of the tunnel. Examples of continuous struggle include:

- Chronic illness (including untreated thyroid disease)
- Unhealthy relationships
- Poverty and/or economic worries
- Job stress

A third trigger for situational depression is an absence of resolution regarding past traumas and abuses you suffered as a child or younger adult.

In the absence of thyroid disease, one out of five people in North America suffers from at least one episode of depression in their lifetime. At least twice as many women suffer from depression as men, perhaps because of the social roles women play in our society. For example, in 1994 through 1997, 72 percent of reported depressive episodes were in women.

Sadness Versus Depression

The million-dollar question is, are you depressed or "just sad"? Everyone experiences sadness, bad days, and bad moods. Feeling sad is not the same thing as depression. Sadness is characterized by sad feelings, which is opposite from numbness—the main feature of depression.

The main thing to remember about sadness versus depression is this: sadness lifts, depression persists. That's how you can tell if you're just feeling sad or are actually depressed. Feelings of sadness and grief are definitely common and normal in an infinite variety of circumstances.

Signs of Unipolar Depression

It's impossible to define what a "normal mood" is since we all have such complex personalities, and exhibit different moods throughout a given week or even a given day. But it's not impossible for *you* to define what a "normal" mood is for *you*. You know how you feel when you're functional: you're eating, sleeping, and interacting with friends and family and you're being productive, active, and generally interested in the daily goings-on in life. In a state of depression, you feel you've lost the ability to function for a prolonged period of time, or if you're functioning at a reasonable level to the outside world, you've lost *interest* in participating in life.

The symptoms of unipolar depression can vary from person to person, but can include some or all of the following:

- Feelings of sadness and/or "empty mood"
- Difficulty sleeping (usually waking up frequently in the middle of the night)
- Loss of energy and feelings of fatigue and lethargy
- Change in appetite (usually a loss of appetite)
- Difficulty thinking, concentrating, or making decisions
- Loss of interest in formerly pleasurable activities, including sex
- Anxiety or panic attacks (This may also be a symptom of thyrotoxicosis, discussed in Chapter 4 and later in this chapter.)
- Obsessing over negative experiences or thoughts
- Feeling guilty, worthless, hopeless, or helpless
- Feeling restless and irritable
- Thinking about death or suicide

When You Can't Sleep

The typical sleep pattern of a depressed person is to go to bed at the normal time, only to wake up around 2 A.M. to find that she can't get back to sleep. Endless hours are spent watching infomercials to pass the time or simply tossing and turning, usually obsessing over negative experiences or thoughts. Lack of sleep affects our ability to function and leads to increased irritability, lack of energy, and fatigue. Insomnia, by itself, is not a sign of depression, but when you look at depression as a package of symptoms, the inability to fall or stay asleep can aggravate all your other symptoms. In some cases, people who are depressed will oversleep, requiring ten to twelve hours of sleep every night.

When You Can't Think Clearly

Another debilitating feature of depression is finding that you simply can't concentrate or think clearly. You feel scattered, disorganized, and unable to prioritize. This usually hits hardest in the workplace or a center of learning, and can severely impair your performance on the job. You may miss important deadlines or important meetings, or find you can't focus when you do go to meetings. When you can't think clearly, you can be overwhelmed with feelings of helplessness or hopelessness. "I can't even perform a simple task such as X anymore" may dominate your thoughts, while you become more disillusioned with your dwindling productivity.

Anhedonia: When Nothing Gives You Pleasure

One of the most telling signs of depression is a loss of interest in activities that used to excite you, enthuse you, or give you pleasure. This is known as *anhedonia*, derived from the word *hedonism* (meaning the "philosophy of pleasure"); a hedonist is a person who indulges his or her every pleasure without considering (or caring about) the consequences. *Anhedonia* simply means "no pleasure."

Different people have different ways of expressing anhedonia. You might tell your friends, for example, that you don't "have any desire" to do X or Y, you can't "get motivated," or X or Y just doesn't "hold your interest or attention." You may also notice that the sense of satisfaction from a job well done is simply gone, which is particularly debilitating in the workplace or in a place of learning. For example, artists (photographers, painters, writers, and so on) may find the passion has gone out of their work.

Managing Unipolar Depression

When your depression is related to life events, talk therapy is the first logical step. (See the section "Finding Someone to Talk To" further on.) Talk therapy can be combined with antidepressant medications. That said, life events and hypothyroidism can collide. It's imperative that all people who have been diagnosed with depression have a thyroid function test (see Chapter 2) to detect for mild, moderate, or severe hypothyroidism. Many diagnosed with depression who have mild hypothyroidism report improvement when they are treated with thyroid hormone, discussed in Chapters 3 and 10. When you have a thyroid condition and depression independently of one another, the fact that your depression persists after your thyroid problem is treated does not necessarily mean your thyroid is acting up again.

Antidepressants

Many people with hypothyroidism are prescribed antidepressants, which work on brain chemistry. However, it makes sense to first treat hypothyroidism and see if depression resolves once thyroid hormone is restored to euthyroid levels.

Antidepressants are sometimes prescribed to those who have real social causes for their depression, anxiety, or other normal mood responses to difficult circumstances, which could be alleviated through real social changes. There is a role for antidepressants, but they should be reserved for more severe cases of depression, where possible.

Several types of prescription antidepressants are available, and newer generations become available each year. Please refer to our resource section in Appendix B for more information on antidepressants. We also urge you to review Chapters 10 and 11, which discuss drug interactions, as well as Chapter 21 on informed consent.

Support Groups

Whether or not your depression is related to a thyroid problem, social support can do wonders. The "sharing" approach has been shown to be highly beneficial—particularly in cases where people share difficult circumstances or have difficulties in common. One example is the support many coping with thyroid disease find online or through thyroid organizations.

Family Support

Depression changes spousal/partner relationships, as well as other family relationships. When you're going through a depression, knowing that things won't "fall apart" can be the source of greatest comfort. Unfortunately, too many people are treated to family harassment in the sense that they are not given the space to go through their depression. Being continuously told to "snap out of it," "get out of the house," "go for a walk," or "What you need is a nice big cup of tea" isn't what family support is about. There are things family members can do that *are* supportive, which will give you the space to feel you are allowed to go through what you are going through. The following small gestures can work wonders to support a depressed family member:

- **Help with homemaking without having to be asked.** When family or friends look after as many of the meals or chores as they can, it takes pressure off of the depressed or hypothyroid person. People who are depressed have trouble asking for help and may worry about how to get everything done, which only adds to the burden; it may also increase anxiety, which frequently accompanies depression.
- **Offer to go to support groups or counseling with the depressed family member.** This says, "I want to understand what's going on with you."
- **Check in instead of checking up.** Asking how someone is feeling is a supportive gesture. But badgering someone with unwanted opinions or advice, or asking, "What did you do today?" in a judgmental tone is not fine or supportive.
- **Let the depressed person feel allowed to set the pace of his or her day.** When family members try to force a depressed person to go on an outing, eat, and so on, it just puts more pressure on the person and emphasizes his or her inability to function or cope.
- **If the depressed person wants to talk about his or her depression or feelings, help him or her feel supported to do so.** People have different ways of coping, and some really choose to be more open about mood disorders. So if your family member wishes to talk about his or her depression, don't feel as though it's a dirty secret, and don't hide the fact that depression is at your house.

Finding Someone to Talk To

Talk therapy for depression can be of enormous value. When you're looking for a therapist, you should focus on finding someone you can relate to, and who is a "good fit." The pitfall you want to avoid is winding up with a therapist who is not helpful. Unhelpful therapy does not mean that your therapist is a poor therapist or unethical; it means that the style of therapy is not well-suited to you, and/or your therapist is not someone with whom you feel entirely comfortable. There can be many reasons for this, and they are often difficult to nail down. In other words, what one person finds helpful therapy another may not. Therapists and styles of therapies are highly individual and so is their impact. Here, we outline styles of therapy some thyroid patients have found helpful:

Biologically Informed Psychotherapy
In *biopsychiatry*, medication combined with talk therapy is the preferred approach. A therapist who practices biopsychiatry will see your anxious or depressive thinking, for example, as a side effect of a mood disorder, which is viewed as a medical condition. Thus, your anxiety or depression is removed from your circumstances and treated like a medical condition, such as pneumonia. The belief is that once your brain chemistry is restored you will begin to think rationally and reasonably again, and you may even be able to shift your perspective on life, which could be done through talk therapy.

Cognitive-Behavioral Therapy
Cognitive-behavioral therapy is more oriented toward upbeat thinking and correcting what is referred to as *disordered thinking*. Instead of dwelling on negative thoughts, this form of therapy is based on the premise that how you think can affect how you feel. People suffering from panic attacks (discussed later) can especially benefit from cognitive therapy.

Feminist Therapy
Feminist therapy means "woman-centered therapy." Feminist therapy is not one specific style of therapy, but an overall philosophy of therapy that takes women's social roles and social situations into account when looking at the symptoms that comprise women's emotional well-being. In a nutshell, a feminist therapist appreciates that you can't win a dog show when you're a cat!

Interpersonal Therapy
Interpersonal therapy is a very specific approach to therapy, based on the idea that malfunctioning relationships surround your symptoms of anxiety or depression. In other words, where there's anxiety and depression, there are "screwed-up" relationships in your life that are interfering with your quality of life. You and your therapist will explore current relationships as well as recent events that may have affected those relationships, such as loss, conflict, or change.

Psychodynamic Therapy
Psychodynamic therapy deals with the "ghosts" of relationships and events from your past, the dynamics of your upbringing, as well as present events and relationships.

Here, your thoughts, emotions, and behavior over a lifetime are examined, and patterns of behavior and aspects of your personality are discussed as possible sources of both internal and external conflict. Couples or groups are often involved in psychodynamic therapy. The adage "The past is history, the future a mystery, and the present a gift" works well in this context.

Anxiety, Panic Disorder, and Thyroid Disease

We discuss both generalized anxiety disorder (GAD) and panic attacks in Chapter 4, because they are commonly confused with, or aggravated by, thyrotoxicosis. In that chapter, we also discuss the hormone system in the body called the *adrenergic* system, which releases adrenaline (also known as epinephrine) and noradrenaline (norepinephrine). Normally, these hormones are released in a "fight or flight" response when you are scared, shocked, or highly excited. It is also these hormones that trigger panic attacks, causing your heart to race, profuse sweating, and all the other symptoms described in Chapter 4. We also discussed in Chapter 4 the concept of beta-andrenergic

Qualified Therapists

The following professionals provide talk therapy for depression:

- Psychiatrist: An M.D. who can prescribe medications.
- Psychologist and psychological associate: These professionals have master's and/or doctorate degrees (such as Ph.D., Ed.D., Psy.D.). They usually work in a hospital or clinic setting, but often can be found in private practice.
- Social worker: A professional with a B.S.W. (bachelor of social work) and/or an M.S.W. (master of social work), and sometimes a D.S.W. (doctor of social work).
- Psychiatric nurse: Sometimes these professionals are trained in psychotherapy.
- Counselor: This professional should have completed certification courses in counseling and obtained a license to practice psychotherapy; a counselor may have, but does not require, a university degree.
- Marriage and family counselor: This professional has completed rigorous training through certification courses in family therapy and relationship dynamics, and has obtained a license to practice psychotherapy. The designation *AAMFT* stands for the American Association of Marriage and Family Therapy.

receptors, which make the heart beat faster and also make you more prone to panic and anxiety.

When you're thyrotoxic, the numbers of beta-adrenergic receptors increase in your body's cells. This makes you much more sensitive to the effects of your own adrenaline, and predisposes people ordinarily able to cope with various stressors to panic attacks and greater anxiety. The key to managing panic attacks and anxiety related to thyrotoxicosis is therapy with a medication known as a *beta-blocker* (see Chapter 11). This medication also helps slow the heart down and prevent severe heart symptoms (discussed more in Chapter 25).

Obviously, not everyone who suffers from anxiety and panic is thyrotoxic. You can be coping with other types of thyroid problems and become anxious as a result of worry over your thyroid condition. And, of course, you have a life outside of your thyroid condition. In the general population, other causes of anxiety are usually normal, garden-variety socioeconomic problems. Worrying about jobs, finances, relationships, and health are all common reasons for anxiety. But when you're under increased stress, normal worries can cross over into anxiety, and low-level anxiety can also worsen or heighten.

Managing Anxiety and Panic

If you've ruled out thyrotoxicosis, and do not require a beta-blocker, talk therapy (specifically, cognitive behavioral therapy), discussed earlier, is an excellent way to manage anxiety and panic. This style of therapy can teach you to anticipate the situations and bodily sensations that are associated with panic attacks; having this awareness can actually help to control the attacks. There are also a number of mental exercises that can help to control hyperventilating or fearful thoughts that could heighten the panic in the throes of an attack. For instance, by replacing the thought "I'm going to faint" with "I'm just hyperventilating—I can handle this," panic attacks can be calmed before fear takes over and the symptoms worsen.

Your doctor may also prescribe antidepressants or tranquilizers, depending on how severe your anxiety and panic are and whether they are affecting your ability to function normally. We cannot devote space to the huge variety of agents available, but you can refer to the resources in Appendix B for further information.

25 Coping with Heart Disease

Both untreated hypothyroidism (see Chapter 3) and thyrotoxicosis (see Chapter 4) can lead to cardiovascular complications (complications involving the heart, arteries, and veins) or a worsening of risk factors for cardiovascular disease. The term *heart disease* generally refers to any type of heart trouble, including irregular or rapid heart rhythms; blockages of the blood supply to the heart muscle causing chest pain (angina) or a heart attack (myocardial infarction); or weakening of the pumping of the heart, causing congestive heart failure. *Atherosclerotic cardiovascular disease* (ASCVD) refers to fatty blockages of blood vessels anywhere in the body. When it occurs in the coronary arteries that feed the heart muscle, it puts you at risk for a heart attack. When ASCVD occurs in blood vessels in the brain, it puts you at risk for having a stroke, in which part of the brain fed by the blocked blood vessel dies. When ASCVD affects arteries that feed your arms or your legs, it causes a problem known as *peripheral vascular disease*. In addition, some people have heart disease that may not be related to ASCVD that affects the way the heart beats. Normally, the heart beats at a regular rhythm with between fifty and ninety beats per minute. Any disturbance of this rhythm is called an *arrhythmia*, with rapid rhythms called *tachyarrhythmias*.

In thyroid patients who are otherwise healthy, these cardiovascular complications disappear or resolve as soon as you return to a euthyroid state, or normal thyroid function. In thyroid patients with preexisting cardiovascular disease, or who have risk factors for cardiovascular disease (obesity, smoking, and so on), untreated hypothyroidism or thyrotoxicosis can be dangerous by accelerating the worsening of cardiovascular problems. This chapter outlines the cardiovascular complications associated with hypothyroidism and thyrotoxicosis and discusses ways to manage them until you become euthyroid.

Heart Complications from Hypothyroidism

As we explained in Chapter 3, hypothyroidism slows down the heart, causing a slow pulse (known as *bradycardia*). This might cause decreased exercise tolerance, shortness of breath, or a feeling of being "winded" when you try to exert yourself. Prolonged hypothyroidism will also lead to the accumulation of fluids, called *lymphedema*, which can swell your hands and feet and mimic the type of edema seen with congestive heart failure. Because your arteries require thyroid hormone to relax, hypothyroidism causes them to tense up, resulting in high blood pressure. People with chronically weakened hearts from underlying ASCVD may not be able to pump blood very easily through these constricted blood vessels, worsening congestive heart failure with fluid accumulating in the lower limbs or in the lungs. Hypothyroid-induced edema can aggravate any existing congestive heart failure or might even be mistaken for congestive heart failure.

Heart Failure or Hypothyroidism?

Some people with hypothyroidism are misdiagnosed with ordinary heart failure, when treatment with thyroid hormone may more easily relieve heart complications. Also, sometimes the swelling of a person's arms and legs from hypothyroidism is confused with edema from congestive heart failure. Here are some ways to tell the difference:

- People in congestive heart failure (CHF) have a diminished cardiac response to exercise; people with hypothyroidism have a normal cardiac response to exercise. This means that hearts in CHF are already working at their limits of activity and are unable to increase their rate or pumping ability in response to exercise, while the otherwise normal hearts of hypothyroid people can make these changes in response to the demands of exercise.
- People in heart failure have a faster pulse than normal; the hypothyroid heart is slower than normal, usually fewer than 60 beats per minute.
- The hypothyroid heart will normalize in response to thyroid hormone, but does not respond as well to treatments used in heart failure, such as the medication digoxin (a form of digitalis, used to try to strengthen hearts with CHF), ACE inhibitors (angiotensin-converting enzyme inhibitors, a potent type of blood pressure medication), or diuretics.
- There is no pulmonary (lung) congestion in hypothyroid people, but it is quite common in heart failure.
- Other hypothyroid symptoms are usually not present in people with congestive heart failure.

For most people with hypothyroidism, the most serious early complication is high blood pressure, which can increase the risk for a heart attack or stroke, as well as congestive heart failure. Hypothyroidism also increases cholesterol levels, which can increase the development of blockages in arteries (atherosclerosis), likewise leading to a heart attack or stroke as well as congestive heart failure.

Congestive Heart Failure

Congestive heart failure means that the heart is weakened and not pumping well. This is usually caused by long-standing problems such as damaged heart valves, high blood pressure, damage to the heart muscle, or, in rare cases, a variety of heart defects that could have been present at birth (congenital heart defects).

Your heart's job is to pump blood through the lungs to pick up oxygen and release carbon dioxide, then throughout the body to provide oxygen and nutrients. If your heart isn't pumping well, then your body's cells are deprived of oxygen and nutrients, seriously interfering with your quality of life. Breathing, moving around, and other activities become labored and difficult.

Congestive heart failure can involve either or both of the heart's main pumping chambers, the left and right ventricles. Most of the time, the left ventricle is the main one involved. Each of the heart's two ventricles has its own "reception room," the left atrium and the right atrium, where the blood gathers before it is pumped into its ventricle. Heart failure occurs when the ventricles are not working properly, with blood unable to be pumped sufficiently in a forward direction and backing up, causing congestion in the body region that had supplied its blood. Blood from most of the body returns to the heart into the right atrium, entering the right ventricle to be pumped into the lungs. Blood from the lungs, after entering the left atrium, goes into the left ventricle to be pumped to the entire body.

When congestive heart failure involves a failed left ventricle, the blood from the lungs is unable to be completely pumped into the body and tends to back up into the lungs. The increased pooling of blood in the lungs' blood vessels increases the pressure in these blood vessels, causing fluid to leak from them into the lungs' air spaces, a condition known as *pulmonary edema*. When the right ventricle's ability to pump decreases, blood backs up in tissues throughout the body, causing a doughy puffiness of body tissues, known as *peripheral edema* generally and *pedal edema* when it involves the feet and ankles. Since the entire cardiovascular system is a continuous and connected system, failure in one ventricle eventually strains the ability of the other ventricle. In this way, congestive heart failure can be specific to a ventricle, causing pulmonary edema with left ventricular failure or peripheral edema with right ventricular failure, or can involve the entire heart, causing both types of edema.

Heart failure is usually not sudden and develops over a period of years. When people with heart failure become hypothyroid, the heart weakens further and this condition can worsen. In addition, since the blood vessels throughout the body require thyroid hormone to relax, hypothyroidism makes it more difficult to push blood through them, a condition known as *increased peripheral vascular resistance*. This makes it even more difficult for the left ventricle to pump blood forward and worsens the heart failure. Also in people with normal thyroid function, the heart enhances its pumping action by beating faster. In hypothyroidism, the heart beats much more slowly and cannot compensate for heart failure by beating faster.

Causes of Heart Failure

The health problems that increase the risk of heart failure are the same problems that cause other heart problems, hypertension and clogged arteries from atherosclerotic cardiovascular disease (ASCVD), which in turn are worsened by obesity (see Chapter 16), smoking, and diets high in saturated fat (see Chapter 20). Heart valve defects, caused by infections, are also a cause of heart failure. Some unfortunate people catch a virus infection of their heart that weakens it to the point of causing heart failure. In the absence of a heart valve problem, most people with heart failure already have underlying significant heart disease and hypertension and may also have diabetes or chronic lung disease (from smoking). In unusual cases, people with severe anemia, untreated thyrotoxicosis, and abnormal heart rhythms can develop heart failure.

Treating Heart Failure in Hypothyroidism

The first step in treating heart failure is to take the appropriate medications prescribed by your physician that decrease the workload of the heart and make it perform more efficiently. This includes reducing the peripheral vascular resistance (seen as high blood pressure or hypertension), decreasing the volume of blood backing up (by using diuretics), and taking medication that enhances the strength of the heart muscle. When hypothyroidism is present and contributing to the heart failure, treatment with thyroid hormone should be started as soon as possible; however, it takes several weeks to fully take effect, and it is important to make sure that you are taking the proper heart medication in the meantime. It is very unusual for hypothyroidism, on its own, to be able to weaken the heart sufficiently to cause heart failure. This makes it very important to continue looking for primary heart problems and treat them in addition to treating the hypothyroidism. If you have underlying heart failure that predated hypothyroidism or was unveiled as a result of hypothyroidism, treatment with lifestyle changes, blood pressure and cholesterol-lowering medications, or possibly surgery may be needed.

Hypertension (High Blood Pressure)

About 10 to 20 percent of people with hypothyroidism suffer from hypertension (high blood pressure), which can lead to heart failure if severe and left untreated for long periods of time. It can also lead to a heart attack or stroke.

To understand high blood pressure, it's useful to explain what blood pressure is. The blood flows from the heart into the arteries (blood vessels), pressing against the artery walls. The simplest way to explain this is to think about the streets of a small city. During the evening rush hour everybody drives home using the same major streets that head to the suburbs. Normally, all of the traffic is easily handled by the multilane streets and roads, or the "arteries" of the city; however, as the city ages, and more people move there, roads develop potholes and areas of disrepair. This results in lane closures, and the traffic backs up as the diminished road capacity is forced to accept the same flow of cars returning home. The increased "pressure," manifested by elevated tempers and rapid, jerky accelerations of cars trying to get through intersections, reflects the constricted roadways.

This is much like the constricted blood vessels, some partially blocked by fatty deposits of ASCVD, attempting to handle the full flow of blood needed by your body. Over time, the left ventricle enlarges and thickens as it works harder than normal to squeeze the blood through the constricted and narrowed arteries. The thickened heart muscle is more difficult to feed through its own coronary arteries and demands greater sustenance from these coronary arteries, placing it at greater risk of a heart attack (death of a section of the heart muscle) should the coronary arteries have fatty narrowing or blood clots.

Since each pumping chamber of the heart, each of the two ventricles and their respective atria, has one-way heart valves that let blood flow only in the proper forward direction, the increased pressure of the blood places greater strain on the valves. Any leaking of blood backward through any of the valves, worsened by hypertension, adds to the backward congestion of blood in the body regions feeding that side of the heart (lungs feeding the left side and the rest of the body feeding the right side). This shows itself as worsening congestive heart failure.

Hypertension refers to the tension or force exerted on your artery walls. (*Hyper* means "too much," as in "too much tension.") Blood pressure is measured in two readings: X over Y. The X is the systolic pressure, which is the pressure that occurs during the heart's contraction. The Y is the diastolic pressure, which is the pressure that occurs when the heart rests between contractions. In the general population, target blood pressure readings are less than 140 over 80 (140/80). Readings greater than 140/85 are considered too high, although readings of just under 144/88 are sometimes considered borderline in an otherwise healthy person. For the general population, 140/85 is "lecture time," when your doctor will begin to counsel you about dietary and lifestyle habits. By 150/90, many people are prescribed an antihypertensive drug, which is designed to lower blood pressure.

In the absence of thyroid disease, it's known that obesity, smoking, and a high-sodium diet can put you at risk for hypertension. Genetic factors are very important, so that your risks for hypertension are much higher if it runs in your family, and there are certain ethnic groups with greater risks. High blood pressure can also be caused by kidney disorders (prevalent in people with diabetes) or during pregnancy.

Blood Pressure–Lowering Medications

If you have underlying high blood pressure that persists, despite taking the appropriate thyroid hormone therapy to treat hypothyroidism, you may be a candidate for some of the following classes of blood pressure–lowering drugs (listed in alphabetical order):

- **ACE inhibitors.** ACE inhibitors (standing for angiotensin converting enzyme inhibitors) lower blood pressure by preventing the formation of the hormone angiotensin II, which causes the blood vessels to narrow. ACE inhibitors are also used to treat heart failure. Possible rare side effects include a cough or swelling of the face and tongue.
- **Alpha-blocking agents.** Alpha-blocking agents block the effects of noradrenaline, a stress hormone, preventing it from activating the alpha-receptors on the muscle lining blood vessels, allowing the blood vessels to relax. Blood pressure decreases with treatment. A possible side effect is blood pressure variation when standing versus reclining.
- **Angiotensin receptor blockers (ARBs).** Similar to ACE inhibitors, ARBs block the effects of angiotensin II on the cells of the blood vessel wall. Essentially ARBs act further down the angiotensin pathway. They're popular because they may have fewer side effects than ACE inhibitors, but appear to be equally effective in terms of blood pressure control.
- **Beta-blockers.** These are used frequently in thyrotoxicosis to slow the heart by blocking the effects of adrenaline (see Chapter 11). Another use of beta-blockers is to reduce blood pressure.
- **Calcium-channel blockers.** Calcium-channel blockers reduce the transport of calcium entering special channels in muscle cells lining the blood vessels, allowing the muscles in the blood vessels to relax. Possible side effects include ankle swelling, flushing, constipation, and diminished strength of the heart muscle.
- **Centrally acting agents.** These drugs act through centers in the brain to reduce the release of adrenaline, slow the heart rate, and relax the blood vessels. Possible side effects include stuffy nose, dry mouth, and drowsiness.
- **Diuretics.** Diuretics are the most commonly used blood pressure medication. Also known as *water pills*, diuretics work by flushing excess water and salt out through your kidneys. Diuretics may increase the risk of heart rhythm problems by causing the kidneys to lose potassium. This can be avoided with diet changes or potassium supplements.
- **Vasodilators.** Vasodilators dilate, or relax, the blood vessels, thereby reducing blood pressure.

High Cholesterol (Hypercholesterolemia) and Hypothyroidism

Cholesterol is a whitish, waxy fat made by the liver and also absorbed from food in your diet. It is also known as a *lipid*, the umbrella name for the many different fats found in the body. Cholesterol is needed to make many hormones as well as cell membranes. Hypothyroidism can increase cholesterol in people whose cholesterol levels would ordinarily be normal while euthyroid. But if you have high cholesterol that predates your hypothyroidism, your already high cholesterol level can jump "off the charts." High cholesterol is dangerous because the excess cholesterol in your blood can lead to narrowed arteries (ASCVD), which in turn can lead to a heart attack or stroke. In the absence of hypothyroidism, saturated fat (see Chapters 16 and 20) is often a culprit when it comes to high cholesterol, but the highest levels of cholesterol are the result of genetic features affecting the creation or disposal of cholesterol in the liver. *Familial hypercholesterolemia* refers to a genetic cause for high cholesterol that does not respond adequately to diet modification.

Total blood cholesterol levels are often provided as general guidelines only. You also have to look at the relative proportion of high-density lipoprotein (HDL) or "good cholesterol" to low-density lipoprotein (LDL) or "bad cholesterol" in the blood. If you're over thirty, an LDL reading of less than 100 mg/dL (in Canada, 3.4 mmol/L) and an HDL reading of more than 40 mg/dL (in Canada, 0.9 mmol/L) is considered desirable. That means you want an LDL reading that is low and an HDL reading that is high; the total cholesterol is not as meaningful as the individual LDL and HDL readings.

The major effect of hypothyroidism is to increase the levels of LDL cholesterol in the blood. Much of this is caused by increasing the absorption of cholesterol from bile (a substance made by the liver), preventing the usual loss of the body's own cholesterol in the intestines. Also, since the liver is the organ responsible for ridding the body of cholesterol (as well as making it), the hypothyroid liver seems unable to effectively clear this cholesterol, contributing to its increased levels. After a few months from starting the appropriate dosage of levothyroxine, sufficient to make your TSH level normal, the effects of hypothyroidism on elevating cholesterol levels should be gone. Of course, if you have underlying elevated cholesterol levels, you may still need specific treatment of this with modification of your diet and cholesterol-lowering medications.

Heart Complications from Thyrotoxicosis

Thyrotoxicosis, as explained in Chapter 4, speeds up the heart rate by increasing the sensitivity of the heart to catecholamines (adrenaline and related hormones). In otherwise healthy people, this can lead to palpitations and tachycardia (fast pulse). In people with underlying cardiovascular disease or risk factors for cardiovascular disease, it can lead to atrial fibrillation and arrhythmias (abnormal heart rhythms). Even in situations with few symptoms of thyrotoxicosis, such as apathetic hyperthyroidism (see Chapter 17), heart symptoms from thyrotoxicosis are frequently seen. The stress placed on the heart can aggravate angina (chest pain) and lead to a type of congestive heart failure (high-output CHF).

High-output CHF is not completely understood. Clearly, this type of CHF can happen in thyrotoxicosis, even without any underlying heart disease. When there is too much thyroid hormone, the heart rate increases and the amount of blood pumped by the heart increases also. The peripheral vascular resistance (the tightening of the blood vessels in the body) is reduced a great deal. In addition, in the case of hyperthyroidism from Graves' disease, the blood vessels feeding the thyroid gland are enlarged and a large portion of the blood flow goes through the gland. All of this stimulation of the heart's rate and the increased flow of blood through the blood vessels may contribute to an overworking of the heart, accounting for this type of heart failure.

Palpitations and Racing Heart (Tachycardia)

The classic heart complications associated with thyrotoxicosis are a very fast pulse and heart palpitations. In people who are hyperthyroid as a result of Graves' disease (see Chapter 6), once excess thyroid hormone levels are reduced to normal, these symptoms disappear. Treatment with either antithyroid medication (see Chapter 11) or beta-blockers (see Chapter 11) can slow the heartbeat and prevent the consequences of a racing heart, such as heart failure or atrial fibrillation. Once thyroid function is restored to normal, you can usually go off beta-blockers.

In people like me (Sara), who are on a TSH suppression dose of thyroid hormone, mild tachycardia or palpitations can persist, along with adrenaline surges that can cause or worsen panic attacks (see Chapter 24). For people in this situation, beta-blockers are usually given lifelong to prevent these complications. If you're thyrotoxic and suffering from these symptoms, but are also asthmatic or have chronic obstructive lung disease from smoking, other medications can be used to slow the heart, since beta-blockers may worsen your breathing in such conditions.

Irregular Heart Rhythm (Arrhythmia and Atrial Fibrillation)

In people with underlying heart disease, thyrotoxicosis can lead to an irregular heart rhythm (arrhythmia), and atrial fibrillation. Normally, each heartbeat is stimulated by an electrical impulse starting in the upper heart chambers, the atria, carried through to the ventricles below through a conduction system in the heart muscle, much like the wiring of your house. There is a "fuse box" at the place where this impulse passes from the right atrium into the ventricle in an ordered fashion, the *atrioventricular node* (AV node). If the conduction system in the atria becomes diseased, electrical impulses in the atria become disordered and rapid, a condition called *fibrillation*. Instead of a one-to-one conduction of the impulses from the atria through the AV node to the ventricles, the AV node can't handle the rapid and erratic impulses, providing a slower, yet very irregular impulse to the ventricles. It's this irregular impulse that makes the ventricles beat in a very irregular rhythm. Blood flow through the heart also becomes very irregular, and this situation can cause the blood to form clots that travel through the body until they lodge into smaller blood vessels, blocking their flow. This can result in a stroke or a heart attack. Also, thyrotoxicosis seems to increase the ability of blood clots to form, worsening the risk of this happening. Until a normal heart rhythm is restored (if possible), it is important to be on special medications that thin your blood, preventing it from clotting inappropriately.

Complications with Amiodarone

Amiodarone is a potent medicine used to treat heart rhythm disturbances. It is infamous for causing three different types of thyroid problems. This is partly because the amiodarone drug contains a large amount of iodine and tends to stay inside the body for many months, even though you may stop taking it. It is also because some people have a reaction of the amiodarone in which it causes an inflammation of the thyroid gland, releasing stored thyroid hormones.

In parts of the world that are iodine deficient, such as mountainous regions of Europe or other regions (see Chapter 3), some elderly people with heart disease have underlying autonomous toxic thyroid nodules (ATN; see Chapter 8). Since they are iodine deficient their ATN does not make them thyrotoxic. After receiving amiodarone for the first time, however, sufficient iodine is released by the drug to permit them to become thyrotoxic from their ATN.

In North America, and other regions of the world with sufficient dietary iodine, there are two different thyroid problems caused by amiodarone. The most common situation is that the person starting the amiodarone has underlying Hashimoto's thyroiditis (see Chapter 5) but has not yet become hypothyroid. In this situation, the excess iodine released by the amiodarone is high enough to worsen the Hashimoto's thyroiditis to the point of causing hypothyroidism. This is easy to treat by providing thyroid hormone therapy.

On the other hand, there is an unusual situation when the amiodarone seems to "poison" the thyroid gland, causing an intense irritation that releases stored thyroid hormones from the gland. Many medical treatments have been tried, most to no avail, to alleviate this problem. If this occurs, most of the time, the two treatment options are to either provide sufficient beta-blockers and medical support for the person to survive the thyrotoxicosis or to have a surgeon remove the thyroid gland, then start thyroid hormone replacement therapy. Determination of the proper approach requires the consultation of expert thyroid specialists and cardiologists.

Chest Pain (Angina)

Chest pain or discomfort because of coronary heart disease is called *angina*. The chest pain is caused when not enough blood and oxygen get to the heart muscle. It's also known in clinical circles as *myocardial ischemia*. The word *ischemia* means "not enough blood flow." A person with angina feels an uncomfortable pressure, fullness, squeezing, or pain in the center of the chest. Some people feel it in the neck, jaw, shoulder, back, or arm. Physically exerting yourself usually brings on the pain; in cases where angina is linked to exertion, it's called *stable angina*. In people with *unstable angina*, the pain can come during periods of rest, or even while sleeping. In these cases, an angina attack should be treated as a heart attack, and the person experiencing it should be rushed to the hospital for treatment.

Chest pain from insufficient blood flow to feed the heart, via the coronary arteries, is usually not seen unless these arteries are partially blocked to begin with (from underlying ASCVD). It is easy to see why people with underlying heart disease may have worsening of angina when thyrotoxic. The heart's metabolism is increased by the excess thyroid hormone, increasing the oxygen and sugar demands of the muscle. In addition, the acceleration of the heart rate places additional demands on the heart muscle. Partially blocked coronary arteries are unable to meet this increased demand for heart-feeding blood. The chest pain of angina (*angina pectoris*) is the sign that there is not enough blood feeding the heart. If left untreated, it can turn into a heart attack (*myocardial infarction*) in which part of the heart muscle dies, putting the person at risk of death if it is severe enough. Treatment consists of efforts to reduce the stress and demands of the heart using beta-blockers and enhancement of the blood flow through the coronary arteries using drugs that expand their diameter or with a balloon catheter to reduce blockages.

26 Coping with Fatigue

I f you look at the list of symptoms in Chapter 3 that comprise hypothyroidism, as well as the symptoms of exhaustion in thyrotoxicosis (see Chapter 4), many of them can exacerbate normal fatigue that is part of daily life. Hypothyroid symptoms can also be confused with chronic fatigue. This chapter discusses normal versus unusual or chronic fatigue, and suggests ways to manage both fatigue that is thyroid-related and fatigue that is unrelated to but can aggravate your thyroid condition.

It's important to note another cause of fatigue common in people with thyroid disease; there's a real risk that exhaustion may be caused by problems with your adrenal glands. The adrenal glands, located above each of your kidneys, make cortisol, the steroid hormone essential for life. They also make adrenaline and related hormones. Just as the thyroid gland is often afflicted by autoimmune disease, causing Hashimoto's thyroiditis or Graves' disease, the adrenal gland is sometimes similarly afflicted by the immune system, causing the adrenal gland to make too little cortisol. This can cause a profound fatigue, known as Addison's disease. Likewise, if hypothyroidism is caused by pituitary or hypothalamic disease, since these organs also control the adrenal gland, trouble here can also cause loss of adrenal gland function. Specific tests must be done to test for this if it's suspected. This is discussed later in this chapter.

Normal Fatigue

Like almost everyone, both Ken and I (Sara) wage daily battles with fatigue. When Ken is tired, we assume it's because of sleep deprivation (he sleeps less than five hours per night most of the time). When I am tired, Ken suggests I get my TSH checked, only to be met with the retort, "Maybe I'm just *tired*!" (As I write this, I'm just back from the lab to rule out whether my "writer's fatigue" is thyroid-related!) The point is this: lifestyle factors are largely responsible for most people's fatigue. We are all aware of lifestyle measures that can remedy fatigue, but we ignore them because we have more things to do than we have the time to do them. However, when hypothyroidism is added to normal fatigue, it can be overwhelming. In these cases, lifestyle changes that can remedy normal fatigue can help you feel less fatigued while going through a bout of untreated hypothyroidism. That said, there are a number of sleep disorders that contribute to what we call "normal fatigue." Some sleep disorders, such as apnea, can even point to an unrecognized thyroid problem, as the apnea can be caused by a goiter (see Chapter 7) or even a large nodule (see Chapter 8) that may be obstructing breathing at night. This section outlines some of the factors responsible for normal fatigue that can be remedied by making lifestyle changes or investigating a potential sleep disorder.

Sleep Deprivation

Sleep deprivation refers to being deprived of the recommended hours of sleep for healthy adults. Sleep deprivation can dramatically worsen fatigue in people who are hypothyroid. In people who are thyrotoxic, sleep deprivation can contribute to exhaustion, but sleep is difficult anyway because the body is working too hard at night, which interferes with a good night's sleep.

In the absence of hypothyroidism or thyrotoxicosis, people who have multiple demands and/or jobs that require long hours are often sleep deprived, which can have serious health repercussions. In fact, some research suggests that chronic fatigue as well as fibromyalgia may be directly linked to chronic sleep deprivation. One Canadian study deliberately deprived a group of medical students of non-REM sleep over a period of several nights. Within the next few days, each of the study participants developed symptoms of CFS and/or fibromyalgia.

There are two phases of sleep: rapid eye movement (REM) and non–rapid eye movement. REM sleep is when researchers believe we dream, an important component in mental health. Non-REM sleep is when we are in our deepest sleep, which is when, researchers believe, various hormones are reset and energy stores are replenished.

Sleep is therefore an active state that affects our physical and mental well-being. Insufficient restful sleep can result in mental and physical health problems.

There is a misconception that as we get older, we need less sleep. This is not so; we need just as much sleep as always, but we often get less sleep. What happens is that our ability to achieve quality sleep for long periods of time diminishes as we age. The older we get, the more fragile our sleep becomes, which can be more easily disturbed by light, noise, and pain (from arthritis, and so on). It's common for various medical conditions to interfere with sleep, and in the case of thyroid disease, this is usually the result of restlessness, anxiety, and racing heart from thyrotoxicosis. Whether you're euthyroid, hypothyroid, or thyrotoxic, for a better sleep, try the following:

- Regular bedtime hours. Go to bed at the same time every night.
- Regular wakeup hour. Try to wake up around the same time every morning.

- Daily sun exposure. Exposure to natural outdoor light during the day helps with sleep.
- A cool, dark, and quiet room at bedtime. Lower the temperature at night or open a window. Use earplugs if necessary and pull down shades or draw curtains.

If you're getting regular sleep and are euthyroid but find you're dozing off during the day or still feel tired, this could be a sign of a sleep disorder, which is present in roughly forty million North Americans. That said, there are two times during a twenty-four-hour period when we are most inclined to feel sleepy regardless of how much sleep we've had. The first period is between about midnight and 7 A.M., when most of us do sleep. But the second period is after lunch, which in many cultures is siesta time or naptime, between 1 and 3 P.M. If you're getting less sleep at night, taking a nap between 1 P.M and 3 P.M can help to combat fatigue in people with more flexible hours, or in people who work night shifts.

Sleep Disorders

A lot of people think they're getting enough sleep but, in fact, are not. They may have a sleep disorder that interrupts deep, restful sleep. For example, if you were treated for hypothyroidism and also have a sleep disorder, you may insist that you feel hypo when you're not, because of daytime fatigue. The following is a brief overview of common sleep disorders.

Sleep Apnea

Sleep apnea is a breathing disorder in which there are breathing interruptions during sleep. *Apnea* means "want of breath" in Greek. There are two types of sleep apnea: central and obstructive. *Central sleep apnea* occurs when the brain fails to send the appropriate signals to the breathing muscles that cause you to breathe in and out. More common, however, is *obstructive sleep apnea*. This occurs when air cannot flow in or out of your nose or mouth. This can be linked to a growth or tumor in the neck or throat area such as a goiter (see Chapter 7) or a large thyroid nodule. In other people, apnea is the result of throat and tongue muscles relaxing during sleep, which can partially block airways. Obesity (see Chapter 16) can also lead to apnea, as an excess amount of tissue can narrow breathing airways. Signs that you may have sleep apnea are persistent loud snoring at night and daytime sleepiness. Frequent long pauses in breathing during sleep, followed by choking and gasping for breath, are an obvious sign of sleep apnea. Some people may be unaware they have apnea, but may find they wake up frequently because of the brain forcing arousal each time they stop breathing. Ultimately, this leads to daytime fatigue because of lack of sleep. Far more serious problems are also linked to sleep apnea, including higher rates of hypertension, heart disease, heart attack, and stroke. If you think you have sleep apnea, a pulmonary specialist (a doctor who specializes in lungs and breathing) can treat it with various methods. (See Appendix B for a list of resources.)

Insomnia

Insomnia is when you are aware of poor quality sleep because you cannot fall asleep; wake up a lot during the night and cannot fall back asleep (also a sign of depression); wake up too early in the morning; or have the sense that your sleep is "fitful" or unrefreshing. Most causes of insomnia are linked to mental or emotional stress, and it is seen more frequently in people over sixty, women, and people who suffer from depression.

Most people have only transient or intermittent bouts of insomnia that resolve once a particularly stressful period has passed. Insomnia can also be linked to medication side effects, caffeine, smoking, or alcohol before bedtime.

Chronic insomnia is often linked to depression, but is also seen in people with arthritis (because of nighttime discomfort), kidney disease, heart failure, asthma, sleep apnea, restless legs syndrome (described later), and Parkinson's disease. Insomnia is generally treated through behavioral therapy and lifestyle modification. When you are thyrotoxic, you may think you have insomnia, when, in fact, your anxiety and restlessness is the result of too much thyroid hormone. A thyroid function test for anyone on thyroid hormone medication should rule out thyroid-related insomnia.

Restless Legs Syndrome (RLS)

RLS is a sleep disorder characterized by tingling sensations in the legs or arms while sitting or lying down. The sensations appear to worsen at night, and to relieve them, a person has to get out of bed and move. The sensations are described as creeping, crawling, tingling, pulling, or painful. In this case, the sensations interfere with your ability to fall asleep or stay asleep. The calf, thigh, and ankle areas are where most people feel these sensations. There is usually an urge to move, rub, or massage the legs when the sensations occur. Knee bends and hot baths before bed are often the best solution.

People with RLS often have another sleep disorder called *periodic limb movements in sleep* (PLMS). In this case, involuntary jerking of the legs can occur every minute or so, which causes people to wake up, or have difficulty falling or staying asleep.

Partners with Sleep Disorders

Fatigue and sleep deprivation can also occur when your partner has a sleep disorder, or simply snores heavily at night. In this case, seeking out treatment for the partner (when possible) is the best route to resolving your own daytime fatigue.

Burnout

Burnout usually occurs in people who are in caregiving roles or professions, such as nursing, therapists of any kind (including occupational therapists or speech therapists), clinicians, and unpaid caregivers. Child-care workers, teachers, and elder-care workers are also vulnerable to burnout. The term *burnout* is now a common term in all healthcare literature; it is characterized by physical and emotional exhaustion, feeling personally disconnected with one's friends and family, and feeling nonproductive. Signs of burnout include low morale, exhaustion, poor concentration, feelings of helplessness and depression, and physical problems such as bowel problems, poor appetite, cramps, headaches, and so on. Clearly, bouts of untreated hypothyroidism or thyrotoxicosis can dramatically magnify burnout.

Burnout is common in caring and caregiving because when people are around nonstop suffering, they can become "drained," meaning that all energies are being poured into meeting the needs of others, leaving no room to fulfill one's own needs. Some articles refer to burnout as *carer's fatigue.*

Burnout is a major contributing factor to fatigue, and if you're going through a bout of untreated hypothyroidism or thyrotoxicosis, taking time off from your job, or in cases of unpaid caregiving, arranging to pay someone for temporary home care to enable some time off is a good idea.

Reducing Fatigue Through Lifestyle Changes

If your thyroid hormone levels are normal, and you have ruled out sleep disorders that may be causing unrecognized sleep deprivation, fatigue is often overcome by making lifestyle changes. If you are going through a bout of untreated hypothyroidism or thyrotoxicosis, these lifestyle changes can help reduce thyroid-related fatigue and exhaustion as well.

Slowing Down Your Job

When you look at the time you spend commuting to work and being at work, there may be several lost hours. For many, commuting to work increases fatigue. If you spend most of your time at work on the computer or on the phone, try to negotiate telecommuting with your employer.

Some people simply look into moving closer to work. Have you considered this? When people calculate car expenses, gas expenses, and so on, moving within walking distance to work may be the answer.

Reducing the workweek is another way of slowing down. Moving down from a five-day workweek to a four-day workweek greatly reduces fatigue for many, and often the financial loss is negligible compared to the psychological benefit of having one day to yourself.

Other ways to negotiate a reduced workweek include using vacation and sick days as "Mondays off" for a year. Some people have weeks of vacation time never used, which can be used for reduced workweeks. In some companies, being away from the office for long periods of time actually creates more "catch-up" fatigue for the employee.

Eliminate Energy Drains

Usually, energy drains come in the form of people. When you're surrounded by people who take energy from you, rather than people who give you energy (in the form of support, love, and so forth), the result is fatigue. Relationships that compromise your values or give you nothing but aggravation should be eliminated—at least temporarily—when you're going through untreated bouts of hypothyroidism or thyrotoxicosis.

Energy drains also come from procrastinating and overbooking yourself. We procrastinate over things we really don't want to do—such as taxes. We overbook ourselves when we're afraid of saying no. The problem is, few people will ever say no. Instead of "No," try "Let me check my schedule and see if I'm already committed." Then, "Sorry, looks like I'm committed elsewhere" or if it's a task, "I've got a deadline on that date for something of equal importance."

Finally, simply doing too much, and expecting too much from ourselves, drains our energy. When possible, hire someone to do the things you can't or don't want to do.

And at home, consider hiring someone to:

- Clean your house or apartment
- Declutter your house by going through closets, filing things, and so on
- Organize your tax receipts
- Garden and/or take care of your lawn

Abnormal Fatigue: Chronic Fatigue Syndrome

A number of people are diagnosed with the general label *chronic fatigue syndrome*. Seventy percent of people who suffer from chronic fatigue are women under age forty-five. Many of them may be misdiagnosed with chronic fatigue when, in fact, they are hypothyroid. In general, chronic fatigue is still a bit of a mystery, and much of the current research points to sleep deprivation, often with unrecognized sleep disorders as the main cause. This section briefly summarizes the accepted theories and definitions.

Chronic fatigue syndrome (CFS) has been around longer than you might think. In 1843, for example, a curious condition called *fibrositis* was described by doctors. It was characterized by symptoms similar to those now seen in fibromyalgia (chronic muscle and joint aches and pains) and CFS. The term *rheumatism*, now outdated, was frequently used as well to describe various aches and pains with no specific or identifiable origin.

What we now call CFS was once known as *Epstein-Barr virus*. In the late 1970s and early 1980s, a mysterious virus, known as Epstein-Barr virus, was diagnosed in thousands of young, upwardly mobile professionals—at the time known as *yuppies*—the so-called baby boom generation. People called this condition the *yuppie flu*, *yuppie virus*, *yuppie syndrome*, and *burnout syndrome*. Many medical professionals were stumped by it, and many disregarded it as a phantom illness or psychosomatic illness, especially in women.

In the early 1980s, two physicians in Nevada who treated a number of patients who shared this curious condition (after a nasty winter flu had hit the region) identified it as *chronic fatigue syndrome*. This label is perhaps the most accurate (and the one that has stuck).

But there are other names for CFS such as the United Kingdom label, *M.E.*, which stands for *myalgic encephalomyelitis*, as well as *post-viral fatigue syndrome*. CFS is also known as *chronic fatigue immune deficiency syndrome* (CFIDS), because it's now believed that CFS sufferers are immune suppressed, although this fact is still being debated. But for the purposes of this chapter I'll refer to the simpler label that seems to tell it like it is: chronic fatigue syndrome.

A lot of people with CFS have been misdiagnosed with various other diseases that share some of the symptoms we now define as CFS. These diseases include mononucleosis, multiple sclerosis, HIV-related illnesses, Lyme disease, post-polio syndrome, and lupus. If you have been diagnosed with any of these diseases, please take a look at the established symptom criteria for CFS outlined here. You may have been misdiagnosed—an extremely common scenario. And, of course, hypothyroidism classically shares many CFS symptoms.

Chronic Fatigue Syndrome or Thyroid?

The following symptoms can indicate chronic fatigue syndrome (CFS) as well as hypothyroidism, or thyrotoxicosis.

- An unexplained fatigue that is "new"
- Poor memory or concentration*
- Sore throat (possible if you have inflammation of the thyroid gland)*
- Mild or low-grade fever
- Tenderness in the neck and underarm area (tenderness in the neck may occur with an enlarged thyroid gland)*
- Muscle pain*†
- Pain along the nerve of a joint*
- A strange and new kind of headache you have never suffered from before
- You sleep but wake up unrefreshed*
- You feel tired, weak, and generally unwell for a good twenty-four hours after you have had even moderate exercise*

*Signs of hypothyroidism
†Signs of thyrotoxicosis

Testing for Adrenal Deficiency

Sometimes, deficiency of the adrenal gland can cause an insidious and gradually severe fatigue. There are two tests that can be done to check for this. The simplest test is called a *cosyntropin (Cortrosyn) stimulation test*. Cosyntropin is a drug that is similar to ACTH (adrenocorticotropic hormone), a hormone made by the pituitary gland to stimulate the adrenal gland, much like TSH stimulates the thyroid gland. To do this test, your physician obtains a blood test for cortisol, then gives you an injection of cosyntropin. Your cortisol level is checked after thirty minutes, and then after another thirty minutes (an hour in total). Normal adrenal glands will be able to produce a cortisol level greater than 20 after the cosyntropin injection. If the cortisol level does not rise sufficiently, then it may be necessary to take cortisol replacement therapy for life.

Three different steroid drugs can be used for cortisol replacement therapy, the two best being hydrocortisone and cortisone acetate. They are given as a pill in the morning and half of this dose in the evening. An alternative drug, prednisone, is sometimes used as a single pill each morning. If both adrenal glands are not working at all, then it may be necessary to take an additional medication to provide another type of steroid hormone, known as a mineralocorticoid, to keep the blood pressure from getting too low.

Sometimes, the cosyntropin stimulation test may not be accurate if there is pituitary or hypothalamic disease as the cause of low adrenal function. Two other tests that work better for this situation are the metyrapone suppression test and insulin-hypoglycemia test. Detailed discussions of these tests are beyond the scope of this book, but they should be well known to the endocrinologists who administer them.

Fibromyalgia Versus CFS

Fibromyalgia is a soft-tissue disorder that causes you to hurt all over—all the time. It appears to be a condition that is triggered and/or aggravated by stress. If you notice fatigue and more general aches and pains, this suggests CFS. If you notice primarily joint and muscle pains, *accompanied* by fatigue, this suggests fibromyalgia.

Fibromyalgia is sometimes considered to be an offshoot of arthritis, and it is not unusual to be misdiagnosed with rheumatoid arthritis. Headaches, morning stiffness, and an intolerance to cold, damp weather are common complaints associated with fibromyalgia. It is also common to suffer from irritable bowel syndrome or bladder problems with this disorder.

Appendix A
Thyroid Links on the Web

The following are good places to start for thyroid resources. If you do not own a computer or you do not have access to one, all public libraries in North America provide free access to the Internet. (Librarians can help you conduct your searches.) There are also many commercial Internet cafes that allow you access for very reasonable prices.

Finding a Thyroid Specialist

American Thyroid Association (thyroid.org; specific URL: thyroid.org/patients/specialists.php3)

American Association of Clinical Endocrinologists (aace.com; specific URL: aace.com/memsearch.php)

The Endocrine Society (hormone.org; specific URL: hormone.org/resources/specialist.php3): the public education arm of the Endocrine Society

Dr. Kenneth Ain (thyroidcancerdoctor.com): allows you to arrange a consultation with Dr. Kenneth Ain regarding thyroid cancer

The American Academy of Otolaryngology—Head and Neck Surgery (entnet.org; specific URL: entnet.org/ent_otolaryngologist.cfm): lists head and neck surgeons (for thyroid surgery)

The American Academy of Ophthalmopathy (aao.org; specific URL: aao.org/aao/eyemd_disclaimer.cfm): lists eye specialists (for thyroid eye disease)

Medicare Participating Physician Directory (www2.medicare.gov/Physician/Search/PhysicianSearch.asp; 1-800-MEDICARE): provides listings of Medicare-participating specialists

Thyroid Websites of Interest

American Thyroid Association (thyroid.org)

American Association of Clinical Endocrinologists (aace.com)

EndocrineWeb.com (endocrineweb.com): an endocrine site maintained by Dr. James Norman, an endocrine surgeon

The American Thyroid Association (thyroid.org)

Thyroid Home Page (thyroid.com): website of the Santa Monica Thyroid Diagnostic Center, founded by Dr. Richard B. Gutler

MyThyroid.com (mythyroid.com): thyroid site maintained by Dr. Daniel J. Drucker

Thyroid Organizations for Patients

American Foundation of Thyroid Patients (thyroidfoundation.org)

Thyroid Foundation of America Inc. (allthyroid.org)

Thyroid Foundation of Canada (thyroid.ca)

European Thyroid Association (eurothyroid.com)

Latin American Thyroid Society (lats.org)

Thyroid Federation International (TFI) Member Patient Organizations

Australia: Australian Thyroid Foundation (thyroidfoundation.com.au) and Thyroid Australia (thyroid.org.au)

Brazil: Thyroid Foundation of Brazil (e-mail: medneto@uol.com.br)

Denmark: Thyreoidea Landsforeningen (thyreoidea.dk)

Finland: Thyroid Foundation of Finland (kolumbus.fi/kilpirauhasliitto)

France: l'Association Française des Malades de la Thyroïde (thyro-asso.org)

Germany: Schilddrüsen Liga Deutschland e.V. (SLD) (schilddruesenliga.de)

Italy: Associazione Italiana Basedowiani e Tiroidei (e-mail: emma99@libero.it)

Japan: Thyroid Foundation of Japan (hata.ne.jp/tfj)

The Netherlands: Schildklierstichting Nederland (schildklier.nl)

Norway: Norsk Thyreoideaforbund (stoffskifte.org)

Republic of Georgia: Georgian Union of Diabetes and Endocrine Associations (e-mail: diabet@access.sanet.ge)

Russia: Thyroid Foundation of St. Petersburg (gasparyan@peterlink.ru)

Sweden: Sköldkörtelförening i Stockholm (skoldkortelforeningen.se) and Västsvenska Patientföreningen för Sköldkörtelsjuka (vpfs.info)
United Kingdom: British Thyroid Foundation (btf-thyroid.org)

Graves' Disease

National Graves' Disease Foundation (ngdf.org)

Thyroid Eye Disease

The TED Association (thyroid-fed.org/members/TED.html)
Thyroid Eye Disease (thyroid-eye-disease.com): the website run by Your Health Press, which publishes the only patient book on TED: *Thyroid Eye Disease: Understanding Graves' Ophthalmopathy*, by Elaine Moore; includes FAQs and many links

Thyroid Cancer

ThyCa: Thyroid Cancer Survivors' Association (thyca.org): Here you'll find local chapters, and links to the following support groups:
Advanced Thyroid Cancer Support Group
America Online Thyroid Cancer Support Group
Anaplastic Support Group
Caregivers Support Group
Long-Term Survivors Support Group
Medullary Support Group
Pediatric Support Group
ThyCa: Thyroid Cancer Support Group
The Thyroid Cancer Online Email Support Group
Canadian Thyroid Cancer Support Group Inc (Thry'vors) (thryvors.org): To join Thry'vors support listserv, go to http://groups.yahoo.com/group/thryvors
The Light of Life Foundation (checkyourneck.com)
The Head and Neck Cancer Foundation (headandneckcanada.com)
Johns Hopkins Thyroid Tumor Center (thyroid-cancer.net)

Thyrogen Website (thyrogen.com)

The Thyroid Cancer Book (thyroidcancerbook.com): website run by Your Health Press, which publishes *The Thyroid Cancer Book*, by M. Sara Rosenthal, which includes the entire low-iodine cookbook of the Light of Life Foundation; also has FAQs and many links

Low-Iodine Cookbooks

lidcookbook.com: website run by Your Health Press, which publishes *The Low Iodine Diet Cookbook* by well-known cookbook author Norene Gilletz; contains FAQs and many links

ThyCa: Thyroid Cancer Survivors' Association (thyca.org): downloadable recipes in PDF

Light of Life Foundation Low Iodine Cookbook (checkyourneck.com/cookbook.asp): posted recipes and link for ordering fifteen-page cookbook

Parathyroid Gland

Parathyroid.com (parathyroid.com): site maintained by Dr. James Norman, a parathyroid surgeon

Hypoparathyroidism Association (hypoparathyroidism.org): provides information that will be helpful if you have calcium problems after thyroid surgery

Appendix B
Links to Other Conditions Related to Thyroid Disease

Depression and Emotional Health

American Counseling Association (counseling.org)
American Psychological Association (apa.org)
National Depressive and Manic-Depressive Association (ndmda.org)
The National Association of Social Workers (NASW) (naswdc.org)
American Institute of Stress (stress.org)
International Stress Management Association (stress-management-isma.org)
The Anxiety Disorders Association of America (adaa.org)

Women's Health

Pregnancy.org (pregnancy.org): nonprofit site with many links to good information
Childbirth.org (childbirth.org): site that is run by childbirth educators and has many good links to other sources
The Hormone Foundation (hormone.org; 1-800-HORMONE): the public education division of the Endocrine Society
North American Menopause Society (menopause.org)
National Osteoporosis Foundation (nof.org)

Heart Health

American Heart Association (americanheart.org)

Obesity

American Obesity Association (obesity.org)
Association for Morbid Obesity Support (obesityhelp.com/morbidobesity;
207-685-3320)

Sleep Disorders and Fatigue

National Center on Sleep Disorder Research (nhlbi.nih.gov/about/ncsdr)
Sleepnet.com (sleepnet.com): a good commercial site for sleep disorders
The CFIDS Association of America (cfids.org): works to conquer chronic fatigue and
immune dysfunction syndrome

Dieting and Weight

Glycemic Index (glycemicindex.com)
dietician.com
Partnership for Healthy Weight Management (consumer.gov/weightloss/bmi.htm):
offers a good body mass index calculator
eDiets.com (ediets.com): a good commercial site that can help you build a
healthy diet

Alzheimer's Disease

Alzheimer's Disease Education and Referral Center (alzheimers.org)
Alzheimer's Association (alz.org)

Complementary Medicine

National Center for Complementary and Alternative Medicine (http://nccam.nih.gov):
a reliable site run by the National Institutes of Health; click on "Health
Information"

Glossary

acute suppurative thyroiditis: a rare form of bacterial *thyroiditis*, where pus and inflammation occur; treated with antibiotics.

Adam's apple: the thyroid cartilage.

ALARA: acronym for "as low as reasonably achievable."

Amiodarone: a potent medicine used to treat heart rhythm disturbances, infamous for causing different types of thyroid problems.

anaplastic thyroid cancer: a very rare but aggressive, hard-to-treat thyroid cancer with poor outcomes; accounts for about 1.6 percent of all thyroid cancers.

angina: chest pain resulting from blockages of the blood supply to the heart muscle.

antithyroglobulin antibody: An antibody associated with *Hashimoto's thyroiditis* that sticks to *thyroglobulin*; interferes with the ability of a laboratory to measure the level of thyroglobulin in the blood, which can be important for thyroid cancer patients.

antithyroid medication: drugs that are used to treat *Graves' disease* in some people by preventing the thyroid from manufacturing thyroid hormone, and occasionally leading to a remission of Graves' disease; *propylthiouracil (PTU)* and *methimazole (Tapazole)* are commonly used antithyroid drugs.

antithyroid peroxidase (TPO): thyroid antibodies that attack the portion of the thyroid cell responsible for making thyroid hormones, associated with *Hashimoto's thyroiditis*.

apathetic hyperthyroidism: refers to *hyperthyroidism* without clear symptoms of *thyrotoxicosis*; usually diagnosed in older individuals (over sixty).

arrhythmia: disturbance of the heart rhythm.

atherosclerotic cardiovascular disease: refers to fatty blockages of blood vessels anywhere in the body; can put you at risk for a heart attack or stroke.

atrial fibrillation: a type of disordered, rapid, irregular heart rhythm.

autoimmune: means "self-immune" or self-attacking.

autoimmune disease: a disease where the body attacks its own tissue.

autoimmune thyroid disease: a thyroid disease involving thyroid antibodies that attack the thyroid gland, as in *Hashimoto's disease* or *Graves' disease*.

benign: noncancerous.

beta-blocker: a type of drug that blocks the effects of adrenaline and slows the heart rate; used in people with *thyrotoxicosis*.

bisphosphonates: drugs that help to form bone; recommended to postmenopausal women.

body mass index (BMI): the best measurement of appropriate weight, this is calculated by dividing your weight (in kilograms) by your height (in meters) squared.

bradycardia: slow heartbeat; associated with hypothyroidism.

carcinoembryonic antigen (CEA): a protein made by medullary thyroid cancer cells, which can be measured and used as a marker for the presence of this type of cancer.

catecholamines: adrenaline and related hormones.

chemosis: bloodshot, red, irritated eyes.

choriocarcinoma: when a molar pregnancy becomes cancerous; also known as cancer of the chorion (the chorion secretes the vital hormone human chorionic gonadotropin—HCG); this can cause thyrotoxicosis.

congenital hypothyroidism: hypothyroidism that is present from birth.

congestive heart failure: weakening of the pumping of the heart.

cretinism: stunted physical and mental development because of severe *hypothyroidism* in the fetus and in childhood; usually caused by iodine deficiency in underdeveloped regions.

CT scan: an x-ray using computerized axial tomography.

cyst: a fluid-filled lump.

Cytomel: the brand name of liothyronine sodium, also known as L-T3 by physicians, which is the pharmaceutical version of *triiodothyronine*, or T3.

differentiated thyroid cancer cells: cancer cells that retain the functional features of normal *thyroid follicular cells*.

dry eye syndrome: when tear production is inadequate or the tears evaporate so quickly that your eyes are left gritty and irritated with every blink; sometimes the result of an autoimmune disease.

dysthyroid orbitopathy: another term for *thyroid eye disease.*

ectopic thyroid gland: thyroid gland found in the wrong place, such as the middle of the chest, sometimes even inside the heart, or lower in the body; results in defective thyroid function and *congenital hypothyroidism.*

endemic goiter: a *hypothyroid goiter* caused by iodine deficiency.

euthyroid: normal levels of thyroid hormone.

euthyroid diffuse goiter: *goiter* without any evidence of *nodules* or *cysts* that makes the proper amount of thyroid hormone.

euthyroid Graves' disease: a type of *Graves' disease* where there are no symptoms of *thyrotoxicosis*; however, there is distinctive *exophthalmos.*

euthyroid multinodular goiter: goiter with multiple *nodules*, feels like a bag of marbles.

exophthalmometer: an instrument that measures the degree to which the eyes protrude out from the skull; used in people with *exophthalmos.*

exophthalmos: bulging eyes; a symptom of *thyroid eye disease.*

fine-needle aspiration biopsy: where a very thin needle, attached to a plastic syringe, is pushed through your skin and into a nodule while the syringe plunger is gently pulled back, taking out material from the nodule, and smeared on glass slides to be viewed under a microscope and evaluated by a pathologist.

FNA: fine-needle aspiration.

follicular thyroid cancer: a type of thyroid cancer that accounts for about 10 percent of all thyroid cancers.

free T4: the only portion of all of the *T4* that is not bound to blood proteins and is able to be taken up into each body cell and do the job of effective thyroid hormone.

free T4 test: the appropriate blood test to measure *free T4* levels.

generalized anxiety disorder (GAD): a psychiatric/psychological disorder where you suffer from persistent worry and anxiety without any relief, despite good reasons for relief from such worry.

gestational hyperthyroidism: when *hyperthyroidism* develops during pregnancy.

gestational hypothyroidism: when *hypothyroidism* develops during pregnancy.

gestational thyroid disease: when any thyroid disease develops during pregnancy.

gestational thyrotoxicosis: refers to a transient form of *thyrotoxicosis* caused by rising levels of human chorionic gonadotropin (HCG), which stimulate the thyroid gland to make thyroid hormone.

gestational trophoblastic neoplasia: when the placental tissue transforms into small cysts, which overtake the womb, usually destroying the fetus within the first few months of pregnancy; results in *thyrotoxicosis*.

glycemic index (GI): measures the rate at which various foods convert to glucose, which is assigned a value of 100; higher numbers indicate a more rapid absorption of glucose, which helps to distinguish simple carbohydrates (or simple sugars) from more complex, or nutrient-dense carbohydrates (such as grains).

goiter: enlarged *thyroid gland*.

goitrogens: substances that can block thyroid hormone formation, found in a variety of foods, such as cabbage or other foods from the Brassica family.

Graves' disease: an autoimmune thyroid disease that causes *hyperthyroidism*.

Graves' ophthalmopathy (GO): another term for *thyroid eye disease*.

Hashimoto's disease: another term for *Hashimoto's thyroiditis*.

Hashimoto's thyroiditis: a major cause of *hypothyroidism*, this type of thyroiditis is an autoimmune thyroid disease, where antibodies attack the thyroid gland, causing it to become dysfunctional and usually resulting in *hypothyroidism*.

Hashitoxicosis: a type of Hashimoto's disease, where thyroid hormone leaks out from the gland, causing *thyrotoxicosis*.

high-density lipoprotein (HDL): this is the "good cholesterol"; should be at least 40 mg/dL.

hypercholesterolemia: high cholesterol.

hypertension: high blood pressure.

hyperthyroid: overactive thyroid gland usually causing *thyrotoxicosis*.

hyperthyroidism: the state of having an overactive thyroid gland, or being *hyperthyroid*.

hypocalcemia: low calcium levels, which can lead to debilitating symptoms.

hypoparathyroidism: when your parathyroid glands do not make sufficient amounts of parathyroid hormone (PTH), usually the result of damage during thyroid surgery, resulting in *hypocalcemia*, which can be temporary or permanent.

hypoplastic thyroid: a thyroid smaller than normal; usually results in *congenital hypothyroidism*.

hypothalamic-pituitary dysgenesis: a failure in the normal formation or function of the *pituitary gland* and/or *hypo-*

thalamus which can lead to *congenital hypothyroidism*.

hypothalamus: a part of the brain that is just above the *pituitary gland*, which helps control the pituitary gland and the thyroid gland by releasing *TSH-releasing hormone* (TRH).

hypothyroid: inadequate levels of thyroid hormone, causing a range of debilitating symptoms, associated with low energy and a slowing down of body cells.

hypothyroid goiter: the most common type of *goiter* in the world, caused by inadequate thyroid hormone levels resulting in subtle or dramatic elevations of *TSH* levels, which stimulates the thyroid gland to grow; can be *endemic* or caused by *Hashimoto's disease*.

hypothyroidism: the state of having an underactive thyroid gland, or being *hypothyroid*.

I-131: one type of iodine isotope used in thyroid scans and treatment.

I-131 dosimetry: the name of the method used to figure out the maximum safe I-131 dose, beyond which there are unacceptable effects on the bone marrow.

iodine: a crucial element the thyroid gland needs to make thyroid hormone.

iodine deficiency: when not enough iodine from food is available to the thyroid, causing *hypothyroidism*, *goiter*, and in children or infants, mental retardation, short stature, or *cretinism*.

isotope: a form of an element, such as iodine, which is often radioactive, or unstable.

isthmus: middle part of the thyroid gland.

levothyroxine sodium: *thyroid hormone* made by a pharmaceutical company in pill form; also called L-T4 by physicians or T4 by the public.

lobectomy: surgical removal of one lobe of the thyroid gland.

low-density lipoprotein (LDL): this is the "bad cholesterol"; should be less than 100 mg/dL.

low-iodine diet (LID): a special diet low in iodine (*not* sodium), which can maximize the sensitivity and effectiveness of radioactive iodine (RAI) scans or treatments for thyroid cancer.

lymph nodes: small *nodules* containing small white blood cells that stimulate the immune system to fight infection; cancer cells may grow in lymph nodes, which are removed during the course of thyroid cancer surgery.

malignancy: cancer.

malignant: cancerous.

medullary thyroid cancer: a type of thyroid cancer that is sometimes genetically inherited, treated with surgery and comes from the parafollicular cells of the thyroid.

metastatic: spreading beyond the site of origin, as in metastatic cancer.

methimazole (Tapazole): one commonly used brand of *thionamides*.

mild hypothyroidism: another term for *subclinical hypothyroidism*.

millicurie: a unit of measurement of radioactivity used for dosing radioactive iodine for scans or treatment.

molar pregnancy: *gestational trophoblastic neoplasia*, also known as a hydatidiform mole.

MRI: a scan using magnetic resonance imaging.

myocardial infarction: another term for heart attack.

neck dissection: performed during a *thyroidectomy*, where the surgeon systematically removes any deposits of tumor that has spread to lymph nodes in the neck.

neonatal hypothyroidism: hypothyroidism that develops within the first twenty-eight days of life of a newborn; if left untreated, it can lead to *cretinism*.

nodules: lumps.

obesity: defined as a *body mass index (BMI)* between 30 and 34.9.

oncology: the study of cancer.

orbital decompression surgery: a surgical procedure that can remove bone from the eye socket and expand the area alongside the eyeball so that swollen tissue can move into it; a corrective surgery in cases of severe *thyroid eye disease*.

osteoporosis: bone loss.

palpitations: rapid, forceful heartbeat.

panic attack: a cascade of physical symptoms associated with adrenaline and the "flight or fight" response (feelings of nausea, vertigo, cold sweat, choking sensations, *palpitations*, and shakiness).

papillary thyroid cancer: a type of thyroid cancer that is usually treatable with surgery and *radioactive iodine*; accounts for about 80 percent of all thyroid cancers.

parathyroid gland: means "near the thyroid," these are other glands close to the thyroid gland which make *parathyroid hormone (PTH)*.

parathyroid hormone (PTH): this hormone causes the kidneys to retain calcium in the blood while releasing phosphorus into the urine; also increases the activation of vitamin D, which enhances the absorption of calcium and phosphorus from food and beverages.

Pendred syndrome: a condition in which an affected person is deaf-mute with a large goiter, the result of a dysfunctional inner ear as well as deficient thyroid hormone production, causing *goiter* and *hypothyroidism*.

peripheral vascular disease: when *atherosclerotic cardiovascular disease* affects arteries that feed your arms or your legs, causing circulation problems and numbness.

pituitary gland: acts as a "hormone thermostat," this gland is located in the brain, and makes thyroid stimulating hormone (TSH) as well as other hormones.

postpartum thyroiditis: a general label referring to *silent thyroiditis* occurring after delivery, causing mild *hyperthyroidism*, and a period of *hypothyroidism*.

propranolol: a commonly used brand of *beta-blocker*.

proptosis: protrusion, or bulging of the eyeball, associated with *thyroid eye disease*.

propylthiouracil (PTU): one commonly used type of *thionamides*.

radioactive iodine: iodine that is radioactive; also called a radioactive *isotope* of iodine.

RAI: *radioactive iodine*.

RAIU: radioactive iodine uptake, which is the percentage of a dose of *radioactive iodine* that is taken up by the thyroid over the course of a day.

recurrent laryngeal nerve: a nerve that supplies the voice box and vocal cords; can be damaged during a *thyroidectomy*.

resistance to thyroid hormone (RTH): another term for *thyroid hormone resistance*.

Riedel's thyroiditis: the rarest form of *thyroiditis*, in which the thyroid gland is invaded by scar tissue, infiltrating throughout the gland and binding it to surrounding portions of the neck.

salivary stones: refers to the swelling of one or more salivary glands (located under the ears and under the lower jaw) because of partial blockage of the salivary ducts by dried saliva; a complication of *RAI* treatment for thyroid cancer.

selective estrogen receptor modulators (SERMs): a class of drugs that help to prevent bone loss; recommended in postmenopausal women.

SESTAMIBI: a type of scan used in nuclear medicine, sometimes used in thyroid imaging.

silent thyroiditis: a form of *thyroiditis* so named because it avoids detection until symptoms of *thyrotoxicosis* (and sometimes *hypothyroidism* thereafter) become severe; usually resolves on its own.

sleep deprivation: being deprived of the recommended hours of sleep for healthy adults.

sleep disorder: a physical disorder that interrupts deep, restful sleep; often not recognized by the sufferer, who may have *sleep deprivation*.

stable iodine: normal, or nonradioactive, iodine.

subacute thyroiditis: also called "painful thyroiditis," this is a rare type of short-lived *thyroiditis* that may be viral in origin; symptoms are pain and inflammation of the thyroid and transient *thyrotoxicosis*.

subclinical hyperthyroidism: mild *hyperthyroidism* with few or no symptoms or *thyrotoxicosis*.

subclinical hypothyroidism: refers to *hypothyroidism* that is very mild, meaning that you have few or no symptoms.

T3: short for *triiodothyronine*.

T4: short for *thyroxine*.

tachycardia: fast heartbeat (or racing heart); associated with *thyrotoxicosis*.

technetium: a type of isotope used for thyroid scans.

thionamides: a class of drugs used as *antithyroid medication*.

Thyrogen (rhTSH): a pharmaceutically prepared version of *TSH* made using recombinant DNA technology; this is synthetic TSH, and is used in whole body scans and other tests for thyroid cancer patients.

thyroglobulin: a protein that is unique to thyroid cells and is the source of thyroid hormone formation.

thyroglobulin test (TG test): a test that measures the amount of *thyroglobulin* in the blood, useful as a marker for thyroid cancer cells.

thyroid antibodies: antibodies from white blood cells that target the thyroid gland, causing an *autoimmune disease*.

thyroid antibody testing: a blood test that checks for the presence of *thyroid antibodies*.

thyroid-associated ophthalmopathy: another term for *thyroid eye disease*.

thyroid dysgenesis: abnormal formation of the thyroid gland; a common cause of *congenital hypothyroidism*.

thyroid dyshormonogenesis: a term encompassing a variety of conditions in which the thyroid gland is unable to manufacture thyroid hormone; a cause of *congenital hypothyroidism*.

thyroid extract: a preparation from dried, cleaned, powdered thyroid glands from cows or pigs; also known as natural thyroid hormone.

thyroid eye disease (TED): also known as Graves' ophthalmopathy (GO) or Graves' orbitopathy, tends to strike people with *Graves' disease*, and is an eye disease causing bulging, grittiness, redness, double vision, and a range of other eye symptoms.

thyroid follicular cells: the cells that produce thyroid hormone, which have receptors for TSH.

thyroid gland: butterfly-shaped gland typically located in front of the windpipe (trachea) just above the midline bony notch in the top of the breastbone (sternal notch).

thyroid hormone: a hormone made by the thyroid gland that serves as the "speed control" for all body cells; types of thyroid hormone are *thyroxine (T4)* and *triiodothyronine (T3)*.

thyroid hormone resistance syndrome (Refetoff syndrome): a rare, inherited disease that results in a person being born with a resistance to his or her own thyroid hormone; caused by a mutation in the gene that makes the receptor for thyroid hormone.

thyroid hormone suppression therapy: a high dosage of *levothyroxine* for the purposes of suppressing *TSH*.

thyroid lobe: one side, or lobe, of the thyroid; as it is butterfly-shaped, a lobe would be one "wing."

thyroid lymphoma: an extremely rare type of thyroid cancer caused by cancerous white blood cells; accounts for less than 3 percent of all thyroid cancers.

thyroid scan: a test where an image or picture is taken, using special radiation detection cameras and radioactive isotopes that "light up" the thyroid for the camera.

thyroid self-exam: a self-exam of the neck area, which can help find suspicious thyroid lumps or an enlargement of the thyroid that should be evaluated by a doctor.

thyroid stimulating hormone (TSH): a pituitary hormone that controls the level of thyroid hormone; high or low TSH levels reflect thyroid function.

thyroid stimulating immunoglobulin (TSI or TSA): A thyroid antibody that sticks to the TSH receptor in the place of TSH, overstimulating the thyroid gland, causing *Graves' disease*, or sticks to parts

of the eye muscle, causing *thyroid eye disease*.

thyroid storm: when symptoms of severe *thyrotoxicosis* can manifest into a "storm" of severe cardiovascular symptoms that warrant emergency attention and admission to an intensive care unit.

thyroidectomy: surgical removal of the thyroid gland; can be total or partial.

thyroiditis: inflammation of the thyroid gland; usually causes *hypothyroidism*.

thyrotoxic: describes someone who suffers from *thyrotoxicosis*.

thyrotoxic goiter: goiters associated with prolonged *thyrotoxicosis*, caused by *Graves' disease* or *toxic nodules*.

thyrotoxicosis: means "too much thyroid hormone," caused by *hyperthyroidism*, overdose of thyroid hormone medication, toxic nodules, and other types of thyroid conditions causing a speeding up of bodily processes; leads to a range of debilitating symptoms associated with overstressed, exhausted body cells.

thyroxine (also known as T4): the inactive early form of thyroid hormone; called T4 because it contains four iodine atoms for each hormone molecule, and is converted by the body's cells into T3, the active form of thyroid hormone.

total T3 test: the appropriate blood test to measure the amount of active thyroid hormone, or *T3* levels.

toxic adenoma: Single thyroid *nodules* that independently make too much thyroid hormone.

toxic multinodular goiter: when the thyroid gland forms multiple nodules that produce too much thyroid hormone.

toxic nodules: lumps that make thyroid hormone on their own, and which do not respond to *TSH*; can be single nodules or multinodular.

triiodothyronine (T3): made by the body's cells out of T4, this is the active thyroid hormone that activates genes and does the job of thyroid hormone.

TSH: short for *thyroid stimulating hormone.*

TSH-releasing hormone (TRH): a hormone made by the *hypothalamus* when the thyroid hormone levels are low and causing the pituitary to produce TSH.

TSH test: a sensitive blood test that assesses whether you have high or low TSH levels, an indicator of whether you have normal levels of *thyroid hormone* or abnormally high or low levels of thyroid hormone; this test assesses how the body "feels"— *euthyroid, hypothyroid,* or *thyrotoxic*—by looking at the body's own natural "thermostat" for thyroid hormone.

ultrasound: a device that uses high-frequency sound waves to produce an echo picture of structures in your body.

undifferentiated thyroid cancer cells: cancer cells that do not retain the functional features of normal *thyroid follicular cells.*

unipolar depression: most common type of depression, characterized by one low, flat mood; frequently a complication of *hypothyroidism.*

WBS: *whole body scan.*

whole body scan: a scan involving pictures of the whole body, used to track thyroid cancer recurrence.

Supportive Literature

Ain, K. B. "Anaplastic Thyroid Carcinoma: Behavior, Biology, and Therapeutic Approaches." *Thyroid* 8, no. 8 (1998): 715–26.

Ain, K. B. "Management of Thyroid Cancer." In *Diseases of the Thyroid*, edited by L. E. Braverman, 287–317. Totowa, NJ: Humana Press, Inc., 1997.

Ain, K. B. "Management of Undifferentiated Thyroid Cancer." *Baillieres Best Practice and Research Clinical Endocrinology and Metabolism* 14, no. 4 (2000): 615–29.

Ain, K. B. "Thyroid Malignancies." In *Oncologic Therapies*, edited by E. E. Vokes and H. M. Golomb, 977–1000. Berlin: Springer-Verlag, 1999.

Ain, K. B. "Unusual Types of Thyroid Cancer." *Reviews in Endrocrine and Metabolic Disorders* 1, no. 3 (2000): 225–31.

Ain, K. B., F. Pucino, T. M. Shiver, S. M. Banks. "Thyroid Hormone Levels Affected by Time of Blood Sampling in Thyroxine-Treated Patients." *Thyroid* 3, no. 2 (1993): 81–85.

Anders, H., and C. Keller. "Pemberton's Maneuver—a Clinical Test for Latent Superior Vena Cava Syndrome Caused by a Substernal Mass." *European Journal of Medical Research* 2, no. 11 (1997): 488–90.

Bartalena L., and J. Robbins. "Thyroid Hormone Transport Proteins." *Clinics in Laboratory Medicine* 13, no. 3 (1993): 583–98.

Benua R. S., and R. D. Leeper. "A Method and Rationale for Treating Metastatic Thyroid Carcinoma with the Largest Safe Dose of 131I." In *Frontiers in Thyroidology*, edited by G. Medeiros-Neto and E. Gaitan, vol. 2, 1317–21. New York: Plenum Medical Book Co., 1986.

Bunevicius, Robertas, et al. "Effects of Thyroxine as Compared with Thyroxine plus Triiodothyronine in Patients with Hypothyroidism." *New England Journal of Medicine* 340, no. 6 (February 11, 1999).

Chakravarthy, M. V., and F. W. Booth. "Eating, Exercise, and 'Thrifty' Genotypes: Connecting the Dots Toward an Evolutionary Understanding of Modern Chronic Diseases." *Journal of Applied Physiology* 96, no. 1 (Jan. 2004): 3–10.

Cheng, T. O. "The Mediterranean Diet Revisited." *QJM—Monthly Journal of the Association of Physicians* 94, no. 3 (March 2001): 174–75.

Cooper, D. S. "Antithyroid Drugs in the Management of Patients with Graves' Disease: An Evidence-Based Approach to Therapeutic Controversies." *Journal of Clinical Endocrinology and Metabolism* 88, no. 8 (2003): 3474–81.

Damcott, C. M., et al. "The Genetics of Obesity." *Endocrinology and Metabolism Clinics of North America* 32, no. 4 (Dec. 2003): 761–86.

Demers, L. M., and C. A. Spencer. "Laboratory Medicine Practice Guidelines: Laboratory Support for the Diagnosis and Monitoring of Thyroid Disease." *Clinical Endocrinology (Oxford)* 58, no. 2 (2003): 138–40.

Dong, B. J., et al. "Bioequivalence of Generic and Brand-Name Levothyroxine Products in the Treatment of Hypothyroidism." *Journal of the American Medical Association* 277, no. 15 (April 16, 1997): 1199–200.

Edwards, C. M. B., J. P. D. Cox, and S. Robinson. "Psychological Well-Being of Patients on L-Thyroxine." *Clinical Endocrinology* 59 (2003): 2, 264–65.

Emanuel, Ezekiel J., and Linda L. Emanuel. "Four Models of the Physician-Patient Relationship." *Journal of the American Medical Association* 267, no. 16 (1992): 2221–26.

Enserink, Martin. "The Vanishing Promises of Hormone Replacement." *Science* 297, no. 5580 (July 19, 2002): 325–26.

Etchells, E., et al. "Disclosure." *Canadian Medical Association Journal* 155 (1996): 387–91.

Etchells, E., et al. "Voluntariness." *Canadian Medical Association Journal* 155 (1996): 1083–86.

Etchells, E., Gilbert Sharpe, et al. "Consent." *Canadian Medical Association Journal* 155 (1996): 177–80.

Friedman, Jeffrey M. "A War on Obesity, Not the Obese." *Science* 299, no. 5608 (2003): 856–58.

Garton, M., et al. "Effect of L-Thyroxine Replacement on Bone Mineral Density and Metabolism in Premenopausal Women." *Clinical Thyroidology* 8, no. 1 (January-April 1995).

Geffner, D. L., and J. M. Hershman. "Beta-Adrenergic Blockade for the Treatment of Hyperthyroidism." *The American Journal of Medicine* 93, no. 1 (1992): 61–68.

Gharib, H. "Changing Concepts in the Diagnosis and Management of Thyroid Nodules." *Endocrinology and Metabolism Clinics of North America* 26, no. 4 (1997): 777–800.

Gruters, A., H. Biebermann, and H. Krude. "Neonatal Thyroid Disorders." *Hormone Research* 59, suppl. 1 (2003): 24–29.

Hegedus, L., S. J. Bonnema, and F. N. Bennedbaek. "Management of Simple Nodular Goiter: Current Status and Future Perspectives." *Endocrine Reviews* 24, no. 1 (2003): 102–32.

Henderson, L., Q. Y. Yue, C. Bergquist, B. Gerden, and P. Arlett. "St. John's Wort (Hypericum Perforatum): Drug Interactions and Clinical Outcomes." *British Journal of Clinical Pharmacology* 4, no. 4 (Oct. 2002): 349–56.

Heyerdahl, S., and B. Oerbeck. "Congenital Hypothyroidism: Developmental Outcome in Relation to Levothyroxine Treatment Variables." *Thyroid* 13, no. 11 (2003): 1029–38.

Hill, James O., Holly R. Wyatt, George W. Reed, and John C. Peters. "Obesity and the Environment: Where Do We Go from Here?" *Science* 299, no. 5608 (2003): 853–55.

Hu, F. B., and W. C. Willett. "Optimal Diets for Prevention of Coronary Heart Disease." *Journal of the American Medical Association* 288, no. 20 (Nov. 27, 2002): 2569–78.

Kaplan, Michael, et al. "Editorial: In Search of the Impossible Dream? Thyroid Hormone Replacement Therapy That Treats All Symptoms in Hypothyroid Patients." *Journal of Clinical Endocrinology and Metabolism* 88, no. 10 (2003): 4540–42.

Kelner, Katrina, and Laura Helmuth. "Obesity—What Is to Be Done?" *Science* 299: no. 5608 (2003): 845.

Knobel, M., and G. Medeiros-Neto. "An Outline of Inherited Disorders of the Thyroid Hormone Generating System." *Thyroid* 13, no. 8 (2003): 771–801.

Knudsen, N., P. Laurberg, H. Perrild, I. Bulow, L. Ovesen, and T. Jorgensen. "Risk Factors for Goiter and Thyroid Nodules." *Thyroid* 12, no. 10 (2002): 879–88.

Kraiem, Z., and R. S. Newfield. "Graves' Disease in Childhood." *Journal of Pediatric Endocrinology and Metabolism* 14, no. 3 (2001): 229–43.

Langley, R. W., and H. B. Burch. "Perioperative Management of the Thyrotoxic Patient." *Endocrinology and Metabolism Clinics of North America* 32, no. 2 (2003): 519–34.

Linden, Wolfgang, J. David Spence, Peter A. Barnett, Vivian Ramsden, and Paul Taenzer. "Recommendations on Stress Management." *Canadian Medical Association Journal* 160, no. 9 (May 4, 1999): S46–S49.

LiVolsi, V.A. *Surgical Pathology of the Thyroid.* Philadelphia: W. B. Saunders Co., 1990.

Macchia, P. E., M. De Felice, and R. Di Lauro. "Molecular Genetics of Congenital Hypothyroidism." *Current Opinion in Genetics and Development* 9, no. 3 (1999): 289–94.

Marx, Jean. "Cellular Warriors at the Battle of the Bulge." *Science* 299, no. 5608 (2003): 846–49.

Maxon, H. R., and H. S. Smith. "Radioiodine-131 in the Diagnosis and Treatment of Metastatic Well Differentiated Thyroid Cancer." *Endocrinology and Metabolism Clinics of North America* 19, no. 3 (1990): 685–718.

Mazer, N. A. "Interaction of Estrogen Therapy and Thyroid Hormone Replacement in Postmenopausal Women." *Thyroid* 14, suppl. 1 (2004): 27–34.

McDermott, M. T. "Thyroid Disease and Reproductive Health." *Thyroid* 14, suppl. 1 (2004): 1–3.

Montuenga, L. M. *The Diffuse Endocrine System: From Embryogenesis to Carcinogenesis*, 158–272. Jena, Germany: Urban & Fischer, 2003.

Nestle, Marion. *Food Politics: How the Food Industry Influences Nutrition and Health.* Berkeley: University of California Press, 2002.

Olveira, G., et al. "Altered Bioavailability Changes in the Formulation of a Commercial Preparation of Levothyroxine in Patients with Differentiated Thyroid Carcinoma." *Clinical Endocrinology* 46 (June 1997): 707–11.

Quadbeck, B., J. Pruellage, U. Roggenbuck, H. Hirche, O. E. Janssen, K. Mann, and R. Hoermann. "Long-Term Follow-up of Thyroid Nodule Growth." *Experimental and Clinical Endocrinology and Diabetes* 110, no. 7 (2002): 348–54.

Redmond, G. "Thyroid Dysfunction and Women's Reproductive Health." *Thyroid* 14, suppl. 134 (2004): 5–16.

Robbins, J. *Treatment of Thyroid Cancer in Childhood*, x, 171. Bethesda, MD: National Institutes of Health, 1994.

Roman, S. A. "Endocrine Tumors: Evaluation of the Thyroid Nodule." *Current Opinion in Oncology* 15, no. 1 (2003): 66–70.

Rovet, J., and D. Daneman. "Congenital Hypothyroidism: A Review of Current Diagnostic and Treatment Practices in Relation to Neuropsychologic Outcome." *Paediatr Drugs* 5, no. 3 (2003): 141–49.

Sachiko T., R. D. St. Jeor, Barbara V. Howard, Elaine Prewitt, Vicki Bovee, Terry Bazzarre, and Robert H. Eckel for the AHA Nutrition Committee. "Dietary Protein and Weight Reduction." A Statement for Healthcare Professionals from the Nutrition Committee of the Council on Nutrition, Physical Activity, and Metabolism of the American Heart Association. *Circulation* 104 (2001): 1869–74.

Saravanan, P., W. F. Chau, N. Roberts, K. Vedhara, R. Greenwood, and C. M. Dayan. "Psychological Well-Being in Patients on 'Adequate' Doses of L-Thyroxine: Results of a Large, Controlled Community-Based Questionnaire Study." *Clinical Endocrinology* 57, no. 5 (Nov. 2002): 577–78.

Sawka, A.M., et al. "Does a Combination Regimen of T4 and T3 Improve Depressive Symptoms Better than T4 Alone in Patients with Hypothyroidism? Results of a Double-Blind, Randomized Controlled Trial." *Journal of Clinical Endocrinology and Metabolism* 88, no. 10 (2003): 4551–55.

Schlosser, Eric. *Fast Food Nation: The Dark Side of the American Meal.* New York: Houghton Mifflin, 2001.

Siegmund, W., K. Spieker, A. I. Weike, T. Giessmann, C. Modess, T. Dabers, G. Kirsch, E. Sanger, G. Engel, A. O. Hamm, M. Nauck, and W. Meng. "Replacement Therapy with Levothyroxine Plus Triiodothyronine (Bioavailable Molar Ratio 14:1) Is Not Superior to Thyroxine Alone to Improve Well-Being and Cognitive Performance in Hypothyroidism." *Clinical Endocrinology* 60 (2004): 6, 750–57.

Singer, P. A., D. S. Cooper, E. G. Levy, P. W. Ladenson, L. E. Braverman, G. Daniels, F. S. Greenspan, I. R. McDougall, and T. F. Nikolai. "Treatment Guidelines for Patients with Hyperthyroidism and Hypothyroidism." Standards of Care Committee, American Thyroid Association. *Journal of the American Medical Association* 273, no. 10 (1995): 808–12.

Toft, Anthony. "Thyroid Hormone Replacement—One Hormone or Two?" (editorial). *The New England Journal of Medicine* 340, no. 6. (February 11, 1999).

Walsh, John, et al. "Combined Thyroxine/Liothyronine Treatment Does Not Improve Well-Being, Quality of Life or Cognitive Function Compared to Thyroxine Alone: A Randomized Controlled Trial in Patients with Primary Hypothyroidism." *Journal of Clinical Endocrinology and Metabolism* 88, no. 10 (2003): 4543–50.

Weiss, R. E., and S. Refetoff. "Resistance to Thyroid Hormone." *Reviews in Endocrine and Metabolic Disorders* 1, no. 1–2 (2000): 97–108.

Whitley, R. J., and K. B. Ain. "Thyroglobulin: A Specific Serum Marker for the Management of Thyroid Carcinoma." *Clinics in Laboratory Medicine* 24, no. 1 (2004): 29–47.

Williams, D. "Cancer After Nuclear Fallout: Lessons from the Chernobyl Accident." *Nature Reviews: Cancer* 2, no. 7 (2002): 543–49.

Your Health Press Series

Note: these are books M. Sara Rosenthal publishes herself on orphan or stigmatizing health topics. Available at online bookstores or phone toll-free: 1-866-752-6820.

Stopping Cancer at the Source (2001)
Women and Unwanted Hair (2001)
Living Well with Celiac Disease (2002) by Claudine Crangle
The Thyroid Cancer Book (2nd edition, 2003)
Living Well with Ostomy (2003) by Elizabeth Rayson
Thyroid Eye Disease (2003) by Elaine Moore
Healing Injuries the Natural Way (2004) by Michelle Schoffro Cook
Menopause Before 40: Coping with Premature Ovarian Failure (2004)
  by Karin Banerd

Index

neonatal and congenital, 39–40
in newborns and infants, 204–7
in older individuals, 225–27
prevalence of, 37
primary, 37–38
secondary, 41
signs of, 38–39, 45–50, 51
subclinical, 40–41
symptoms that persist, 59–60
tertiary, 42
thyroiditis and, 40
treating, 52–59

Iatrogenic hypothyroidism, 38
Indeterminate nodules, 119
Infertility, 66
Inflammatory bowel disease (IBD),
    89
Informed consent, 273–74
Informed decision-making
    beneficence and nonmaleficence,
        275–76
    confidentiality, 274–75
    doing the right thing, 276–77
    informed consent, 273–74
    justice, 276
    respect for persons, 272–73
    standards of care, 269–72
    steps toward, 277–78
Inherited predisposition, 80. *See also*
    Genetic link
Insomnia, 303, 322
Insular carcinomas, 132–33
Interpersonal therapy, 306
Iodide, stable, 159–61
Iodine, 9
Iodine deficiency, 42–43, 160

Iodine diet, low-, 262–63, 255
Iodine excess, 43–44
Ischemia, 317
Isotopes, 165, 166
Isthmus, 5

Jackson, Michael, 76
Justice, 276

Kennedy, John F., 95
Kennedy Jr., John F., 95
Ketosis, 223–24

Langer, Stephen E., 244
Legal standard of care, 269–70
Leptin, 219
Levothyroxine (L-T4)
    best way to take, 148–49
    description of, 9, 14, 53–59, 143
    misuse of, 73
    mixtures of T3 and, 58–59, 152
    name brands vs. generics, 55,
        144–46
    pill sizes, 54, 146–47
    storage and heat sensitivity, 57,
        147–48
    thyroid cancer and, 140
    thyroid extracts, 57–58, 152–53,
        243–44
Lid lag, 292, 295
Lipids, 14. *See also* Fat, dietary
Lithium carbonate, 161
Liver problems, 157
Low blood sugar, 71
Low-iodine diet (LID), 255, 262–63
Lupus, 89–90
Lymph nodes, 7